Designs for
the Pluriverse

New Ecologies for
the Twenty-First Century

Series Editors: Arturo Escobar, University of North Carolina, Chapel Hill
Dianne Rocheleau, Clark University

THIS SERIES ADDRESSES TWO TRENDS: critical conversations in academic fields about nature, sustainability, globalization, and culture, including constructive engagements between the natural, social, and human sciences; and intellectual and political conversations among social movements and other non-academic knowledge producers about alternative practices and socio-natural worlds. Its objective is to establish a synergy between these theoretical and political developments in both academic and non-academic arenas. This synergy is a sine qua non for new thinking about the real promise of emergent ecologies. The series includes works that envision more lasting and just ways of being-in-place and being-in-networks with a diversity of humans and other living and non-living beings.

NEW ECOLOGIES FOR THE TWENTY-FIRST CENTURY aims to promote a dialogue between those who are transforming the understanding of the relationship between nature and culture. The series revisits existing fields such as environmental history, historical ecology, environmental anthropology, ecological economics, and cultural and political ecology. It addresses emerging tendencies, such as the use of complexity theory to rethink a range of questions on the nature-culture axis. It also deals with epistemological and ontological concerns, building bridges between the various forms of knowing and ways of being embedded in the multiplicity of practices of social actors worldwide. This series hopes to foster convergences among differently located actors and to provide a forum for authors and readers to widen the fields of theoretical inquiry, professional practice, and social struggles that characterize the current environmental arena.

Designs for the Pluriverse

Radical Interdependence, Autonomy,
and the Making of Worlds

Arturo Escobar

DUKE UNIVERSITY PRESS
Durham and London
2018

© 2017 Duke University Press
All rights reserved
Printed in the United States of America on acid-free
paper ∞
Designed by Matthew Tauch
Typeset in Arno Pro by Westchester Publishing Services

Cataloging-in-Publication Data is available from the
Library of Congress.
ISBN 978–0–8223–7090–1 (hardcover : alk. paper)
ISBN 978–0–8223–7105–2 (pbk. : alk. paper)
ISBN 978–0–8223–7181–6 (ebook)

Cover art: Gabriel Orozco, *Piñanona 1*, 2013. Tempera
and burnished gold leaf on linen canvas on wood.
40 × 40 × 4 cm. © Gabriel Orozco/kurimanzutto, Mexico
City. Image courtesy of the artist and kurimanzutto,
Mexico City. Photo by Studio Michel Zabé, 2013.

To Bob Marley, a prophet of our times

To the Zapatistas of Chiapas, for their pluriversal imagination

To the indigenous, Afrodescendant, and peasant communities of the Norte del Cauca region of Colombia, for their steadfast determination to defend the *tejido de la vida* (the relational weave of life) against rampant destruction by modern worlds.

Contents

Preface and Acknowledgments

The times they are a-changin,' chanted Bob Dylan in a prophetic song back in 1964, at the dawn of the North American counterculture movement. That was well before intensive globalization with its increasingly conspicuous collateral damage, including climate change, widespread extractivism, extensive conflict and social dislocation, and the inexpressible devastation of the Earth. Today we would have to say, with climate justice activist Naomi Klein (2014), that *this changes everything.* For both Dylan and Klein, as for so many visionaries and activists worldwide and some farsighted designers, all of whom will be among the protagonists of this book, Klein's injunction is to be taken not only seriously but literally. What this means is that what is at stake is not just a given economic model (neoliberal capitalism), nor a set of cultural traits inimical to life on the planet (say, rampant individualism and consumerism), high-level policy reform (e.g., more comprehensive climate change protocols), geopolitical power struggles for re- and de-Westernization, or the ever-growing military-industrial complex. As Latin American indigenous, black, and peasant activists are wont to say, the contemporary crisis is a crisis of a particular *modelo civilizatorio,* or civilizational model, that of patriarchal Western capitalist modernity. This is a striking claim, but one that more and more social groups on the planet, in both the Global South and the Global North, are taking to heart in the defense of their places, territories, and cultures. As we shall see in the conclusion, the implication is none other than *everything has to change.* For those for whom the current conjuncture "changes everything," what needs to change is an entire way of life and a whole style of world making. It goes deeper than capitalism.

This book is about this civilizational conjuncture, its implications for design theory and practice, and the practical potential of design to contribute to the profound cultural and ecological transitions seen as needed by a mounting cadre of intellectuals and activists if humanity is to face effectively the interrelated crises of climate, food, energy, poverty, and meaning. The book is based on the belief that this potential is real, as suggested by some trends within the design profession as a whole, particularly among a small but perhaps growing subgroup of designers who are actually already embarked on the project of "design for transitions." Some of these designers claim that the crisis demands nothing less than a reinvention of the human. Bold claims indeed. The book finds its main epistemic and political inspiration and force, however, in the political struggles of indigenous, Afrodescendant, peasant, and marginalized urban groups in Latin America who mobilize with the goal of defending not only their resources and territories but their entire ways of being-in-the-world. Some of them do so in the name of their collective alternative "Life Projects," a concept that is also finding a propitious home in transition design circles. The second wellspring of inspiration and ideas is the discourses and practices of the visionaries and activists who, in so many places and spheres of life, are engaged in bringing about the transitions. That's at least how many of them see it. A main goal of the book is to ask whether design can actually contribute to enabling the communal forms of autonomy that underlie these transition visions and Life Projects. This is to say that one of the major goals of the book is to place cultural and political autonomy, as defined by the mobilized grassroots communities in Latin America, firmly within the scope of design, perhaps even at its center in the case of those wishing to work closely with communities in struggle.

To nourish design's potential for the transitions, however, requires a significant reorientation of design from the functionalist, rationalistic, and industrial traditions from which it emerged, and within which it still functions with ease, toward a type of rationality and set of practices attuned to the *relational* dimension of life. This is why the approach taken is ontological. Design is ontological in that all design-led objects, tools, and even services bring about particular ways of being, knowing, and doing. This ontological dimension of design will be discussed at length in the book. Major sources for the reorientation of the rationalistic tradition lie within the nondualist and relational forms of life effectively present among many of the peoples engaged in territorial struggles against extractive globalization. These struggles evince the strong communal foundations still present at the basis of these people's social life. Insights for thinking about relationality are also found within certain postdualist trends in academic circles of late, often described as the ontological turn. Relationality is also present, in the last instance, in the Earth itself, in the endless and ceaselessly changing weave of life on which all life depends. At some point in the book, we will speak about "the political activation of relationality" to signal the emergence of these vital knowledges and forces.

These are the main themes of the book, then: cultural, civilizational, and ecological transitions; an ontological approach to design and design for transitions; and the relations among autonomy, design, and the political activation of relational and communal logics at the center of the transitions. Can design's modernist tradition be reoriented from its dependence on the life-stifling dualist ontology of patriarchal capitalist modernity toward relational modes of knowing, being, and doing? Can it be creatively reappropriated by subaltern communities in support of their struggles to strengthen their autonomy and perform their life projects? Can ontologically oriented design play a constructive role in transforming entrenched ways of being and doing toward philosophies of well-being that finally equip humans to live in mutually enhancing ways with each other and with the Earth? Such are the overall questions explored in this book.

Situating This Book's Emergence within Epistemological and Political Contexts

This book is the result of seven years of research and teaching on design, relationality, and transitions at the upper-division and graduate levels; the background, however, goes much farther back. Given that I am not a professional designer nor a theorist within a design school, I feel it is important to situate this work and to convey its emergent character within design and scholarly trends, as well as within my ongoing intellectual-political projects. Making explicit the genealogy of my interest in design will also help me explain the ways in which my take on design is necessarily idiosyncratic and purposeful. I have worked around design themes for many decades. Chemical engineering (my undergraduate major) is about the design of production systems (chemical plants and operations) based on the thermodynamic analysis of the flows of matter and energy that go into these systems.[1] Paradoxically, the engineering professions have been a central agent in the creation of the structural unsustainability of the contemporary world.

During my PhD years at Berkeley in the 1980s, I worked closely with one of the pioneers of systems thinking, C. West Churchman, who in the mid-1950s had coauthored the first textbook of operations research with Russell Ackoff and with two systems planners and designers close to Churchman, the British planner Leonard Joy and the Finnish designer Ritva Kaje. West (as he was universally known) wrote a difficult book, entitled *The Design of Inquiring Systems* (Churchman 1971), and ever since I read it in the late 1970s the notion of the design of knowledge systems has stuck in my mind as one of the most fundamental aspects of intellectual work. Since then, I have been reading in a sustained fashion, albeit largely on my own, in the vast and heterogeneous area of systems thinking, including cybernetics, self-organization, emergence, and complexity. Today, as we shall see, living-systems theory figures prominently in transition visions and novel design frameworks. One highlight for me in this regard was my conversations with the late biologist of complexity Brian Goodwin on several occasions at Schumacher College, an ecological transitions think tank in southern England. The works of Goodwin and those of Humberto Maturana and Francisco Varela on self-organization, autopoiesis, and complexity have influenced my approach to design, as will be abundantly reflected in this book. I see this engineering and systems background as the first thread in the genealogy of my design concerns.

Between the mid-1980s and the early 2000s, I collaborated with groups in Colombia working within the popular communications field, by then a rising professional and activist space. One of the key concepts of this field was that of *diseño de culturas* (the design of cultures), applied to political and professional work with grassroots organizations concerning literacy, popular art, and alternative development projects, particularly with indigenous and Afrodescendant communities for whom oral traditions were still predominant.[2] The popular education and popular communications movements were strong among activists in many parts of Latin America, and, inspired by Paulo Freire's pedagogy of the oppressed, Orlando Fals Borda's participatory action research movement, and liberation theology, activists roamed the land engaging in cultural work with peasant and ethnic subaltern communities. My acquaintance with these trends was decisive for the work I came to do with Afro-Colombian activists in southwestern Colombia beginning in the early 1990s, which continues to this day. Thinking about alternative economies and alternatives to development with these activists, and contributing actively to the defense of their territories and life projects, has been a primary space to think about design for me. This second thread informs my current research project (explained in chapter 6 of this book), centered on a transition imagination exercise for the Cauca River valley region (around the city of Cali), where I grew up and where I continue to collaborate with Afro-Colombian, women's, and environmental collectives.

This transition imagination exercise comes at the end of three decades of critical engagement with questions of development, which involved detailed analyses of the ways in which policy and planning, as design tools par excellence, deeply structure people's realities and everyday lives. Today we would say (ontologically) that development policy and planning, as well as much of what goes on under the banner of design, are central political technologies of patriarchal capitalist modernity and key elements in modernity's constitution of a single globalized world. But I reached this realization only after a series of detours and nonlinear reorientations of my work, as one might call them today, leaning on the language of complexity, including Heideggerian phenomenology and Foucauldian poststructuralism. These philosophical currents, among others, helped me to understand clearly how the so-called underdevelopment of Asia, Africa, and Latin America was actually the result of a complex discursive invention that took place in the early post–World War II period, the consequences of which we are still currently living out. Today I would say that development has been one of the most portentous social experiments of the past seventy years—a grand design gone sour.

Ecology provides a third thread. My interest in ecology started in the early 1980s at Berkeley, where I served for several years as a teaching assistant for the yearlong introductory course for the conservation and resource studies major, which gathered many of the students wishing to engage in environmental activism in the Bay Area and beyond. I continued my ecological learning with James O'Connor and the founding group of the *Capitalism, Nature, Socialism* journal in Santa Cruz in the second half of the 1980s, and with colleagues in the Anthropology Department at the University of Massachusetts, Amherst, in the 1990s, who were by then pioneering a "biocultural synthesis" of biological and cultural approaches to the environment and to questions such as health, nutrition, and poverty.[3] It branched into a substantial interest in political ecology, still one of my main fields—a field often defined as the study of the interconnections among culture, nature, power, and politics. Today this thread feeds directly into the work that I, along with colleagues Mario Blaser and Marisol de la Cadena, call political ontology. An important crystallization of these ecological interests was the codesign in 1998 of a weeklong workshop on ecological river basin design for river communities of the Pacific rain forest in Colombia, in which I applied a systems approach to the "territorial ordering" of river spaces. I designed the workshop and implemented it with activists of the Proceso de Comunidades Negras (Process of Black Communities). The workshop was the first statement of what I then started to call *autonomous design*, to be featured in the last chapter of this book.

There is one more important line of work shaping my design concerns, also dating to my years at Berkeley, and directly connected with how I came to conceptualize the present work. In the early 1980s, I became acquainted with Maturana and Varela's notion of autopoiesis, with Fernando Flores and his work on ontological coaching, and eventually with Flores and Terry Winograd's concept of ontological design (Winograd and Flores 1986).[4] These all marked significant influences on me. The notion of ontological design outlined in Flores and Winograd's book stayed with me throughout the years, and I attempted to develop it in the first version of this book, completed in the spring of 2012. Since then, I have come across the work of a loosely connected network of scholars for whom this notion has also been important, although not necessarily in connection with Flores and Winograd's work, and their work has come to inform the present version significantly. With the emergence of the ontological turn in social theory over the past decade, I have been cultivating the convergence, in my own thinking, of design ontologies and the ontological turn in the academy, anchored in the notions of relational and nondualist ontologies. This book has thus also become an exploration of the design dimension of the ontological turn. My acquaintance with Buddhism and nondualist forms of spirituality over the same period has kindled my interest in relationality (through related concepts such as dependent coarising and interbeing), in turn enriching my understanding of the ontology of design. I should mention another element of importance that has also influenced my design concerns. Since the early 1990s, my interest in information and communication technologies put me in touch with the digital dimension of design through the work of thinkers like Brenda Laurel, Pierre Lévy, and Paul Virilio, particularly the last's caustic yet lucid critique. Thinking about the digital from relational perspectives became part and parcel of the cultural studies of design I develop in this book.

I would be remiss if I did not mention, in ending, that one particular attraction of design for me is that I feel design thinking describes my own scholarly work and writing process. True, there is a lot of hype about the somewhat mysterious abilities underlying the creative work of (famous, mostly male) designers. There is nothing mysterious about it, however, as recent ethnographies of designers at work show (e.g., Cross 2011; Murphy 2015), although this does not mean that it is not complex. I find more compelling the description of how design works than, say, that of how Cartesian models explain scientific thinking as allegedly based on logical reasoning, induction and deduction, and so forth. This doesn't mean that logical reasoning is not important—it is—but that intuition, feelings, and emotions are often as important. Above all, the "abstract reasoning" account of knowledge leaves out of the picture a hugely important feature of knowledge production that design thinking does not: the fact that creation is always emergent, in the two registers of emergence: self-organized and other-organized, the latter qualifier meaning that the scholar/designer also lays down elements and makes decisions that enable the self-organizing dynamic to take off and do its thing. As I hope the previous account of my multiple locations shows, my scholarly and political work has evolved in great part through self-organizing emergence over the years, much more than as a result of any conscious research plan.

There have been the proverbial moments of inspiration, but overall, from the early 1980s (if not before) until today, all the pieces that have come into the *making* of this book have coevolved through manifold "local" interactions that I could not have predicted in advance—from my dissatisfaction at a young age in Cali with "catching up" with the West and becoming "modern" and the seemingly incongruous encounter with systems thinking, ecology, and social movements, to the engagement with, say, Maturana and Flores and, more recently, transition thinkers and designers and ontological turn theorists and things digital and the dire realities at play in the work with Afro-Colombian activists and . . . All of these threads are responsible for this book, which means that this book is itself a temporary crystallization of this emergence (in fact, this book was just supposed to be an input into the other book I was writing; in a way, it just happened). Perhaps one might call the composition of the emergent heterogeneous assemblage that is this book, design.[5]

I emphasize "making" above because, as designers would have it, intellectual work is about making. There is an embodied character to writing that is often disregarded, a tactility almost and a phenomenology of writing that partakes more of a makers' culture than of the isolated "mind at work" celebrated in popular accounts of scientists and innovators (the "Steve Jobs genius" phenomenon). Most of what we do as scholars is refashioning, often through bricolage, by making novel connections, reconfiguring, reframing, and rearticulating ideas that were already proposed by others or that just float in the historically accumulated noosphere, and with some luck this refashioning sets off emergent logics that end up in, say, a good book.[6] The process evolves through *composition*, in Jacques Attali's (1985) sense of this term—even more, this book has been designed or composed in this way. To put it differently, all creation is collective, emergent, and relational; it involves historically and epistemically situated persons (never autonomous individuals), and this ineluctable relationality is acknowledged now by designers in the age of "design, when everybody designs," in Ezio Manzini's (2015) skillful title. I suspect that many scholars would agree with the view just sketched of how intellectual making takes place.

To conclude, I can say, in retrospect, that my overriding concern is with difference, and how difference is effaced or normalized—and, conversely, how it can be nourished. This concern embraces difference in the biological realm (hence, my interest in biodiversity), epistemic difference (coloniality), cultural difference, and—as one might say today—ontological difference, or the pluriverse. Today, difference is embodied for me most powerfully in the concept of the pluriverse, *a world where many worlds fit,* as the Zapatista put it with stunning clarity. This has been the central problem that, largely intuitively, has reverberated throughout my intellectual life. It has also been about "living fearlessly with and within difference," as feminists from the Global South often put it (e.g., Trinh 1989; Milczarek-Desai 2002), that is, about an ethical and political practice of alterity that involves a deep concern for social justice, the radical equality of all beings, and nonhierarchy. It's about the difference that all marginalized and subaltern groups have to live with day in and day out, and that only privileged groups can afford to overlook as they act as if the entire world were, or should be, as they see it.

Here we find a powerful design connection, as both design and difference are about the creation of form. They are about morphogenesis, in the broad sense of the term, which involves a broad range of processes, from how the leopard changed its spots or how the butterfly acquired its wings—and so many instances of emergent natural order and "design," such as the ubiquitous fractal and dendritic structures found even in the Amazon River basin taken as a whole—to the architect's concern with form in the design of the built environment, to landscapes, cities, art, and so forth.[7] Between "the life of form" and the "form of life" (Goodwin 1994, 2007) an entire design space opens up; it includes the "world-within-the-world" of human creation (Fry 2012) for sure, but it goes beyond, as intuited by cultural studies of design scholar Brenda Laurel: *"When one steps back from the marketplace, things can be seen in a different light. While time passes on the surface, we may dive down to a calmer, more fundamental place. There, the urgency of commerce is swept away by the rapture of the deep. Designers working at that depth choose to delve into the essence of design itself. Form, structure, ideas and materials become the object of study"* (2003, 13; my emphasis). This "acquired disposition" of the designer is poetically described by Australian design theorist Susan Stewart as "the deep pleasure experienced by the designer, in the blossoming or unfolding of felicitous material conjunctions and effects; in the embodied recognition of what is both transformative and fitting within the material context in question" (2015, 275).

We restate the question: can design be reoriented from its dependence on the marketplace toward creative experimentation with forms, concepts, territories, and materials, especially when appropriated by subaltern communities struggling to redefine their life projects in a mutually enhancing manner with the Earth?

Acknowledgments

Acknowledging the multiple influences on the ideas presented in this book is essential to explaining its writing in multiple geographic, epistemic, and social locations. As I have already suggested, my sources of inspiration are twofold: the cogent notions stemming from Latin American social struggles, on the one hand, and theoretical and political debates in the academy in Latin America, the United States, and elsewhere, on the other. To begin with the first category, my first debt of gratitude goes to the brilliant and committed group of Afro-Colombian activists belonging to the organizational network Process of Black Communities, particularly Charo Mina Rojas, Marilyn Machado, Francia Márquez, Carlos Rosero, Yellen Aguilar, Danelly Estupiñan, Karin Banguero, Felix Banguero, María Ginés Quiñones, José Santos, and Libia Grueso, with most of whom I have maintained a friendship and collaboration that goes back to the early 1990s. My thanks also to those academics and intellectuals who are fellow travelers in the work with the Process of Black Communities, particularly Patricia Botero, Axel Rojas, Gladys Jimeno, Anthony Dest, Irene Vélez, Sheila Grunner, Viviane Weitzner, Hildebrando Velez, Jeanette Rojas, David López Matta, and Ulrich Oslender, and the entire Grupo de Académicos e Intelectuales en Defensa del Pacífico Colombiano, created in 2010 by academics and activists with the goal of advancing an international campaign,

Otro Pazífico Posible (Another Pacific Is Possible). My deep appreciation to Betty Ruth Lozano, María Mercedes Campo, and Natalia Ocoró, of the Cali-based Colectivo Cultural Afrodiaspórico (Afrodiasporic Cultural Collective), for their important work on the brutal impact of extractivism and patriarchal capitalism on black women in urban contexts. Comrades and activist intellectuals in Colombia and elsewhere from the field of social struggles who have been important to the ideas presented here include Manuel Rozental, Vilma Almendra, Gustavo Esteva, Xochitl Leyva, Patrick Bond, and Ashish Kothari.

Shifting to the academic domain, although the separation is hardly sharp, this book owes a first debt of gratitude to Marisol de la Cadena, Mario Blaser, Eduardo Gudynas, and Michal Osterweil, with whom I have maintained an active agenda of collaborative research and writing on relationality, political ontology, and the Latin American resistance to extractivism and transitions to postextractivism. The thinking space created by this group has been central to the book's imagination, despite the healthy skepticism that some of them, and other friends, maintain regarding the idea of design. Also important in this regard have been my conversations over the years with Cristina Rojas, J. K. Gibson-Graham, Herman Greene, Laura Ogden, John Law, Boaventura de Sousa Santos, Sonia Alvarez, Wendy Harcourt, Philip McMichael, Enrique Leff, Walter Mignolo, and Catherine Walsh.

I have been fortunate to draw on conversations with a growing number of friends and colleagues working in design fields. Of crucial importance has been my acquaintance with Tony Fry and Anne-Marie Willis in Australia, pioneers of ontological design, and their ideas are amply reflected in this book. Similarly important has been the group at Carnegie Mellon School of Design (Terry Irwin, Cameron Tonkinwise, Gideon Kossoff, and Peter Scupelli), who kindly invited me to participate in their Transition Design Workshop in March 2015, with Ezio Manzini as a main speaker. I would also like to thank, in the United States, Juan Obando (Massachusetts College of Art and Design, Boston), Ignacio Valero and Lynda Grose (California College of the Arts, San Francisco), Elizabeth Chin (Art Center College of Design, Pasadena), Kenny Bailey (Design Studio for Social Intervention, Boston), Lucy Suchman (Department of Sociology, Lancaster University, Lancaster, UK), Damian White (Rhode Island School of Design, Providence), Silvia Austerlic (Santa Cruz), and Fernando Domínguez Rubio (Department of Communications, University of California, San Diego). Conversations with anthropology colleagues Peter Redfield, Ana María Ochoa Gautier, Diane Nelson, and Anke Schwittay have been particularly relevant to understanding the growing fields linking anthropology and design, and so were the discussions held at the Innovent session "Design for the Real World. But Which 'World'? What 'Design'? What 'Real'?," that I co-organized with Eeva Berglund and Debbora Battaglia as part of the American Anthropological Association Annual Meeting in San Francisco in 2012. My special thanks to the co-organizers and to Brenda Laurel for accepting our invitation and for her inspiration. I have maintained a fruitful conversation on anthropology and design with Eeva Berglund in Helsinki. Also in Helsinki, Andrea Botero and Kari-Hans Kommonen at the Media Lab, Aalto University, have been sporadic but important interlocutors for the past ten years. Thanks to Alison Clarke and Martina Grünewald (Department of Design Theory and History, University of Applied Arts, Vienna), for inviting me to participate in their anthology on the anthropology of design. Finally, old and new acquaintances in Colombia are becoming newly meaningful for my design interests, including Alvaro Pedrosa, Andrés Burbano, Astrid Ulloa, Alfredo Gutiérrez, and Felipe C. Londoño y Adriana Gómez Alzate, from the Doctorado en Diseño y Creación (Design and Creation PhD program) at the Universidad de Caldas in Manizales.

Students in both the United States and various parts of Latin America have been a significant motivating force and a source of insight for many of the ideas presented here. I thank deeply the undergraduate and graduate students who took my formal courses at Chapel Hill when many of the ideas presented here were half-baked hypotheses at best, and the scores of Colombian and Latin American students who have attended lectures or short courses on aspects related to the book over the past eight years, particularly in Colombia and Argentina. I would like to acknowledge a number of outstanding former undergraduate students at the University of North Carolina at Chapel Hill— Amy Zhang, Katie Cox-Shrader, Kari Dahlgren, Tess Pendergrast, Karina Hernández, Laura Barros, Stephanie Najar, Courtney Shepard, Cameron Trimpey-Warhaftig, Tess Maygatt, Luis Gonzales, and Ariana Lutterman— all of whom are pursuing their own remarkable intellectual-political projects. The graduate students at Chapel Hill and in Latin America have become too numerous to mention by name, but their engagement with earlier versions of this work was critical to its current shape. Friends elsewhere I'd like to thank include Claudia von Werlhof, Jeremy Gould, Thomas Wallgren, Marianne Lien, Janet Conway, Lee Cormie, Ariel Salleh, Federico Demaria, and Irène Bellier. Over the past six years, I have given numerous presentations at universities in Europe and Latin and North America on the various aspects of the political ontology of territorial struggles, transitions, relationality, and design, and I thank those who invited me and the audiences, who often provided highly valuable feedback.

Joan Martínez-Alier, Enrique Leff, Dianne Rocheleau, Carlos Walter Porto Gonçalves, David Barkin, and Víctor Toledo have all enriched immensely my understanding of the ecological and territorial dimensions of neoliberal globalization and social struggles. Thanks to the Research & Degrowth group spearheaded by ICTA scholars in Barcelona (Institut de Ciència y Tecnologia Ambientals) for sharing their work on degrowth with me, to Marco Deriu for his timely invitation to the third International Degrowth Conference in Venice in September 2012, to Silke Helfrich and David Bollier for including me in their important work on commoning and the commons, and to Rob Hopkins for his inspirational work on the Transition Town Initiative, all to be discussed in chapter 5. The Latin American dimension of the book has benefited immensely from the work of many friends and colleagues, including María Lugones, Natalia Quiroga, Alberto Acosta, Verónica Gago, Diego Sztulwark, Colectivo Situaciones, Rita Segato, Raquel Gutiérrez Aguilar, José Luis Coraggio, Raúl Zibechi, Julieta Paredes, Yuderkis Espinosa, Maristella Svampa, and Pablo Mamani. In Colombia, I would like to thank Eduardo Restrepo, Patricia Vargas, Aída Sofia Rivera, Darío Fajardo, María Victoria Uribe, Marta Cardona, Iván Vargas, Laura Gutiérrez, Diana Gómez, Eloísa Berman, Miguel Rocha, Irene Alejandra Cabrera, Chris Courtheyn, and the research group on Nation, Culture and Memory at Universidad del Valle in Cali (particularly Luis Carlos Arboleda). Thanks to Chris as well for his excellent assistance with the manuscript at various stages of writing. My deep thanks to the group of colleagues at the Universidad del Cauca in Popayán, who have crafted an incredibly vital interepistemic space where community and activist knowledges occupy a place of pride, for welcoming this work in their midst, including Olver Quijano Bolívar, Javier Tobar, Adolfo Albán Achinte, Olga Lucía Sanabria, Axel Rojas, Lorena Obando, and Cristóbal Gnecco.

My immediate scholarly environment in Chapel Hill has been nourished by a supportive and engaging group of colleagues, of whom I'd like to thank Larry Grossberg, Don Nonini, Michal Osterweil, Dottie Holland, Eunice Sahle, John Pickles, James Peacock, Peter Redfield, Mark Driscoll, Gabriela Valdivia, Federico Luisetti, Emilio del Valle Escalante, and Rudi Colloredo, as well as Orin Starn, Diane Nelson, and Michaeline Crichlow at Duke. Thanks to Larry for his insightful and useful comments on the manuscript. Pavithra Vasudevan, Cassandra Hartblay, Ahsan Kamal, Marwa Koheji, and Kathleen Kenny engaged with the manuscript from the perspective of their own work as

PhD students in Chapel Hill in enriching and constructive ways. My gratitude in Chapel Hill also goes to Megan and Tim Toben, founders of the Pickards Mountain Eco-Institute, for cultivating the transition spirit in our immediate environment through their creative ecological work and their deep concern for the future of life. My very special thanks to Gisela Fosado, my editor at Duke University Press, for her decided interest in this work, her constant encouragement, and her unfailingly wise and timely advice; to Maryam Arain for her proactive editorial assistance at the press; and to Kim Miller and Lisa Bintrim for their enormously careful copy editing of the manuscript, which made of this book a more accomplished work. At home, where most of these ideas became crystallized in multiple handwritten notebooks and on the screen, my *compañera* Magda Corredor provided not only unfailing support but daily insights on so many aspects of life that helped me clarify what is at stake in the pages that follow. To her, my deepest love and gratitude. Finally, as always, to the musicians, for keeping the pluriverse alive: to the haunted musics of Mali and Senegal and the musics of Africa, the continent that gave us the rhythm that dwells at the heart of all life; to the marimba music of the Colombian Pacific; and to so many vibrant hybrid musics that day and night unfailingly keep so many worlds in movement with the indubitable conviction that there is still much in life that refuses to yield to the ontology of devastation that has become so pervasive with neoliberal globalization and its vacuous notion of progress.

Introduction

In 1971, as industrialism and U.S. cultural, military, and economic hegemony were coming to their peak, Victor Papanek opened *Design for the Real World* with the following caustic indictment of the field: "There are professions more harmful than industrial design, but only a very few of them. . . . Today, industrial design has put murder on a mass-production basis"; even more, "designers have become a dangerous breed" (1984, ix). Reflecting on the watered-down governmental agreements at the much-talked-about summits on the environment and sustainable development (Rio +20 in June 2012 and the Paris COP 21 in December 2015), just to mention two prominent recent attempts at "redesigning" global social policy, one might think that not much has changed, but this would be too quick a judgment. To be sure, much of what goes on under the guise of design at present involves intensive resource use and vast material destruction; design is central to the structures of unsustainability that hold in place the contemporary, so-called modern world. But despite crucial continuities, today's social and design contexts are significantly different than in the 1970s. Informed by a rich international experience in "Third World development," which enabled him to witness failure after failure in design, Papanek called for taking the social context and responsibility of design with utmost seriousness. A growing number of contemporary designers are heeding this call today. This book can be seen as a contribution to this ongoing redefinition of design; it will do so from a particular vantage point, here referred to as *ontological* or, more precisely, *politico-ontological*.

The global boom of design with postmodernism and globalization has certainly had its ups and downs, its high and low moments. Reflections on design by its theorists and practitioners over the past decade, however, converge on some realizations and novel emphases. The first is the ubiquity of design—design is literally everywhere; from the largest structures to the humblest aspects of everyday life, modern lives are thoroughly designed lives. Second, social context is important for successful design, well beyond products' functional or commercial applications, or for effective services. Third, ecologically oriented fields in particular have realized design's vital role in creating a more livable world, with the concomitant need to come up with types of design that make a difference. The fourth signals what is perhaps the most radical change: the need to take seriously the notion that everybody designs, leading to a whole range of proposals for ethnographic, participatory, and collaborative design, and indeed a rethinking of the entire concept of design, "when everybody designs," as Italian design theorist and practitioner Ezio Manzini (2015) pronounced in the very title of his most recent, and compelling, book. Similarly, the spread of digital technologies has pushed designers into embracing unprecedented rules for design, based on interactivity and user participation; design comes to be seen as collaborative, plural, participatory, and distributed. In short, as Tim Brown—a design guru from the famed San Francisco firm IDEO—puts it, design "has become too important to be left to designers" (2009, 8). All of the above is seen as requiring new methods, approaches, and ways of thinking—a novel "design thinking" (T. Brown 2009; Cross 2011), a manner of approaching not only the task at hand but the world that is more ethnographic and relational. Designers discuss the changing status of "the object" (Lukic and Katz 2010) and "things" (Ehn, Nilsson, and Topgaard 2014), echoing current debates in science and technology studies, anthropology, and geography. Finally, as exemplified by Anne Balsamo (2011) for the case of technological innovation, there is an important focus on the relation between design and culture: the fact that design is about creating cultural meanings and practices, about designing culture, experience, and particular ways of living (see also Manzini 2015; Julier 2014; see Laurel 2001; Suchman 2007; and Sparke 2004 for important precedents on this relation). Whether all of this warrants claiming that a new design culture has emerged remains a matter of debate, although the acute sense of change in critical design studies is itself a factor to be considered.

One thing should be clear from the outset: while any design discussion inevitably summons established design imaginaries, it should be clear that in this book *design* refers to much more than the creation of objects (toasters, chairs, digital devices), famous buildings, functional social services, or ecologically minded production. What the notion of design signals in this work—despite *design*'s multiple and variegated meanings—is diverse forms of life and, often, contrasting notions of sociability and the world.

The Argument and the Book's Outline

The book is divided into three main parts. Part I introduces some elements from the design literature at present and offers an outline for a cultural studies approach to design. I pay particular attention to those works that imagine a new social role and modes of operation for design (chapter 1). There are abundant ideas about how design is being transformed in practice, and how to hasten the change, although as we shall see few of these works question the cultural-philosophical armature from which design practice itself emerges (broadly, patriarchal capitalist modernity). Taken as a whole, these trends reveal the existence of a critical design studies field under construction. In chapter 2, recent theoretical trends and design debates in anthropology, ecology, architecture and urbanism, digital studies, development studies, political ecology, and feminist theory are reviewed to ascertain their contribution to an understanding of the nexus among design, culture, and the construction of reality specific to the current historical conjuncture. The aim of this part is to introduce diverse literatures to diverse audiences: design literatures to non-design readers and, conversely, up-to-date social theory approaches to design experts with little background in the social sciences and the humanities.[1]

Part II proposes an ontological reading of the cultural background from which design emerges, and it goes on to outline an ontological approach to design. Chapter 3 presents a particular analysis of the background that enables a unique answer to the question of design's reorientation. Inspired by a "minor" perspective within the biology of cognition (spearheaded by the original work of Chilean biologists Humberto Maturana and Francisco Varela, 1980, 1987), this chapter develops a reading of the background in terms of the "rationalistic tradition," often associated with the objectifying epistemology of Cartesianism. It summarizes well-known arguments about the dualist ontology that, linked to such a tradition, characterizes the prevailing versions of Western modernity. What is new here is the idea that such a critique of dualisms (mind/body, self/ other, subject/object, nature/culture, matter/spirit, reason/emotion, and so forth) is arising from many different intellectual and activist domains, not just academic critiques. My argument is that the convergence of these tendencies is fostering the creation of an ontological-political field that questions anew, and goes beyond, these dualisms. The multisited emergence of such a field is making progressively perceptible—theoretically and politically—a range of alternatives, increasingly conceptualized in terms of the notion of relationality. This concept offers a different, and much-needed, way of re/conceiving life and the world, and a potential new foundation for design.

With these pieces and a renewed mode of access to the question of reorienting design in place, chapter 4 moves on to outline the concept of ontological design. Initially proposed by Terry Winograd and Fernando Flores in the mid-1980s, it has remained little developed, with the few exceptions featured prominently in this book. Ontological design stems from a seemingly simple observation: that in designing tools (objects, structures, policies, expert systems, discourses, even narratives) we are creating ways of being. A key insight here is what Anne-Marie Willis (2006, 80) has called "the double movement of ontological designing," namely, that we design our world, and our world designs us back—in short, design designs. The ontological design approach is found at the basis of Tony Fry's proposals for a transition from sustainability to "Sustainment," as well as a handful of recent transition design proposals. In this chapter I present ontological design as a means to think about, and contribute to, the transition from the hegemony of modernity's one-world ontology to a pluriverse of socionatural configurations; in this context, *designs for the pluriverse* becomes a tool for reimagining and reconstructing local worlds.

Part III explores this proposition in depth. Chapter 5 brings to the forefront the cultural-political background within which a pluriversal design practice arises as a tangible possibility and as more than just a figment of the intellectual imagination. This chapter takes a sweeping look at the rich production, over the past decade, of cultural and ecological transition narratives and discourses in both the Global North and the Global South. It summarizes emergent notions and movements in the Global North, such as degrowth, commoning, conviviality, and a variety of pragmatic transition initiatives. For the Global South, it examines current debates and struggles around *Buen Vivir* (well-being), the rights of nature, communal logics, and civilizational transitions, particularly as these debates are taking place in some Latin American countries, pondering whether they can be seen as instances of the pluriverse re/emerging. The argument here is that these transition imaginations, which posit the need for radical transformations in the dominant models of life and the economy, might constitute the most appropriate framework for an ontological reframing of design. Two interconnected reframings are then presented: an evolving "Transition Design" framework being developed as a graduate training and research program at Carnegie Mellon University's School of Design, and Manzini's conceptualization of design for social innovation and transition to a new civilization.

Finally, chapter 6 develops the notion of autonomous design as a particular ontological design approach in dialogue with the transition visions and design frameworks. The basic insight is, again, seemingly straightforward: that every community practices the design of itself. This was certainly the case with traditional communities (they largely endogenously produced the norms by which they lived their lives), as it is today with many communities, in both the Global South and the Global North, that are thrown into the need of designing themselves in the face of ever-deepening manifestations of the crises and the inescapable techno-economic mediation of their worlds. In other words, if we accept the thesis—voiced by social movement activists, transition visionaries, and some designers—that the current crises point at a deeper civilizational crisis, then the autonomous design of new forms of life and their own life projects appears to many communities as an eminently feasible, perhaps unavoidable, theoretico-political project; for some, it is even a question of their survival as distinct worlds. I will illustrate this notion of autonomous design with a transition exercise for a particular region in Colombia's southwest, envisioning a transformation from the ecologically and socially devastating model that has been in place for over a hundred years to a codesign process for the construction of a life-enhancing regional pluriverse.

A fundamental aspect of autonomous design is the rethinking of community or, perhaps more appropriately, the communal; this rekindled concern with the communal is in vogue in critical circles in Latin America and in transition movements in Europe concerned with the relocalization of food, energy, and the economy and with transition towns and commoning, among others.[2] Hence, this chapter attempts to place autonomy and the communal at the center of design. (That this has nothing to do with the individual autonomy imagined by liberalism will become clear throughout the book. In fact, the opposite is the case.) The inspiration for this proposition comes from the view that autonomy is the most fundamental feature of the living; in Maturana and Varela's terminology, to be explained in chapters 3 and 6, autonomy is the key to *autopoiesis*, or the self-creation of living systems. This proposition will serve as a partial anchor for proposing a particular practice and way of thinking about the relation among design, politics, and life, to be called *autonomous design.*

From "Development" to the Pluriverse

At the dawn of the development age, a group of reputable United Nations experts characterized the project to come as follows: "There is a sense in which rapid economic progress is impossible without painful adjustments. Ancient philosophies have to be scrapped; old social institutions have to disintegrate; bonds of caste, creed, and race have to burst; and large numbers of persons who cannot keep up with progress have to have their expectations of a comfortable life frustrated. Very few communities are willing to pay the full price of economic progress" (United Nations, Department of Social and Economic Affairs 1951, 15). In hindsight, we can consider this pronouncement as a daring, albeit utterly arrogant, design vision. The notion of underdevelopment was just being concocted, and the "Third World" had not yet been born. A new design dream was overtaking the world; we are still engulfed by it, even though, for many, as for the Earth itself, the dream has increasingly turned into a nightmare. What the United Nations envisioned was a sweeping "elimination design" (Fry 2011) of its own, aimed literally at scrapping the vernacular design and endogenous practices that for centuries had nourished, for better or worse, the lives of millions throughout the centuries. Almost overnight, a diverse range of rich and vibrant traditions were reduced to being worth, literally, nothing: nondescript manifestations of an allegedly indubitable fact, "underdevelopment." Yet this dream made perfect sense to millions and was embraced by elites almost worldwide. Such was the power of this design imagination. Not only that, the discourse still holds sway today, as witnessed by the newest round of self-serving debates and policy maneuvers set in place in 2015, and for the next fifteen years, under the rubric of the post-2015 development agenda and the scuffle over a new set of sustainable development indicators. As Fry puts it, "the world of the South has in large part been an ontological designing consequence of the Eurocentric world of the North" (2017, 49). Thus, it is necessary to liberate design from this imagination in order to relocate it within the multiple onto-epistemic formations of the South, so as to redefine design questions, problems, and practices in ways more appropriate to the South's contexts.

Today, faced with the realities of a world transformed by a changing climate, humans are confronted with the irrefutable need to confront the design disaster that development is, and hence to engage in another type of elimination design, this time of the structures of unsustainability that maintain the dominant ontology of devastation. The collective determination toward transitions, broadly understood, may be seen as a response to the urge for innovation and the creation of new, nonexploitative forms of life, out of the dreams, desires, and struggles of so many groups and peoples worldwide. Could it be that another design imagination, this time more radical and constructive, is emerging? Might a new breed of designers come to be thought of as transition activists? If this were to be the case, they would have to walk hand in hand with those who are protecting and redefining well-being, life projects, territories, local economies, and communities worldwide. These are the harbingers of the transition toward plural ways of making the world. *The order is rapidly fadin' / And the first one now will later be last / For the times they are a-changin.'* Perhaps the pluriverse is indeed rising, as the Zapatista of Chiapas and those engaged in so many other popular struggles have been saying for over two decades now.

The Stakes

In 1980, as neoliberalism and unfettered market-led globalization were coming firmly into place with the conservative regimes of Margaret Thatcher and Ronald Reagan, elected with seemingly overwhelming popular support, Bob Marley sent a powerful message in the perfect rhythm of Jamaican reggae:

> *Check out the real situation:*
> *Nation war against nation.*
> *Where did it all begin?*
> *When will it end?*
> *Well, it seems like: total destruction the only solution.*
> *And there ain't no use: no one can stop them now.*
> *Ain't no use: nobody can stop them now.*[3]

Where did it all begin, indeed? What are the stakes? Can "they" be stopped? There are scores of answers to these questions, of course. I would like to consider two particular takes on them, far from the current limelight of critical analyses, but perhaps more radical, to end this introduction. The first, by cultural critic Ivan Illich, involves as much a theory of crisis as a transition framework. The second, by several Latin American and European feminists, lucidly unveils the longest historical roots of the contemporary malaise, locating patriarchy at the center of it. Besides their farsighted vision, which makes them particularly appropriate for thinking about transitions, they have the additional value of embodying a strong dissenting design imagination. Reading the feminists' critical theory of patriarchy and Illich's acerbic but enlightening analyses of today's machine-centered civilization, one could reach the conclusion that indeed *Ain't no use: nobody can stop them now.* Yet, at the same time, their insights about transitions to relational and convivial ways of being, knowing, and doing are concrete and real, as in many other transition narratives on which we will draw.

Illich is best known for his trenchant criticism of the deleterious character of expert-based institutions, from medicine and education to energy and transportation, and of the disempowering effects of the feminization of work and the narrowing down of gender struggles to a matter of individual economic and political equality. Published in 1973, *Tools for Conviviality* summarized many of his critiques, setting them in the context of a political vision, namely, the reconstruction of convivial modes of living, or what he termed *conviviality.* The book was self-consciously written as "an epilogue to the industrial era," in the conviction that "in the advanced stage of mass production, any society produces its own destruction" (2015, 7, 9).[4] His key concept, that of the industrial mode of production, enabled him to conceptualize the threat to the human that arises when tools, broadly understood, reach thresholds beyond which they become irremediably damaging to people and the environment. The steady erosion of limits started in the seventeenth century with the harnessing of energy and the progressive elimination of time and space, gained force with the Industrial Revolution, and accomplished a complete restructuring of society in the twentieth century. Many technologies or "tools" based on specialized knowledge, such as medicine, energy, and education, surpassed their thresholds sometime in the early to mid-twentieth century. Once these thresholds were passed, the technologies became not only profoundly destructive in material and cultural terms but fatally disabling of personal and collective autonomy. The concentration of power, energy, and technical knowledge in bureaucracies (the State) resulted in the institutionalization of these tools and enabled a tight system of control over production and destruction. Illich referred to this process as *instrumentation* and showed how it systematically destroys convivial modes of living. The result was a mega-tooled society embedded in multiple complex systems that curtail people's ability to live dignified lives.

The corollary is that society has to be reinstrumentalized to satisfy the twin goals of conviviality and efficiency within a postindustrial framework. This goal requires facing head-on the threats that accelerated growth and the uncontrollable expansion of tools pose to key aspects of the human experience, including the following: humans' historical localization in place and nature; people's autonomy for action; human creativity, truncated by instrumentalized education, information, and the media; people's right to an open political process; and humans' right to community, tradition, myth, and ritual—in short, the threats to place, autonomy, knowledge, political process, and community. Anticipating degrowth debates (chapter 5), Illich spoke about the need for an agreement to end growth and development. To a world mired in ever-increasing production, while making this production seem ever easier, Illich counterposed not only the fallacy of the growth imperative, thus making its costs visible, but the cultivation of a joyful and balanced renunciation of the growth logic and the collective acceptance of limits.[5]

What Illich proposed was a radical inversion, away from industrial productivity and toward conviviality. "To the threat of technocratic apocalypse, I oppose the vision of a convivial society. Such a society will rest on social contracts that guarantee to each person the broadest and freest access to the tools of the community, on the condition of not hampering others' equal freedom of access.... A plurality of limited tools and of convivial organizations would foster a *diversity of modes of living that would acknowledge both memory and the inheritance from the past as creation*" (2015, 26–28; emphasis added). This ethical position involves an alternative technical rationality; as we shall see, it lends support to the emphasis by social movements on ancestrality as the basis for autonomy, and by transition designers on futurality, or the creation of futures that have a future, as a fundamental design principle. As Illich adds, convivial tools will have to be efficacious in fostering people's creative autonomy, social equity, and well-being, including collective control over energy and work. This means that tools need to be subjected to a political process of a new kind. As science and technology create new energy sources, this control becomes all the more important. To achieve these goals, in Illich's view, it is imperative to impose limits on the expansion of production; these limits have the potential to enable the flourishing of a different kind of autonomy and creativity. At the end of the process, there might emerge a society that values sobriety and austerity, where people relearn dependence on others instead of surrendering to an altogether powerful economic, political, and technocratic elite. The process is eminently political:

> Convivial reconstruction implies the dismantling of the current industrial monopoly, not the suppression of all industrial production. . . . A continuous process of convivial reconstruction is possible on the condition that society protects the power of persons and collectivities to change and renew their lifestyles, their tools, their environments; said otherwise, their power to give their reality a new face. . . . We are talking about a society that diversifies the modes of production. Placing limits on industrial production has for us the goal of liberating the future. . . . A stagnant society would be as untenable as a society of endless acceleration. In between the two, there lies the society of convivial innovation. . . . Threatened by the omnipotence of the tool, the survival of the species thus depends on the establishment of procedures that enable everybody to clearly distinguish between these two forms of rationalizing and using tools, thus inciting people to choose survival within freedom. (94–97)

Let us leave Illich for a moment and consider Claudia von Werlhof's account of patriarchy as the source of the contemporary civilizational model that is wreaking havoc on humans and nature. If one were to ask people on the street to name the main crisis sources, very few would name patriarchy. Why, then, go there? There is no doubt that, for von Werlhof, the roots of the Western civilizational crisis lie in the long development, over the past five thousand years, of patriarchal cultures at the expense of matriarchal ones. For this author, patriarchy goes well beyond the exploitation of women; it explains the systematic destruction of nature. Conversely, matriarchy is not defined by the predominance of women over men, but by an entirely different conception of life, not based on domination and hierarchies, and respectful of the relational fabric of all life. This is why, for all cultures, it can be said that "in the beginning, there was the mother" (in the last instance, Mother Earth), that is, the relation, as tends to still be the case today for many indigenous peoples, who retain a range of matriarchal practices. Progressively, however, men undermined this fundament of life in their attempt to usurp women's power to create life through what von Werlhof labels "the patriarchal alchemy." While in its original connotation *alchemy* referred to a mode of knowledge based on observation of the natural rhythm of life, for the patriarchs it became a practice of destruction, the fragmenting of the elements of matter to eventually produce, out of the isolated elements, what was considered most valuable, such as gold or the philosopher's stone. Destruction progressively became the program to be advanced, contradictorily in the name of creating life; eventually, with modernity and the dominance of the machine, the program transmuted into the search for endless progress and the promise of a ceaselessly better world. Monotheistic religions have been a main component of this program, with the pater as a godlike figure. After more than five hundred years of patriarchal Western modernity, this "alchemic civilization" based on "creation through destruction" has seemingly become global, always at war against life. From von Werlhof's perspective, capitalism is the last phase of this patriarchal civilization.[6]

According to several Latin American feminists, the origin of this last phase is found in the Conquest of America and the instauration of the modern/colonial world system. Looking at this historical process from the perspective of patriarchy is essential to understand the transformations ushered in by modernity. To this end, Argentinian feminist anthropologist Rita Segato (2015) introduces a distinction between the "world-village" (*mundo-aldea*) of communal worlds, with their dual-gender ontology (based on complementary dualities, organized on the basis of relations of reciprocity, and not on a binary between intrinsically independent pairs), and the "world-state," with its dualist ontologies, which progressively occupies communal worlds through the constitution of a public sphere dominated by men and an increasingly subordinated feminine private sphere. It was thus that the low-intensity patriarchies of communal worlds gave way to what Segato calls the high-intensity patriarchy of capitalist modernity. From this perspective, patriarchy is at the root of all forms of subordination, including racial, colonial, and imperial domination, along with the resulting pedagogy of cruelty, as Segato names it, imposed on all societies. There is agreement among the growing cadre of Latin American autonomous, decolonial, and communitarian feminists, as Aymara intellectual-activist Julieta Paredes (2012) puts it, that it was on the bodies of women that humanity learned how to dominate. The corollary is to always analyze historically the entanglement of diverse forms of patriarchy, from the autochthonous and indigenous to the modern.[7]

Patriarchal alchemy engulfs most aspects of life; as individuals, we see ourselves in terms of a type of self-realization that is also a process of self-alchemization, of always re/making ourselves through production and self-improvement. Our spirituality often gets impoverished, trapped in the separation between matter and spirit; the body is debased by patriarchal religions, far from the spirituality of Earth. Progressively, humans start to experience a distancing from all life, which includes, unwittingly, those claiming equality within the same life-destroying patriarchal regimes. Once in the modern period, the world comes to be increasingly built without attachment to place, nature, landscape, space, and time—in short, without reference to the hic et nunc (the here and now) that has shaped most human existence throughout history.[8] From these feminist perspectives, what is thus needed is a politics for an other civilization that respects, and builds on, the interconnectedness of all life, based on a spirituality of the Earth, and that nourishes community because it acknowledges that love and emotion are important elements of knowledge and of all of life.

The notion of the interconnectedness of all life is central to ecology, to most transition narratives, and to the theoretical currents discussed in this book in terms of relationality (chapter 2). All living, human or not, takes place within a relational matrix. The forgetting of this fact led to the development of patriarchal cultures. North Carolina ecologist and theologian Thomas Berry (one of the transition thinkers discussed in chapter 5) echoes von Werlhof's analysis in a profound sense. For him, "a new interpretation of Western historical development is emerging through the concept of patriarchy.... The entire course of Western civilization is seen as vitiated by patriarchy, the aggressive, plundering, male domination of our society" (1988, 138–140). This expanded role ascribed to patriarchy, he adds, has yet to reach the public so that it becomes possible to imagine a postpatriarchal, genuinely ecological ("omnicentric") world. Emerging from the analysis is the need for a new historical mission, that of ushering in "a period when a mutually-enhancing human-earth relationship might be established" (145). This can be arrived at only by working against the grain of the four key establishments that support the modern patriarchal vision: governments, corporations, universities, and organized religion.

These lessons resonate with the systematic comparison of "European patriarchal culture" and "matristic cultures" by Humberto Maturana and German psychologist Gerda Verden-Zöller (1993). Like the feminist writers just discussed, these authors adopt an ontological conception of the cultures of matriarchy and patriarchy: "In a patriarchal culture both women and men are patriarchal, and in a matristic culture, both men and women are matristic. Matristic and patriarchal cultures are different manners of living, different forms of relating and manners of emotioning, different closed networks of conversation that are realized in each case by both men and women" (2008, 112).[9] Placing the rise of Indo-European patriarchal culture within a historical and evolutionary context, these authors arrive at some seemingly startling conclusions within an overall perspective they call "the biology of love." Patriarchal culture is defined as characterized by actions and emotions that value competition, war, hierarchies, power, growth, procreation, the domination of others, and the appropriation of resources, combined with the rational justification of it all in the name of truth. In this culture, which engulfs most modern humans, we live in mistrust and seek certitude through control, including control of the natural world.

Conversely, historical matristic cultures were characterized by conversations highlighting inclusion, participation, collaboration, understanding, respect, sacredness, and the always-recurrent cyclic renovation of life. With the rise of pastoral societies, the transition from one culture to the other started and has not ceased ever since. Matristic modes of being persist in contemporary cultures, despite the prevailing patriarchal approach. They survive, for instance, and however partially and contradictorily, in mother-child or parent-child relations, in love relations, in science, and in participatory democracy. Of crucial importance in this conception is the recognition that the basis of biological existence is the act of emotioning, and that social coexistence is based on love, prior to any mode of appropriation and conflict that might set in. Patriarchal modern societies fail to understand that it is emotioning that constitutes human history, not reason or the economy, because it is our desires that determine the kinds of worlds we create.[10]

Matristic thought and culture arise and thrive within this biology of love; they take place "in the background of the awareness of the interconnectedness of all existence; hence, they can only be lived in the continuous implicit understanding that all human actions have implications for the totality of existence" (Maturana and Verden-Zöller 1993, 47). In this view, the change in human emotioning from interconnectedness to appropriation and control thus emerges as a crucial cultural development justified, with the advent of modernity, by a certain rationality. Hence, it is necessary to cultivate again the harmony of coexistence through the equality and unity of all living beings within the ongoing, recursive, and cyclical renovation of life. The ethical and political implications are clear:

> Hence, if we want to act differently, if we want to live in a different world, we need to transform our desires, and for this we need to change our conversations.... This is possible only by recovering matristic living.... The matristic manner of living intrinsically opens up a space for coexistence where both the legitimacy of all forms of existing and the possibility of

agreement and consensus on the generation of common projects of coexistence are accepted. . . . It allows us to see and to live within the interaction and coparticipation of everything that is alive in the living of all the living; patriarchal living [on the contrary] restricts our understanding of life and nature because it leads us to search for a unidirectional manipulation of everything, given the desire to control living. (105)

Retaking this "neglected path" implies reversing the devaluing of emotioning in relation to reason, which inevitably undermines social coexistence. For von Werlhof, the implications are equally momentous:

It turns out that—whether we want to or not—*we cannot continue living within modernity* because it robs us of the very basis for life, including our mere survival! . . . There are two alternatives: to go deeper [within modernity] or to exit from it, to reform it or to revolutionize the situation, toward an alternative *to* modernity rather than *of* modernity. But we know well that this is the greatest taboo all over the world, that is, to leave behind the so-called Western civilization, because it means leaving patriarchy as such behind. This rupture is almost unimaginable anywhere, except within the indigenous worlds. (2015, 159)

"There is only one solution," she continues, considering the Zapatista experience: "the reconstruction of a nonoccidental civilization not only in Mexico but also in the West and throughout the entire planet" (195). We will have to wait until the last chapters of this book to ascertain whether this seemingly utopian call has any purchase with concrete social actors. Suffice it to say for now that this notion of civilizational change is being seriously entertained by many transition theorists and visionaries, from ecologists and climate activists to spiritual teachers. Overcoming patriarchy requires an internal cultural healing, the revitalization of traditions and the creation of new ones, the realization that a civilization based on the love of life is a far better option than one based on its destruction. Some indigenous peoples in the Americas see themselves as engaged in the *Liberación de la Madre Tierra* (the Liberation of Mother Earth), well beyond the traps of the alchemic civilization of corporate and market globalization, which they often refer as the "project of death." For them, it is time to abandon "the superstitious belief in progress and in the modern epoch as the best of all worlds, that is, in the *alchemic project*" (von Werlhof 2015, 85). This is also the meaning of the "new matriarchies" that von Werlhof and others intuit, those that while inspired by matriarchal principles of the past are becoming transformative forces appropriate to the worlds of today.

It bears emphasizing that the importance of this long-term analysis of patriarchy and Western modernity as the background of the contemporary crisis lies in the fact that these authors see patriarchy as *an active historical reality*; it is not a thing of the past. Patriarchal ways of being are central to the historicity of our being-in-the-world at present. This awareness needs to be brought to bear in any significant reorientation of design. As Susan Stewart remarks, "the excision of history from design thinking isolates the understanding that informs the design act from any understanding of the temporal trajectories in which it participates" (2015, 276). Recognizing those historical aspects of our historicity that seem buried in a long-gone past—which requires paying attention to the realm of myth and story in shaping our worlds—is part and parcel of design's coming to terms with the very historicity of the worlds and things of human creation in the current tumultuous age.

Design with/out Futures?

Readers might rightly wonder what these ideas about autonomy, relational living, and so forth have to do with design, ontological or otherwise. Moreover, is *autonomous design* not an oxymoron? The possibility I am trying to ascertain is quite straightforward in principle: whether some sort of ontologically oriented design could function as design for, and from, autonomy. Here again we confront one of the key issues of this book: can design be extricated from its embeddedness in modernist unsustainable and defuturing practices and redirected toward other ontological commitments, practices, narratives, and performances? Moreover, could design become part of the tool kit for transitions toward the pluriverse? What would that imply in terms of the design of tools, interactions, contexts, and languages in ways that fulfill the ontological design principle of changing the ways in which we deal with ourselves and things so that futuring is enabled?

We find distinct yet complementary clues to these questions in the activist and scholarly worlds. If the conditions ever existed for constructing a design agenda from within the theoretico-political space of the social struggles of the day, that moment is today. In 2001 the World Social Forum already announced this historical possibility in the Brazilian city of Porto Alegre; its call to action still reverberates: *Another world is possible.* The World Social Forum echoed what the Zapatista of Chiapas had already voiced with amazing lucidity and force:

Queremos un mundo donde quepan muchos mundos (We want a world where many worlds fit). Is it possible to read in these popular slogans the seeds of a radical design imagination? "Queremos ser nosotros los que diseñemos y controlemos nuestros proyectos de vida" (We ourselves want to be those who design and control our life projects), says the Mapuche poet Elicura Chihuailaf (quoted in Rocha 2015, 97). One can see instances of this determination up and down Latin America, from the Zapatista of Chiapas and the autonomous communities in Oaxaca to the *nasa* and *misak* in Colombia's southwest and the Mapuche in Chile and Argentina, but also among a growing number of campesino and Afrodescendant communities in a number of countries and equally in some urban settings. This determination experienced a veritable takeoff around 1992, coinciding with the five-hundredth anniversary of the so-called discovery of America and the renaming of the continent by indigenous movements as *Abya Yala.*[11] With this renaming, the indigenous peoples achieved a *madurez telúrica,* or civilizational coming-of-age, as their activists put it.

This coming-of-age is foregrounding a range of forms of *pensamiento autonómico,* or autonomous thought. Together with the recrafting of communal forms of knowing, being, and doing, these notions—*autonomía* and *comunalidad*—and their associated practices may be seen as laying the ground for a new design thought with and within communities. Experiences embodying the search for autonomy can be witnessed in many corners of Latin America and the Caribbean, particularly in locations where brutal forms of extractive globalization are being resisted: in struggles for the defense of seeds, commons, mountains, forests, wetlands, lakes, and rivers; in actions against white/ mestizo and patriarchal rule; in urban experiments with art, digital technologies, neoshamanic movements, urban gardens, alternative energy, and so forth. Taken as a whole, these manifestations of multiple collective wills evince the unwavering conviction that another world is indeed possible. Many of these social movements can be seen as processes of "matriarchalization," of defending and re/creating relational and cooperative modes of living with humans and nature.

Let us shift to the world of design scholarship. Australian design theorist Tony Fry speaks of the "defuturing effects" of modern design, by which he means design's contribution to the systemic conditions of structured unsustainability that eliminate possible futures. It is thus important to recover our future-imagining capacity, for which he proposes a transition from the Enlightenment to a new horizon of "Sustainment," a new age capable of nourishing those relational ways of being-in-the-world capable of countering the on-tology of defuturing. Design theorists Anthony Dunne and Fiona Raby (2013) likewise argue for design practices that enable collective discussion about how things could be—what they term *speculative design.* "Design speculations," they write, "can act as a catalyst for collectively redefining your relationship to reality" by encouraging—for instance, through what-if scenarios—the imagi-nation of alternative ways of being (2). Such critical design can go a long way, in their view, against design that reinforces the status quo. "Critical design is critical thought translated into materiality. It is about thinking through design rather than through words and using the language and structure of design to engage people. . . . *All good critical design offers an alternative to how things are*" (35; emphasis added). That we are in the age of "speculative everything" is a hopeful thought, assuming it fuels the kinds of "social dreaming" (169) that might result in "the multiverse of worlds our world could be" (160). The on-tological impetus of speculative design will be explored at length in subse-quent chapters, particularly through the notion of design for transitions to the pluriverse.

Speculation is rampant in all kinds of directions. It is useful to identify two opposing design fictions as a heuristic, with a whole range in between. At one end we find matristic, convivial, futuring, and, broadly speaking, relational visions that highlight the re/creation of worlds based on the horizontal rela-tion with all forms of life, respecting the human embeddedness in the natu-ral world. At the other end of the spectrum there lies the dream, held by the flashy techno-fathers of the moment, of a posthuman world wholly created by Man. This is the world, for instance, of synthetic biology, with its gene-centric view of life; of booming techno-alchemies for genetic enhancement and the prolongation of life; of robotics, cyborgian fantasies, space travel, nanotech-nology, unlimited 3-D printing, and much more; of the bizarre geoengineering schemes concocted in corporate boardrooms as solutions to climate change; and of those advocating for the "Great Singularity," a technologically induced transformation "when humans transcend biology," in which life would finally be perfected, perhaps as in the world-without-mothers of artificial intelligence fictions such as those portrayed in the film *Ex-Machina,* where women's ability to give life is finally completely usurped since wo/man is wholly created by man through the machine.[12] Are these masculine imaginaries of creation—design imaginations for sure—really universal, or unavoidable, as their fathers pretend? One thing is certain: were it to succeed, this world would cease to have any resemblance to the original nature from which all life stemmed

(Plumwood 2002). Here we find the possibility at least of a bifurcation between two design paths, between two modes of civilizational regulation, matriarchal and patriarchal.

Have these tawdry fathers, with their narrow vision of innovation, robbed us of different visions of the future? Given that their views stem from centuries-old civilizational narratives and practices, they capture most of the political force and media attention. Yet in between the Silicon Valleys of the world and struggling communities, one finds all kinds of instrumentations and technological developments, including those informed by an ecological awareness of planetary limits and global climate change. These will be crucial for a design imagination that avoids the traps of capitalistic industrial instrumentation and goes beyond the ontology of separation that thrives on hierarchy, competition, aggression, and the control of humans and nature. Coming to terms anew with "the question concerning technology" (Heidegger 1977) is indeed one of the greatest challenges faced by any kind of critical design practice. As Clive Dilnot (2015) puts it, we need to address head-on the exponential increase in the destructive capacity of technology but in ways that do not cede humans' ability to construct an entirely different set of relations with other living beings through technology.[13] To the naturalized destructiveness that has accompanied the anthropocene, and faced with the emergence of the artificial as the ineluctable mode of human life, he argues, we need to oppose the cultivation of qualitatively new modes of becoming through the very futuring potential offered by the artificial. *Possibility* here means "the negotiation with actuality and not the escalation of what is" (Dilnot 2015, 169), as in the techno-alchemic imaginations just mentioned. As he adds, this implies "negotiation of the possible through the artificial, just as it is also *negotiation with the conditions of natural existence*" (169; emphasis added); these are crucial distinctions. This offers the only chance to overcome "the abject capitulation to what-is [that] is maintained by our inability to grasp what is emerging" (170). The current conjuncture brought about by the full emergence of the artificial confronts us with the need to think anew about the intersection of ethics, design, and politics. We shall take up these vital questions again in the book's conclusion.

The expansion of the artificial also challenges us to "unfold the political capacities of design" by going against the analytical tendency in critical design studies to examine primarily how design, through its very materiality, "hardwires" particular kinds of politics into bodies, spaces, or objects (Domínguez Rubio and Fogué 2015, 143). In contrast, one might focus on design's ability to broaden the range of possible ways of being through our bodies, spaces, and materialities. This unfolding may be seen as based on "designers' acquired orientation to the pursuit of attentive and open-ended inquiry into the possibilities latent within lived material contexts" (Stewart 2015, 275). It thus becomes appropriate, as suggested here, to think about design's capacities and potentiality through a wide spectrum of imaginations—in terms of matristic cultures with feminists; in terms of autonomy and communal modes of living with those struggling to defend landscapes and territories worldwide; or in terms of the artificial, with design thinkers striving to steer a course between the prevailing defuturing practices and the futuring potential of science and technology.

These debates signal a still-unresolved issue in social theory, and a source of tensions and contradictions in activist worlds: the question of modernity or modernities, including the seemingly simple question, is life better today than it has ever been for the human majorities?, as medical advances, the rights of women, life expectancies, communication technologies, and improvement in livelihoods for many seem to suggest. Will there still be "modern solutions to modern problems"? Or has modernity's ability to even imagine the questions that need to be asked to effectively face the contemporary ecological and social crisis been so fatally compromised, given its investment in maintaining the worlds that created it, as to make it historically necessary to look elsewhere, in other-than-modern world-making possibilities? But are these other possibilities, as far as we know them (e.g., those that emerge from relational and place-based forms of living), still viable alternatives? Or have they become, rather, historical impossibilities given their relatively small scale and scope when compared with the globalization juggernaut? We will take up these questions again in the conclusion.

Here, then, is the argument in a nutshell:

1 The contemporary crisis is the result of deeply entrenched ways of being, knowing, and doing. To reclaim design for other world-making purposes requires creating a new, effective awareness of design's embeddedness in this history. By examining the historical and cultural background from within which design practice enfolds, the book aims to contribute to the collective reflection on that practice. To this end, the book is a contribution to the cultural studies of design.

2 Today the most appropriate mode of access to the question concerning design is ontological. Designing this mode of access involves both understanding the dualist ontology of separation, control, and appropriation

that has progressively become dominant in patriarchal capitalist modernity, on the one hand, and inquiring into existing and potential rationalities and modes of being that emphasize the profound relationality and interconnectedness of all that is, on the other. This book contributes to developing this ontological approach to design.

3 The contemporary conjuncture of widespread ecological and social devastation summons critical thought to think actively about significant cultural transitions. Two hopeful forms of transition thinking within design theory and practice are arising as a result: design for transitions, with a broad view of transition ("civilizational," or "the great transition"); and design for autonomy, centered on the struggles of communities and social movements to defend their territories and worlds against the ravages of neoliberal globalization. This book contributes to outlining the fields of design for transitions and autonomous design.

4 This book, finally, seeks to contribute to design discourse through the elaboration of the cultural background of design, at a time when designers are rediscovering people's ability to shape their worlds through relational and collaborative tools and solutions. It is, however, a Latin American contribution to the transnational conversation on design, that is, a contribution that stems from contemporary Latin American epistemic and political experiences and struggles.[14]

I would like to add one final caveat. This book should be read as belonging to a long set of conversations in both Western philosophy and sociopolitical spaces in the West and beyond. The preoccupation with relationality and with the limitations of binary thinking was not invented with the "ontological turn," needless to say; on the contrary, they have received a lot of attention in modern philosophy, at least from the time of Immanuel Kant's humanism and Hegelian and Marxist dialectics, if not before. At the same time, the recent thinking on relationality makes visible the limitations of previous approaches to escaping dualism, particularly how far past authors were willing to push dualism's implications in terms of envisaging significant transformations from the perspective of radical interdependence. There are also genuinely new emphases, particularly the concern with the agency of nonhumans and a certain renewed attention to materiality. These have opened fresh paths for moving intellectually, socially, and politically beyond dualisms and, perhaps, decolonizing Western thought. To put it in Western academic terms, I would say that this book is more anthropological Heideggerianism than deconstructive posthumanism or relentless Deleuzian deterritorialization. This is so because of its commitment to place, the communal, and other practices of being, knowing, and doing, and no doubt also because of its critical approach to technology and its commitment to notions of the human capable of harboring a genuine care for the world.

I also believe there is greater clarity today than in the recent past that the notion of relationality involves more than nondualism; that reimagining the human needs to go beyond the deconstruction of humanism (still the focus of most posthumanist thought) in order to contemplate effective possibilities for the human as a crucial political project for the present; and that to the awareness of how we live in a world (or worlds) of our own making (again, a prevalent theme in Western philosophy) we now need to add a sharper consciousness of how those worlds make us—sometimes with deeply troubling results.

The book should thus be read as constructed along three axes: ontology, concerned with world making from the perspective of radical interdependence and a pluriversal imagination; design, as an ethical praxis of world making; and politics, centered on a reconceptualization of autonomy precisely as an expression of radical interdependence, not its negation.

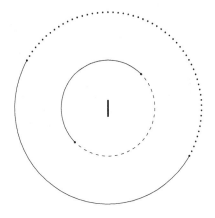

Design for
the Real World

But Which "World"?

What "Design"?

What "Real"?

1

Out of the Studio
and into the Flow
of Socionatural Life

Design is evolving from its position of relative insig-
nificance within business (and the larger envelope
of nature), to become the biggest project of all. . . .
Massive Change is not about the world of design; it's
about the design of the world.

· **Bruce Mau and the Institute without Boundaries,**
Massive Change

A purely technocentric view of innovation is less sustainable now than ever. . . . What we need is an approach to innovation that is powerful, effective, and
broadly accessible . . . that individuals and teams can
use to generate breakthrough ideas that are implemented and that therefore have an impact. Design
thinking, the subject of this book, offers just such an
approach.

· **Tim Brown,** *Change by Design*

In a world in rapid and profound transformation, we
are all designers. . . . The more tradition is weakened,
the more subjects must learn to design their own
lives and shift from a prevalence of activities carried
out in a traditional way to one in which choices are
mainly of design.

· **Ezio Manzini,** *Design, When Everybody Designs*

Statements on the rapidly changing, and increasingly transformative, character of design abound in the literature of the past decade. The intensification of the globalization of images and commodities fostered by markets and technology has led today's critical design theorists to advocate for new kinds of engagement between design and the world. This starts with everyday life but moves on to infrastructures, cities, the lived environment, medical technologies, food, institutions, landscapes, the virtual, and, in the long run, experience itself.[1] The claims about design's potential new roles range from the significant to the earth shattering. A key question becomes: how does one design for a complex world? Instead of keeping on filling the world with stuff, what design strategies will allow us—humans—to lead more meaningful and environmentally responsible lives (Thackara 2004)? As some design researchers contend, we all live within a design cluster, that is, immersed in designs of all kinds, which means that design becomes "a category beyond categories" (Lunenfeld 2003, 10), opening up new spaces for linking theory, practice, and purpose, connecting vision and reality. This brings forth the endless process of discovering new territories for design through research (Laurel 2003).

To be sure, the majority of design treatises still maintain a fundamental orientation that is technocratic and market centered, and do not come close to questioning design's capitalistic nature. Many navigate in between, alternating between uncritical celebration and venturesome ideas and critiques.[2] Design has its caustic critics as well, although few and far between. A well-known text by Hal Foster, for instance, finds that the pervasive, almost total character taken on by design today not only "abets a near-perfect circuit of production and consumption" but instantiates a "pan-capitalist present" (2002a, 192). According to Foster, this type of present effects a perpetual profiling of the commodity that drives the contemporary inflation of design. Whatever transgressive character postmodernism might have had, Foster argues, it has become routinized by design, contributing to the exhaustion of any critique under the label of the *post* or the *neo*. This "wising up" of commercial culture has fashioned the designed subjects of pancapitalism (Foster 2002b). Design has certainly been fully integrated into the neoliberal model of capitalism that has become pervasive since the 1980s (Dunne and Raby 2013). For Sanford Kwinter, the resulting "pop-libertarian aesthetic," according to which every aspect of our daily lives is susceptible to becoming a design objective (in affluent societies), has been accompanied by the capitulation of criticism in the academy and the public sphere to such trends. Nevertheless, asserting that "much more than our living rooms and silverware are at stake" (2007, 17) and acknowledging that it implies a highly developed form of rationality, Kwinter considers that design is also a vehicle for the deepest human aspirations and as such should be a matter of widespread concern.

This chapter looks at some of the most salient critical trends in design studies and practice. It discusses recent proposals for transforming design from an expert-driven process focused on objects and services within a taken-for-granted social and economic order toward design practices that are participatory, socially oriented, situated, and open ended and that challenge the business-as-usual mode of being, producing, and consuming. It highlights design frameworks that pay serious attention to questions of place, the environment, experience, politics, and the role of digital technologies in transforming design contexts. The chapter ends with a discussion of whether a critical design studies field—one that emerges at the intersection of critical social theory and design studies—can be said to exist. A main goal of the chapter is to prepare the ground for more detailed discussions of ontological design, transition design, design for social innovation, and autonomous design, particularly for those readers with little background in design studies. I start with an intuitive, but I believe analytically suggestive, entry into the nature of design.

"When Old Technologies Were New": Design's Arrival in Gabriel García Márquez's Macondo

It is often the case that highly accomplished literary works reveal essential aspects of human life and history with a sharpness and clarity that philosophy and the social sciences can hardly aspire to match. Such is the case, for instance, with *One Hundred Years of Solitude*, by Colombian writer Gabriel García Márquez (1970), a novel that hides unsuspected lessons about the early phases of the deployment of technology and design in so-called traditional societies. Let us start by recalling the book's beginning, often considered one of the most perfect opening paragraphs of world literature:

> Many years later, as he faced the firing squad, Colonel Aureliano Buendía was to remember that distant afternoon when his father took him to discover ice. At that time Macondo was a village of twenty adobe houses, built on the bank of a river of clear water that ran along a bed of polished stones, which were white and enormous, like prehistoric eggs. The world was so recent that many things lacked names, and in order to indicate them it was necessary to point. Every year during the month of March a family of

ragged gypsies would set up their tents near the village, and with a great uproar of pipes and kettledrums they would display new inventions. First they brought the magnet. . . . (1)

But the magnet and the ice were just the beginning of what turned the pre-modern, seemingly designless reality of the poor people of Macondo topsy-turvy. A long paragraph at the start of a later chapter brings us up to date on the dialectic of wonder and disappointment, enthrallment and confusion, felt by the town's people in response to so many modern inventions, such as electricity, the cinema, the phonograph, and the telephone. Let us listen to this amazingly lucid summary paragraph:

Dazzled by so many and such marvelous inventions, the people of Macondo did not know where their amazement began. They stayed up all night looking at the pale electric bulbs fed by the plant that Aureliano Triste had brought back when the train made its second trip, and it took time and effort for them to grow accustomed to its obsessive toom-toom. They became indignant over the living images that the prosperous merchant Bruno Crespi projected in the theater with the lion-head ticket windows, for the character who had died and was buried in one film and for whose misfortune tears of affliction had been shed would reappear alive and transformed into an Arab in the next one. The audience, who paid two cents apiece to share the difficulties of the actors, would not tolerate that outlandish fraud and they broke up the seats. The mayor, at the urging of Bruno Crespi, explained in a proclamation that the cinema was a machine of illusions that did not merit the emotional outbursts of the audience. With that discouraging explanation many felt that they had been the victims of some new and showy gypsy business and they decided not to return to the movies, considering that they already had too many troubles of their own to weep over the acted-out misfortunes of imaginary beings. Something similar happened with the cylinder phonographs that the merry matrons from France brought with them as a substitute for the antiquated hand organs and that for a time had serious effects on the livelihood of the band of musicians. At first curiosity increased the clientele on the forbidden street and there was even word of respectable ladies who disguised themselves as workers in order to observe the novelty of the phonograph from first hand, but from so much and such close observation they soon reached the conclusion that it was not an enchanted mill as everyone had thought and as the matrons had said, but a mechanical trick that could not be compared with something so moving, so human, and so full of everyday truth as a band of musicians. It was such a serious disappointment that when phonographs became so popular that there was one in every house they were not considered objects for amusement for adults but as something good for children to take apart. (164)

As anthropologist Tim Ingold (2011) says, we moderns who have science can feel a certain degree of astonishment at novel discoveries—the newest iPad or electric vehicle, a seemingly miraculous drug just hitting the market—yet no real sense of wonder, as the people of Macondo did then. So, when the telephone was finally introduced, "it was as if God had decided to put to the test every capacity for surprise and was keeping the inhabitants of Macondo in a permanent alternation between excitement and disappointment, doubt and revelation, to such an extreme that no one knew for certain where the limits of reality lay" (164). That was to change significantly with the passage of time, especially as more and more marvels and strangers came to town on the weekly train. And here, at the very end of this page-and-a-half-long paragraph, one hears that "among those theatrical creatures, wearing riding breeches and leggings, a pith helmet and steel-rimmed glasses, with topaz eyes and the skin of a thin rooster, there arrived in Macondo on one of so many Wednesdays the chubby and smiling Mr. Herbert, who ate at the house" (164–165). Those who have read the book will recall what happened next: Mr. Herbert took his scientific instruments to study the banana he was served at the Buendías' house, and, as the saying goes, the rest is history, for shortly thereafter he returned to stay, along with the entire banana company, which eventually caused what García Márquez describes as a leaf storm or whirlwind. For the writer, the banana company represents the political economy of modern technology and design, the main driving engine for the whirlwind of modernity.

I grew up in Cali, Colombia, already with many of the technologies that so marveled and at the same time disappointed the people of Macondo, but in a predigital age. My family did not own a TV until I was fifteen. Before that, kids in our middle-class neighborhood would crowd together in the early part of the evening in the living room of one of our luckier neighbors to watch TV for an hour or so, an occasion for much merriment and communion among the kids; then we would go out to play on the street. By the time I finished college in 1975—still living at home, as was and still is the custom—my parents had acquired, with significant financial sacrifice, our first, low-tech stereo player. That was one of the technological highlights of those years for me, and little by little I started to build a small collection of the vinyl records of my favorite

artists. I would stay up late at night in my bedroom studying and doing homework, after everybody else had gone to sleep, while listening at low volume to
my favorite station on an old, worn-out radio that surely had seen better days.
In college I learned to program in Fortran IV; we would write up by hand
in pencil the simple programs that would enable the endless calculations for
our engineering homework, and each of those programs was converted into a
large number of punch cards with little holes in them that would then be read
by our huge, brand-new, and resplendent IBM 360, which lay impassively in a
large, air-conditioned room of its own. We would look at the reddish machine
in awe from behind the room's glass windows as the young technicians ran our
programs and we waited for the results, which came in the form of long reams
of paper put out by the dot matrix printers of the time, with a unique sound
that quickly became part of our technological sensual repertoire. By the time
I was doing my PhD at Berkeley in the 1980s, all of this had changed dramatically, of course. Yet I invariably wrote the first draft of my dissertation chapters
by hand, at a café on Clement Street in San Francisco, before typing them up
on my first PC at home nearby, a large and heavy Kaypro 4, somewhat popular among academics at the time (it operated with two 64K floppy disks, one
containing the word processing program, the other the data).

The point of this microethnography of my own practices around technology as well as García Márquez's account is not just anecdotal. Nor is it nostal-
gia for times and things (or lack of things) past, and certainly is not intended
to convey a reified account of the rapid pace of technological innovation.[3]
My first goal in telling these stories is simple: to make us aware, before I go
on to discuss contemporary design in some detail, of the complex entanglement of science, materials, technologies, capitalism, and culture that makes
up the matrix of modern design. My second goal, more pertinently for now,
is to highlight the social and cultural histories of the body that surround all
design, the fact that design is a key element in who we become because of the
kinds of practices designed objects and tools call on us to perform. (Does it
matter whether we write with pencils or on an iPad? Whether we engage in
activities collectively in the neighborhood or in the solitude of our individual
rooms in nuclear homes? Whether we dance and make music with others or
listen to it in silence through our earphones? In what ways do these diverse
practices construct different selves and societies? Does it matter?) To be sure,
it doesn't have to be either-or, and certainly it is not a question of finding out
whether things were better before than they are now, or the other way around,
but of foregrounding the indubitable ethnographic fact of the diverse ways of

being-through-practices with which our tools have much to do. Toys are us, aren't they?

The power of tools and design to shape being and identity is eloquently attested by the buzz caused by the world's fairs, from the mid-nineteenth century till today, which became showcases for designs embodying the technological and cultural accomplishments of the age. The famous Crystal Palace Exhibition in London in 1851 (Stocking 1987; Bürdek 2005) paraded for the first time in a specially designed space the technologies, trinkets, and prototypes of the day—power looms, pumps, steam engines, industrial machines. As visitors made their way through the glass cathedral, it became clear to them that not all peoples in the world had achieved the same level of "development," for there was no way the arts from "the stationary East" nor the handicrafts from "the aborigines" could ever match the "progress" of the West. Machines, after all, were "the measure of men" (Adas 1989). World's fairs were not only shrines for the collective adoration of the "civilization" and progress brought about by the Enlightenment era but also machines for effecting what in current Latin American critical theory is called *coloniality*, that is, the hierarchical classifications of peoples in terms of race and culture.

We no longer point at things, of course, as in Macondo's times; design gives us their names, and in this naming we are given to them, too. We rarely think these days about the ways in which our lives are thoroughly designed. Previous inventions constitute, too, the history of our designing—of both their making and our being made by them. It is a sedimented, and thus invisible, history, yet no less effective because of that. From time to time scholars remind us that old technologies were once new, to paraphrase Carolyn Marvin's (1988) wonderfully imaginative title, and that technological development is about "implementing the future" (Marvin 1999).[4] Objects and products are of course central to this. This is strikingly the case with all the design innovations for the home space, from the mid-nineteenth-century Singer sewing machine to the entire range of modernist innovations in the 1920s–1950s (plywood chairs, table lamps, Bauhaus-style furniture, door handles, stackable dishes, vacuum cleaners and washing machines, Braun toasters and kettles, cars of course, Swedish furniture, Finnish glass, and those iconic brand objects of Italian Bel Design, such as Olivetti typewriters and that most beautiful device for modern mobility, the Vespa, introduced in 1946).

These are but a few of the hundreds of objects one is likely to find in lavishly illustrated design history books. They are the stuff of design. And yet design is much more, perhaps even more so today than in the heyday of modernism. Let us now discuss what else there is in the world of design and how it contributes to shaping the design of the world and of our lives.

Reengaging with the World: Toward Participatory, Human-Centered, and Socially Oriented Design

Any serious inquiry into contemporary design must be a journey into the trials and tribulations of capitalism and modernity, from the birth of industrialism to cutting-edge globalization and technological development. This is of course beyond the reach of this short book, yet some general remarks are in order. Design has doubtlessly been a central political technology of modernity. Regardless of where one situates the origin of design—whether with the first use of tools by early humans, the budding technological imagination of the Renaissance, the Industrial Revolution, or nineteenth-century modernism—the fact remains that as an aspect of everyday life design takes off with modernity. Why? Because only with modernity, particularly after the end of the eighteenth century, did societies become thoroughly pervaded by expert knowledges and discourses and transformed by them. Both Jürgen Habermas and Michel Foucault refer to this aspect of modernity, whether in terms of the "colonization" of the lifeworld by such knowledges or the bureaucratization and governmentalization of life by expert institutions linked to the State. What this means is that previously taken-for-granted practices, from child rearing and eating to self-development and of course the economy, became the object of explicit calculation and theorization, opening the door to their designing. This is an aspect that often escapes the attention of design critics, too mired perhaps in design's relation to capitalism. In short, with the development of expert knowledge and modern institutions, social norms were sundered from the lifeworld and defined heteronomously through expert-driven processes; they were no longer generated by communities from within (ontonomy) nor through open political processes at the local level (autonomy).[5]

With the full development of the Industrial Revolution in the mid-nineteenth century, industrial design came to the fore as a field. After a period of uneasy relations with the arts and crafts movement, which tried to counteract the ascendancy of "the world of machines" during the second half of the nineteenth century, by the time modernism emerged in the twentieth century design had become inextricably wedded to functionalism. During the first half of the twentieth century, first with the Bauhaus and then with the Ulm school of design, as well as design schools in other European cities, modern design articulated a new view of the intersection of art, materials, and technology at the same time that it instilled in working people new ways of living through the design of lived environments and the functionality of objects. Functionalism, however, carried the day.[6] Even then, oftentimes the designers' aim was to improve mass-produced goods and people's quality of life through the use of new materials and techniques. One may see in these practices a nascent preoccupation with the relation between design and politics, to be discussed fully in the last chapter of this book.[7]

This also means that, from the outset, design has been inextricably tied to decisions about the lives we live and the worlds in which we live them, even if this awareness seldom accompanies "design as usual." Not only design but the academy, with its penchant for neutrality, shies away from these normative questions: "The question we humans must face"—says Humberto Maturana, on whom we'll draw a lot in subsequent chapters—"is that of what do we want to happen to us, not a question of knowledge or progress" (1997, 1). As Colombian cultural critic Adolfo Albán puts it, speaking about the seemingly intractable social and ecological problems facing most societies, "el problema no es de ciencia, sino de las condiciones de la existencia" ("the problem is not one of lack of knowledge, but of the conditions of existence"; this goes as well for sustainability and climate change: far more than instrumental knowledge and technological adaption is required!).[8] Today some leading critical designers are beginning to tackle this issue in earnest. What world do we want to build? What kinds of futures do people really want? (Thackara 2004; Laurel 2001; Dunne and Raby 2013). How can we strive for "a new, hopefully wiser, civilization" (Manzini 2015, 15)? These normative questions are central to ontologically oriented design.

If we start with the presupposition, striking perhaps but not totally far-fetched, that the contemporary world can be considered a massive design failure, certainly the result of particular design decisions, is it a matter of designing our way out? In an oft-quoted definition by Herbert Simon, design offers the means to "devise courses of action aimed at changing existing conditions, into preferred ones" (quoted in Thackara 2004, 1).[9] Ezio Manzini has proposed a variation on Simon's formula. "Design," he says, "is a culture and a practice concerning how things ought to be in order to attain desired functions and meanings" (2015, 53). Manzini's emphasis on design's role in meaning creation (to be discussed at length in chapter 5) leaves no doubt that "more-of-the-same" or "business-as-usual" approaches are not what is called for. More-of-the-same solutions can at best lead to reducing unsustainability. The good news, however, is that a lot of "going beyond the same" is already happening, in so many social, political, and technological spheres; the bad news is that it might not be happening fast enough, if we heed the criteria of climate change scientists and activists, or with the degree of purposefulness required. More worrisome, most of the policy design that goes on at the level of the State and international organizations sits comfortably within the same epistemic and cultural order that created the problems in the first place. How to go beyond the aporias caused by the fact that we are facing modern problems for which there are no modern solutions (Santos 2014) is one of the key questions that radical design thinking needs to tackle.

There are areas of agreement about how to go on. Let me mention a few. As design moves out of the studio and the classic design professions (industrial design, engineering, and architecture and art) and into all domains of knowledge and applications, the distinction between expert and user/client breaks down. Not only does everyone come to be seen as a designer of sorts, but the argument for a shift to people-centered (and, to a lesser extent, earth-centered) design is more readily acknowledged. Designing people and the environment back into situations also means displacing the focus from stuff to humans, their experiences and contexts. From mindless development to design mindfulness (Thackara 2004), from technological fixes to more design, from object-centered design to human-centered design, and from "dumb design" to "just design"—all of these notions become new guiding ideas (e.g., Laurel 2003; T. Brown 2009; McCullough 2004; Chapman 2005; Simmons 2011). Some of the features of the new design thinking are summarized by Paola Antonelli, the architecture and design curator at the Museum of Modern Art in New York; contemporary design approaches, she says, are critical, activist, organic, and political; they are about thinkering (thinking with your hands, doing hands-on conceptual work), about problem finding and problem framing more than problem solving, and about functional social fictions rather than science fiction; they are guided by ethics more than by user-friendliness. Design has developed a new sensitivity to the environment and to human predicaments, and is more attuned to its ability to contribute to creating a better world; it becomes a medium in the service of society rather than solution-making expertise in the service of industry.[10]

These principles summon to the discussion unprecedented methodological and epistemological issues, opening up a welcoming space for disciplines such as anthropology and geography. New methods highlight front-end research, with the designer as facilitator and mediator more than expert; conceive of design as eminently user centered, participatory, collaborative, and radically contextual; seek to make the processes and structures that surround us intelligible and knowable so as to induce ecological and systems literacy among users; and so forth. Above all, to go back to the normative question, there is an attempt to construct alternative cultural visions as drivers of social transformation through design.

Design as a Situated and Interactive Practice

The increasingly pervasive character of computing in everyday life has fostered concrete questions and design challenges—from "Are 'smart devices' really smart, or are they rather making people more stupid?" to questions about interactivity, networks, space and place, and embodiment. The mood is to go beyond the early fascination with information and communication technologies of the 1980s and 1990s (and allied concepts such as virtual reality and cyberspace; see Escobar 1994; Laurel 2001) and a narrow focus on human-computer interfaces toward a more expansive field, variously referred to as "information technologies and creative practices" (Mitchell, Inouye, and Blumenthal 2003) or "interaction design practices" (McCullough 2004; see, e.g., p. 163 for a "manifesto for interactive design"). In Malcolm McCullough's view, interaction design practices articulate interface design, interaction design, and experience design. Imbued in phenomenological tenets, he sees this articulation in terms of situated technologies that, rather than being decontextualized and value neutral, are embodied, place based, convivial, and conducive to care (see also Manzini 2015; Ehn, Nilsson, and Topgaard 2014). This conception resituates digital technologies within human- and place-centered design, thus counteracting modernity's proclivity to decontextualized speed, efficiency, mobility, and automation. In architecture and other domains, this means designing systems that are easy to operate—a situated design practice that is grounded in place and community but that through embedded systems nevertheless addresses how people navigate the world through their mobile devices. Design thus becomes a critical localized practice, but one that joins the open-source dimension of technology to the cultural practice of design. From these debates it is important to remark on the salience that designers like McCullough, Manzini, and Pelle Ehn, Elizabeth Nilsson, and Richard Topgaard give to questions about place, locality, and community in their revisioning of design practice, both as a corrective to the uncritical embrace of mobile technologies and as a way to redefine their role in daily life—all of this without disavowing the existence and potential of the new technologies.

There is no doubt, from this hasty and purposeful review, that a relatively new brand of design theorist is emerging; the new theories are to some extent a result of taking design practices beyond their established domains, including in social service and environmental arenas, for-profit consulting firms staffed by interdisciplinary research teams, community-based nongovernmental organizations and design outfits, and even social movements.[11] Design thinking has become a key trope in this context. As the editorial in a recent issue of *Design Studies* devoted to the concept put it, the great popularity gained by design thinking outside the design professions stems precisely from the perception of design's real or potential contribution to addressing "wicked" (intractable, unbounded) problems, and of design as an agent of change (Stewart 2011). This brings about a shift from design's functional and semiotic emphasis to questions of experience and meaning.[12] While some designers manifest unease with this trend, many assess it in a positive light. As a key figure in the spread of design thinking from the well-known Bay Area design company IDEO puts it,

> design thinking begins with skills designers have learned over many decades in their quest to match human needs with available technical resources within the practical constraints of business. By integrating what is desirable from a human point of view with what is technologically feasible and economically viable, designers have been able to create the products we enjoy today. Design thinking takes the next step, which is to put these tools into the hands of people who may have never thought of themselves as designers and apply it to a vastly greater set of problems. . . . [There is a] difference between *being* a designer and *thinking* like a designer. (T. Brown 2009, 4)[13]

There isn't much of a self-critical look here in terms of the political economy and cultural politics of design, yet the descriptive character of the analysis—often with a degree of ethnographic detail—is interesting in itself.

Architecture and Urbanism: Experimentation, Unsettlement, and the Reinvention of the Vernacular

There are three topics to be touched on very briefly in what remains of this chapter before a concluding reflection on whether a field of critical design studies can be said to be emerging. These are architecture and urbanism, ecological design, and the relation between design and politics. To start with architecture: there is no doubt that architecture has always been central to design, as witnessed by its role in design education and as richly exemplified by traditions in many world regions (e.g., Italy, Finland, Catalonia in Spain, some Latin American countries, East Asia, or cities like Chicago and San Francisco) where architects have customarily included as part of their practice the design of furniture, fashion, music, materials, and even utopias. There is also a sense that architecture has ceased to be a poor relative of social theory, becoming an important space for discussions about globalization, urbanization, the environment, modernity, and media and digital culture; architects are often attuned to the pressing social issues of the day, including globalization and the anthropocene (e.g., Turpin 2013), and to the theoretical and philosophical problems with which the social sciences and humanities deal (e.g., Sykes 2010).[14] Also readily recognized by critics, however, is the fact that a certain style of architecture has contributed to the inflation of design—a sort of "Bilbao effect," after Frank Gehry's famous Guggenheim Museum in this city. Foster contrasts this "master builder" (Gehry) with Dutch-born and New York–based architect Rem Koolhaas, whose design writings and architectural practice aim rather to rethink globalization from alternative architectural and urban principles. Koolhaas's practice is contradictory, to be sure, as reflected in his work of cultural-architectural criticism *Contents* (2004), a tour de force that combines in intricate ways deconstructive analyses, exposés, post-9/11 geopolitics, diatribes (e.g., on architecture and war), and, of course, a dazzling and ever-proliferating and bifurcating graphic display of images, fonts, photographs, drawings, and so forth.[15] For Tony Fry (2015, 87–89), however, Koolhaas's version of posturbanism continues to abide by the "signature architecture" tendency that spells out the abandonment of the urban as a project and hence the unquestioned character of the city as the locus of the unsustainable.

At the other end of the spectrum, one would be remiss to overlook pleas for the renewal of vernacular architectural practices, for mobilizing the elements of the earth along with those of place and culture to deal with the seemingly intractable problems of urban poverty and environmental degradation, as in the case of the amazing architecture of dwelling in parts of West Africa, beautifully illustrated, described, and theorized by Jean-Paul Bourdier and Trinh T. Minh-ha (2011). *Vernacular*, in these contexts, no longer indexes a rigid traditionalism but a space of possibility that could be articulated to creative projects integrating vernacular forms, concrete places and landscapes, ecological restoration, and environmental and digital technologies in order to deal with serious problems of livelihood while reinvigorating communities.

The tiny house movement, in its multiple instantiations, could be said to be inaugurating a new vernacular thoroughly infused with ecological and cultural design knowledge. Various hybrids of vernacular, self-made, and functional housing are emerging, for instance, in the well-known "half-houses" of Chilean architect Alejandro Aravena.[16] Vernacular forms of design may be particularly relevant when used in design projects intended to strengthen communal autonomy and resilience.

This is just the tip of the iceberg of discussions at the intersection of architecture, art, and design. An exhibit at the Venice Architecture Biennale in 2012 under the rubric "Traces of the Past and Future Steps" showcased a range of tendencies at this intersection; many of the works on display demonstrated ecological sensibility as well as an acute awareness of philosophical and cultural issues such as space and place, temporalities, objects, materiality, locality, scale, agency, and so forth. Innovative designs and experimentation with materials, forms, and patterns embodied reflections on topics such as the relation between the natural and the artificial (moving back from the excessive concern with the virtual toward an ecological sensibility), self-organization, popular knowledge of the built environment, the cultural dimension of architecture (e.g., issues of identity), aesthetic diversity (e.g., the multiplicity of pattern making, including vernacular forms), and of course sustainability. In some cases, however, the lack of a deliberate discussion of capitalism and globalization does not mean a lack of awareness of their importance as much as indicate that architectural discourse gets at them in other ways (through artistic expression, concern with individual behavior, or hints of the spiritual value of space situations, the fate of traditional forms, the destruction and reconstruction of seemingly obsolete spaces or dilapidated neighborhoods, and so forth). Some works explored new imaginaries for living by rethinking long-standing practices (e.g., courtyards in China) through innovative building designs (maintaining the courtyard principles but going beyond its bounded form to propose new structures). Some of the works could be said to be deeply attuned to relational ways of being-in-the-world, starting with the materials themselves (the great wonder in the transfiguration of materials at the microscale, whether wood, glass, or metal, as the narrative of one of the exhibits put it) and the role of objects and surfaces as dwelling topographies that open up toward a deep understanding of place and attention to communal logics and interrelations with the environment.[17]

The tension between those architects for whom place is a crossroads of flows and events and an inevitable space of transformation on an always-shifting ground (e.g., Koolhaas) and those who continue to adhere to an existential conception of place continues to be productive. Nobody has perhaps broached this tension with more passion than Finnish architect Juhani Pallasmaa (e.g., 2016). Influenced by his famous countryman, the architect Alvar Aalto, and building on what is perhaps still the most profound phenomenological reflection on space and place—the inspiring *The Poetics of Space*, by French philosopher Gaston Bachelard (1969)—Pallasmaa provides us with a thoroughly contemporary meditation on the act of dwelling as the fundamental medium of our being-in-the-world. Architecture, for him, has forgotten this basic fact of existence, causing him to pen disparaging reflections on the profession. As he argues, architects are now taught to design houses, not homes, thus contributing to the uprooting that feeds into our growing inability to genuinely connect with the world. There is a "poetics of home"—linked to memory, emotions, dreams, identity, and intimacy—that functional architecture and "modern living" have foreclosed (e.g., "in the contemporary house, the fireplace has been replaced by the TV" [35]; or, as Bachelard might say, the modern apartment has given up on its oneiric function and is no longer capable of fostering our dreams).

Pallasmaa draws substantial implications from this situation, including the loss of our ability to truly imagine alternative worlds. Against architecture's growing instrumentalization and aestheticization, without deep roots in our existential experience, he arrives at a conclusion that has significant design implications. "A building is not an end in itself. A building conditions and transforms the human experience of reality," he states; "it frames, structures, articulates, links, separates and unites, enables and prohibits" (96). This is because buildings possess "a tectonic language" (97); we interact with them actively with our entire body and senses. Partaking more of the nature of a verb (*to inhabit, to dwell*) than that of a noun, "every meaningful building is at the same time about the world, about life, and about the very discipline of architecture" (98).[18] Something of the sort can be found in writings about Japanese architecture, at least in its traditional instantiations. In his book on aesthetics and architecture, *El elogio de la sombra* (In Praise of Shadows, 1994), writer Junichirō Tanizaki discusses central aspects of the materialist phenomenology of the traditional house, from the woods, ceramic, and paper (e.g., those wooden lattices of translucent paper that serve as doors or room dividers, the texture of which transmits "a little warmth that recomforts the heart" [25]) to the bathroom ("which our ancestors, who rendered everything poetic, paradoxically transmuted into a space of the most exquisite taste") and, above all, the alternation between life and shadow, which serves as a principle for all aspects of interior design, every experience, even that of eating (e.g., the gleam of cooked rice, or of traditional porcelain dishes, which is lost with Western-style lighting).[19] These principles reached an incredible level of development in the traditional temples, such as the fourteenth-century Buddhist temple outside of Kyoto so splendidly described by anthropologist Norris Johnson (2012), with its meticulously designed buildings, gardens, and ponds, where even stones respond to an animist perspective in which everything is alive and partakes of our emotions, calling for an ethic of compassion and love. Here land, landscape, and the spirit of place achieve a most harmonious interrelation, perhaps because it is based on the principle of their sacredness.

Today, however, the real challenge lies in urbanism. As Fry harshly puts it, "gestural egocentric architectural statements and master planning fictions measured against the scale of imperative [climate change and generalized unsettlement] are not merely misplaced, they are crimes against the future" (2015, 48).[20] Much more than reactive adaption and retrofitting of buildings that serves the interests of the affluent will be needed to face the universally but differentially experienced condition of unsettlement that has come about as a result of the combined action of climate change, population growth, global unsustainability, and geopolitical instability. As he vehemently states, "destruction has gained the upper hand" (25) in a world that is made structurally unsustainable by colonialist forms of Western capitalist modernity. The development of new modes of earthly habitation has become an imperative, which means changing the practices that account for our dwelling in ways that enable us to act futurally instead of insisting on the strategies of adaptation to defuturing (future-destroying) worldly conditions that are on offer at present. What is required is a new kind of metrofitting made up of design strategies capable of bringing about new infrastructures of life. Adaptation and resilience will have to be revisited through the creation of grounded, situated, and pervasive design capacity by communities themselves who are bound together through culture and a common will to survive when confronted with threatening conditions, not by global experts, bureaucrats, and geoengineers who can only recommend the business-as-usual approaches that emerge from impoverished liberal mind-sets. All of this will call into question the notion of the city as an enduring sociomaterial form—perhaps the end of the modernist city, once the symbol of dynamism and progress. In short, the "recreation of urban life should occupy a central position in the structural changes that must occur if 'we' humans are to have a viable future" (82). The destructive metabolic nature of cities implies going beyond the model of the modernist city. Fry's urban design imagination provides important leads with regard to "the question of finding futural modes of dwelling" (87). Reimagining the city along these lines will have to be part of any transition vision and design framework.

Design and the Rise of the Digital

The digitalization of so many dimensions of social life is one of the most important social facts of the last few decades. Digital technologies and information and communication technologies have to do with all aspects of everyday life, and design's role in the ever-expanding and always-changing digital territories is one of the most poignant questions for critical design studies. Succinctly stated, "doing digital design also means designing society, and designers ought to take a stand as a driver of social change" (Kommonen n.d., 2). For Kari-Hans Kommonen, a theorist at the Aalto University Media Lab in Helsinki, the principle of digital design should be the critical awareness that "digital products also live in the social world and change it. Digital design cannot operate outside its social context, because files, systems and media only gain meaning as part of a community's practice. Effective, meaningful design is a social activity, in which the designer is one actor among many. In addition to computers, software, digital information and media, the materials of digital design also include communities, processes, practices and culture, and designers need to be equipped with the right skill to deal with these elements" (1). More than technological expertise, open-source approaches and certainly the celebration of new media is at stake.[21]

The democratizing potential of information and communication technologies has been exaggerated. Let us recall that the 1990s was the high decade of things cyber. Digital technology designer Brenda Laurel's (2001) list of "four revolutions" usefully marks the changes in the digital field: the PC, computer games, virtual reality and cyberspace, and of course the Internet and the web (see also McCullough 2004). Over the past ten to fifteen years, at least in the Anglo-American science and technology studies field, the focus on the digital was displaced by attention to things "bio," particularly as a result of the ontological turn in social theory (see the next chapter). Social science studies of the digital continue to be done, although perhaps with less excitement than during the first wave; the seeming consolidation of digital technologies in so many aspects of life (ubiquitous computing) has robbed this field of its previous glamour as a source of epistemic, social, and cultural analyses. Now the cyber is just one more field of practice among many. That said, there is a lot of interesting work being done at the interface of the digital and the cultural that contributes to illuminating, and continuously reappraising, the meaning of being digital; these include both theoretical and ethnographic studies. There are interesting works on postcolonial theory and computing (Irani et al. 2010), the digital divide, digital technologies and the body, social media, virtual environments and communities, and so forth. Some of this work involves ethnographic investigations of the manifold intersections of digital technologies and cultural practices, originating a new field of digital anthropology (Boellstorff 2008; Balsamo 2011; Horst and Miller 2012; Pink, Ardèvol, and Lanzeni 2016).

Questions about the digital have not been salient in ontologically oriented research, with the possible exception of those who follow in the tradition of Terry Winograd and Fernando Flores (1986) on ontological design, such as Harry Halpin and Alexandre Monnin's (2014) work on the philosophy of the web. Halpin (2011) draws on Heideggerian phenomenology and on Humberto Maturana and Francisco Varela's (1980, 1987) biology of cognition to reformulate the so-called four Es in the artificial intelligence field—cognition as embodied, embedded, enactive, and extended.[22] Challenging conventional views of representation and individual cognition in the artificial intelligence field, he advocates for a notion of collective intelligence in terms of a collective understanding of cognition that extends into an equally collectively shaped environment. The notion of cognition as embodied (to be explained at length in chapter 3) is central to this "neo-Heideggerian program" in artificial intelligence. The web itself comes to be seen as collective intelligence, while embodiment is redefined away from the individual toward the constitution of assemblages.

A persuasive framework for the digital that has ontological implications is being developed by Benjamin Bratton in San Diego. Bratton's (2014) concern with the geopolitics of planetary-scale computation leads him to posit the existence of an "accidental megastructure," the Stack. On first inspection, the Stack looks like an updated version of cyberspace, only much more comprehensive and totalizing, for it includes myriad dimensions of life, from mineral sourcing to the cloud, from interfaces to robots, from platforms to users, and from governmentality to surveillance. The Stack is the new *nomos*, or political geography of the Earth. It is the dimension one needs to add to the analytical triad of the State, civil society, and the market—so now we also have the Platform, or the Stack. Within the Stack, the cloud and the user enable a substructure that Bratton refers to as the Black Stack, a hardware and software "computational totality" that produces an accelerated geopolitics that shapes economies as much as subjectivities, transforming the meaning of the human by proliferating the world's nonhuman inhabitants and users (see also Invisible Committee 2015). This geopolitics/biopolitics of the digital has profound implications for design.

Sustainability by Design?

At the other end of the spectrum from the digital, we have the concern with the natural. Both demand equal attention from design perspectives. Since the inception of the sustainability movement in 1987 with the publication of the Brundtland Report, *Our Common Future*, where the term *sustainable development* was first defined as development that meets the needs of the present without compromising the ability of future generations to meet their own needs (World Commission on Environment and Development 1987), critics have pointed out that such a definition is oxymoronic in that the interests of development and the needs of nature cannot be harmonized within any conventional model of the economy (e.g., Redclift 1987; Norgaard 1995). Despite the moment of hope and the actual achievements at the Earth Summit held in Rio de Janeiro in 1992, the contradictions and criticisms have only multiplied through the years, peaking around the disappointing twentieth-anniversary conference of the Earth Summit (known as Rio + 20), held in Rio in June 2012, where the notion of the green economy was presented by governments from the North and by international organizations as the panacea for reaching the ever-elusive goal of sustainable development. The notion of a green economy corroborated critics' view that what is to be sustained with sustainable development, more than the environment or nature, is a particular capitalistic model of the economy and an entire dualist ontology.

We will touch on sustainability again when discussing ontological design, but even a cursory map of design trends must include a mention of ecological design. It took almost three decades after the publication of landscape architect Ian McHarg's anticipatory *Design with Nature* (1969) for a field of ecological design properly speaking to take off.[23] Approaches range from the conceptual to the technocratic, with the latter predominating, particularly economic and technological perspectives; the range among the latter category is wide, from proposals that could be said to push the envelope in envisioning a significant transformation of capitalism (as in the well-regarded proposal for "natural capitalism" by Paul Hawken, Amory Lovins, and L. Hunter Lovins [1999]) to the plethora of greenwashing proposals coming out of the World Bank, the United Nations, and mainstream environmental think tanks in the Global North around climate change, sustainable development, and the green economy.[24] A counterintuitive example comes from the field of fashion and sustainability; in this field, one finds designers taking seriously the social and ecological challenges of the industry in an attempt to transform it (from reductions in the environmental impact of materials and processing to reuse and refashion strategies, place-based production, and biomimicry), as well as proposing creative notions like codesign through active crafting, hacking, and the tackling of difficult issues related to alternative knowledges, politics, and transitions to other cultural and ecological models for society (see the excellent book by Kate Fletcher and Lynda Grose [2011]; see also Shepard 2015).

There have been significant conceptual strides in ecological design, largely through collaborations among architects, planners, and ecologists with on-the-ground design experience. A readily accepted principle is that ecological design involves the successful integration of human and natural systems and processes; whether this integration is seen as based on learning from several billion years of evolution and from nature's designs, or as needing to rely on, and hence reinvent, technology to deal with contemporary situations, the starting point is the realization that the environmental crisis is a design crisis and that humans need to change their practices radically to avert it.[25] There are a number of shared notions, notably the belief that ecological sustainability goes well beyond economic sustainability, ultimately requiring a significantly new culture. Living-systems theory is seen by many as the basis for design competence for conservation, regeneration, and stewardship; these goals involve seeding all socionatural systems with diversity and creating resilience through intelligent webs, building on the self-organizing potential of natural and social systems. Going against the expert-driven dominance of design, some ecological theorists argue for "a deeply participatory process in which technical disciplinary languages and barriers are exchanged for a shared understanding of the design problem. Ecological design changes the old rules about what counts for knowledge and who counts as a knower. It suggests that sustainability is a cultural process rather than an expert one, and that we should all acquire a basic competence in the shaping of our world. . . . For too long we have expected the design professions to bend an inert world into shape. The alternative is to try to gently catalyze the self-designing potentialities of nature" (van der Ryn and Cowan 1996, 147, 130). In this framework, "solutions grow from place," and cultivating design intelligence becomes a key aspect of democracy based on locality. This marriage of ecology and direct democracy manifests itself best in bioregionalism but also in the redesign of cities to foster forms of human habitation through which people can relocalize a range of activities in place and community, integrated with the environment.[26] Some envision a "design process where mutualism is extended from locality to locality across continents" (Hester 2006, 61). While all this might sound a bit utopian and lacking in self-critique, a valuable feature is that these frameworks are accompanied by concrete examples of re/design embodying ecological design principles. At their best, they acknowledge that unsustainability springs from the cultural structure of modernity itself (Ehrenfeld 2009, 7, 210); modern solutions in the form of so-called sustainable development and the green economy will not do. John Ehrenfeld's ontological design approach leads him to conclude that sustainability will be brought about only if "a cultural upheaval" takes place (211). For many ethnoterritorial social movements, sustainability involves the defense of an entire way of life, a mode of being~knowing~doing. These are among the most important contributions to the network of recurrent conversations arising in response to the ecological crisis and attempts to redress it.

Critical Design Studies and Speculative Design

Critical design studies must embrace, at its best, the vital normative questions of the day, and they should do so from out-of-the-box perspectives. This type of inquiry can be found in instances of engaged research at the interface between design and activism, or where modern designs seem to break down or become inoperative. Feminist disability scholars (e.g., Hartblay 2017) are reframing the concept of universal design (a sort of barrier-free design for individual accessibility) in both collective and relational terms. These scholars argue for participatory, bottom-up, situated design methods that build on a close examination of the interrelations between differently abled bodies and design outcomes. Thus reinterpreted, the idea of diverse bodies becomes a stimulating epistemic and material-discursive basis for design practice. By constructing ableism as an ontological issue, they suggest, designers might arrive at a materialist ontology that is mindful of the relationality that necessarily brings together bodies, spaces, environments, tools, and so forth. For this to happen, however, a nonableist ethnography of in/accessibility is required (e.g., of ramps, buildings, and living spaces), one that reveals the meanings and practices of disability and its accompanying designs.[27] In another revealing study, an ecological concern with the wastefulness of modern toilets leads the author to unconceal a veritable domestic culture of shit, steeped in modernist understandings of the body, waste, cleanliness, and so forth, calling for significant ecological-ontological redesign (Dimpfl 2011). These examples can be said to be situated within the critical cultural studies of design; they engage the speculative design imagination in ways that may lead to a significant reconstruction of cultural and material practices.

After this purposeful review, can a field of critical design studies be said to be emerging? By *critical* I mean, following academic usage, the application of a panoply of critical theories to design (from Marxist and post-Marxist political economy to feminist, queer, and critical race theory, poststructuralism, phenomenology, postcolonial and decolonial theory, and the most current postconstructivist and neomaterialist frameworks). Adopting this criterion, one could say that a critical design studies field is indeed emerging. Several caveats are in order. First, as should be clear, the elements and contours of the field are far from being restricted to the academy; many of its main contributions stem from design thinking and activism, even if often in some relation with the academy. Second, despite these thought-provoking ideas, it is not far-fetched to suggest that such a field is still nascent. Not only is there still a dearth of critical analyses of the relation between design practice and capitalism, gender, race, development, and modernity, but the limits of Western social theory's ability to generate the questions, let alone answers, needed to face the unprecedented unraveling of modern and most other forms of human life on the planet at present are becoming patently clear (at least to this author). Third, the relations among design, politics, power, and culture still needs to be fleshed out.

Design and Politics

We will end this chapter with a preliminary discussion of design and politics. Is design at present inextricably tied to capitalism and a liberal conception of politics?[28] Conversely, can design be infused with a more explicit sense of politics, even a radical politics? We already mentioned in passing the socialist orientation of some design pioneers during the heyday of modernism. Climate change is, of course, pushing a wide sector of the design profession toward ecological forms of design consciousness. Humanitarian crises are creating unprecedented spaces where capitalist production and liberal politics no longer work, or at least not entirely, and designers are finding an unusual niche there. Some ecologically minded architects and urbanists are thinking deeply about the relations among design, Earth, and democracy. By giving up expert control over service design in the nongovernmental organizations and the public sector, designers, it can be argued, are exercising a kind of epistemic politics. These are instances in which more explicit connections between design and politics are being tried out. But the vexing question of the relation between design and the making of deeply unequal, insensitive, and destructive social orders seems to remain design's own "wicked problem."

This is beginning to change. Contemporary Scandinavian design has been more successful at pairing social democratic goals and design, for instance, as superbly analyzed in Ehn, Nilsson, and Topgaard (2014a) and by Keith Murphy (2015) for the Swedish case. Their exploration of the relation between design and innovation contains a much-needed critique of the elitist notions of culture industries and creative classes, which de facto reduce innovation to a matter of expertise at the service of capital. "There is a genuine call for innovation through user-centered design, and even a belief that innovation is getting democratized," Ehn, Nilsson, and Topgaard claim. "At the same time, inventive as it may seem, the new paradigm is surprisingly traditional and managerial," that is, oriented toward markets and profits (2014b, 3). Fostering a different conception of innovation, for these authors, demands assiduous and committed work with marginalized publics, adapting design methods such as makerspaces, fabrication labs (fab labs), and friendly hacking while exposing the class basis of the professionals and positioning the knowledge and experience of the subordinated groups as legitimate. This is a constructive call to take into account in relation to all the tendencies discussed in this chapter.

Carl DiSalvo's (2012) framework of adversarial design makes a cogent case for approaches that broach explicitly the agonistic connection among design, technology, democracy, policy, and society. These are important steps. Further inroads into the design-politics relation are being made, as we shall see, in the fields of transition design and design for social innovation. The class and race character of design has barely begun to be tackled, for instance, by Damian White (2015) and Elizabeth Chin (2017). As Chin unequivovally states, there are few social spaces more unrelentingly white than the art and design studio. For her, this unreflective whiteness in design territories is unable to excavate the racist and sexist ideologies embedded in Bauhaus-derived aesthetics that constitute good design for many (2). Radicalizing design politics will require dealing openly with these issues, situating design squarely in relation to inequality, racism, sexism, and colonialism. It will also imply moving at the edges of the Western social theory episteme, beyond the rationalistic, logocentric, and dualist traditions of modern theory. The rest of this book is in many ways devoted to substantiating this latter proposition. At some point we'll get back to the questions with which we started: Which "design"? What "world"? What "real"? But this will come after a particular problematization of our ways of thinking about, and enacting, "world" and "real." That will be the basis for an ontological approach to design.

To sum up: important tendencies have emerged in the design world over the past decade, aiming to reorient design practice from its traditional meaning as linked to objects, technological change, the individual, and the market and carried out by experienced experts, toward a conception of design as user centered, situated, interactive, collaborative, and participatory, focused significantly on the production of human experience and life itself. It is fair to say, however, that taken as a whole the U.S. variants of these changes—most aptly summarized in the concept of design thinking—are less critical in their analysis of politics, governmentality, power, and capital than some of their European counterparts. We will arrive at the perspectives from the Global South only in the last two chapters and the conclusion.

Brenda Laurel, whose work over the decades constitutes a critical cultural studies of design, has provided an imaginary for furthering the dissenting imagination within design that is apt for concluding this first chapter: "New paradigms continue to be explored by people who poke at the edges; the public responds by reframing hopes and expectations; and the character of a new medium begins to emerge. The process of maturation in new media requires creativity, time, investment, optimism" (2001, 8). Transition and autonomous design proposals are "poking at the edges" of capitalist modernity's onto-epistemic formation and may thus be considered an integral part of the CDS (Critical Studies of Design) field.

2 Elements for a Cultural Studies of Design

Conventional discipline-based design education cannot contribute to substantial change unless students are inducted into understanding theories of power, social structure and social change, and the like. If one were to design a postgraduate (or even undergraduate) degree course in, say Meta-Design or Transition Design, it might, on the surface, look more like Humanities than design.

· **Anne-Marie Willis,** "Transition Design: The Need to Refuse Discipline and Transcend Instrumentalism"

By general consent [in anthropology] the organizations of production, distribution, governance, and knowledge that have dominated the modern era have brought the world to the brink of catastrophe. In finding ways to carry on, we need all the help we can get. But no one—no indigenous group, no specialist science, no doctrine or philosophy—holds the key to the future, if only one could find it. We have to make the future for ourselves, but that can only be done through dialogue. Anthropology's role is to expand the scope of this dialogue: to make conversation of human life itself.

· **Caroline Gatt and Tim Ingold,** "From Description to Correspondence: Anthropology in Real Time"

Psychoanalysis and ethnology occupy a privileged position in our knowledge . . .
because, on the confines of all the branches of knowledge investigating man, they
form an undoubted and inexhaustible treasure-hoard of experiences and concepts,
and above all a perpetual principle of dissatisfaction, of calling into question, of criticism and contestation of what may seem, on other respects, to be established. . . .
Ethnology, like psychoanalysis, questions not man himself, as he appears in the human
sciences, but the region that makes possible knowledge about man in general. . . .
[It] is situated within the particular relation that the Western ratio establishes with all
other cultures. . . . [Ethnology and psychoanalysis] are directed towards that which,
outside man, makes it possible to know, with a positive knowledge, that which is given
to or eludes his consciousness. . . . One thing in any case is certain: man is neither the
oldest nor the most constant problem that has been posed for human knowledge.

· **Michel Foucault,** *The Order of Things*

Design theory and design education take place at the edges of social theory,
conventionally the province of the social science and the humanities. It thus
makes sense to affirm that the development of an ontological approach to design, one that destabilizes its comfortable niche within naturalized modern
orders, demands a recentering of design education in order to bring it fully
into the critical social theory space. As Anne-Marie Willis maintains, however,
this task entails more than a straightforward extension or application of social
theory to the design field. It is worth completing the above quote from her as
we start this chapter to convey the sense of what is at stake. Such a program

> would teach on: Theories of Power, Change and the Political; Culture/
> Sociality; History and Philosophy of Technology; Theories of Subjectiv-
> ity, Mind/Mentalities; Theories of Making and Designing and contextual
> studies ("history") such as Modernity/Enlightenment. But of course these
> subjects would not have this title; they would not be taught as conventional
> Humanities courses or "complementary studies." The challenge would be
> how to make connections to design, but not in an appropriative way, reduc-
> ing, decontextualizing, and hollowing out the radical nature of deep ideas,
> old and new. . . . The framework for teaching from this body of knowledge
> would need to be meta-designing along with an implicit, at times explicit,
> critique of the design professions: "these are the historical forces that have
> created the context in which design has emerged as a particular kind of
> delimited practice. This is what has designed design and is still designing
> design. *This is what we need to understand so as to create a practice of counter-
> designing.*" (2015, 73; emphasis added)

Herein lies an entire program for redesigning design education (see also Fry 2017), a task to which this chapter purports to make a modest, and clearly situated, contribution. It does so from the perspective of a cultural studies of design. By this, following Lawrence Grossberg (2010), we mean the examination of the ways in which people's everyday lives are articulated with culture within and through particular design practices. The cultural studies of design will also study design's role in the current cultural-historical conjuncture—how design practices participate in fundamental processes of the production of reality and their articulation with forms of power. It does so "by taking culture as its starting point, its entrance into the complex balance of forces constructed out of the even more complicated relations of culture, society, politics, economics, everyday life, etc." (24). Cultural studies' radical contextuality implies its connection to transformative social practices and struggles. It is, finally, about the cultural work that needs to take place for the creation of new futures. Design is no doubt a main player in the making of the modern onto-epistemic formation, and hence a most appropriate subject for cultural studies.[1]

Many of the debates and contributions sketched in the previous chapter may be considered important contributions to the cultural studies of design. This chapter extends this investigation by looking at a number of trends arising from fields that, while not central to design practice or design education, nevertheless have a direct bearing on the conditions within which design theory and practice unfold, especially when one takes an ontological approach to design. These fields include anthropology, development studies, political ecology, and feminist theory. These trends complement the discussion of elements from the previous chapters, such as sustainability and digital culture. They are not presented as explicit content for design education but as elements that may enter into educational and training strategies for design schools wishing to make forays into the ontological and transition design projects. Conversely, students from the social sciences and the humanities might find in the notes that follow useful ideas for bringing social theory to bear on design-related problems, which I believe are often present in the situations in which we work.

The first, and main, part of the chapter focuses on the diverse engagements between anthropology and design, alternating between the more applied or action-oriented "design anthropology" and the critical "anthropology of design." The second part moves on to consider recent design inroads into the fields of development and humanitarian aid; it looks at the ways in which designers are attempting to position themselves within development projects, including in the rapidly growing, and distinctive, space of humanitarianism.

Finally, the third part discusses the scholarly transformation, known as the ontological turn, that ensued from the encounter between the field of political ecology and the evolving concerns with ontology (objects, things, matter, the real, immanence, process) in postconstructivist social theory. Arising out of this intersection, the nascent field of political ontology, this chapter suggests, constitutes a constructive space for rethinking design ontologically. Political ontology will be used in subsequent chapters to reframe two issues of importance for ontological and autonomous design: unsustainability, on the one hand, and the struggles of territorial-based social movements, on the other. Thinking about design from the vantage point of political ontology will also enable us to ascertain its relation with the decolonial project of moving toward "a world where many worlds fit." This reflection will be an important element in the notion of designs for the pluriverse, to be discussed in the last part of the book.

To anticipate a bit, an ontological approach to design will, on the one hand, show how modern design has been pivotal to the systematic creation of unsustainability and the elimination of futures—bringing the world to the brink of catastrophe, as described in the epigraph from Caroline Gatt and Tim Ingold (2013, 147); on the other, it will put forward the question of whether design practices stemming from nondualist conceptions might be capable of leading to futuring strategies for transitions beyond the nature/culture rift, within a dialogical pluriverse. This is part of the big picture of design at present, but just the beginning. If the figure of Man as the foundation of all knowledge—modern Man or, as Donna Haraway puts it, "Man the Modern" (1997, 78)—emerged, in Michel Foucault's (1970) argument, at the end of the eighteenth century, when a new configuration of knowledge (a new episteme) finally crystallized, this same Man is the design subject, "Man the Designer," one might say. Design has had an easy and largely celebrated existence within what we usually refer to nonchalantly as the modern age. This age, however, is a complex constellation of coevolving processes, including a particular episteme, an ensemble of social forms among which patriarchal capitalism and coloniality occupy pride of place, and an ontological architecture structured around the founding dualisms of nature/culture and West/non-West. It is this onto-epistemic and social formation that is at the foundation of design.

Extricating "designer man" from this complex of forces so that humans can again play a more constructive role in the praxis of being alive is thus intimately entangled with the passing of Man as the center of all knowledge and as the measure of life. It requires no less than a new notion of the human, a veritable posthuman understanding of what it means to be a living being in the age of climate change, generalized unsettlement, and a growing insurrection against the defuturing effects increasingly evident in the so-called globalized world.

Between Design Anthropology and the Anthropology of Design

Social/cultural anthropology (in the Anglo-American and Latin American usage; *ethnology* in French, as in Foucault's quote above) is the science that, at the edges of but at the same time central to Western knowledge, makes evident the historicity of any and all cultural orders, their arbitrary and historically constructed character, including that of the West itself. This is why anthropology might be particularly useful to design studies, because it enables us to examine any social order as the result of design processes involving the interplay of materiality, meanings, and practices. Moreover, as Foucault says, "the general problem of all ethnology is in fact that of the relations (of continuity or discontinuity) between nature and culture" (1970, 377). The relation between nature and culture—its different regimes, the multiple forms it takes, and the consequences of those various forms and regimes—will reappear persistently throughout this book, whether in the analysis of the ontological dualism between nature and culture that became consolidated at the time of the founding of Western modernity or, conversely, in the discussion of the relational ontologies underlying the worlds of those peoples thought to be without history, for whom the relation between nature and culture has little to do with the sanitized modern ontology that keeps them separate. It will also resurface in the irrefutable emergence—out of so many "unarchived histories," to use the wonderful expression of one of the founders of the subaltern studies group in India, Gyanendra Pandey (2014)—of the multiple territorial struggles being waged by peoples in defense of their relational worlds. The concern with the nature/culture relation will resurface, finally, in the discussion of un/sustainability from design perspectives.

The rapprochement between anthropology and design has gained force over the past decade. As Keith Murphy states in his retrospective look at this relation, "even though designed phenomena have received significant anthropological attention since the discipline's earliest days, the basic fact that they are designed has not received much attention" (2016, 440). The changing attitude is seen as both promising and troublesome, and this is reflected in the three main forms that the relation has taken: bringing anthropological insights into design (design anthropology), bringing design insights into anthropology (ethnography as design), and applying critical social theory to design practice (anthropology of design). A fourth variation is proposed in this book, and this is the possibility of reorienting design on the basis of anthropological concerns, broadly speaking, by which I mean infusing design with the perspective of the multiplicity of onto-epistemic formations, or worlds, within which anthropological work often takes place (traditionally understood as "native" cultures). Whereas this also includes modern worlds, of course, this fourth option is particularly concerned with the knowledges and desires of subaltern subjects and the social movements they create.[2]

Design Anthropology

The most salient of these trends at present is design anthropology, involving the use of anthropological concepts and methods in design; positions range from applied (market-driven) to activist (socially conscious) design. A good deal of the literature on design anthropology advocates for the incorporation of anthropology into design practice based on an argument about relevance and professional opportunities. This is an interesting trend largely led by anthropologists practicing in the design world (see, e.g., Tunstall 2011; Whitemyer 2006; and some of the chapters in A. Clarke 2011a and Laurel 2003). The web-based literature on this trend is growing rapidly. While highlighting the necessarily action-oriented character of the field, the more academic-oriented versions of design anthropology emphasize the role of theory in informing action. Two recent volumes develop this design-oriented theoretical and methodological perspective (A. Clarke 2011a; Gunn, Otto, and Smith 2013). The authors in these volumes rearticulate the anthropological insight of the cultural embeddedness of all artifacts to suggest why design anthropology "is emerging as a methodology as much as a discourse" (Clarke 2011b, 10). Design anthropology should thus not be seen merely as an applied field (although this clearly happens as well, as in industrial or business anthropology); in fact, the thrust of the matter is the realization that contemporary critical designers, combining anthropological-style observation and speculation on emergent social practices, are developing a distinct style of knowledge (Gunn, Otto, and

Smith 2013). This particular way of doing both anthropology and design is yielding new methods, such as ethnographic approaches to design contexts that make it possible to tack back and forth between action and reflection; participatory design orientations (Ehn, Nilsson, and Topgaard 2014); political preoccupations, including the decolonization of design practice (Tunstall 2013); and ethical discussions about the role of values in human-centered design.

This trend has resulted in the creation of a dynamic and growing field with its own set of concerns that feed back into both anthropology and design. A case in point is the notion of prototyping the social as a means to critically look at, and construct, more inclusive worlds (A. Clarke 2011b, 11). A recent anthropological group project looked precisely at the rise of a "prototyping paradigm" in a variety of fields, including of course design but also art, science, software development, and engineering. "The experimental and open-ended qualities of prototyping," as one of the group's conveners hypothesized, "have become a surrogate for new cultural experiences and processes of democratization" (Corsín Jiménez 2013, 382). By examining prototyping as an emergent complex cultural practice, and by introducing a metareflection on "prototyping prototyping," this project examined critically the historicity of this practice while highlighting the productivity of a design practice based on a logic of experimentation, imagination, user-centeredness, and collaboration that, they argue, could fruitfully inform anthropological work (ARC Studio 2010).[3] Above all, these trends suggest that, while still nascent, the coming together of design and anthropology is creating a rich arena for a rapidly developing field (Chin forthcoming; Otto and Smith 2013).

Ethnography and Design

The attention to the relation between ethnography and design is a reflection of the evolving relation between anthropology and design (e.g., Bichard and Gheerawo 2011; Plowman 2003 for an early statement on interface anthropology and research on "the vibrant new villages of computing" [Laurel 1989, 93]; Suchman 2007 on the ethnography of human-machine reconfigurations; plus the Clarke and Gunn, Otto, and Smith volumes already mentioned). This brings us to the second trend, which looks at the actual or potential contributions of design to anthropology—how design thinking and research provide resources for ethnographic inquiry in particular, within an overall framework conceptualized as the "anthropology of the contemporary" (Rabinow and Marcus 2008; Suchman 2011). This development has been spearheaded by George

Marcus's project "Rethinking Ethnography as a Design Process" at the Center for Ethnography, University of California, Irvine.[4] The basic insight—that ethnography can be rethought as a design process on the basis of certain trends in design practice and education such as collaboration, diverse partnerships, and outcome orientation—has yielded insightful ethnographic tools beyond established methods such as participant observation and informant interviews, thus making the field better equipped to understand contemporary worlds and imagine constructive courses of action. This trend could be said to have an important predecessor in the work of Donald Schön and Martin Rein (e.g., Schön 1987; Schön and Rein 1994). Working in the field of urban studies from a Deweyian perspective, Schön developed an entire framework for dealing with the limitations of technical rationality that he saw (somewhat ethnographically) as dominant in architectural and craft design and moving toward a "reflection-in-action" type of training for professionals. His conceptualization of the design process as reflection-in-action, and of the studio as a model for it, remains relevant.

An original counterpoint to the relation between ethnography and design has been proposed by Gatt and Ingold (2013), who argue for a shift from anthropology and ethnography as design, or for design, to anthropology *by means of* design. Imbued in phenomenological tenets and relational perspectives, these authors elaborate a notion of correspondence that foregrounds the processual character of all living. "To correspond with the world, in short," they suggest, provocatively, "is not to describe it, or to represent it, but to *answer* to it"; hence their corollaries: first, they consider a shift from anthropology and ethnography as description to "*anthropology-by-means-of-design [as] a practice of correspondence*" (2013, 145; see also Ingold 2011). Second, they argue that "design, in this sense, does not transform the world. It is rather part of the world's transforming itself" (Gatt and Ingold 2013, 146). Whether one considers this conception of design as merely poetic or a valid and clairvoyant response to how life actually works, this proposed framework offers rich insights into how phenomenologically minded designers, by working alongside the world as it unfolds, might think about issues such as improvisation, foresight, dwelling, and nondeterministic goals and directions for transformation. In fact, as these authors conclude, thinking about design in terms of correspondence affords paths for shifting anthropological practice from its emphasis on academic texts to collaboration with ethnographic subjects in their world-making projects. We shall ask later whether this notion of anthropology-by-means-of-design offers insights for the explicitly activist and political transition design and autonomous design conceptions to be developed in the context of collaboration with, say, indigenous communities.

The Anthropology of Design

The third tendency—the anthropology of design—entails the critical analysis of design as a domain of thought and practice, using contemporary critical theories to this end (Suchman 2011). It looks critically at what goes on "under the increasingly flexible banner of design," as Finnish anthropologist and design theorist Eeva Berglund descriptively puts it.[5] While it engages seriously with design fields, it is more cautious about what is taking place at the intersection of anthropology and design. Not all of the work in the anthropology of design takes the form of a distanced critique, however. As Berglund (2011, 2012) suggests in her analysis of Helsinki's architecture and Finnish environmentalism and design, the crossovers between design and anthropology suggest room for intellectually stimulating engagement. This does not do away with all the problems, such as the persistence of unquestioned binaries between nature (e.g., the forest) and culture (e.g., the city) in much environmentally oriented design, and a certain depoliticization of issues that comes from reliance on design discourse. This might feed into activist conceptions of design, which anthropologists, inside and outside academia, are in a particularly strong position to assess and contribute to developing. For Berglund, while the popularity of design and design thinking invites critique, it also calls for a cautious assessment of how the two fields might enrich each other and coimagine projects in diverse areas of socionatural life. Elizabeth Chin brings out the tensions inherent to the rapprochement between anthropology and design: while design's action-oriented ethics questions anthropology's inability to engage effectively with the actors with whom it works, the latter easily deconstructs the former's often-uninformed "first-world" sensibility and proclivity for "productification and marketing" (2017). These tensions notwithstanding, the search for mutual learning at the anthropology/design interface is on and is likely to continue in the near future.[6]

The depoliticization of much design work is, needless to say, real. As Lucy Suchman rightly states, anthropology may contribute to redressing this situation by "bringing into view the politics of design, including the systemic placement of politics beyond the limits of the designer's frame" (2011, 4). A related inquiry, proposed by design theorists Fernando Domínguez Rubio and Uriel Fogué (2015), examines how objects and things embed logics of power, leaning on Foucault's analyses of the creation of disciplinary societies through normalizing practices in schools, hospitals, armies, factories, and so forth. The disciplinary society, in Foucauldian terms, is indeed a designed society. This research program probes designers' understanding of innovation and creativity, to the extent that these are often entangled with the reproduction of the (capitalist and colonial) status quo. In other words, how design can be infused with a more explicit sense of politics—a radical politics—is one of the most important questions critical theory can pose to design practice.

Questions of class, gender, race, and coloniality are notoriously absent from most design theory and practice, and so is that of design's dependence on capitalism (White 2015; Tunstall 2013; Chin forthcoming; Kalantidou and Fry 2015). We already mentioned Chin's (2017) assessment of design as a white cultural practice. As she argues, looking at design in terms of the intersection of class, gender, race, coloniality, and other markers of identity must be an integral component of the decolonization of design (see also Tunstall 2013). These questions are being taken up explicitly by designers working in intellectual-activist spheres, oftentimes with community-oriented design organizations. For the Design Studio for Social Intervention group, led by Kenneth Bailey in Boston, "the designer's stance is experimental and proactive. It helps propel us beyond merely addressing existing problems with existing forms into imagining entirely new terrains of possibility. Equally important, design invites widely disparate ways of knowing into a single co-creative practice."[7] This design studio, which is working toward social justice, is developing innovative methodologies at the interface of community, art, planning, and activism.[8] Community-level design is also being used to connect environmental justice, memory, performance, materiality (e.g., toxins in the soil), and land and landscape to keep alive, and renew, a community's long-standing experience of protest and resistance while reimagining its future, for instance, in the context of environmental justice struggles in North Carolina (Vasudevan 2011).

As these and other cases demonstrate, work being done with marginalized communities often ends up radicalizing participatory methods through interaction design research in which local knowledges and insights are genuinely taken as the starting point of the design process. Based on their teamwork with homeless youth in Southern California, Chin and collaborators note that most design work with the homeless results in projects that are either a version of a tent or a shopping cart (Chin et al. 2016). The ability of this type of "do-gooder," socially oriented design to address questions of social justice and inequality—let alone to take seriously the homeless's voices and perspectives—is very limited, in these authors' view. What the latter requires is an epistemic "getting out of the way," as Michael Montoya (2013) descriptively puts it in his work on *acompañamiento* (accompaniment) in the planning and design of health interventions with Latinas/os in the same part of the United States. Chin's and Montoya's teamwork approaches vividly demonstrate how difficult it is to quell sufficiently the designers' or researchers' own categories so that they can even begin to understand the often-counterhegemonic categories of subaltern groups. Both researchers invoke Latin American traditions of participatory research in this endeavor. The notion of autonomous design to be developed in the last part of this book resonates with these projects.

Discussions of the relation between design and politics reflect the fact that design has become a formidable political and material force; the corollary is whether design is becoming, or can become, a promising site for the transformation of the entrenched cultures of unsustainability toward pluriversal practices. Reframing design practice ontologically is intended as a contribution to this discussion. It is also an attempt to locate design politics in its capacity to generate new entities and relations, that is, to unveil design's capacity "to 'propose' new kinds of bodies, entities and sites *as political*" (Domínguez Rubio and Fogué 2015, 148), thus expanding established understandings of the political.

Design in the Development and Humanitarian Field

International development is another field in which the presence of design debates and practices is growing noticeably. As already suggested by the quote from the United Nations report from 1951 in the introduction to this book, it can be argued that the entire project of development, in which the industrialized countries were to aid poor countries to adopt strategies for "modernization" and, eventually, join the ranks of the First World, was an immense design project. For seven decades, development discourses and strategies have kept in place the idea that much of Africa, Asia, and Latin America is underdeveloped and that it is the duty of well-intentioned governments and institutions to help them develop and modernize. That this dream turned into a nightmare for many has been sufficiently shown. The development discourse, along with the huge knowledge-power apparatus it created (from the World Bank to national and local development agencies all over the Third World, nongovernmental organizations, and so forth), became instead a highly efficient mechanism for the economic, social, and cultural production of Asia, Africa, and Latin America in particular ways (Escobar 2011). It is intriguing that design, as an expert discourse, has had little explicit presence in development activities or their critique until recently.

The entry of design into development is both troublesome and hopeful, depending on how one looks at it. Peter Redfield has begun to map a particularly critical area, based on the examination of a number of "humanitarian goods" and "modest designs" when basic survival is at stake (including "ready-to-use" therapeutic food such as Plumpy'nut, a personal water-filtering system named LifeStraw, a simple human sanitation device called Peepoo, and inexpensive treatment for diseases such as Ebola and AIDS). Based on a decade of engagement with Médecins sans Frontières (Doctors without Borders), Redfield discusses the nexus of Enlightenment rationality, secularism, capitalism, and colonialism that constitutes the cultural and political background of humanitarian aid. Redfield and colleagues (Redfield 2012, 2013; Redfield and Bornstein 2010) engage in a sustained analysis of the thorny issues raised by humanitarianism, including how to bear witness and practice "active neutrality" in contexts of massive dislocation where saving a few lives seems to be all one can do. The design of many humanitarian goods takes shape amid austere constraints such that durability, simplicity, and portability are essential. More critically, these goods circulate according to a new commodity logic; while the "approach remains openly commercial," the producers are aware of what it means to work in "an explicitly humanitarian market" (Redfield 2012, 175, 168). Consequently, Redfield shows how this design practice can neither be reduced to being an instrument of neoliberal globalization nor be assimilated into well-established forms of governmentality or developmentalist intervention. Something else, potentially new, seems to be happening in this field of "minimal biopolitics" emerging at the intersection of anthropology, humanitarian practice, and design; this process is unfolding within a veritably sacrificial international order. Here, design questions not infrequently become a matter of life and death.[9]

Humanitarian design has opened the way for a still-small but growing tendency, namely, the reframing of development and poverty alleviation in terms of innovation and design. Here, professional designers use collaborative "development design thinking" to develop poor-appropriate interventions, with the poor participating as clients in the process of innovation. Big design firms, in this way, are getting into development as an expanded frontier for lucrative contracts and the application of expertise, whereas smaller organizations are more interested in socially conscious design. Design for development has thus become an interesting domain in which to investigate "the afterlives of development," as anthropologist Anke Schwittay (2014, 31) puts it in a recent reflective piece on this trend. In her analysis of microfinance or "financial inclusion" schemes—well known owing to the alleged success of the Grameen Bank in Bangladesh at "empowering poor women" to become microentrepreneurs—she shows the tensions that arise in the codesign process; many of these stem from the fact that participation in these schemes still functions within a colonizing politics of development knowledge. She concludes, "Application of Western expertise and technology to solve the problems of development privileges outsider, technological, and often commercial solutions over political action or indigenous practice. In this way, humanitarian design constitutes a continuation of modernist development interventions and also shows their current embrace by global market forces. However . . . humanitarian design can begin to create alternative development figures within the existing apparatus. It acknowledges the messiness and complexity of any project of change and recommends proceeding with caution" (43).[10]

Schwittay's caution is a wise one. To mention just two of the most recent incarnations of the development dream: first is the amazing machinery set in place to discuss and agree on the set of post-2015 sustainable development indicators after the fifteen-year Millennium Development Goals expired in 2015, with questionable results.[11] The second is the sad and, frankly, ludicrous framework proposed by the World Bank (2013) in *World Development Report 2014: Risk and Opportunity—Managing Risk for Development*. The hardworking economists at this institution have just come to the realization that what keeps poor people in their poverty is that they have not yet learned how to manage the risks they face, so that they can then take advantage of their opportunities! Page after page of the report vividly describes and illustrates a world increasingly full of risks, all of which is presented as if risks just happen, and the report then goes on to propose schemes by which the poor can finally learn to "manag[e] risk for a life full of opportunities" (2). It is hard to decide whether such an amazingly simplistic approach (which nevertheless, even more sadly, influences policy worldwide) is one more proof of the World Bank's amazing capacity for cynicism or yet another sign of its incapacity to understand power dynamics and poor people's lives, or both.

Caution is thus definitely in order when considering the expansion of design into development. It is frequently the case that development design recycles colonialist representations—for instance, the notion that "Africa has little to offer, but much to receive" (Pereira and Gillett 2015, 118), which obscures the incredibly resourceful everyday design agency of Africans—or ends up endorsing strategies in which the "values of design thinking draw from a progressive narrative of global salvation that ignores non-Western ways of thinking rooted in craft practices that predate yet live alongside modern manufacturing techniques" (Tunstall 2013, 236). A decolonial perspective on development is thus essential for approaching codesign with subaltern groups in ways that strengthen, rather than undermine, their collective autonomy. Only by attending to the entrenched geopolitics of development knowledge can designers become more critical of how design operates within unequal world orders and in the borderlands of the modern/colonial world system and become a force for change alongside those groups most negatively affected by modern designs, grand or small.

Political Ecology, Feminist Political Ecology, and the Emergence of Political Ontology

There is a certain clarity about the political economy of design—design's dependence on, and contribution to, capitalism, exploitation, and other forms of power, both broadly speaking and in specifically in terms of design's contribution to maintaining particular forms of work and divisions of labor, an issue that design theorist Damian White (2015) has examined with insight. There is also a political ecology to it, stemming from design's fundamental role in the exploitation of natural resources, its participation in energy-intensive and consumerist lifestyles, and its propagation of specific ideas about nature and the built environment, among other areas. There is not much contemporary design that is done "with nature," to put it mildly. It thus befits this field to develop a sophisticated political ecology of its own practice; for this task, it is useful to consider the main elements—theories, concepts, and issues—with which this field has dealt since its inception.

There are many ways to define political ecology (PE) and tell its genealogy.[12] There is broad agreement about its starting point in the 1970s, when a number of social scientists began to analyze the relation between society and nature by combining ecological frameworks (largely from the cultural and human ecology schools of the 1950s–1970s, centered on the analysis of the relation between humans and the environment) with social theory frameworks, particularly Marxism and systems theory. Some of the early critiques of sustainability were influential in this early PE.[13] Since then, the field has remained intensely interdisciplinary, with geography, anthropology, ecological economics, sociology, and environmental history playing the most prominent roles. Since the 1990s, poststructuralism has favored a shift in focus toward the various regimes of representation and power through which nature has been culturally constructed, historically and in place (science, patriarchy, whiteness, and colonial narratives). In general terms, what came out of these two very productive phases was an understanding of PE as the field that studies the multiple intersections among nature, culture, power, and history. Emphases oscillated between "the social production of nature" (more prevalent in Marxist geography) and "the cultural construction of nature" (in poststructuralist-inflected anthropology). Ecological economics centered on reframing economic theory through material-energetic analyses and questions of valuation. It became explicitly linked with PE through its concern with environmental struggles, chiefly in terms of what Joan Martínez-Alier (2002) calls ecological distribution conflicts (see also Healy et al. 2013; Escobar 2008). All of these inquiries are useful for crafting the types of hybrid political ecologies appropriate to design's concern with enabling different socioecological futures (White 2015; White, Rudy, and Gareau 2015).

These approaches or phases overlap today in the work of many authors; a certain theoretical eclecticism characterizes PE. The current moment can nevertheless be considered a distinct third phase. This phase can broadly be described as postconstructivist and neomaterialist. While it incorporates many of the insights of the constructivist moment (nature is historically and culturally constructed) and continues to pay attention to the social production of nature by capital under globalizing conditions, the center of attention is now an entire range of aspects that were largely bypassed by the social and human sciences as a whole. The category that perhaps most aptly captures these diverse tendencies is the *ontological turn*; it has become salient in geography, anthropology, and political theory during the past decade. What defines this turn is the attention to a host of factors that deeply shape what we come to know as reality but that social theory has rarely tackled—factors like objects and things, nonhumans, matter and materiality (soil, energy, infrastructures, weather, bytes), emotions, spirituality, feelings, and so forth. What brings together these very disparate items is the attempt to break away from the normative divides, central to the modern regime of truth, between subject and object, mind and body, reason and emotion, living and inanimate, human and nonhuman, organic and inorganic, and so forth. This is why this set of perspectives can properly be called postdualist. More colloquially, it can be said that what we are witnessing with postdualist, neomaterialist critical theories is the return of the repressed side of the dualisms—the forceful emergence of the subordinated and often feminized and racialized side of all of the above binaries.[14]

The most important targets of a postdualist PE are the divide between nature and culture, on the one hand, and the idea that there is a single nature (or world) to which there correspond many cultures, on the other. The deconstruction of the first divide started in the 1980s, with the works of Tim Ingold, Marilyn Strathern, Philippe Descola, Donna Haraway, John Law, and Bruno Latour (and many others in other parts of the world). The more recent scholarship, however, makes a concerted effort at reconnecting nature and culture, and humans and nonhumans, through a rich variety of theoretical and ethnographic proposals and investigations. This task of reconnection may take the form of visualizing networks, assemblages, naturecultures, or socionatures, or through and analyzing the composition of the more-than-human worlds always in the process of being created by all kinds of actors and processes. Distributed agency (e.g., Bennett 2010) and relational ontologies are key concepts here. Whether these postdualist trends finally manage to leave behind the anthropocentric and Eurocentric features of modern social theory and their particular accentuation in the Anglo-American academy is still a matter of debate. In the remainder of this section, I discuss two lines of work that are tackling this problematic: feminist political ecology (FPE) and political ontology.

It is not a coincidence that the most interesting research taking place at the interface of the ontological turn and PE is being done by feminist geographers, anthropologists, and political theorists.[15] Perhaps it could be said that they are the "most consistently relational" among the academics working across the nature/culture divide, while being mindful of not "re-worlding everything into one lens," as Paige West puts it (as many of us academics are prone to do).[16] Feminists from the Global South are particularly attuned to the manifold relational politics and ways of being that correspond to multiple axes of power and oppression.[17] Though not strictly located within PE or FPE (but see some of the contributions in Harcourt and Nelson 2015; Harcourt 2016; Salleh 2009b), their relational writings are very important for radicalizing the insights of postdualist FPE. Carolyn Shaw (2014) proposes the African feminist notion of *negofeminism*—a feminism that is not ego based—as a basis for relational thinking and writing, a notion that recalls that of the "expanded ecological self" of deep ecology. Something similar can be said of the potential contributions to FPE and postdualist PE by decolonial Latin American feminists, for whom an essential part of any feminist work is the deconstruction of the colonial divide (the us-versus-them divide that was introduced with the conquest of America, slavery, and colonialism and is alive and well today with modernizing globalization and development; see Espinosa, Gómez, and Ochoa 2014; Lugones 2010a, 2010b; von Werlhof 2015). Whether the concept of gender is even applicable to preconquest societies, or even to contemporary non-Western and nonmodern societies, remains a matter of debate, given the relational fabric that, to a greater or lesser extent, continues to characterize such societies, which admits of no strictly separate and preconstituted categories of masculine and feminine (Lugones 2010a, 2010b; Paredes 2012).

Of course, feminists have a strong living genealogy on which to construct their theoretical-political projects in a "high-relationality" mode, from their willingness to ask questions about the situatedness of knowledge, the historicity of the body, and the intersectionality of forms of oppression, to the salience of emotions and affect and the relevance of the voices of women from the Global South. This heritage is reflected today in the feminist commitment to and creativity in exploring other ways of worlding, including new insights about what keeps the dominating ontologies in place. Today FPE can be said to be a transnational practice space of understanding and healing (e.g., Harcourt and Nelson 2015; Baksh and Harcourt 2015). It builds on the realization that attachments (to body, place, and nature) have ontological status. In some versions, there is an explicit aim to build effective bridges across worlds by bringing to the fore community, spirituality, and intimacy with places as ways to repair the damage inflicted by the ontology of disconnection and oppression. Gloria Anzaldúa's (2002) powerful call for all of us humans to be *nepantleras*—bridge builders and reweavers of relationality—is shared by some of these new orientations. All of these feminist concerns pose challenges to design practice and provide useful concepts for a feminist and relational rethinking of design. One might extend Wendy Harcourt's (2009) consistent concern with the body politics of development to the design field in order to direct designers' attention to the ways in which the multiple actual or possible design/body intersections do or might play out in the kinds of worlds we end up inhabiting.

Along with decolonial FPE, political ontology (PO) examines political strategies to defend or re-create those worlds that retain important relational and communal dimensions, particularly from the perspective of today's multiple territorial struggles. The term *political ontology* was coined by anthropologist Mario Blaser (2009, 2010, 2014) and continues to be developed by him along with de la Cadena and myself (de la Cadena 2010, 2015; Escobar 2014; Blaser, de la Cadena, and Escobar 2014), as well as by others (e.g., Jackson 2014). The emphasis is on worlds and ways of worlding in two senses: on the one hand, PO refers to the power-laden practices involved in bringing into being a particular world or ontology; on the other hand, it refers to a field of study that focuses on the interrelations among worlds, including the conflicts that ensue as different ontologies strive to sustain their own existence in their interaction with other worlds. It should be emphasized that PO is situated as much within critical trends in the academy as within ongoing struggles for the defense of territories and worlds. It is this active and profound commitment to thinking from the space of struggles involving ecological-ontological conflicts that gives PO its specificity at present. The notion of ontological struggles, in this context, signals a problematization of the universalizing ontology of the dominant forms of modernity—what John Law (2011) has descriptively called the "One-World World" (OWW). In addition, PO is intended to make visible the ontological dimension of the accumulation by dispossession that is going on today in many parts of the world through extractivist development models, principally large-scale mining, agrofuels, and land grabbing linked to commercial agriculture (McMichael 2013). Against the will to render the world one, PO asserts the importance of enhancing the pluriverse, and to this end it also studies the conditions for the flourishing of the pluriverse.

While PO is very much influenced by the more-than-human trend of late (de la Cadena 2015; Tsing 2015), it also seeks to scrutinize human-centered assemblages. By placing PO deeply (ethnographically and politically) within worlds that are not constructed solely on the basis of the nature/culture divide, even if partially connected with the OWW and hence also making themselves in terms of the divide, PO scholars and intellectual-activists hope to render visible those heterogeneous assemblages of life that enact nondualist, relational worlds. Also, PO has a decided decolonial orientation in that it rearticulates the colonial difference (the hierarchical classification of differences created historically by the OWW's domineering ontology) into a vision of multiple onto-epistemic formations, ineluctably coconstituted within power relations. This rearticulation exposes anew the OWW's epistemic inability to recognize that which exceeds it, and renovates our understanding of the human.

The historicity of PO at the present moment, finally, is given by the utter necessity, as gleaned from mobilizations in Latin America, of defending relational territories and worlds against the ravages of large-scale extractivist operations, such as mining and agrofuel production (but one could mention as well the Sioux struggle against the Dakota Access Pipeline and surely other indigenous struggles in North America). Against the ontological occupation and destruction of worlds effected by the globalization project, PO emphasizes the importance of thinking from, and within, those configurations of life that, while partially connected with the globalizing worlds, are not fully occupied by them (Escobar 2014; de la Cadena 2015).

PO and Epistemologies of the South

There is one more social theory framework I would like to review before shifting to an explicitly applied register. This framework could prove to be particularly useful for critical and cultural design studies given that it involves a sustained inquiry into how social change happens. This is the framework of Epistemologies of the South (ES), developed by one of the architects of the World Social Forum, the sociologist and legal scholar Boaventura de Sousa Santos (2014), possibly one of the most compelling and practicable proposals for social transformation to emerge at the intersection of the Global North and the Global South, theory and practice, and the academy and social life. It outlines trajectories for thinking otherwise, precisely because it carves a space that enables thought to reengage with the amazing diversity of forms of knowledge held by those groups whose experiences can no longer be rendered legible by academic Eurocentric knowledge, if they ever could. Ontologically oriented design proposals such as transition design and design for social innovation will also find ES valuable in their determination to develop non-Eurocentric practices.

The ES framework is based on a series of premises and strategies, often effectively summarized by its author in compact and seemingly straightforward formulations—insightful reversals—which nevertheless point at crucial problems within contemporary social theory (Santos 2007, 2014).[18] Perhaps the best starting point for our purposes is the maxim that *we are facing modern problems for which there are no longer modern solutions.* Ontologically speaking, one may say that the crisis is the crisis of a particular world or set of worldmaking practices, the dominant form of Euro-modernity (capitalist, rationalist, liberal, secular, patriarchal, white, or what have you), or, as already mentioned, the OWW—the world that has arrogated for itself the right to be "the" world, subjecting all other worlds to its own terms or, worse, to nonexistence.

If the crisis is largely caused by this OWW ontology, it follows that addressing the crisis implies transitioning toward the pluriverse. This is precisely another of the major premises of ES, that *the diversity of the world is infinite;* succinctly, the world is made up of multiple worlds, multiple ontologies or reals that are far from being exhausted by the Eurocentric experience or being reducible to it.

The invisibility of the pluriverse points at one of the major concepts of ES, namely, the sociology of absences. Here again we find an insightful formulation: *what doesn't exist is actively produced as nonexistent or as a noncredible alternative to what exists.* The social production of nonexistence signals the effacement of entire worlds through a set of epistemological operations concerning knowledge, time, productivity, and ways of thinking about scale and difference. Conversely, the proliferation of struggles in defense of territory and cultural difference suggests that what emerges from such struggles are entire worlds, what in this book we call relational worlds or ontologies. This gives rise to a sociology of emergences. There are clear ontological and design dimensions to the two main strategies introduced by ES, namely, the sociology of absences (the production of nonexistence points at the nonexistence of worlds) and the sociology of emergences (the enlargement of those experiences considered valid or credible alternatives to what exists involves the forceful emergence of relational worlds through struggle).

Another principle of ES brings up the connection between theory and ontology. This is that *the understanding of the world is much broader than the Western understanding of the world.* This means that the transformation of the world, and the civilizational transitions adumbrated by many indigenous, peasant, and Afrodescendant activists, might happen along pathways that might be unthinkable from the perspective of Eurocentric theories. Said differently, there is a glaring gap between what most Western theories today can glean from the field of social struggles, on the one hand, and the transformative practices actually going on in the world, on the other. This gap reveals a limit faced by mainstream and leftist theories alike, a limit that stems from the mono-ontological or intra-European origin of such theories. To think new thoughts, by implication, requires stepping out of the epistemic space of Western social theory and into the epistemic configurations associated with the multiple relational ontologies of worlds in struggle. It is in these spaces that we might find more compelling answers to the strong questions posed by the current conjuncture of modern problems with insufficient modern solutions.

We may draw some implications for design praxis from ES. Do design practices participate in the sociology of absences by overlooking nonexpert subaltern knowledges or by treating them as unable to provide the basis for other designs and design otherwise? Or by measuring productivity and efficiency through the monocultural yardstick of market economics? Conversely, can design practice contribute to broadening, and drawing on, the rich spectrum of experiences that should be considered viable alternatives to what exists? More generally, what would it entail to construct a non-Eurocentric design imagination? What kinds of epistemic and ontological platforms would this project require? What would it take for design practitioners to search for repertoires of design ideas from the perspective of social and cognitive justice (including, but going beyond, the more easily detectable forms of vernacular design)? Tackling these questions might require a significant reorientation of the rationalist and modernist cultural background from which design emerged and within which it continues to operate.

Design under Ontological Occupation: The PO of Territorial Struggles

From a PO perspective, it can be argued that globalization *has taken place at the expense of relational and nondualist worlds* worldwide. Today, economically, culturally, and militarily we are witnessing a renewed attack on anything relational and collective. Indeed, the twin forces of expulsion (Sassen 2014) and occupation can be said to constitute the chief logic of the current pattern of global domination.[19] The occupation of people's territories by capital, the State, and at times armed actors implies economic, technological, cultural, ecological, and often military aspects, but its most fundamental dimension is ontological. From this perspective, what occupies territories is a particular ontology, that of individuals, expert knowledge, markets, and the economy. This is the merciless world of the 1 percent (or, say, 10 percent) denounced by the Occupy and Spain's *indignados* movements, foisted on the 90 percent and the natural world with ever-increasing virulence, cynicism, and illegality, since more than ever *legal* signals only a self-serving set of rules that imperialize the desires of the powerful (from the World Trade Organization and the invasion of countries with the acquiescence of the so-called international community of occupiers, to the legal ongoing police occupation of poor ethnic neighborhoods, as the case of Ferguson and others finally made clear to many people in the United States).

Conversely, however, the perseverance of communities and the commons, and the struggles for their defense and reconstitution—particularly, but not only, those that incorporate explicitly ethnoterritorial dimensions—involve resistance and the defense of territories that, at their best and most radical, can be described as pluriversal, that is, as fostering the coexistence of multiple worlds. By resisting the neoliberal globalizing project, many marginalized communities are advancing *ontological struggles* for the perseverance and enhancement of the pluriverse. Let me mention a few examples to make this point more tangible (we will return to these and other examples in chapter 6).

A striking case of ontological occupation of territories comes from the southernmost area of the Colombian Pacific, around the port city of Tumaco. There, since the early 1980s, the mangrove and rain forests have been under progressive occupation by outsiders, and communities have been displaced, giving way to oil palm plantations and industrial shrimp cultivation. Nonexistent in the 1970s, by the mid-1990s oil palm plantations had expanded to over thirty thousand hectares, and the industry projected that the area would double in a few years. The monotony of the plantation—row after row of palm as far as you can see, a green desert of sorts—has replaced the diverse, heterogeneous, and entangled worlds of forest and communities. There are two important aspects of this dramatic change to note: first, the plantation form effaces the relations maintained with and by the forest-world; emerging from a dualist ontology of human dominance over nature, the plantation is one of the most effective means to bring about the ontological occupation of local relational worlds. Second, plantations are *unthinkable* from the relational perspective of forest-worlds; within these worlds, forest practices take on an entirely different form that ecologists describe in terms of agroecology and agroforestry. Not far from the plantations, industrial shrimp companies were also busy in the 1980s and 1990s, transforming the mangrove-world into a disciplined succession of rectangular pools, "scientifically" controlled. A very polluting and destructive industry, especially when constructed on mangrove swamps, this type of shrimp farming constitutes another clear example of ontological occupation and politics at play (Escobar 2008).

Mangrove forests are primary examples of relational ontologies. The mangrove-world is enacted minute by minute, day by day, through an infinite set of practices carried out by a multiplicity of beings and life forms, involving complex weavings of water, minerals, degrees of salinity, forms of energy (sun, tides, moon), human activity, spiritual beings, and so forth. There is a rhizome-like logic to these entanglements, very difficult to map and measure, if at all; this logic reveals an altogether different way of being and becoming in territory and place. Said otherwise, things and beings *are* their relations;

they do not exist prior to them.[20] From a capitalist perspective, transforming them from "worthless swamp" to agroindustrial complexes is a laudable aim (Ogden 2011). In these cases, the insatiable appetite of the OWW spells out the progressive destruction of the mangrove-world, its ontological capture and reconversion by capital and the State (Deleuze and Guattari 1987; Escobar 2008, 2014). The OWW, in short, denies the mangrove-world the possibility of existing as such. Local struggles constitute attempts to re/establish some degree of symmetry to the partial connections that the mangrove-worlds maintain with the OWW.

Elders and young activists in many territorial communities worldwide passionately express why they defend their worlds even at the price of their lives. In the words of an activist from the Afrodescendant community of La Toma, in the Norte del Cauca region of Colombia, south of Cali, who has been waging a courageous struggle against illegal gold mining for over five years, "It is patently clear to us that we are confronting monsters such as transnational corporations and the State. Yet nobody is willing to leave her/his territory; I might get killed here, but I am not leaving."[21] Such resistance takes place within a long history of domination and resistance, and this is essential for understanding territorial struggles as ontological political practices and as the background for autonomous design. La Toma communities have knowledge of their continued presence in the territory since the first half of the seventeenth century. It is an instructional example of what activists call *ancestrality*, referring to the ancestral mandate that inspires today's struggles and that persists in the memory of the elders, amply documented in oral traditions and scholarly studies (Lisifrey et al. 2013). This mandate is joyfully celebrated in oral poetry and song: *Del Africa llegamos con un legado ancestral; la memoria del mundo debemos recuperar* (From Africa we arrived with an ancestral legacy; the world's memory we need to recuperate).[22] Far from being an intransigent attachment to the past, ancestrality stems from a living memory directly connected to the ability to envision a different future—a "futurality" (Fry 2012) that struggles for the conditions that will allow them to persevere as a distinct world.

Back to La Toma: from November 17 to 27, 2014, a group of twenty-two women marched from La Toma to Bogotá, a distance of 440 kilometers, to protest the continued illegal and destructive gold mining in their territories, despite the agreements to stop it that the government had signed from 2009 on. Many people joined in along the way or offered solidarity, in small towns and larger cities such as Cali and Ibagué. Upon arriving at the cold Andean *sabana,* the high-altitude plateau where Bogotá is located, and facing the indifference and dilatory tactics of the bureaucrats of the Ministry of the Interior, the women decided to occupy the building, which they proceeded to do for close to two weeks, despite threats of forced eviction and the intense *frío sabanero,* or the region's cold (which affected the occupiers, especially at night), until they finally reached a new signed agreement with the government. The agreement called for, among other things, the removal of all the *retroexcavadoras* (large backhoe-type excavating machines) used for gold extraction and a plan to protect the communities from threats by the backhoe owners and other armed actors. By mid-January, however, and despite timid attempts by various government agencies, it was clear that the agreements were not going to be fulfilled. In mid-April Francia Márquez, one of the main leaders of the march, penned two brave and lucid open letters to the government and the public at large. "Everything we have lived," she said in her first letter, "has been for the love for our territories, the love we feel when we see the plantain germinate, when we have a sunny fishing day, of knowing your family is close by. . . . Our land is the place where we dream of our future with dignity. Perhaps that's why they [armed actors, including the army, paramilitaries, and guerrillas] persecute us, because we want a life of autonomy and not of dependency."[23]

Written in the context of the tense peace negotiations between the government and the Fuerzas Armadas Revolucionarias de Colombia (FARC) guerrillas, the letter also contained a direct indictment of the government's national development plan, one of whose pillars, or *locomotoras* (locomotives), is precisely mining. For Márquez, this model can only generate hunger, misery, and war. The implication is clear: without transforming this model radically, and without conditions of autonomy for the territories, peace will be illusory. There can never be peace, she had said in an earlier letter, "if the government is not able to create the conditions to take care of life, if it does not privilege the life of all beings above all private interests and the interests of the transnationals." As she reminded everyone in the letter, "we started on this march to let you all know that illegal mining is leaving us without our families, robbing from us the possibility of continuing to live in the territory where our umbilical cords are buried."[24] Addressed "to those women who take care of their territories as if they were their daughters and sons. To the women and men who care for a Dignified, Simple, and Solidary Life," the letter ended with the march's slogan: "The territory is our life, and life is not sold—it is loved and defended" (*El territorio es la vida y la vida no se vende, se ama y se defiende*).

A third example comes from the struggle of the indigenous Nasa and Misak peoples, also from the Norte del Cauca region, who describe the goal of their struggle as the *Liberación de la Madre Tierra* (the Liberation of Mother Earth).[25] Both groups have maintained a steady resistance to colonization from the time of the conquest; this resistance has experienced a sharp resurgence since the early 1970s with the creation of regional indigenous organizations. Ever since, their strategy to recover their ancestral territories—expropriated by sugarcane plantation barons beginning in the middle of the nineteenth century and by other interests more recently—has met with relative success, even if at a high cost in terms of lives lost and violent repression on the part of the State and armed actors. The strategies and "cosmoactions" of these *pueblos* (peoples) have been centered on the recovery and defense of territories and their *Planes de Vida* (Life Plans). As they put it, the territory is "the vital space that ensures our survival as a people and as a living culture in harmony with nature and the spirits. The territory is our true history book, since it keeps alive the traditions of those who inhabit it. As the collective space of existence, it also makes possible the harmonious coexistence among the pueblos. It grounds the indigenous cosmovision as the raison d'être of our survival" (Consejo Regional Indígena del Cauca [Cric], quoted in Quijano 2012, 219). Their strategy is motivated by the following principle: "to recover the land in order to recover everything: authority, justice, work; this is why we need to think with our own heads, speak our language, learn our history, and analyze and pass on our experiences as much as those of other peoples" (257). Similarly, the Life Plan of the Misak people is explained in terms of "the construction and reconstruction of a vital space in which to be born, grow, persist, and flow. The Plan is a narrative of life and survival, the construction of the path that enables the transit through life; it is not a simple planning scheme" (Cabildo, Taitas, y Comisión de Trabajo del Pueblo Guambiano 1994, quoted in Quijano 2012, 263).

The defense and recovery of their territories is thus actively seen and pursued by these groups as the necessary means for the reconstitution of their worlds, and involves the articulation of cultural, economic, environmental, and spiritual processes. The Misak Life Plan "posits a type of development based on our distinct culture and cosmovision, organized under five rubrics: Our Territory; Our People (*Mamuy misak*); Culture and the Cosmovision; Authority; and Our Customary Law (*derecho mayor*). These are rendered concrete through programs along four axes: Territory, Land, and Territoriality; Education and Culture; Economy (*economía propia*); Health and Food Autonomy" (Cabildo Indígena Guambía 2007, quoted in Quijano 2012, 208).

The Life Plans and the autonomous economy, just as much as the defense of the territory, are strategies of relocalization, that is, strategies for the persistence of the place-based and communal weave of life. These are strategies for ontological difference and against the modern capitalism's pretension of rendering all communities delocalized and economized consumers. Autonomy is a counternarrative to the ongoing pressures to delocalize. One of the most notable regional indigenous organizations, for instance, the Regional Indigenous Confederation of Cauca (Consejo Regional Indígena del Cauca), has maintained the banner of "Unity, Land, Culture, Autonomy" since its inception in the early 1970s. For the other major regional organization (the Association of Northern Cauca Indígenas Cabildos [Asociación de Cabildos Indígenas del Norte del Cauca, ACIN]), "the Life Plan seeks to consolidate the construction of our ancestral process with full freedom and autonomy, ensuring the participation of everybody in the community" (ACIN 2009, quoted in Quijano 2012, 236). The organizing principle of this association, tellingly, is *tejer en libertad la vida* (to weave life in liberty), and it is enacted through five *Tejidos de Vida* (Life Weavings) concerning economy and the environment, people and culture, justice and harmony, the defense of life, and communications and external relations that support truth and life. In this perspective we find the other main element to be developed as part of the concept of autonomous design, namely, the community or the communal.

The last example comes from an altogether different region of Colombia and constitutes another incredibly inspiring instance of autonomous and territorial indigenous struggle in the country. It concerns the Kogui, Arhuaco, Wiwa, and Kankuamo peoples of the Sierra Nevada de Santa Marta in Colombia's northeast, by the edge of the Caribbean Sea. These groups have also maintained a radical struggle for their cultural difference, based on a relational ontology founded on the notion that "the territories are living entities with memory" (Ulloa 2012, n.p.); it is in them that "the geographies of people's relations with nature are inscribed, through the exercise of territoriality and the articulation of symbolic, political, economic and social relations" (Ulloa 2010, 81). These groups' political strategies are geared to the defense of their territories, which they describe in terms of *Madre Tierra* (Mother Earth), ancestral territories, and sacred territories. In short, the territory

> is seen and felt as the existential space for the sacred and the everyday alike, for their knowledge and customary law and the relation with other beings, including the management of relations with other humans. . . . The

territory is comprehended in an integral fashion, as the space where the physical and the spiritual are articulated and where all actors [human and not] have their own unique place and set of relations. The territory is cognized in terms of the interpretation of ancestral marks inscribed in long-standing sacred sites; this perception orients present-day actions and the integrated management of the entire territory in order to ensure its environmental and cultural preservation. (Ulloa 2010, 81)

The contrast between these "other territorialities," constructed on the basis of relational ontologies, and the ontology of separation and fragmentation maintained by mainstream economic actors and the State could not be sharper. In fact, the ultimate goal of the mobilization of the peoples of the Sierra Nevada de Santa Marta is none other than ensuring *the circulation of life*, as Colombian anthropologist and geographer Astrid Ulloa has admirably shown through her sustained ethnographic research with these communities. The circulation of life is enacted through a series of practices involving knowledge, sacred sites, seeds, rituals, and customary law. A well-known fact in the Colombian and Latin American ethnology of the Kogui and Arhuaco peoples is that they see themselves as the elder brothers of all other humans and as such are charged with the mandate of keeping universal equilibrium through the circulation of all life, starting with their own territory. It is on the basis of this ontology of life circulation—a genuine framework for sustainability—that they elaborate their project for autonomy, under very adverse conditions and extreme pressures on their territories (Ulloa 2011; chapter 6, this volume).

These examples demonstrate the continued existence of socially significant experiences that do not conform to the mainstream Euro–Latin American modern ontology. They can be properly seen as instances of economic, cultural, and epistemic insurgency that aim to re/create and maintain practices of cultural, economic, and ecological difference (Walsh 2009, 2012). The difference is, in the last instance, ontological, and it is expressed most eloquently with the metaphor and practices of weaving. Weaving, it goes without saying, can also serve as an organizing metaphor for life-centered design. Toward the end of the book we will introduce the idea of transition design as one that enables us to become effective weavers of the mesh of life, with the Liberation of Mother Earth as one of its central principles.

There are many such examples worldwide, involving almost every territorial community where the extraction of natural resources is taking place. The key design question, to be tackled in chapter 6, is whether it is possible to even think about a design praxis under conditions of ontological occupation. Given that occupation is a worldwide phenomenon, and bound to become more acute as the living conditions of large numbers of people on the planet worsen and as their territories become ever more the target of expulsion and occupation by extractive forms of capital, this question is of utmost importance. As will be argued, an ontological approach to design provides paths toward imagining design practices that contribute to people's defense of their territories and cultures. We will call this approach autonomous design.

We haven't strayed too far from where this chapter started, namely, the investigation of the relation among design, culture, and power specific to the current conjuncture, as the examples from this section are instances of this intersection and point at how we might think about it otherwise. This is why we defined this conjuncture, from a cultural studies perspective, in terms of the ontological occupation of relational worlds by a dominant world, on the one hand, and the limitations of modern social theory and the modern sciences to provide compelling solutions to today's wicked problems, on the other. As I hope to have shown, one can find elements for rethinking design culturally and ontologically in a number of scholarly trends in anthropology, geography, development studies, political ecology, feminist theory, and political ontology, among other fields. Some of the insights they afford will come in handy in subsequent chapters, as we go on to consider design frameworks intended to support transitions toward sustainability and communal autonomy within a pluriversal perspective.

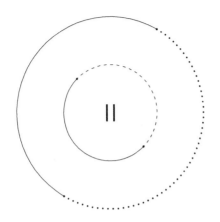

The Ontological
Reorientation
of Design

3

In the Background
of Our Culture

Rationalism, Ontological Dualism, and Relationality

Thus we confront the problem of understanding how
our experience—the praxis of our living—is coupled
to a surrounding world which appears filled with
regularities that are at every instant the result of our
biological and social histories.

· **Humberto Maturana and Francisco Varela,** *The Tree of*
Knowledge: The Biological Roots of Human Understanding

The ecological crisis requires from us a new kind of
culture because a major factor in its development has
been the rationalist culture and the associated human/
nature dualism characteristic of the West. . . . Rationalist culture has distorted many spheres of human
life; its remaking is a major but essential cultural en-
terprise. . . . The ecological crisis we face is thus . . . a
crisis of the culture of reason or of what the dominant
culture has made of reason.

· **Val Plumwood,** *Environmental Culture: The Ecological*
Crisis of Reason

Más allá de la razón hay un mundo de colores.

"There is a world of colors beyond reason."

· **Adolfo Albán Achinte,** *Más allá de la razón hay un*
mundo de colores

To pose the question of a redirection of design in a fundamental manner, it is necessary to venture into the cultural and philosophical tradition from which it arises and within which it functions with such ease. Contemporary philosophy and cultural theory abound in critical analyses of this tradition, usually under the guise of the critique of metaphysics (the illustrious tradition from Friedrich Nietzsche and Martin Heidegger to Gianni Vattimo and Michel Foucault) or the critical analysis of modernity (Jürgen Habermas, Ulrich Beck, Anthony Giddens, Charles Taylor, Donna Haraway, and Bruno Latour, to mention just a few in European and Anglo-American scholarship, to which we should add contributions from the fields of cultural studies and postcolonial and decolonial theory). In this section, however, I will draw on a little-known set of authors precisely because they foreground the question of design. The preferred term utilized by these authors to refer to the pervasive cultural background within which much of our contemporary world unfolds is the *rationalistic tradition*. I should make it clear, however, that what I am trying to make here is not a philosophical argument per se, but a claim about a broader cultural phenomena: the effects of a "tradition" in orienting people's (including designers') ways of thinking and being. My interest also lies in making connections among this tradition, the ecological crisis, and the cultural and political struggles around nature and difference in Latin America.[1]

Rationalism and the Cartesian Tradition

The tradition we are talking about is variously referred to as *rationalistic, Cartesian,* or *objectivist* and is often associated with related terms such as *mechanistic* (worldview), *reductionistic* (science), *positivistic* (epistemology), and, more recently, *computationalist* (model). For Francisco Varela, the term that best captures the tradition is *abstract,* by which he means "this tendency to find our way toward the rarified atmosphere of the general and the formal, the logical and the well defined, the represented and the foreseen, which characterizes our Western world" (1999, 6). This is an apt definition of *logocentrism,* or the belief in logical truth as the only valid (or main) grounds for knowledge about an objective world made up of things that can be known (and hence ordered and manipulated at will; see Vattimo 1991). For now, suffice it to say that at the basis of the tradition are assumptions about the correspondence between language and reality, or representation/thought and the real. In organized science as much as in daily life, this tradition operates in pervasive ways (see Winograd and Flores 1986, ch. 2; Nandy 1987). In science it is connected to what biologist Lynn Margulis and collaborators have descriptively called the "Cartesian license" (Sagan, Margulis, and Guerrero 1997, 172), which not only placed "man" on the highest rung of the ladder of being but led science to investigate reality by separating mind and matter, body and soul, and life and nonlife—what they call a kind of forgery that imagined a dead cosmos of inanimate matter.

This is, of course, well-trodden terrain in Western philosophy. We shall see, however, why Varela views this feature of our knowledge practices as limiting in some fundamental ways, *including for the very philosophical traditions that call it into question.* We shall also see how it shapes some of the strongest structures of the dominant form of Euro-modernity (the belief in the individual, in the real, in science, and in the economy as self-constituted entities). Finally, we will discuss the extent to which the tradition is deeply connected to a determining feature of such modernity, namely, ontological dualisms. These dualisms underlie an entire structure of institutions and practices through which the oww idea is enacted, effecting at the same time a remoteness from the worlds that we inevitably weave with others and from the natural world, a feature that we will locate at the basis of not only the ecological crisis but also attempts to redress it, whether through relational practices of design (see the next chapter) or political action informed by the relational and communal logics of some social movements (chapter 6). There is thus a concrete purpose in introducing the rationalistic tradition here before tackling these other issues.

Let us start with a peculiar reading by Varela and colleagues of the Cartesian/rationalistic tradition: "It is because reflection in our culture has been severed from its bodily life that the mind-body problem has become a topic for abstract reflection. Cartesian dualism is not so much one competing solution as it is the formulation of this problem" (Varela, Thompson, and Rosch 1991, 30). As a formulation of the question of the relations among mind, body, and experience, it is partial at best. A clear example of the shortcomings of this approach is the standard conceptualization of cognition as the representation by a discrete mind of a preexisting, separate world (cognition as the manipulation of symbols). For Varela and colleagues, this is fundamentally mistaken; for them, rather than "the representation of a pregiven world by a pregiven mind," cognition is "the enactment of a world and a mind on the basis of a history of the variety of actions that a being in the world performs" (9). When you think about it, it makes perfect sense: mind is not separate from body, and both are not separate from the world, that is, from the ceaseless and always-changing flow of existence that constitutes life (or can you really separate them out?). By positing the notion of cognition as representation, we are all cut off from the stream of life in which we are ineluctably and immediately immersed as living beings.

They call this view *cognition as enaction* (embodied action). It is based on the assumption of the fundamental unity of being and world, of our inevitable thrownness into the world (or *throwntogetherness*, to use geographer Doreen Massey's [2004] wonderful neologism).[2] It also assumes that the primary condition of existence is embodied presence, a dwelling in the world (see also Ingold 2000, 2011). By linking cognition to experience, our authors lead us into an altogether different tradition. In this tradition we recognize in a profound way that "the world is not something that is given to us but something we engage in by moving, touching, breathing, eating" (Varela 1999, 8). A number of consequences follow. The first is that while there is indeed a distinction between self and world in this view, there is also a fundamental continuity between them (emphatically expressed in the dictum that there is an "unbroken coincidence of our being, our doing, and our knowing"; Maturana and Varela 1987, 25); the rationalistic tradition remains at the level of the divide, thus missing much of what goes on in life. Second, while we live in a world accessible through reflection, this accessibility is limited; here lies one of the traps.

As Humberto Maturana tellingly underscores, there is an emotional side to all forms of rationality in that every rational domain is founded on emotional grounds, "and it is our emotions that determine the rational domain in which we operate as rational beings at any instant" (1997, 5); in other words, even the decision to be rational is an emotional decision. The consequences are far from negligible: "We are rarely aware that it is our emotions that guide our living even when we claim that we are being rational . . . [a]nd in *the long run we do not understand our cultural existence*" (6; emphasis added). In addition, all modes of knowledge based on reason get at only part of the human experience, the reflexive part, bracketing its immediate, lived aspects, that is, our essential historicity. This historicity is most cogently expressed by Maturana and Varela in the quote that opened this chapter: "Thus we confront the problem of understanding how our experience—the praxis of our living—is coupled to a surrounding world which appears filled with regularities that are at every instant the result of our biological and social histories." The implication for knowledge of this inevitable immersion is that we need to find "a *via media*: to understand the regularity of the world we are experiencing at every moment, but without any point of reference independent of ourselves" (Maturana and Varela 1987, 241; see also 1980).

This injunction has been anathema to the Western rationalistic tradition, for which the world out there preexists our interactions. In the enactive approach, we are always immersed in a network of interactions that are at every instant the result of our biological and cultural histories. We necessarily cocreate the world with others (humans and nonhumans) with whom we live in coexistence. The ultimate conclusion drawn by Maturana and Varela is no less startling, and equally foreign to modern logocentrism: "*We have only the world that we bring forth with others, and only love helps us bring it forth*" (1987, 248). The Buddhist notion of dependent coarising, the complexity theory concept of emergence, Maturana and Gerda Verden-Zöller's (2008) biology of love, and the feminist emphasis on care and love agree with this view. These are principles of relationality. But before we go there, I'd like to briefly discuss some other consequences of the rationalistic tradition, starting with the individual. Four beliefs—in the individual, science, the economy, and the real—are part of the default setting of design theory and practice as we know it; in other words, design inevitably takes place within such an ontological background.

Four Fundamental Beliefs in the Modern Onto-epistemic Order

The Belief in the Individual

One of the most profound—and even damaging—consequences of the rationalistic tradition is the belief in the individual. This belief, one might say, constitutes one of design's main wicked problems. Throughout the centuries, colonialism, modernization, development, and globalization have been the economic and political projects that carried with them into most other world cultures the Trojan horse of the individual, destroying communal and place-based forms of relating (Esteva and Prakash 1998). This continues to be a neglected dimension in analyses of neoliberal globalization—the fact that it entails a veritable cultural war against relational ways of being and the imperial imposition of the cultural regime of the market-based individual. The genealogy of the modern individual has of course been traced in critical scholarship (e.g., by Ivan Illich, Michel Foucault, and Taylor). It has been linked to the history of needs, disciplinary practices, commoditization (the Marxist theory of labor and alienation), and a whole set of political technologies centered on the self. Despite these analyses, the notion that we exist as separate individuals (the possessive or autonomous individual of liberal theory, endowed with rights and free will) continues to be one of the most enduring, naturalized, and deleterious fictions in Western modernity (see Dreyfus and Kelly 2011 for a compelling recent analysis of the cultural nihilism associated with this belief that resonates with the concerns of this book).

Melanesian and Amazonian ethnography has been particularly effective in unsettling the trope of the modern self by showing the rich gamut of social regimes of personhood that do not conform to Western notions of the self, many of which are deeply relational (e.g., Strathern 1988; Battaglia 1995; Viveiros de Castro 2010). Buddhism, of course, has for over twenty-five hundred years developed a powerful theory and practice of living based precisely on the nonexistence of what we call the self—in fact, for Buddhism, attachment to the self and fixation on an objectivist notion of the real are the fundamental causes of suffering rather than freedom. Mindfulness meditation is geared toward cultivating a nonconceptual wisdom that transcends the subject/object division. A main teaching in this tradition is that all things without exception are empty of essence (a lesson the modern academy has been grappling with for only a few decades through the notion of antiessentialism). A correlate notion, already mentioned, is that nothing exists by itself, that everything interexists; this theory of interbeing is a powerful critique of the modern idea that whatever we perceive is real in and of itself.[3]

The Buddhist realization of the empty self finds a correlate in Varela's notion of the virtual self, derived from the biology of cognition and theories of emergence and self-organization. This virtual self is "a coherent pattern that emerges from the activity of simple local components, which seems to be centrally located, but is nowhere to be found, and yet is essential as a level of interaction for the behavior of the whole" (1999, 53; see also Varela, Thompson, and Rosch 1991). The mind/self is an emergent property of a distributed network, or rather of a patchwork of subnetworks, from neurons to language and symbols, assembled by a complex process of tinkering, which neither has a uniform structure nor is the result of a unified design (e.g., Varela, Thompson, and Rosch 1991, 105; Sharma 2015). In the end, one can say that "*the cognitive self is its own implementation: its history and its action are of one piece*" (Varela 1999, 54; italics in the original). Alternatively, one may say that the self is a nexus "within a continuously unfolding field of relations" (Ingold 2011, xii). The idea of the nonexistence of the self—or a profoundly relational notion of the self—is simpler than it sounds. Sometimes I ask my students, somewhat jokingly, whether they have seen the self; hard to pinpoint, isn't it? This absence of a self, however, does not entail placing in doubt the stability of the world, nor the world's regularities and coherences (more on this later). What it means is that we also have to give up, along with the notion of a personal self, the idea of a world that has a fixed and ultimate ground.[4]

Despite its emphasis on participation and interactivity, the emergent design culture that I described in the last two chapters continues to function within a Cartesian view of the world as made up of individuals and things; this belief shapes the notion of design agency. The hold of the individual as the design agent par excellence is beginning to loosen, however, and the newer tendencies aim to find a balance between disembedded and relational understandings of the person. Two particular notions can be credited for this important change. The first is the idea that design takes place today in systems of distributed agency, power, and expertise, within which it is becoming more difficult to maintain the fiction of the isolated individual, and even that of the designer genius at work in the studio. Closely related are the notions of codesign and dialogic collaboration, through which designers and common folk alike "rediscover the power of doing things together" (Manzini 2015, 24). The reawakening of things local and communal fits into this changing landscape of design conditions. Echoing Ivan Illich's critique of the disabling nature of modern technologies, Ezio Manzini finds in the growing desire to abandon individualistic lifestyles a hopeful condition for collaborative design (94–98). From the design world, then, there is also relational pressure being exerted on that most recalcitrant of modern constructs, the so-called individual. More, however, is needed before relational personhood can become the default setting in a postindividualist world. This takes us into the second strong structure of modernity, the belief in the real.

The Belief in the Real

What can be more real than the world on which we plant our feet, or the surrounding world into which our minds seemingly awake? Fair enough. The issue, however, is how the rationalistic tradition translates this basic datum of experience into the belief in an objective reality or an outside world, prior to, and independent of, the multiplicity of interactions that produce it. This objectivist stance is at the basis of much design practice and needs to be tempered in a nondualist ontological conception of design. For one thing, this belief in the real leads to an ethos of human mastery over nature, a pillar of patriarchal culture. It disempowers us for partnering with nature and other humans in a truly collaborative, earth-wise, and stream-of-life manner. Such a notion of the real also buttresses the idea of a single world that calls for one truth about it. Social movements such as the Zapatistas have pointed to this assumption of One World or of a universe with One Truth as the basis of neoliberal globalization, so it has become a target of many social movements, to which they counterpose a view of a world where many worlds fit. Science and technology studies has discussed at length the process by which the "unfolding but generative flux of forces and relations that work to produce particular realities," which makes up the world as multiple, gets reduced to a "single out-thereness" that then becomes the stuff of our experience (Law 2004, 7). By enacting a One-World World (OWW), this Euro-American metaphysics, as John Law calls it, effaces multiple realities through complex processes of power. By ethnographically showing how different realities are patched together into discrete "out-therenesses," one could hope to counteract the ontological politics of the OWW with another that operates on the basis of radical ontological difference and pluriversality (Law 2011; Mol 1999; Blaser 2010; de la Cadena 2010; Escobar 2014). This politics is crucial for ontological design.

The notion of the OWW signals the predominant idea in the West that we all live within a single world, made up of one underlying reality (one nature) and many cultures. This imperialistic notion supposes the West's ability to arrogate for itself the right to be "the world," and to subject all other worlds to its rules, to diminish them to secondary status or to nonexistence, often figuratively and materially. It is a very seductive notion, however; the best way to dispel it is, perhaps, ethnographically and decolonially, as Law suggests. "[T]here is a difference," he states, invoking a comparative ethnographic argument:

> In a European or Northern way of thinking the world carries on by itself. People don't *perform* it. It's *outside* us and we are *contained* by it. But that's not true for [Australian] aboriginal people. The idea of a reality out there, detached from the work and the rituals that constantly re-enact it, makes no sense. Land doesn't *belong* to people. Perhaps it would be better to say that *people* belong to the land. Or, perhaps even better still, we might say that processes of continuous creation redo land, people, life and the spiritual world altogether, and in specific locations. (2011, 1)

As he hastens to say, what is involved here is not a matter of beliefs (or, worse, the assumption that our Western view is the truth, since it is validated by science, whereas theirs is just a belief) but *a matter of reals*. The question for design remains, what would it take for designers to operate without a purely objectivist and single vision of the real? To embrace the notion that design practices, too, might contribute to creating multiple notions of out-thereness, rather than a single one? And, moreover, to take seriously the view that reality is an ongoing and continuous flow of forms and intensities of all kinds? We will get back to these questions in our discussion of the relational ontologies mobilized in territorial struggles in Latin America.

Nobody within the Anglo-American academy has crafted a view as counter to the ontology of the oww as Tim Ingold (2000, 2011). In this anthropologist's view, the world is anything but static and inanimate, not an inert container. It is rather a meshwork made up of interwoven threads or lines, always in movement. As much as any other living being, humans are immersed in this meshwork. Drawing insights from animist cultures and philosophies, Ingold (like some transition visionaries and biologists and many indigenous and spiritual teachers) arrives at the idea of a sentient universe. The resulting framework cannot but be deeply relational; a sentient universe is one in which "it is the dynamic transformative potential of the entire field of relations within which beings of all kinds . . . continuously and reciprocally bring one another into existence" (2011, 68). To sum up, "things are their relations" (74; see also Strathern 1991). It should be clear that in such a vision of the world *it is practically impossible to demarcate a single, stable real.*[5] To be able to do so, one has to parcel out entire domains of the meshwork as inanimate; this is precisely one of the modern operations par excellence; indeed, moderns imagine the world as an inanimate surface to be *occupied*; for many relational cultures, on the contrary, humans and other beings *inhabit* a world that is alive.[6] While moderns occupy space, nonmoderns dwell in places by moving along the lines and threads that produce the place. It is instructive to quote again from Ingold to dispel once and for all the oww idea: "Rather than thinking of ourselves only as observers, picking our way around the objects lying about on the ground of a ready-formed world, we must imagine ourselves in the first place as participants, each immersed with the whole of our being in the currents of a world-in-formation: in the sunlight we see, the rain we hear and the wind we feel in. Participation is not opposed to observation but is a condition for it, just as light is a condition for seeing things, sound for hearing them, and feeling for touching them" (2011, 129).

One of the most cogent instantiations of this idea was actually developed in the late 1960s and early 1970s by scholars who started to conceptualize the circularity between observer and observed within what came to be known as second-order cybernetics (or the cybernetics of observing systems). Going against the grain of dominant scientific positions that posited the separation of the observer from the observed as the principle of objectivity, these theorists argued that this separation was not only impossible but even undesirable. In his poetic recollection of this development at a conference in Paris in 1991, Heinz von Foerster (perhaps the central figure in the movement) claimed, "I would like you to join me in a land where [the nonseparation of observer and observed] is not forbidden; rather, where one is encouraged to write about oneself. What else can one do, anyway"? (1991, 2). Explaining the historical shift from looking at things "out there" (acting as if one were an independent observer "that watches the world go by," as if "through a peephole") to "looking at looking itself," he concludes, "What is new is the profound insight that a brain is required to write a theory of a brain. . . . [Thus, one is rather] a person who considers oneself to be a participant actor in the drama of mutual interaction of the give and take in the circularity of human relations" (2). His ultimate conclusion is still at the center of debates on the real today: that to act is to change oneself and the unfolding universe as well.[7]

In other words, we are not radically separate from what we commonly conceive of as external reality, but rather such reality comes into being moment by moment through our participation in the world (see also Sharma 2015, 4). Is it even possible to think about design in such a deeply relational, processual, historicized, and seemingly ever-moving and ever-changing life, a world always in formation? This is one of the main questions to be tackled in the next chapter.

The Belief in Science

The belief in the real is largely validated by an equally naturalized belief in the concept of science as the foundation of valid knowledge claims in modern societies. Besides the well-known discussions in modern social theory about the status of science, say, from philosophical (critique of epistemological realism), feminist (phallogocentrism), and other poststructuralist perspectives (the politics of science-based truth claims), there are lesser-known currents that figure infrequently, or too tangentially, in the former set of analyses—for example, debates about indigenous, local, and traditional ecological knowledge; discussions about the geopolitics of knowledge and epistemic decolonization; concerns with cognitive justice; and so forth. Besides showing how the hegemony of modern knowledge works to make invisible other knowledges and ways of being, some of these tendencies highlight the links between hegemonic scientific practices and violence and oppression in non-Western contexts.

Such is the case with what in my mind is one of the most enlightening set of critiques of modern science, namely, that produced somewhat collectively by a group of South Asian cultural critics who offer brilliant examples of the dissenting imagination.[8] Investigating the effects of science in third-world contexts, as the work of these intellectuals shows, provides for a very different reading of science, one that, while acknowledging that metropolitan science might have been associated historically with dissent, demonstrates that not only has this ceased to be the case but science has become the most central political technology of authoritarianism, irrationality, and oppression of peoples and nature. As a reason of state, science operates as the most effective idiom of violent development and even standardizes the formats of dissent. In the face of this, the semiarticulate protests of the subaltern rise, at times becoming creative assessments of Western knowledge, lessening science's hegemony and keeping alive a plurality of consciousnesses. Of particular interest for our concern with relationality and design is the argument that, by splitting cognition and affect and ideas from feelings, in the interest of objectivity, science contributes to heightening modernity's tendency toward pathologies of isolation and violence, enabling scientists to get credit for constructive discoveries while avoiding responsibility for the destructive ones.

Organized science thus becomes ineffective as an ally against authoritarianism and increasingly dependent on market-based vested interests. This motivates the powerful and perhaps startling indictment, by Ashis Nandy, that "of all the utopias which threaten to totalize the human consciousness, the most seductive in our times has been the one produced by modern science and technology" (1987, 10). In this way, science loses sight of its potential role in the search for nonoppressive forms of culture and society. It cannot even enter into dialogue with other forms of knowledge given its de facto claim to have the monopoly on knowledge, compassion, and ethics. Awareness of this epistemic politics that characterizes mainstream science becomes a required element when designers and others are working with marginalized groups.

The Belief in the Economy

It is not surprising to find a most acerbic assessment of economics from the same pen: "Our future is being conceptualized and shaped by the modern witchcraft called the science of economics" (Nandy 1987, 107). The issue goes well beyond economics per se in the sense that the rise of this science since the late eighteenth century hides an even more pervasive civilizational development, namely, the invention of something called *the economy* as a separate domain of thought and action, linked to another powerful fiction, the self-regulating market—with the science of economics purportedly capable of telling us the truth about it.[9] It might well be the case that neoliberal economics has been shaken by the financial crisis of 2007–2008, but its imaginary—individuals transacting in markets, unfettered production of commodities, unlimited growth, accumulation of capital, progress, scarcity, and consumption—goes on unhindered. The result, as Tony Fry puts it, is that "the future is being butchered on the slaughter bench of economic growth" (2015, 93).

This highly naturalized discourse undermines most of the current proposals for sustainability and for moving to a postcarbon age, and will need to be tackled as such in critical design frameworks. The denaturalization of the economy is an area of active critical work, for instance, in the imagination of diverse economies beyond the capitalistic one (Gibson-Graham 2006) and social and solidarity economies (largely in Latin America; see, e.g., Coraggio, Laville, and Cattani 2013; Coraggio and Laville 2014), or in proposals for *decroissance* (degrowth) in Europe and for alternatives to development in South America. More tellingly, it can be discerned at the grassroots level; as Gustavo Esteva provocatively puts it, "those marginalized by the economic society in the development era are increasingly dedicated to marginalizing the economy" (2009, 20). Decentering the economy from social and ecological life is a sine qua non for all transition activism and design. It is expressed in many of the ongoing experiments with relocalization of food production, for instance.

With the consolidation of "the economy" from the late eighteenth century on, we have in place a tightly interconnected set of crucial developments in the cultural history of the West, namely, the individual, objective reality, truthful science (rationality), and self-regulating markets. The ensemble of the individual, the real, science, and the economy (market) constitutes the default setting of much of socionatural life in late modernity; they are historical constructs, to be sure, but also beliefs to which we are deeply attached in our everyday existence because of the pervasive social structures, processes, and practices that hold them in place, without which we cannot function. They reveal our commitment to individualism, objectivism, and economism; in fact, they are varieties of essentialism and, in the case of the market at least, fundamentalism. It would take a relatively profound ontological transformation on our part to alter this default setting at the individual, let alone collective, level. Said otherwise, the notions of the individual, the real, and the economy as having intrinsic existence by themselves, independent of the relations that constitute them, and of us as observers, are instances of "folk essentialism," as Kriti Sharma (2015, 12) wonderfully puts it. They seem to us completely real, yet they depend on an entire complex set of operations. It is precisely this impression of reality that we need to probe more deeply to arrive at a view of their ineluctable contingency.

Whereas science imposes its criteria of rationality and objectivity on all forms of knowledge, supported by a Euclidean view of independent reality anchored materially in space and time, economics performs a related operation by taking the sphere of production out of the flow of socionatural life, and technology sediments this ontology with its nonconvivial, industrial instrumentations. Humans, finally, learn how to operate like individuals by construing themselves as raw materials for endless improvement ("self-alchemization" in Claudia von Werlhof's [2015] terms). It is thus that within modern patriarchal capitalist societies we learn from childhood to prioritize production and consumption (at the expense of other manners of valuing existence), individual success (instead of collective well-being), orientation toward the future (instead of mindfulness to the present and dwelling in the hic et nunc of quotidian existence), and the subordination of spirituality and the awareness of the unity of all that exists to the materialism of commodities, of being to possessing. All of this has the cost of making us see ourselves as separate and distant from nature and others (whether in terms of gender, race, culture, or what have you), thus bracketing, if not denying, their coexistence in a relation of mutual respect.

It is this onto-epistemic formation in which we are enmeshed, largely without our knowing it. *This, too, is the meaning of our ontological commitment to "being modern."* The question we need to ask, in ever more refined and enabling ways, is whether it is possible to imagine other forms of knowing~being~doing without losing our ability to navigate skillfully the meanderings of the modern constellation structured by the four beliefs so sketchily analyzed. Pursuing this goal implies significant ontological work on our part. We cannot place this entire historical circumstance at the doorstep of the rationalistic tradition, of course, but the process is deeply intertwined with that rationality and its associated ontology. To this topic we dedicate the next section.

Issues and Problems with Ontological Dualism

Questions of ontology were sidestepped in much of contemporary theory after the linguistic turn and the concern with epistemology after the rise of poststructuralism in the academy. However, the relation between understanding and ontology has been central to philosophical traditions such as phenomenology, and perhaps it is no surprise that the concern with ontology is coming back in social theory and in fields such as geography, anthropology, political philosophy, and science and technology studies. Part of this return is due to intra-academic trends, but a good deal of it finds its impetus in social and ecological concerns and movements beyond the academy, and it is important to have both sources in mind.

Terry Winograd and Fernando Flores define *ontology* simply as concerned with "our understanding of what it means for something or someone to exist" (1986, 30).[10] Ontology has to do with the assumptions different social groups make about the kinds of entities taken to exist "in the real world." Notice that this definition does not entail a strong realist position (the assumption of a common or universal underlying reality); at the same time, this does not mean that "the mind" constructs the world (a kind of subjectivism); the definition tries to get at the existence of multiple worlds while maintaining a nonobjectifying notion of the real. Our ontological stances about what the world is, what we are, and how we come to know the world define our being, our doing, and our knowing—our historicity. Here it is important to keep in mind the distinctions among epistemology (referring to the rules and procedures that apply to knowledge production, including what counts as knowledge and what the character of that knowledge is), the episteme (the broad, and largely implicit, configuration of knowledge that characterizes a particular society and historical period and that significantly shapes the knowledge produced without the awareness of those producing it), and ontology.[11]

Mario Blaser (2010, 2013) proposes a three-layered definition of ontology, where the first layer is the one already hinted at: the assumptions about the kinds of beings that exist and their conditions of existence—a sort of inventory of beings and their relations. The second layer refers to ways in which these ontologies give rise to particular socionatural configurations: how they "perform themselves," so to speak, into worlds. In other words, ontologies do not precede or exist independently of our everyday practices; worlds are enacted by practices. Finally, ontologies often manifest themselves as stories, and these make the underlying assumptions easier to identify. This layer is amply corroborated by the ethnographic literature on myths and rituals (of creation, for instance). It also exists in the narratives that we moderns tell ourselves about ourselves, which are repeated over and over by politicians in their speeches or, invariably, in the six o'clock news' rendition of "what is happening in the world." This "what is happening" invariably refers back to the ontological ensemble of the individual, the real, science, and the market, that is, to the fact that *we see ourselves as self-sufficient subjects confronting an "external world" made up of preexisting, self-standing objects that we can manipulate at will,* or at least hope to. In short, what CNN or the BBC reports on, from an ontological perspective, is the status of this ensemble, including threats to it, though these are invariably explained in terms of the same categories, never allowed to drift too far out into other cultural worlds.

This argument holds for all areas of social life; for instance, the divide moderns make between nature and culture, which entails seeing nature as inert, informs the agroindustrial model of agriculture that from the time of slave plantations and "scientific forestry" in Germany in the eighteenth century to today's transgenic seeds, pushed by agribusiness corporations, has become dominant in many parts of the world. From a relational ontology, something like a plantation of a single crop produced for profit and the market does not make any sense. On the contrary, relational ontologies are performed into cultivation practices more akin to what peasants have traditionally done (multicropping, with production for subsistence as well as the market; a diverse landscape, with links to communities and gods, etc.), or to the kinds of localized, organic, resilient, and democratic agricultural systems that today's agroecologists propose as the way out of the food crisis. But this is getting ahead of the story of relationality, and it is time to say something more general about dualism before moving on to the next section.

A number of authors emphasize three fundamental dualisms in what I have referred to here as the dominant form of Euro-modernity: the divide between nature and culture, between us and them (or the West and the Rest, the moderns and the nonmoderns, the civilized and the savages, etc.), and between subject and object (or mind/body dualism) Latour's (1993) characterization of the first two divides as central to the constitution of modernity is well known. Blaser (2010) adds that the second divide is in turn essential to the making and functioning of the first and refers to it as "the colonial divide." This is not the place to trace the genealogy of these divides; suffice it to mention that ecologists and feminists place emphasis on the mind/body, culture/nature, and man/woman divides as foundational to patriarchal cultures, reductionist forms of science, disembodied ways of being, and today's ecological crisis. Some biologists argue that the pervasive binarisms have led to a reduction of complexity in our accounts of the world that has consequences for our understanding of, and interactions with, such a world, and so forth. The literature is huge, but here again I purposefully want to identify three points that are seldom emphasized or even flagged in Euro-American academic scholarship.

The first point is that *the problem is not that dualisms exist*; after all, many societies have been structured around dualities, although in most cases these are treated in terms of the complementarity of nonhierarchical pairs (e.g., yinyang dualities). The problem is with the ways in which such divides are treated culturally, particularly the hierarchies established between the two parts of each binary, and the social, ecological, and political consequences of such hierarchies. In the argot of a current Latin American perspective, this feature is referred to as *coloniality*, the central feature of which is *the categorization and hierarchical classification of differences*, leading to the suppression, devaluing, subordination, or even destruction of forms of knowledge and being that do not conform to the dominant form of modernity. Coloniality cemented the dichotomy between the human/civilized (European) world, further classified in terms of gender, and the nonhuman/uncivilized (the nonmodern, racialized dark peoples of the world, described, like animals were, in terms of their biological sex) (Lugones 2010a, 2010b).

These systems of classification became the crux of the projects for bringing "civilization," "modernity," and, later on, "development" to much of Asia, Africa, and Latin America. In short, there is no modernity *anywhere* without this coloniality; coloniality also implies a pervasive Eurocentrism—a hegemonic representation and mode of knowing that claims universality for itself, derived from Europe's claimed position as the center. A corollary of this conceptualization of modernity/coloniality is that the very process of enacting it always creates types of "colonial difference"—encounters, border zones, processes of resistance, hybridization, assertion of cultural difference, or what have you—where dominant modern forms fail to fulfill themselves completely as such, revealing simultaneously the arbitrariness (and often brutality) of many aspects of the modern project, and the multiple assertions of pluriversality, what in the decolonial perspective is called "worlds and knowledges otherwise." We will discuss later on the implications of the colonial difference for ontological design and designs for the pluriverse.[12]

Australian feminist and environmental philosopher Val Plumwood has drawn out the implications of dualist thinking in terms of what she calls the ecological crisis of reason. For her, the ecological crisis is a crisis "of what the dominant culture has made of reason" (2002, 5). This form of rationality, which claims mastery over nature, relies on multiple "centrisms" (anthropocentrism, self-centrism, Eurocentrism, androcentrism) and has produced, in the age of global markets, "ratiogenic monsters." Blind to our ecological embeddness, this reason-centered culture supports elite forms of power, strengthens the illusion of the autonomous individual, and idolizes an economic rationalism that ingrains masculinity and invisibilizes the agency of nonhumans and subordinated groups. Rather than relying on "the same elite culture and developmentalist rationality that led us into the mess" (16) in the first place—in other words, rather than intensifying the same reason-centered culture, as solutions such as the purported green economy do—her advocacy is for a form of nondualist, noncolonialist rationality that resituates human practice within ecology, and nonhumans within an ethics of respect and responsibility (see also Leff 2002, 2015, for a related argument and proposal).

The second observation is that these three salient dualisms work themselves out into a whole series of other divides, including the following (not an exhaustive list): human and nonhuman, live (life/organic) and inert (matter/inorganic), reason and emotion, ideas and feelings, the real and its representations, the secular and the sacred or spiritual, what is alive and what is dead, the individual and the collective, science (rationality, universality) and nonscience (belief, faith, irrationality, culturally specific knowledge), facts and values, form and content, developed and underdeveloped. In both academic and activist worlds, we are witnessing a renewed interest in the subordinated side of the dualisms across an entire spectrum of their manifestations, a sort of return of the repressed sides of the pairs as *important dimensions of what constitutes life itself*—for example, growing attention to emotions, feelings, the spiritual, matter, nonscientific knowledges, body and place, nonhumans, nonorganic life, death, and so forth. Taken together, the recent emphases can be seen as mapping an emerging *ontological-political field* with the potential to reorient cultural and social practice in ways that clearly foster the intersecting goals of ecological sustainability, social justice, and pluriversality.

The Political Activation of Relationality

We hypothesize that this process amounts to a *political activation of relationality* (Blaser, de la Cadena, and Escobar 2014).[13] This activation can be gleaned from developments in fields as varied as local food and environmental activism, opposition to extractivism, alternative economies, digital technologies, and some varieties of urban environmentalism, as well as from emerging transition frameworks, such as degrowth in the Global North and "alternatives to development" and Buen Vivir in the Global South; actors operating within these various fields are crafting a lexicon for a significant cultural and ecological transition, driven in part by an emphasis on nondualist, postcapitalist, and nonliberal ways of being and doing (more on this in the last two chapters).

The academic critical perspectives that could be said to fall within the project of unsettling dualisms have been growing over the past decade, largely under the headings of postconstructivist, postdualist, neorealist, and posthuman approaches (related to the ontological turn discussed in the previous chapter). More explicitly concerned with both epistemology and ontology, the recent perspectives seek to transcend the limits of deconstructive and discursive analyses by venturing into the positive project of how the world can be—and be understood—otherwise; in so doing, they afford new concepts, questions, and resources. Some of these works aim to theorize the productivity of life in all of its dimensions and ineluctable immanence (Bennett 2010; Coole and Frost 2010; Luisetti 2011); others underscore the vast range of agency associated with nonhumans and the manifold ways in which the world gets to be assembled (actor-network theory; e.g., Law 2004; Latour 2007). Still others return to issues of embodiment and corporality, through which subjects make themselves and their worlds (e.g., Grosz 2010); explore social life from the angles of temporality, openness, and becoming (Connolly 2011); or develop novel conceptualizations of interspecies relations and communities (e.g., Haraway 2008). Some related trends focus on rethinking cognition in order to underscore the radical contingency of all reality (Sharma 2015), explore the ways in which cognition can be extended through biotechnical couplings supported by digital technologies (Halpin, Clark, and Wheeler 2010; Halpin and Monnin 2014), discuss ontological emergence from the perspective of neo-cybernetics (B. Clarke and Hansen 2009), and draw implications from the affirmation of the sentience of all living beings not only for how we understand consciousness as a profusely distributed property of all beings but also for how the world (from the Earth to our bodies and ourselves) is ceaselessly cocreated by flows of energy and material (Sagan 2011), which are sometimes also seen in terms of a spirit force that pervades even what moderns consider to be the inanimate world (TallBear 2011).[14]

This brings me to the third aspect of the growing concern with dualisms. This is the extent to which the tendencies so hastily described above can be seen as questioning the modern social theory episteme. If one takes this epis-teme to be structured by a few major practices, the question becomes whether the emergent tendencies are capable of unsettling this epistemic space in more significant ways than has been the case with critical theories so far, or whether they rather continue to function within it.[15] Generally speaking, the recent approaches aim to go beyond an ontology and epistemology of subjects and objects and point at the shortcomings of a politics derived from such a dualist understanding. There is, then, much to learn from them. By focusing on the repressed side of the dualisms, they move at the edges of the Western social theory table (in the Foucauldian sense), yet one may wonder whether, by continuing to appeal to a logocentric understanding, they remain trapped within the table. To explore this question, I return briefly to Varela's argument about the shortcomings of rationalistic styles of thought.

Varela's Move: On the Limits of Modern Social Theory

For science writer Dorion Sagan, modern approaches to the social and natural sciences have "block[ed] out most of the world" (2011); hence, what we are witnessing in the turn to animal, nonhuman, more-than-human, and posthu-man studies is the return of all those unacknowledged aspects of the living that make life possible. In responding to Sagan from the perspective of Vine Deloria's "American Indian metaphysics," Kimberly TallBear (2011) argues that some of these trends and categories still endow nonhumans with human-like biographical and political lives that assume somewhat independent stand-points and, above all, that they are still inadequate to describe all relations among beings. She also pushes us to think about the ways in which some of the cutting-edge trends reproduce some of the modern binaries, including that of life and nonlife, resulting in the exclusion of, say, stones, trees, or thunder from being effective forces in the world, and even perhaps having sentience (on pansentience, see also Rose 2008; Goodwin 2007). Despite their efforts, do the recent tendencies continue to uphold in some fashion an *intramodern* (largely Euro-American) understanding of the world (as decolonial theorists might argue)? Do they continue to function within a much-renewed, but still primarily Western/modern, episteme?[16]

As a provisional hypothesis, I argue that the reliance on long-standing forms of rationality and logocentric analysis remains central to critical academic pro-duction (this book included!) and that, despite its remarkable productivity, it has consequences for finding our way beyond the dominance of dualist ontologies. To develop this hypothesis, I start by recalling Varela, Evan Thompson, and Eleanor Rosch's argument about the limits of abstract rationality and their insistence on joining reflection and experience. This is precisely what phenomenology attempted to do, yet—Varela and coauthors argue—it failed to fully address the radical questions it raised. Why? Their answer is relatively simple, yet the implications are far reaching. Phenomenology breaks down precisely because its analysis of experience remained "quite within the mainstream of Western philosophy. . . . It stressed the pragmatic, embodied context of human experience, *but in a purely theoretical way*" (1991, 19; emphasis added). Could this assessment—that phenomenology is still "philosophy as theoretical reflection" (20) and that, more generally, "even though it has recently become quite fashionable to criticize or 'deconstruct' the standpoint of the cogito, philosophers still do not depart from the basic *practice* responsible for it" (28; italics in the original)—apply to social theory as a whole, perhaps even to those trends that problematize its structuring dualisms?[17]

While this question will remain open in this book, we might find clues for further discussion of the issue in these authors' subsequent move: "What we are suggesting is a change in the nature of reflection from an abstract, disembodied activity to an embodied (mindful), open-ended reflection. . . . What this formulation intends to convey is that reflection is not just *on* experience, but reflection *is* a form of experience itself. . . . When reflection is done in that way, it can cut the chain of habitual thought patterns and perceptions such that it can be an open-ended reflection, open to possibilities other than those contained in one's current representation of the life space" (26). They refer to this form of refection as *embodied reflection*. In other words, for these authors, theoretical reflection does not need to be—or not only—detached. The second element in their formulation of the breakdown of phenomenology, and the actual bold step, is to suggest that "we need to enlarge our horizon to encompass non-Western traditions of reflection upon experience" (21; see also Varela 1999), including philosophy in cultures other than our own. They find a compelling path in one such tradition, the sophisticated and centuries-old Buddhist philosophy of mind, particularly its method of examining experience, called mindfulness meditation, intended to lead the mind back from the abstract attitude to the situation of one's experience.[18]

It is important to emphasize that none of the authors we are reviewing are calling for a wholesale rejection of Cartesian rationality nor of the subject-centered reason so much discussed by the intramodern philosophers of modernity (e.g., Habermas 1987); rather, they advocate for a weakening of its dominance and a displacement of its centrality in the design of the world and our lives. This is done in the name of reorienting the rationalistic tradition (Winograd and Flores 1986); fostering embodied, situated forms of reflection (e.g., Varela, Thompson, and Rosch 1991); imagining nondualist forms of rationality that enable us to resituate humans within an ecological understanding of life (e.g., Plumwood 2002; Leff 2015); arriving at decolonial and genuinely intercultural modes of knowledge production (decolonial theory; see, e.g., Walsh 2009); or moving toward convivial societies where nonconvivial tools have a role to play but do not dominate (Illich 1973). In doing so, these authors are moved by two aims: the first is to point out the consequences of the dualisms, especially how disconnected we normally are from many aspects of everyday existence; the second, perhaps more crucial for this book, is to argue that *the practice of transformation* really takes place in the process of enacting other worlds/practices—that is, in changing radically the ways in which we encounter things and people, not just theorizing about such practice (e.g., Spinosa, Flores, and Dreyfus 1997, 165). In these proposals we find clues toward this path, whether the renovated practice is Buddhist, ecological, political, decolonial, or a reimagined design approach. Let us listen to two final statements on the first aspect before concluding with a brief discussion of relationality.

The New Zealand environmentalist Deborah Bird Rose has powerfully stated the case against dualisms; Western dualisms, she says, sustain "a feedback loop of increasing disconnection. Our connections with the world outside of self are less and less evident to us, and more and more difficult to sustain and to experience as real" (2008, 162).[19] A certain derealization parallels the desacralization that follows from dualist rationality. "If life is always in connection, and if those connections are being destroyed, as they are these days at an enormous rate, what becomes of the remaining of life?" (166). Nandy (1987, 102–109) underscores the effect of organized science in fueling "the human capacity to isolate" and fostering affectless forms of "sanitized cognition" at both the individual and collective levels. All cultures, in his view, however, find means to respond to the pathologies of isolation, to de-isolate themselves in various ways, including through religion. In pondering the construction of nonoppressive societies in ways that do not render them newly oppressive orders themselves, Nandy insists on the need to take into account the "visions of the weak" and their notions of a good society and a desirable world. For Nandy, this has to be done by bearing in mind that "their apparent inability to withstand analytical thought, and their defensiveness and diffidence in the face of Cartesian categories—all contribute to their undervaluation" (18).

Here Nandy spells out one of the most intractable, and damaging, expectations of institutionalized dualist thinking:

> There is a pecking order of cultures in our times which involves every dialogue of cultures, visions and faiths and which tries to force the dialogue to serve the needs of the modern West and its extensions within the non-West. Under every dialogue of visions lies a hidden dialogue of unequals.... *A culture with a developed, assertive language of dialogue often dominates the process of dialogue and uses the dialogue to cannibalize the culture with a low-key, muted, softer language of dialogue.* The encounter then predictably yields a discourse which reduces the second culture to a special case—an earlier stage or simplified vision—of the culture with the assertive language of dialogue. (14–15; emphasis added)

Nandy's warning could help explain the resurgence of fundamentalisms (as a response, sometimes violent, to the skewed distribution of cultural resources in the global political economy of dialogue), or the reenactment of cultural subordination by today's Latin American governments and nongovernmental organizations when they utilize domineering modernist languages in their "negotiations" with indigenous, peasant, and black communities and movements that, historically, could be said to have had less assertive languages of dialogue. This notion also serves as a critique of so-called conflict resolution methodologies developed at elite schools such as Harvard University and exported all over the world, or approaches to "democracy building" and "transitional justice" in "postconflict" regions. In all of these cases, the assertive (Western, allegedly rational) apparatuses of dialogue operate as political technologies to subdue relational visions of peace, dialogue, and life. Said otherwise, discussions of cultural visions, civilizations, and intercultural dialogue involve complex ontological and political processes. This epistemic politics becomes another element in the project of infusing design with a progressive politics.

Relationality: Beyond the Nature/Culture Divide

If not dualism, if life is always in connection, then what? The immediate, obvious answer to disconnection, isolation, and so forth is, of course, to reconnect—with each other, with our bodies, the nonhuman world, the stream of life (e.g., Macy 2007). One rising answer to the problematic of disconnection/reconnection is thus relationality. There are many ways to understand relationality. Dualism is itself a form of relationality but one that, as we have seen, assumes the preexistence of distinct entities whose respective essences are not seen as fundamentally dependent on their relation to other entities—they exist in and of themselves. Network theories imply a more serious effort at taking into account the role of interrelations in making up things and beings. Many network approaches nevertheless still take for granted the existence of independent objects or actors prior to the networking, and despite their thrust toward topological thinking, they fall back into Euclidean geometries of objects, nodes, and flows. As Sharma puts it, speaking about the notion of interdependence in biology, many of these notions still imply "independent objects interacting." There are two shifts, according to Sharma, that have to happen for a genuine concept of interdependence to arise: the first implies going "from considering things in isolation to considering things in interaction"; the second, more difficult to accomplish, is "from considering things in interaction to considering things as *mutually constituted*, that is, viewing things as existing at all only due to their dependence on other things" (2015, 2).

Is it possible, then, to develop a deeper notion of relationality, one in which the relational basis of existence radically pervades the entire order of things? One general principle I find useful is that a relational ontology is that within which *nothing preexists the relations that constitute it*. In these ontologies, life is interrelation and interdependence through and through, always and from the beginning. Buddhism has one of the most succinct and powerful notions in this regard: nothing exists by itself, everything interexists, we inter-are with everything on the planet. This principle of interbeing has been amply developed in Buddhist thought.[20] A different way to look at it, from the perspective of phenomenological biology, is the already-mentioned idea of the "unbroken coincidence of our being, our doing, and our knowing" (Maturana and Varela 1987, 35); in other words, there is a deep connection between action and experience, which in turn instills a certain circularity in all knowledge, which Maturana and Varela summarize with the maxim "*All doing is knowing, and all knowing is doing*" (26), or by saying that "*every act of knowing brings forth a world*" (26). This coincidence of being~doing~knowing implies that we are deeply immersed in the world along with other sentient beings, who are similarly and ineluctably knower-doers as much as ourselves. This equates with Sharma's insistence that genuine interdependence obtains only when we consider all entities as mutually constituted.

More academically—and this has been one of the most fascinating strands of anthropological research since the 1960s, if not before—ecological anthropologists have shown through ethnographic fieldwork that many groups throughout the world do not base their social life on the distinction between nature and culture (or humans and nonhumans), or at least not in the ways in which moderns do. In many cultures, on the contrary, rather than separation, there is continuity between what moderns categorize as the biophysical, human, and supernatural domains. Anthropologists working with indigenous groups in the Amazon or North America, aboriginal groups in Australia, or various groups in Melanesia—including key figures such as Marilyn Strathern, Tim Ingold, Philippe Descola, and Eduardo Viveiros de Castro but many others in many other countries as well—have richly described the local models of nature that underlie ontologically vibrant relational worlds. Eduardo Restrepo (1996) and Astrid Ulloa (Ulloa, Rubio, and Campos 1996; Ulloa 2006), for instance, have provided compelling accounts of the local models of nature of black and indigenous groups in the Colombian Pacific rain forest region; even though all of these groups are of course also coconstituted by modern imaginaries, they sometimes enact worlds in movement for the defense of their territories and difference (Escobar 2008, 2014). In other words, these groups are involved in the political activation of relationality.[21]

The sources of relational thinking are not restricted to the non-West. There are important sources in what could be called "alternative Wests" or "nondominant modernities," and possibly in the worlds being created in urban areas in the Global North as a result of ecological activist commitments. Biologist Brian Goodwin (2007), for instance, speaks of a "Goethean" science of qualities that acknowledges the importance of feelings and emotions as important sources of knowledge creation, and as essential elements in "healing our fragmented culture" (see also Kauffman 2008 on the need to go beyond the dualism of reason and faith). Earlier philosophical or aesthetic traditions in the West are being summoned by scholars and, to a lesser extent, activists in their search for nondualist perspectives, as witnessed by renewed interest in the works of Baruch Spinoza, Henri Bergson, Alfred North Whitehead, William James, and John Dewey and the writings on nature by the American romantics. Boaventura de Sousa Santos (2014) posits the idea of the existence of a nonoccidentalist West in the philosophies of Lucian de Samosata, Nicholas of Cusa, and Blaise Pascal. To these could be added nondualist thinkers from other parts of the world who have had some resonance in the West, such as Jiddu Kirshnamurti and Sri Aurobindo, spiritual teachers from India.

The landscape of explorations of nondualism is thus becoming rich and vast, no doubt a sign of the times, of the very fact that "all our stories are now being deflated thanks to Earth" (Rose 2008, 166). If one thinks about climate change, for instance, one has to agree with Rose, despite the facile positions of geoengineers and green marketers. The growing visibility of nondualism is also a reflection of the fact that nobody really performs as a pure wound-up Cartesian toy. Phenomenologically speaking, we simply can't; we refuse to partition life entirely according to fixed divides. The impetus to re/connect (socially, ecologically, spiritually) is always there, and we activate it daily in many ways, even in our otherwise-objectifying relations with the "natural world" (e.g., in planting a garden) or when we disrupt the constant boundary making we perform as "individuals" (reaching out to others). The question remains, however: what would it mean to develop a personal and collective practice of interbeing? How do we innovate with postdualist ways of inhabiting the planet that are more amicable to the continued existence of all sentient beings, ways in which, to rely once more on Thomas Berry's (1999, 11) inspiring statement, humans become present to the planet in a manner that is mutually enhancing? How do we engage in the "geographies of responsibility" (Massey 2004) that our constitutive interrelatedness with all sentient beings necessarily implies? Can these be fostered in the most modern-driven contemporary settings? Can we find sources of the nonself, and do so not only among those who live in the shadow of the liberal diaspora (Povinelli 2001) in distant lands but also among those of us inhabiting the densest liberal worlds?

We will leave pending the question of whether pointing out the dualisms is in itself sufficient to get rid of the coloniality of the dualisms. As we suggested, for this to happen *it is necessary to step out of the (purely) theoretical space into some domain of experience* (political, contemplative, even policy or design oriented, or what have you)—in other words, it is imperative to *engage with (or perhaps contribute to creating) worlds where it is impossible to speak of nature and culture as separate* (or only in terms of nature/culture in separation, since we cannot avoid the divide altogether; that is, even groups that strive to maintain a relational ontology have to maintain both at the same time: dualist talk and practices of nature, on the one hand, and the nondualistic practices of relational beings, on the other). Said more simply, theorists cannot maintain both feet in the academy and purport that they/we are bringing about a different world; they/we need to put one foot in a relational world (or worlds)—to practice what we preach.

It will likely be objected that in order to speak about relationality I am introducing a new binarism (dualist and nondualist ontologies). Gilles Deleuze and Félix Guattari's partial way out applies here: "We employ a dualism of models only in order to arrive at a process that challenges all models. Each time, mental correctives are necessary to undo the dualisms we had no wish to construct but through which we pass.... [Dualisms are] an entirely necessary enemy, the furniture we are forever rearranging" (1987, 20–21). Sometimes the "mental correctives" do not need to be as complicated as social theory might want them to be; uncommon reversals with simple caveats might suffice. Sometimes I wonder, for instance, why we (critical theorists) are so prone to speak about alternative or multiple modernities but cannot imagine thinking seriously about alternative traditions. I will end this part with an insightful reversal by Nandy that should make us pause and think about such a possibility (Nandy's caveat here is that we need to avoid narrow-minded traditionalisms that demystify modernity while remystifying tradition, and to allow for critical dialogue, interaction, and mutual transformation among cultures within a genuine intercultural communion): "The pathology of relatedness has already become less dangerous than the pathology of unrelatedness" (1987, 51). To paraphrase, the pathologies of modernity have already proven to be more lethal than the pathologies of traditions; ecologically at least, this seems an incontrovertible statement.

It could be said that with the progressive expansion of the dominant forms of modernity "humanity" started its cultural, existential, and political journey into the terrain of ontological dualism. Starting from local histories in some corners of Europe, the journey evolved into a "global design" (Mignolo 2000). Is it possible to reorient such a tradition and to redirect the journey into an altogether different direction? Is this what the planetary ecological and social crisis is all about, or at least one of its important dimensions? Can design play a role in such a reorientation of both the cultural background and the journey itself?

4

An Outline of
Ontological Design

The empire consists of postulating that the hic et nunc [place-based, face-to-face existence] is in the past and that only interactivity remains.

· **Paul Virilio,** *The Administration of Fear*

The idea of ontological designing is gathering momentum, yet, to date, it has not been addressed front-on.

· **Anne-Marie Willis,** "Ontological Designing—Laying the Ground"

We encounter the deep question of design when we recognize that in designing tools we are designing ways of being.

· **Terry Winograd and Fernando Flores,** *Understanding Computers and Cognition*

So you are holding a digital device in your hand, maybe even while you read these pages. Do you know what it is? How it un/does you in particular ways? How it un/does the world? Here is American rapper Prince Ea's passionate plea that we think about it deeply, one might say ontologically:[1]

> Do you know the average person spends four years of his life looking down at
>   a cell phone? Kind of ironic, ain't it? How these touch-screens can make us
>   lose touch.
> With so many iMacs, iPads, and iPhones, so many "i"s, so many selfies
> Not enough "us"s and "we"s
> See, technology has made us more selfish and separate than ever
> 'Cause while it claims to connect us, connection has gotten no better . . .
> Reclassify Facebook for what it is, an antisocial network . . .
> We sit at home on our computers measuring self-worth
> in terms of numbers of followers and likes . . .
> What about me? Do we not have the patience to have a CNVRSTN without
>   ABBRVTN?
> This is the generation of media over stimulation
> Chats have become reduced to snaps, the news is 140 characters, videos of six
>   seconds at high speed, and you wonder why ADD [attention deficit disorder]
>   is on the rise faster than 4G LTE . . .
> This one, my friends, we cannot autocorrect, we must do it ourselves.
> Take control or be controlled, Make a decision . . .
> I am so tired of conforming . . . to this accepted form of digital insanity . . .
> I imagine a world where we smile when we have low batteries,
> 'Cause that will mean we'll be one bar closer—to humanity.

Let me reassure you at the outset that it is not a question of being for or against technology, or even of settling the score on the alleged battle between tradition and modernity, but rather of bringing to the fore the diversity of existential options open to us humans, the multiple ways of being in space/place and time, and of what technologies do to the Earth and to our communities. Prince Ea's slow, carefully worded rapping makes us aware of the anthropological narrowing of existential choices fostered by things digital, paradoxically in the name of freedom, the carefully regulated freedom of neoliberal self-improvement schemes, of the seductive "Be All You Can Be" slogan, which translates as "maximize your interactions, your connectivity, the information you upload into your devices so as to download it again when useful." But it is in so striving to be free that we are, paradoxically, most programmed, most effectively compelled to be and act in particular ways, to conform to the norm of being "free."

What would it mean, then, to be "one bar closer to humanity"? The question is not as simple as it seems; it demands digging deep into the cultural and material background of the seemingly simple act, but actually complex cultural-historical fact, of using a digital device. The media discourse about the digital era is perhaps the best place to start the digging, for it is deeply rooted in modern technological society. According to popular understanding, what's most exciting about our increasingly ubiquitous digital devices is the revolution of sorts in communication, information, and interactivity they brought about.[2] Unpacking fully the meaning of *communications, information,* and *interaction* is beyond the scope of this short introduction, but it should be clear by now to the ontologically minded reader that the background for understanding these notions involves fundamental assumptions about the nature of language, the individual, progress, and life itself. In other words, underlying these constructs there lies the Cartesian/Euclidean onto-epistemology of independent entities that preexist any interaction, of information as made up of discrete and truthful accounts of an objectively existing real, of a world made up of objects that language only denotes but does not help to construct, of rules of logic and forms of rationality benignly intended to make the world a decent and livable place (which are not the result of the mind-set of hyperracist white wealthy politicians with their repeated calls for "security" and "law and order").

This is not to forget that the data on your computer or slick mobile phone depend on the bits of cobalt, gallium, indium, tantalum, platinum, palladium, niobium, lithium, germanium, and so forth lodged in them; that, more than fancy-sounding Latin names, these materials are bits of Africa for sure, sometimes from South America, perhaps from eastern Congo with its bloody wars and brutal forms of eviction of locals to secure a steady supply of these "conflict minerals"; and that these wars create thousands of victims, including through the abuse of young women, and that they are connected to the devastation of forests and rivers, not to speak of the e-waste created by hundreds of millions of discarded screens, mobile devices, and computers that thousands of poor people in China or elsewhere scavenge for any bit of value left in them, under the most hazardous conditions, because the waste of some is the opportunity of others, right? And let us not overlook either the fact that these minerals are housed in geological strata, in a "metallic materiality" that summons capitalists to perform patriarchal alchemy at ever-higher levels, since corporations have come to believe that they can bend the Earth into any form or shape, so that even the geological time of our planet, embedded in deep layers of rock, comes to be disturbed, a resource at the service of our small but powerful machines.[3] What this means is that we impose the Judeo-Christian linear time (of salvation and progress) on allegedly inert geological strata, which perhaps explains why the Earth is screaming, as Brazilian liberation theologian Leonardo Boff has been telling us for decades, most purposely in his book *O grito da Terra, o grito dos pobres* (*Cry of the Earth, Cry of the Poor*; 1997).

Of course, we can venture farther back in order to recall that today's digital devices rely on those discoveries in solid-state physics that gave rise to transistors, semiconductors, microchips, and integrated circuits at the dawn of the digital revolution, to the steady miniaturization that made Silicon Valley explode with possibilities and unbridled celebrations, bubbles, hype, and disappointments, so that slowly but surely we awaken to the ineluctable realization of the colonialist, bloody links among Silicon Valley, Africa, and dramatically underpaid Chinese workers (surely part of Steve Jobs's much-celebrated "genius"). We end up with the complex geo-ontological formation that Benjamin Bratton (2014) calls the Stack, wherein rests the entire political geology of contemporary media and information and communication technologies, and it should make us ponder what are we doing, really, with our fanciest tools, which many of us have come to think we can no longer live without.

There is more. Also implicit in Prince Ea's narrative is the displacement of copresence by telepresence, of face-to-face relations by relations with distant others. But you might say: doesn't life become more exciting this way? Fair enough. Nonetheless, as the philosopher-architect Paul Virilio—by his own acknowledgment not a prophet of doom but a true lover of new technologies (1999, 13)—asks, "How can we really live if there is no more *here* and if everything is *now*? (1997, 37).[4] Surely being free from place and time represents human progress, one might argue. Yet as we plug in to our various interfaces and engage in tele-existence, as we become citizen-terminals of sorts, our bodies are deterritorialized, as in the cyberpunk fantasies of the 1980s, when cyberspace became a metaphor for anything that was cool.[5] Alienated from place, our only recourse is to maximize speed under the tyranny of real-time transmission, trapped in the utopia of the annihilation of duration, of being involved in as many things as possible at the same time, all the time. Corresponding to these changes at the level of subjectivity there are transformations at aggregate levels, including the temporal homogenization of the planet, the imposition of the infosphere on the biosphere, of bytes over bio, a new cybernetics of control that even WikiLeaks can never hope to diffuse. And so we succumb, too, to a global environment of fear (the fear of the terrorist, or of natural disasters) propagated by real-time media, to the "synchronization of emotion on a global scale" (Virilio 2012, 30), and that's how our emotional territories get occupied. Yet, "So what?," you might still ask. And I respond: would the losses caused by all these technocultural changes not outnumber the gains? How would one even know? And one might add: are the rematerialization of the body and the reterritorialization of place still possible? Or are they already historically foreclosed possibilities?

Let me insist that it is really not a question of making value judgments about what's better or worse, but of conveying a sense of why it is critically important that we ask the questions. I do not have a Facebook account; I don't tweet, and I don't even own a smartphone (sometimes I say, jokingly, that my old-fashioned cell phone is the smartest since it doesn't let me get text messages I don't want to read, beeps I don't want to hear, "connections" I'd prefer not to have). I do not claim in the least bit to be a better person than those spending four hours a day on their cell phones. That would be hypocritical of me, for after all I've spent countless hours at a screen just writing this book. At the same time, what difference does it make in terms of my style of being human, or posthuman? This question is part and parcel of the historical ontology of ourselves, of what makes us who we are at present.

So, do you now see why ontology—actually, political ontology—is important? Can design contribute to fulfilling the historic, perhaps vital, task of catalyzing forms of collective intelligence that attend to the kinds of choices confronting us, including design's own role in creating them?

. . . .

Recasting the question concerning new technologies ontologically is certainly not an issue of total rejection but a redirection of the cultural tradition from which they stemmed. Modern societies are already thoroughly theoretically driven. By this I mean that expert knowledges have a profound influence on how we live our lives. In so many domains of life, from eating our food (mediated by nutritional knowledge, including our food fears) and child-rearing practices (mediated by the pediatric, psychological, and health establishments with their battery of experts) to thinking about the economy, we make daily choices based on rational judgment mediated by expert discourses. Our daily reality is textually mediated and produced by all kinds of expert categories, including their unfailing deployment by the media. How this tradition shapes design practice will be further developed in this chapter by taking the ontological argument proposed by Terry Winograd and Fernando Flores as a point of departure.

The first section introduces the notion of ontological design as originally outlined by Winograd and Flores. We then move in the second part to discuss recent ontological approaches to design, particularly the work of Tony Fry and his collaborators. While he does not engage with Winograd and Flores directly, Fry's approach is consistent with these authors' formulation, as they share some sources, particularly Heideggerian phenomenology and analysis of technology. Together, these works constitute a foundation for evolving approaches to the ontology of design. The last part of the chapter deals with another important question posed by Francisco Varela in the third lecture in his short book *Ethical Know-How: Action, Wisdom, and Cognition* (1999): whether nondualist attitudes can be fostered in Western cultures. This reflection will open the way for a discussion of transitions and design for transitions, to be discussed in the following chapter.

What Is Ontological Design?

Why should design be considered "ontological"? The initial answer to this question is straightforward: "We encounter the deep question of design when we recognize that in designing tools we are designing ways of being" (Winograd and Flores 1986, xi). Understood as "the interaction between understanding and creation" (4), design is ontological in that it is a conversation about possibilities. One more way to get at the ontological dimension of design is by addressing "the broader question of how a society engenders inventions whose existence in turn alters that society" (4–5). Digital technologies are of course dramatic cases of radical innovations that opened up unprecedented domains of possibilities (as were printing, the automobile, and television earlier); they transformed an entire set of daily practices. Thus, every tool or technology is ontological in the sense that, however humbly or minutely, it inaugurates a set of rituals, ways of doing, and modes of being (Escobar 1994). It contributes to shaping what it is to be human.

A second sense in which design is ontological, already hinted at by Winograd and Flores, is that, in designing tools, we (humans) design the conditions of our existence and, in turn, the conditions of our designing. We design tools, and these tools design us back. "Design designs" is the apt and short formula given to this circularity by Anne-Marie Willis; "we design our world, while our world acts back on us and designs us" (2006, 80). This applies to the entire range of objects, tools, institutions, and discourses of human creation, no matter how neutral we consider them. Can there be anything more seemingly neutral than a space of habitation, a container for the body? I often give the example of the Amazonian indigenous *maloca* (indigenous longhouse) versus the archetypical nuclear-family house in suburban America. The maloca can house several dozen people under a single roof, even if the act of habitation obeys certain rules of behavior and spatial distribution. As I jokingly say, paraphrasing, "give me a maloca, and I will raise a relational world" (including the integral and interdependent relations between humans and nonhumans); conversely, give me a suburban home, and I will raise a world of decommunalized individuals, separated from the natural world. Design thus inevitably generates humans' (and other Earth beings') structures of possibility.

It is Winograd and Flores's contention that the pervasive way in which we think about technology, coming from the rationalistic tradition, not only constitutes *the implicit understanding of design* but makes it difficult, if not impossible, to come up with new approaches to the design of machines that are better suited to human purposes; it also becomes an obstacle to the creation of the open domains of possibility enabled by computer-mediated networks of human interaction. The rationalistic tradition traps our imagination through constraining metaphors such as that of computers as brains or mere information-processing devices, and that of language as a medium for the transmission of information (see Dreyfus 1979 for a critique of artificial intelligence from this perspective). In unconcealing that tradition, these authors aim at a redirection rather than a debunking of the tradition, but the goal of the redirection is substantial: "to develop a new ground for rationality—one that is as rigorous as the rationalistic tradition but that does not share the presuppositions behind it" (Winograd and Flores 1986, 8).[6]

To this end they weave together theories of biological life (Humberto Maturana and Francisco Varela 1980, 1987), phenomenological frameworks about knowledge and human action (Martin Heidegger 1962, 1977; Hans-Georg Gadamer 1975), and philosophy of language (the theory of speech acts). From these fields come the conceptual pillars of their framework: the notion that cognition is not based on the manipulation of knowledge about an objective world; that the observer is not separate from the world she or he observes but rather creates the phenomenal domains within which she or he acts; and that the world is created through language (again, language is not a mere translation or representation of reality "out there" but is constitutive of such reality, a point underscored by semiology and poststructuralist theory). Similar to the

Indian critics of science discussed earlier, Winograd and Flores find a deep connection between the rationalistic tradition and organized science, a fact that mars understanding in a host of domains, from cognitive science to policy making and even citizenship, entrepreneurship, and activism (Spinosa, Flores, and Dreyfus 1997). The mind-body dualism that posits the existence of two separate domains—the objective world of physical reality and the individual's subjective mental world—is of course one of their targets. Against such a dualism, they uphold the fundamental unity of being-in-the-world, the primacy of practical understanding, and the idea of cognition as enaction.

The background is thus the space of possibilities within which humans act and express their "care" for the world. "This world is always organized around fundamental human projects, and depends upon these projects for its being and organization" (Winograd and Flores 1986, 58). The Cartesian notion of modern subjects in control of an objective world, as much as that of the "flexible" postmodern subject surfing the web, does not, in their view, provide a good basis for the ontological skill of disclosing new ways of being (see Dreyfus and Kelly 2011 for a similar point). This ontological skill of history making— engaging in conversations and interventions *that change the ways in which we deal with ourselves and things*—can be enlivened, as Flores and coauthors Charles Spinosa and Hubert Dreyfus examine in detail in a subsequent work (Spinosa, Flores, and Dreyfus 1997). Rather than the proverbial detached deliberation or desituated understanding characteristic of the public sphere, the skillful disclosing of new worlds demands intense involvement with a collectivity. It requires a different sort of attitude that comes from dwelling in a place and from a commitment to a community with which we engage in pragmatic activity around a shared concern, or around a disharmony. In these notions we can already sense the idea that the designer might be a discloser in this sense; moreover, the designer shows awareness that she or he is a discloser. It is also these authors' contention that while this kind of history making has declined in the West, it is by no means completely lost—again, it is a capacity that needs to be retrieved, and I contend that design is a means to this retrieval (Dreyfus and Kelly 2011; Dreyfus 2014).

Ontological Design as Conversations for Action

It should be stressed that, as for Varela, for Winograd and Flores the entire process is deeply practice oriented. Sensing and holding on to a disharmony in one's disclosive space is not effectively achieved by stepping back from the problem in order to analyze it; on the contrary, when meaningful change is needed, "then disharmonies will be of the non-standard situational kind that is usually passed over by both common sense and [abstract] theory," and in these cases what is required is intense engagement and involved experimentation (Spinosa, Flores, and Dreyfus 1997, 23–24).[7] This resonates with a design philosophy that emphasizes the engaged, experimental, and open-ended practices of design research, including prototyping and scenario building. Winograd and Flores convey this same idea by talking about "breakdowns" rather than "problems," at least in the way the latter are discussed in the rationalistic tradition. Breakdowns are moments in which the habitual mode of being-in-the-world is interrupted; when a breakdown happens, our customary practices and the role of our tools in maintaining them are exposed, and new design solutions appear and are created; we can intuitively feel the appropriateness of this notion for the myriad cases of ecological breakdown in contemporary situations.

It should be emphasized, at the risk of being repetitive, that these authors insist that both the disclosing activity and the act of dealing with breakdowns imply going beyond the commonly held idea that the world functions in terms of individual mental representations of a problem, toward a social perspective of patterned, embedded interaction—that is, a perspective that highlights our active participation in domains of mutual concern. Moreover, all of this takes place through language: "To put it in a more radical form, we design ourselves (and the social and technological networks in which our lives have meaning) in language" (Winograd and Flores 1986, 78); or, to return to Maturana, "languaging" is the fundamental manner of existence of human beings; not only that, but language is intimately connected with the flow of emotions, as languaging and "emotioning" together provide the basis for the recursive coordination of behavior through the creation of consensual domains. Maturana calls "the consensual braiding of language and emotions, *conversation*" (1997, 9; see also Maturana and Verden-Zöller 2008).

It should be made clear that these authors are not saying that we need to get rid of detached modes of knowing in toto, nor that representations are not important. As they put it, "human cognition includes the use of representations, but it is not based on representation" (Winograd and Flores 1986, 99). Similarly, Varela, in stressing the importance of "know-how" (which he says has predominated in the wisdom traditions, such as Buddhism, Taoism, and Confucianism), as opposed to the Cartesian "know-what," is not minimizing the importance of rational analysis but highlighting the salience of concrete, localized forms of ethical expertise based on nondual action for ordinary life, which moderns usually disregard. These notions reveal the assumed one-to-one correspondence between language and reality, representation and the real, which takes us back to the questions of, Which "world"? What "design"? What "real"? The answer, as should be clear by now, points well beyond the objectivist, dualist, and detached understandings of world, design, and real. How can we rethink design on the basis of the reformed understanding of these notions?

For Winograd and Flores, the answer to this question necessitates a rethinking of organizations and their management. True, while a great deal of what managers do conforms to well-known rational decision-making routines as described in systems analysis, remaining at this level narrows the field of possibilities. To start with, a great deal of what managers do daily is to respond actively and concernfully to daily situations in order to secure effective cooperative action. In doing so, managers can be seen as activating networks of commitments; from this perspective, more generally, organizations constitute conversations for action; there is a certain degree of recurrence and formalization in these conversations, which Winograd and Flores characterize in terms of distinct linguistic acts. Organizations are networks of commitments that operate through linguistic acts such as promises and requests. In the end, the central feature of organizations and their design is the development of communicative competence within an open-ended domain for interpretation in ways that make commitments transparent:

> Communicative competence means the capacity to express one's intuitions and take responsibilities in the networks of commitments that utterances and their interpretations bring to the world. In their day-to-day being, people are generally not aware of what they are doing. They are simply working, speaking, etc., more or less blind to the pervasiveness of the essential dimension of commitment. Consequently, there exists a domain for education in communicative competence: the fundamental relationships between language and successful action. People's conscious knowledge of their participation in the network of commitments can be reinforced and developed, improving their capacity to act in the domain of language. (1986, 162)[8]

It could be argued that this approach leans on a rationalistic understanding of reflection, and to some extent this is the case. However, it is also a departure from it based on the implication of cognition as enaction, as spelled out by Maturana and Varela: "Since all cognition brings forth a world, our start-ing point will necessarily be *the operational effectiveness of living beings in their domain of existence*.... [Effective action] enables a living being to continue its existence in a definite environment as it brings forth its world. Nothing more, nothing less" (1987, 29–30; emphasis added). There are two corollaries of importance here for an ontological approach to design that will be explored more fully later on: first, the need to make explicit our de facto ontological commitment to a modernist epistemology and ontology of subjects and ob-jects (made up, to reiterate, of discrete "individuals" operating on the basis of "true (detached) knowledge" about "really existing" economies, and so forth); and, second, the question of whether different ontological commitments, based on a relational understanding, are possible.

Operational effectiveness is of course a key issue for the design of tools, including computers; it is conveyed through the concept of transparency of interaction, and interfaces are crucial in this regard. Here again Winograd and Flores warn that interfaces are not best achieved by mimicking human fac-ulties but that tools' "readiness-to-hand" requires thinking more complexly about the right coupling of user and tool within the space of relevant domains. A sort of interface anthropology is at issue here (Laurel 1989; Suchman 2007). Building on the work of Mexican designer Tomás Maldonado, the Argentinean designer Silvia Austerlic (1997) speaks about the ontological structure of de-sign as made up of the interrelations among tool, user, and task or purpose, all of which are brought together by the interface. The German-Chilean design theorist Gui Bonsiepe (2000) has coined the term *audiovisualistics* as a way to point at the cognitive complexity involved in interface design from the per-spective of operational effectiveness.

Breakdowns are central to Winograd and Flores's notion of design. As a situ-ation of "nonobviousness," a breakdown is not something negative but provides the space of possibility for action—for creating domains where new conver-sations and connections can take place. Breakdowns can be anticipated to a certain extent, but they mostly arise in practice, calling for a back-and-forth between design and experience; the building of prototypes can facilitate this task by helping to generate the relevant domains for anticipating breakdowns and dealing with them when they emerge (1986, 171). This also means that a key aspect of design is the creation through language of the domains in which people's actions are generated and interpreted. This is a main principle of user-centered design, and today it would include taking into account the design of context, and the user's own design, as discussed in chapter 1. If we think about the ecological crisis as characterized by a recurrent pattern of breakdowns, what is at stake is the creation of systematic domains where definitions and rules can be re/defined in ways that make visible interdependencies and commitments (or the lack thereof). This is different from the concept of expert systems as the design of professionally oriented domains, which are unlikely to foster the kinds of conversation for action that are needed to face the crisis. In designing changes in people's space of interactions, the goal of the ecological designer is to trigger changes in individual and collective orientations, that is, changes in the horizon that shapes understanding, a point to be discussed further when we take up the notion of sustainability again.

Toward the end of their book, Winograd and Flores summarize these principles:

> The most important design is *ontological*. It constitutes an intervention in the background of our heritage, growing out of our already-existent ways of being in the world, and deeply affecting the kinds of beings that we are. In creating new artifacts, equipment, buildings, and organizational structures, it attempts to specify in advance how and where breakdowns will show up in our everyday practices and in the tools we use, opening up new spaces in which we can work and play. Ontologically oriented design is therefore necessarily both reflective and political, looking back to the traditions that have formed us but also forwards to as-yet-uncreated transformations of our lives together. Through the emergence of new tools, we come to a changing awareness of human nature and human action, which in turn leads to new technological development. The designing process is part of this "dance" in which our structure of possibilities is generated. (1986, 163)

"In ontological designing," to quote them one final time, "we are doing more than asking what can be built. *We are engaging in a philosophical discourse about the self—about what we can do and what can be.* Tools are fundamental to action, and through our actions we generate the world. The transformation we are concerned with is not a technical one, but a continuing evolution of how we understand our surroundings and ourselves—of how we continue becoming the beings we are" (179; emphasis added). In subsequent chapters we will prod this perspective into a nondualist path by focusing explicitly on the communal and pondering how to transition beyond the rationalistic tradition whose pervasiveness Winograd and Flores do so much to unconceal.

Becoming Human by Design

Most people would intuitively reject the idea that we humans, too, are designed in some fashion. Yet this is one of the most direct and consequential lessons of the ontological approach to design. To paraphrase, in modern societies we design ourselves, although not under conditions of our own choosing. From the resulting allegedly universal but specifically modern notion of the human now emerges the imperative to transcend its anthropocentric, androcentric, and rationalistic foundations, which has yielded an entire spectrum of post-humanist approaches, some of which were discussed at the end of chapter 2.

Fry's design ontology (Fry 2011, 2012, 2015; Fry, Dilnot, and Stewart 2015) can be considered a special case within the posthumanist landscape, for several reasons: first, it is to my knowledge the first and only approach to systematically link posthumanism and design; and, second, concomitantly, it makes a decided effort at crafting a posthumanist notion of the human, one that tackles systematically the consequences of living under structured unsustainability as a civilizational condition. What, Fry asks, "has been lost in the rise of the hegemonic category 'the human'?" (2012, 12). Fry reminds us that the human is the result of three great forces: natural selection, self-organization, and design.[9] This evolutionary view allows Fry to signal the uniqueness of the leap toward unsustainability entailed by modernity. This is a third important feature of the work of Fry and his collaborators, namely, their willingness to imagine beyond modernity, and to do so decolonially, that is, with a profound awareness that one of the most important design consequences of modernity has been the systematic suppression, and not infrequently destruction, of nonmodern worlds. "Writ large," Fry states, "[modernity] did not just take the future away from the peoples it damaged and exploited but set a process in motion that negated the future, and defutured both the born and the unborn" (2015, 23). Thinking decolonially indicates a critique of the notion of a world made of One World and, conversely, upholds the notion that "while the planet is singular, world is plural—for it is formed and seen in difference—as are we" (21). The sensitivity to difference is crucial here, since it refers to the pluriverse and contributes to the argument that what needs to be sustained is precisely the pluriverse.[10]

For Fry, one of the most serious effects of modernity is what he calls *de-futuring*, understood as the systematic destruction of possible futures by the structured unsustainability of modernity. *Futuring*, in contrast, is intended to convey the opposite: a future with futures. The tension between defuturing and futuring is one way used by Fry to suggest a move from the Enlightenment to the "Sustainment," a new imaginary for an age (in the Heideggerian sense of *age*) where different ways of thinking, being, and doing become possible. For Fry, this transition is akin to that from the ancient to the modern world. The imperative for the move toward Sustainment stems from the need to counter the defuturing effects inherent in the economies, cultures, and institutions of the contemporary world, primarily their unquestioned attachment to economic growth. The Sustainment is prefigurative, as was the Enlightenment with its belief in universal reason and the imperative of order and progress, no doubt the civilizational dream that is unraveling under our eyes.

The pervasive conditions of unsustainability and defuturing inherent to the reason-centered culture that became entrenched with the passage to modernity must be destroyed as part of the reestablishment of futuring conditions. This dialectic of destruction and creation is part and parcel of Fry's framework. Moving toward Sustainment calls for an explicit ethics of what to destroy and what to create, materially and symbolically. This is one of the principles for the kinds of designing that need to go on under the dialectic of Sustainment; it involves destroying that which destroys (the unknowing and unthinking that produces unsustainability) and, at the same time, embracing the project of founding a new tradition capable of carrying the Sustainment forward. The former supposes an entire range of actions properly understood as "elimination design." The latter requires disclosing the possible ways of being-in-the-world that do not reenact unsustainability but rather enable acts of imagining, designing, and re/making that are auspicious for Sustainment. Unlike sustainable development, the green economy, or the liberal ethic of saving the planet—all of which continue to function within the defuturing ontology—the Sustainment challenges us moderns to secure futures for the kinds of relational forms of being capable of countering the still-pervasive conditions of defuturing and unsustainability.

The Posthuman Human and the Artificial

The world modern humans have created is "deworlding" under the pressures of globalized capitalism, population, and technology. The project of "reworlding" is thus necessarily ontological in that it involves eliminating or redesigning not just structures, technologies, and institutions but our very ways of thinking and being (Illich 1973). Perhaps one of the most daring, and puzzling, aspects of this task is Fry's unapologetic call for redesigning the human.

Simply put, if it is (certain) humans who are causing unsustainability, we have to redesign the human. Many modern thinkers will reasonably sense in the notion of redesigning the human the ugly ghosts of social engineering, sociobiology, or Foucauldian biopower—a hypermodernity at its worst. Yet Fry is careful to make clear that what he means is a posthuman and postrationalistic idea of the human. As he says, "We are travelling toward a point at which we will have to learn how to redesign ourselves. This is not as extreme as it sounds, for we have always been a product of design—albeit unknowingly. . . . In essence, what is being suggested here is action towards the relational development of a new kind of 'human being'" (2012, 37). The implication is that we need "to consider the ontologically designing forces that constitute subjects with diminished agency and the reverse: an ontologically designed subject beyond the subject" (162). As Cameron Tonkinwise ([2014?]) has explained, this goal does not mean that we are masters of our destiny, nor that we are able to design our existence at will. What it means is that we are historically thrown into our designedness, with particular acuity at present. This might actually be another connotation of the anthropocene. What Fry has in mind, to follow Tonkinwise's argument, is in fact the opposite of "human-centered design" with its "timid [liberal] version of the human," most often concerned with consumer desires and instrumental rationality (Tonkinwise 2014, 7). But "being by design" is not instrumental; it points at the fact that we exist in the space of our designing. Human-centered design should thus not be confused with Fry's idea of becoming human by design.

Equally important, Fry is adamant that, as the planet is confronted with the dramatic consequences of unsustainability and defuturing, such as climate change, the resources at hand—whether afforded by modernity or by traditions of any kind—are no longer appropriate to the task. No amount of evolutionary adaptation or natural design will do. On the contrary, what is required is the design of novel ontologically futuring practices that take us decidedly into the dialectic of Sustainment, beyond the "world-within-the-world" of modern colonialist making, by means of re/makings that radically transform humans' tendency toward the unsustainable. This implicates an anthropogenesis that rearticulates the relational assemblages of the biological (humans' animality), the sociocultural, and the technical. Fry makes clear that for him humans today are constituted within a naturalized artificial ecology created through design and technics; this means that nature becomes a "standing reserve" to be appropriated, thus unknowingly making the world we create a negation of the biophysical world of our absolute dependence. This rate of change, he concludes (2012, 61), "has come to override evolutionary time," thus "the need for humans to adapt has become ever more urgent. But now the only available option is to adapt by artificial means. Survival will thus now become a biosocial ontological design project. . . . Rather than pose the adaptation in the human/animal frame, we must place it in the context of the relation between the human and the artificial." In this way Fry takes us back to the brief discussion in the introduction about design and the future. It would be pertinent to ask whether Fry succeeds in articulating a view of the future different from that of the techno-fathers of geoengineering, synthetic biology, the great singularity, and the like; in other words, whether his proposal gains sufficient distance from the ontology of appropriation and control that so naturally inhabits the techno-futurist visions related to the artificial. While, for Fry, humans became prosthetic beings with the invention of the first tools, from the rise of modernity onward the ontological designing of the body/tool/mind assemblage has resulted in a "world-within-the-world" that has naturalized the artificial dimension of human evolution. For Fry, this means that modern humans are inescapably anthropocentric.

Rather than posit a radical way out of this anthropocentrism, Fry calls for a self-conscious and responsible anthropocentrism that, by necessity, has to invent its own posthuman notion of the human. Evolution in the anthropocene thus needs to be properly understood in terms of natural selection, self-organization, and ontological design. This is partially at odds with those proposals in the ecological design field that give primacy to the organic integration of humans and nature but resonates with the calls to embrace critically the possibilities afforded by contemporary technology found among feminist scholars in the field of science and technology studies (such as Donna Haraway). Despite Fry's rejection of a strict biocentric ethic (e.g., 2015, 57), not anything goes, since design-as-adaptation nevertheless has to take into account the self-organizing dynamics of the Earth. In any case, it will remain pending until the conclusion of this book whether Fry (and this book itself) escapes the ontology of enframing and project orientation that today's rising ethic of the artificial seems to deploy with such force.

The results of the modernist ontological design journey, and the very complexity of the agency of what designs us, can be seen most patently in cities. We referred in passing (chapter 2) to "the question of finding futural modes of [urban] dwelling" (Fry 2015, 87), and we can now return to this notion to conclude this section. Fry locates this question within a large-scale history of earthly habitation, which shifted from nomadism to settlement with farming about ten thousand years ago. In order to envision futures with a future, a third mode of human habitation has to be recognized and actively re/shaped, which Fry calls *unsettlement*. Despite the dramatic changes in urban habitation, settlement is still the default framework in city planning and in discussions of climate change adaptation, as if we were still dealing with the modernist city. But mass mobility and climate change have thrown the situation into an altogether different mode and scale. We can expect abandoned cities, pervasive riots and conflict related to food and the climate, mass deaths, fierce struggles for survival, and all kinds of human-induced disasters as that "world-within-the-world" par excellence that is the modern city unravels under the effects of climate change. Exposing the instability of this mode of habitation—including modernity's misformed and misplaced cities, and the homelessness and structural unsustainability characteristic of the afterlife of the modern city—is the first task of an ontological design strategy concerned with earthly habitation:

> We are "thrown" into these defuturing conditions as the future is sacrificed to the hollow gains of the present. . . . The continuity of this relation is at the heart of Sustainment—the conceptual and practical project beyond the Enlightenment, modernity, globalism, and sustainability (which so often sustains the unsustainable—be it industries, ways of life, products, institutions, built environments, modes of agriculture, and more). All of this adds up to the making of a world of being-in-difference. A post-human world (again in its difference) is demanded wherein the human is not abandoned but rather becomes in tune with the being of Sustainment, and so becomes a futural agent. (Fry 2015, 32)

The practical aspects of rethinking urban design and adaptation are huge and encompass all dimensions of the space and time of the city; Fry explores them at length in *City Futures in the Age of a Changing Climate* (2015).[11] Learning how to dwell in another way will bring with it a sharper recognition of what we (modern humans) actually are, so that we can be otherwise. Fry maps an entire cultural-political project that involves "embracing the ontological status of the city assemblage as post-natural environments of difference together with regimes of ordering and disordering (the formal and the informal, the informational and metabolic, the industrial and post-industrial, the spectacular and hidden). . . . It follows that a very different view of post-urbanism is now to be put forward here" (88), one that makes possible futural modes of dwelling.

Sustainability by Design?

This is a good point to bring back the question of sustainability, this time from an explicitly ontological perspective. Imbued with the major tenets of Heideggerian phenomenology and Maturana's biology, a recent approach to sustainability by John Ehrenfeld develops an ontological framework for ecological design.[12] Ehrenfeld (2009) starts by arguing that current proposals will at best amount to reducing unsustainability rather than creating true sustainability. For the latter to happen, a veritable reinvention of the collective structures that shape our lives and that define our humanness is required. Briefly, in Ehrenfeld's diagnosis, unsustainability springs from the cultural structure of modernity itself. Moreover, approaches intended to deal with environmental problems are based on a reductionist definition of the problem that in turn stems from the narrow understanding of reality, rationality, and technology inherited from the Cartesian tradition. This is causing tremendous breakdowns in not only ecological but also social life, which the author interprets in terms of addiction to consumption. From here he goes on to propose a framework for the redesign of tools, physical infrastructure, and social institutions as a means to foster changes in consciousness and practices based on an ontology of care. The framework revisits the intersection of three domains—the human, the natural, and the ethical—as the space for an alternative approach to sustainability.

From these initial steps follows the definition of sustainability as "*the possibility that humans and other life will flourish on the planet forever*" (Ehrenfeld 2009, 53; italics in the original). In this vision, flourishing, following various philosophical and spiritual sources, "is the most basic foundation of human striving and, if properly articulated, can be the strongest possible driver towards sustainability" (53). Flourishing, he goes on to propose, can be brought about only by shifting to a design mode that is effective at dealing with the culture of unsustainability—in other words, the way out can be no other than sustainability by design (76–77). This is one of Ehrenfeld's stronger contentions, the second being that what needs to be transformed first and foremost, given their overwhelming power, are the economic and technological domains that sustain the modern ontology. This does not mean that the key to sustainability is to be found in scientific breakthroughs or techno-fixes but rather that "the key to sustainability is the practical truths that each of us discovers in our daily life and that contribute to the collective activities of our culture" (95).

How, then, can one design a world that brings forth flourishing in everyday activities? Can cultural practices be changed by design? Echoing pragmatists' understanding (John Dewey and Charles Pearce), Ehrenfeld makes the bold claim that this can indeed be done—"devices" can be designed to gradually transform our primary mode of understanding and being. This conclusion comes close to Charles Spinosa, Fernando Flores, and Hubert Dreyfus's (1997) notion of history making and relies on a particular articulation of the notion of care (for self, others, and the world), arguing that care can be structured into the design of tools and equipment through "presencing." Key to presencing (a concept similar to the hoped-for "ready-to-hand" character of technological interfaces) is the incorporation into tools of ecological habits through design so as to transform routine actions into forms of ecological behavior; this is to be achieved by embedding "scripts" into product design. Designers, in this way, would need to go well beyond the goal of satisfying users' needs, to articulate the concerns of a collectivity in novel ways. New embodied routines slowly become collective, eventually transforming social consciousness and institutional structures.[13]

Generally speaking, what is at play in this proposal is the emphasis in recent design thinking on "making things effective and meaningful" through convivial solutions arrived at via the principle of use-centered effectiveness (Manzini 2015). As Tonkinwise likes to put it, "radical sustainable design just means designing little things a lot, all over" (2013b, 14); in other words, sustainability is such a huge challenge because it reveals the infinite number of small things that will need to change. More theoretically, thinking sustainability through design brings forth the challenging question, "How do you translate a new cognitive paradigm into material environments and everyday practices?" (10; see also Tonkinwise 2013a), which in turn requires a renewed attention to materiality from which there might emerge more sustainable mind-sets, attention to questions of scale, and the reconceptualization of materiality. This brings to the fore the repoliticization of sustainable design, especially if one considers that oftentimes the process takes place through grassroots innovation, calling on design activists to engage in the relocalization of making things and in the socially and culturally complex task of networking sustainable innovations.

The ontological concern with sustainability has been the subject of Mexican ecologist Enrique Leff's decades-long effort at developing an ontological and political framework for sustainability, mentioned in passing in chapter 3 (Leff 2002, 2015; see Escobar 2008, 103–106, 129–132, for a discussion of this author's work). As Leff states, "political ecology constructs its theoretical and political identity in a world of mutation, driven by an environmental crisis: a crisis of being-in-the-living-world. . . . *Something* new is emerging in this world of uncertainty, chaos and unsustainability. Through the interstices opened up in the cracks of monolithic rationality and totalitarian thinking, environmental complexity sheds new light on the future to come. This 'something' emerges as a need for emancipation or a will to live" (2012, 32). For this something to be cultivated, there is a need for a new ecological episteme, one in which sustainability becomes the horizon for purposive living based on a dialogue of knowledges and cultures. Leff's vision, influenced by Heidegger and deconstruction, also signals an ongoing transition with open-ended futuring possibilities.

Ontological Design and the Question of Agency

None of the ontological design approaches discussed so far are very clear about the agency behind the reenvisioned design, and a more satisfactory discussion of this thorny issue will have to await the discussion of transition design and autonomous design, where there is a more explicit sense of agency. While the idea that everybody designs is taken seriously, the proponents of ontological design seem to reserve a special role for a kind of designer who has the necessary disposition and training to carry the ontological undesigning/redesigning project forward. Thinking about agency ontologically calls for a more nuanced understanding of "use," which Mark Titmarsh and Tonkinwise (2013) explore through a reinterpretation of the interrelations between art and design. The roles of research, technology, and the studio as well as the political economy of unsustainability are the subject of much debate from the perspective of the ontological framing, yet the agent who is carrying out these practices remains elusive. Fry comes close in his discussion of the types of people who will emerge in the wake of the radical changes brought about by unsustainability, defuturing, and unsettlement, and of course not all the characters he envisions in his posthuman fiction will play a constructive role toward Sustainment. How the "worldly rematerialization" capable of "enabling the 'being-otherwise' of these [new] beings" will take place is not explicitly discussed (Fry 2012, 208).[14]

The understanding of agency in contemporary theory has been transformed dramatically as a result of the ontological turn. With the arrival of objects, things, nonhumans, spirits, and so forth into theory's orbit, the explanation of what life is and how it gets constituted into worlds has been significantly enriched. The concept of distributed agency—which suggests that agency is not the result of discrete actions by single subjects acting intentionally but largely the effect of complex heterogeneous networks of humans and nonhumans—has profound implications for design, and these will be explored in the next chapter (Manzini 2015). The key ontological design question of "how our tools are part of the background in which we can ask what it is to be human" (Winograd and Flores 1986, 163) thus becomes more complicated; it needs to be broadened at the very least by considering how the designers' understanding of humans and worlds changes when all kinds of nonhumans, and the heterogeneous assemblages of life they bring into existence, are brought into the picture.

One of the thorny issues in discussions about design agency is that of authorship. The emphasis on codesign, of course, takes direct aim at the reified and glorified notion of authorship, whether in product design, urbanism, or architecture. Yet the reliance on a strong notion of authorship is not so easily dispelled. As architectural historian Amy Zhang puts it well, "there is a crucial need in architecture to question the ontology of the designer before directing the attention towards any critical reflexivity on the practice's ontological effects" (pers. comm., July 17, 2015). In addition, she argues, notions of individual authorship are being dramatically eroded by the digital modeling to which architectural practice has become subservient, without even talking about financial dependence and compensation issues. Yet a certain dualism continues to remain in place: author/design (and potential correlates, such as nonauthor/nondesign). Also at stake here are entrenched divisions of labor and issues of race and gender, enabling the (often white and male) author-designer to act with total obliviousness to the material and economic dimensions of production. This type of objectified authorship is inimical to genuine practices of collaboration and design for and from relationality.

A phenomenologically oriented notion of agency is embedded in Otto Scharmer and Katrin Kaufer's concept of "leading from the emerging future" (Scharmer 2009; Scharmer and Kaufer 2012). Their foundational insight about "acting from the presence of what is wanting to emerge" (19) involves a robust notion of relationality and futuring. Their notion of presencing is proposed as a way to counteract the ontology of disconnection ("Ego-System") that is killing the Earth through consumption; it implies an expanded view of the self and might foster design thinking and prototyping that embody the new that is emerging or wants to emerge. This kind of presencing, as the authors argue, is conducive to a transitional space where new kinds of "frontline prac-titioners" tap into emerging social-natural configurations in order to facilitate new communal connections. The frontline practitioner would realize that "the real power comes from recognizing patterns that are forming and fitting with them" (Scharmer 2009, 32). They would face head-on Varela's injunction that modern science does not understand experience—they will delve into (in principle, nondualist) experience as a veritable wellspring for design. Their framework comprises a series of shifts (from downloading, seeing, and sens-ing to presencing, crystallizing, prototyping, and performing) that involve "letting go," "letting come," enacting, and embodying the emergent. These shifts take place within a social space of collective creation (presencing) and destruction (absencing), requiring a significant personal transformation toward more relational modes of being. This proposal can be considered an ontological design framework, and to some extent is presented as such.[15]

Thinking about agency in the context of Sustainment and transitions brings with it its own challenges. In the last part of the chapter I would like to inquire into the possibility of design practices informed by nondualism and relation-ality; from this perspective, the question becomes that of whether nondual-ist action can be fostered under the conditions of deworlding and defuturing mapped by Fry and collaborators. We can lean on Varela once more in search for clues to answer this question, before returning to a final discussion of on-tological design. I should make it clear, however, that this is one particular way to explore the practice and ethics of ontologically oriented design. Along the way, we will find some support for this inquiry in the pluralization of musics happening all over the world today.

Nondualism in Everyday Life? Varela's Question

In the third lecture in *Ethical Know-How* (1999), Varela deals with the absence of a self as we know it in the West, proposing the notion of a selfless or virtual self as an emergent property of a distributed system mediated by social inter-actions (52–63). For Varela, a key question arising from both of these concep-tualizations is whether we can learn to embody the empty self, that is, to really develop *a practical way* to go beyond the assumption of the self-interested autonomous individual and the businesslike and ego-clinging features it com-mands.[16] This is what the Buddhist mindfulness tradition is all about; it aims to provide a means to nonduality as well as principles for groundlessness as compassion. This is not the place to discuss further the Buddhist part of Varela's argument; suffice it to say that he concludes that the acceptance of the nonsolidity of the self brings about an authentic type of care; indeed, "here one is positing that authentic care resides at the very ground of Being, and can be made fully manifest in a sustained, successful ethical training. A thoroughly alien thought for our nihilistic Western mood, indeed, but one worthy of being entertained" (73).[17]

The corollary is stated as a genuine question: "How can such an attitude of all-encompassing, responsive, compassionate concerns be fostered and embodied in our culture?" (73). To be sure, the answer starts by restating that "it obviously cannot be created through norms and rationalistic injunctions," or just through new concepts or self-improvement schemes; on the contrary, "it must be developed and embodied through *disciplines* that facilitate the letting-go of ego-centered habits and enable compassion to become spontaneous and self-sustaining" (73), with each individual growing into his or her own sense of nonduality, authentic caring, and nonintentional action. This will surely sound too esoteric and spiritual to many modern readers (however, the notion resonates with how intellectual-activists from social movements speak about their activist skills for history making, as briefly discussed in chapter 2). We find a sustained answer to this question in the framework for "the work that reconnects" developed by Joanna Macy and colleagues from the perspective of systems thinking, ecology, feminism, and Buddhism (Macy and Brown 1998; Macy 2007; Macy and Johnstone 2012). Macy's goal is to provide an intellectual and practical path for moving from a self-destructive "industrial growth society" to a "life-sustaining" one. This epochal shift, a Great Turning, demands a profound change in our perception of reality, including surrendering our belief in a separate self and adopting an ecological self; abandoning anthropocentrism in favor of a life-centered paradigm; acknowledging the dependent coarising of all things, including the knower and the known, body and mind; fostering structural changes at the level of economic systems and technology; and cultivating shifts in consciousness through various means, such as nondualist spiritualities. Only then can one hope to be "in league with the beings of the future" (2007, 191), a concept that speaks to the concerns of sustainability.

Macy bravely addresses why we keep on failing to make these insights into effective forces in the real world, or how we can. Coincidentally, her most recent book, coauthored with Chris Johnstone, is dedicated "to the flourishing of life on this rare and wondrous planet" (Macy and Johnstone 2012)—another reference to sustainability as flourishing. We will encounter Macy's vision again in the discussion on transition narratives. For now, we can ask: are Varela's question and Macy's insights useful for design? Can design be more attuned to these realizations? To inhabiting spaces of nonduality, nonliberalism, noncapitalism? To finding sources of the nonself in the most contemporary struggles and situations? These are questions for an anthropology and cultural studies of design that takes an ontological approach seriously.

With these questions, we are back within the critical analysis of modernity. Modernity is, indeed, the larger onto-epistemic formation within which the rationalistic tradition has thrived. I have deliberately eschewed in this work a substantial discussion of perspectives on modernity. It is important, however, to put modernity in its place, so to speak. Somehow we seem to have accepted the idea that some version of modernity is here to stay, globally, until the end of times. It is worth quoting Ashis Nandy once more to interrogate this assumption:

> The time has come for us to restore some of the categories used by the victims themselves to understand the violence, injustice and indignity to which they have been subjected in our times.... These neglected categories provide a vital clue to the repressed intellectual self of our world, particularly to that part which is trying to keep alive the visions of a more democratic and less expropriatory mode of living. To that other self of the world of knowledge, modernity is neither the end-state of all cultures nor the final word in institutional creativity. Howsoever formidable and permanent the edifice of the modern world may appear today, that other self recognizes, one day there will have to be post-modern societies and a post-modern consciousness, and those societies and that consciousness may choose to build not so much upon modernity as on the traditions of the non-modern or pre-modern world. (1987, xvii)

One could interpret Nandy's discussion as speaking about the futuring possibilities embedded within, and often articulated by, the most direct victims of modern defuturing. It is important to restate, however, that Nandy is not advocating for an intransigent defense of tradition. His reworking of the concepts of tradition and modernity is much more sophisticated than that; besides, he is interested first and foremost in the dialogue among cultures. Most movements in the South are not interested in a recalcitrant defense of traditions either, even if advocates of modernity on all ends of the political spectrum continue to corner them into such a slot in the name of one or another universalism or dualism. Nandy acknowledges the importance of excavating and fighting for a lost or repressed West (just as I have spoken of alternative Wests that might constitute sources of nondualist ontologies). Perhaps the time has come to stop regarding any reference to tradition as pathological, romantic, or nostalgic. Care should be taken of course not to fall into an uncritical defense of traditions that might shelter one form of oppression or another (e.g., patriarchy). But one can legitimately ask, can some types of tradition not be used today as tools for criticism, futuring, and sustainment? "The choice of traditions I am speaking of involves the identification, within a tradition, of the capacity for self-renewal through heterodoxy, plurality, and dissent. It involves the capacity in a culture to be open-ended, self-analytic and self-aware without being overly self-conscious. . . . Fortunately, cultures are usually more open and self-critical than their interpreters" (Nandy 1987, 120).

Social groups in struggle, at their best, move in several directions at once: adding to, and strengthening, their long-standing practices, while mastering the modern world, its practices and technologies. Bolivian scholar Silvia Rivera Cusicanqui (2014) points at this feature with her notion of *sociedades abigarradas*, referring to the capacity of Latin American popular and indigenous cultures to define their own forms of modernity, more convivial than the dominant ones precisely because they also find nourishment in their own histories, intricately weaving indigenous and local practices with those that are not local, thus resulting in worlds made up of different cultural strands that affect each other without nevertheless fusing into one.[18] From this, in her view, stem more lasting intercultural entanglements because they find sustenance in the complementarities among diverse worlds without overlooking the antagonisms, articulating with market economies while anchored in indigenous knowledge and technologies. Here lies an entire novel view of modernities and traditions, a pluriversal framework.

Design and the Relational Ontologies of Music

Some genres in contemporary popular music are an apt model to describe what many groups and movements today are seeking to accomplish through their innovative cultural and political practices. Usually described as "fusion," these globalized genres involve features that seem utterly contradictory: a commitment to a place-based musical tradition but at the same time an opening up of that tradition more than ever to conversations with other world musics and to the use of a panoply of digital and nonconventional production technologies to achieve the best possible rhythms and sounds.[19] The results are oftentimes unique and original, powerful in the ways in which they engage people's bodies and consciousness, perhaps confirming Jacques Attali's (1985) contention that music, more than theory, heralds the new cultural and political orders to come. Does this prophetic function of music suggest at the very least that some artistic practices such as music might be more attuned to relational being? Can contemporary fusions be considered in any way to be effectively interepistemic and pluriversal and, if so, a source of inspiration for the type of novel collaborative design practices envisioned by design thinkers such as Ezio Manzini (2015)? Are musicians engaging in ontological politics when they collaborate in the making of across-worlds musics? Do contemporary musics of a certain kind open up new possibilities for being-in-sound?[20]

Some of these questions are broached by music and cultural theorist Ana María Ochoa Gautier (2014) in her historical research on the relation between aurality and being. What she finds is that acoustics has been an intensive area of design innovation in the West since at least the nineteenth century. The acoustic collapses form and event, calling forth a rethinking of the relations among process, design, and materiality. Building on Stephen Feld's notion of acoustemology, Ochoa Gautier goes on to discuss how sound confounds the boundaries between epistemology and ontology, revealing the existence of relational regimes of aurality where the physics of sound, musical form, (im)materiality, sound technology, and sound perception all play a part. In her examination of nineteenth-century European accounts of native musics in Colombia, she unveils an entire political ontology of music surrounding these accounts. One of the lessons of her examination of acoustic ontologies is that "local sounds" are not static traits meant to represent a particular place; there has always been a kind of "sonic transculturation" (Ochoa Gautier 2006) that the new fusions bring to new levels of sophistication, thus setting in motion a pluriversal force. By bringing sound and aurality to the forefront, she hopes to redress the overwhelming focus of critical design studies on the visual.

Another interesting attempt at linking design and music is the notion that design might be emerging as a fifth principle of radical musical practice at present. This idea has been suggested by Amy Zhang for the case of some contemporary musics (pers. comm., January 15 2012). She bases this suggestion on Attali's (1985, 20) identification of ritual, representation, repetition, and composition as the four main historical modes of music production from the perspective of the relations between society and power specific to particular historical periods.[21] For Attali, composition, unlike the previous modes, disrupts the dominant codes and political economy of music and inaugurates a real potential for relationality and collective experimentation. Attali quotes the Italian avant-garde composer Luciano Berio: "If we compose music, we are also composed by history, by situations that constantly challenge us" (141); this can be seen as a rendition of the idea that design designs, challenging us into futuring kinds of design. To this Attali adds:

> Music is no longer made to be represented or stockpiled, but for participation in collective play, in an ongoing quest for new, immediate communication, without ritual and always unstable. It becomes nonreproducible, irreversible.... Music is ushering in a new age. Should we read this emergence as the herald of a liberation from exchange-value, or only of the emplacement of a new trap for music and its consumers, that of automanipulation? The answer to these questions, I think, depends on the radicality of the experiment. Inducing people to compose using predefined instruments cannot lead to a mode of production different from that authorized by those instruments. (141)

It could be added, following Zhang's insight, that contemporary music adds novel elements to Attali's compositional principle, including open-endedness, working across musical and cultural difference, collaborative creation, and so forth. If this is so, perhaps one can say that design is the compositional model appropriate to the pluriversal age. For Zhang, composition has fallen short of its promise, given its continued reliance on individual authorship and its immersion in commercial capitalism. Other practices are emerging. This is a trend that ontologically minded designers would do well to keep in mind as they reimagine design practices that avoid the traps of past design modes of operation.

Back to Ontological Design

Let's begin by highlighting some aspects shared by the ontological design conceptions summarized in this chapter. First is the rejection of Cartesianism, broadly speaking, whether in the form of John Law's "One-World World," Heidegger's "Age of the World Picture" (including the enframing effect of the world as object to be appropriated), or the notion of an ontology of autonomous subjects confronting discrete, self-standing objects that the scientist can study in isolation or the designer manipulate at will. This metaphysics is replaced by an ontology in which humans do not discover the world but constitute it, whether through enaction (Varela), language (Winograd and Flores), meshworks (Ingold), or the ineluctable thrownness and engagement with things (e.g., Fry, Willis, Tonkinwise). The various readings represent diverse attempts at developing nondualist approaches to knowledge, cognition, and design. They go beyond critique to offer alternative formulations.

There is also agreement that ontological design is design after the "subject," and certainly after the subject/object divide. It favors modes of being-in-the-world beyond humanism, nihilism, and reason-centered anthropocentrism (Spinosa, Dreyfus, and Flores; Plumwood; Fry). Ontologically oriented design thus necessarily has a critical impetus. It involves "rethinking the way society is organized, shifting values, and significantly altering business models and economic thinking," as Tonkinwise (2012, 8) puts it. Does this mean that ontological design approaches become an integral part of critical design studies? It makes sense to claim that this is the case for several reasons. First, ontological design contributes to a relational understanding of the material, as it aims to dematerialize society through a new awareness of materiality and through the innovation of new ways in which society can "resource itself." This in turn implicates a transformed attention to practice (including the articulation of design and ethnography); a recovery of the agency of things, their "vibrant materiality," as opposed to the alleged inertness of "objects" (Bennett 2010); a resituation of the material within the metabolism of the economy (production and consumption), as ecological economics instructs; and a reintegration of design into larger assemblages stemming from place.

Ontologically oriented design thinkers share a belief in the radical innovative potential of design. Clearly, business-as-usual modes of designing and living have to be superseded. "I want 'business as usual,'" says Tonkinwise, "to just disappear because it's destroying the planet socially and ecologically.... Within design thinking there is an idealistic drive toward anti-capitalism, or at least anti-business-as-usual" (2012, 8, 14). The realization of this radical potential, to continue with this design theorist, requires a profound relational sensibility that links materiality, visuality, and empathy (via practice) in the creation of novel assemblages of infrastructures and devices, skills and know-how, and meanings and identities. Finally, there is a shared emphasis on the need to imbue design education with the tools for ontological reflection in ways that make designers conscious of their own situatedness in the ecologies for which they design.

As a Way of Concluding

The following are some features of the ontological approach to design, as a way to conclude this chapter. The list is purposely elaborated on the basis of the works presented in the chapter. Ontologically oriented design

- Recognizes that all design creates a "world-within-the-world" in which we are designed by what we design as subjects. We are all designers, and we are all designed.
- Is a strategy for transitions from Enlightenment (unsustainability, defuturing, deworlding, destruction) to Sustainment (futuring, reworlding, creation). It embraces ontologically futuring practices, particularly those involving the bringing into being of relational worlds and humans.
- Avoids defuturing into objects and reveals technology's contribution to unsustainability. It brings together imagination and technology ontologically, and it tackles head-on the anthropogenesis of technicity.
- Is postsubject and postobject; it goes beyond the techno-rationalism of the self (user, author) as intrinsically existing; it challenges the hegemonic category of the human while striving for a posthuman practice by raising the question of civilizational transitions.
- Is not a(bout) straightforward fabrication but about modes of revealing; it considers retrieving forms of making that are not merely technological, while embracing new creations. It may do so by looking at the entire range of design traditions (within the West and beyond) non-Eurocentrically and decolonially.
- Is not about "expanding the range of choices" (liberal freedom) but is intended to transform the kinds of beings we desire to be. In this sense, it is potentially noncapitalist or postcapitalist and nonliberal.
- Builds on life's and the Earth's immanent capacity for self-organization. It tackles head-on the question of artificiality but does so while being mindful of the complex webs of life that make up the pluriverse.
- It promotes convivial and communal instrumentations involving human/nonhuman collectives provoked into existence by ecological breakdowns or shared experiences of harm. It imagines designs that take seriously the active powers issuing from nonhumans, and it builds on the positive ontology of vibrant matter, realizing that design situations always involve encounters between human and nonhuman actants of all kinds.
- It involves the design of domains in which desired actions are generated and interpreted; it explicitly contributes to creating the languages that create the world(s) in which people operate. In the creation of domains of conversations for action, it necessarily moves from design to experience and back (through, say, prototyping and scenario analysis). It inquires about the extent to which the creation of new designs enables

better domains of interpretation and action to emerge, without overlooking power dynamics.

- It always entails reconnection: with nonhumans, with things in their thinghood, with the Earth (Earth-wise connections), with spirit, and of course with humans in their radical alterity (decolonially, considering the inclusion of multiple worlds, rather than exclusion). It contributes to dismantling dualisms and takes seriously all forms of nondualist existence. At its best, it discerns paths to (greater) mindfulness and enables ontologies of compassion and care.

- All design is for enactive use (not involving just users), produces operational effectiveness (but not narrowly defined utility), fosters the autopoiesis of living entities and heterogeneous assemblages of life, and is mindful of living in the pluriverse.

We shall revisit some of these features at the very end of this book, particularly after the discussion of autonomous design and the concept of the communal. For now, it is fitting to end this chapter with the following plea by Tonkinwise: "So we, especially we designers, must become much more steeped in ontological accounts of what design means, and what the human that is designed and so designs, is and can be" ([2014?], 7). Herein lies a constructive program for ontological design.

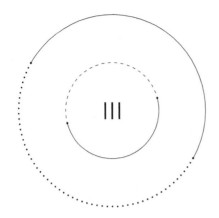

III

Designs for
the Pluriverse

5 Design for Transitions

Transition Design is a proposition for a new era of design practice, study and research that advocates design-led societal transitions toward more sustainable futures. . . . Transition design solutions have their origins in long-term thinking, are life-style oriented and place-based and always acknowledge the natural world as the greater context for all design solutions.

· **Terry Irwin,** "Transition Design: A Proposal for a New Era of Design Practice, Study and Research"

Being a transition designer means adopting different values and perspectives. It is therefore a process of learning, but, for the same reason, a challenge. It requires designers to acknowledge the hypocrisy that comes from being a change agent toward a new system from within the old system.

· **Cameron Tonkinwise,** "Design's (Dis)Orders and Transition Design"

The background of the book is the great transition: a process of change in which humanity is beginning to come to terms with the limits of the planet, and which is also leading us to make better use of the connectivity available to us. . . . Starting with these it is possible to outline a design scenario built on a culture that joins the local with the global (cosmopolitan localism), and a resilient infrastructure capable of requalifying work and bringing production closer to consumption (distributed system).

· **Ezio Manzini,** *Design, When Everybody Designs: An Introduction to Design for Social Innovation*

This chapter draws connections between visions of transitions (civilizational, paradigmàtic, epochal) and design. Together, they create an emergent field, variously called *transition design, design for transitions,* and *design for social innovation.* Given its subject and scope, this field necessarily has ontological implications, for behind any vision of transition there lies, to a greater or lesser extent, a substantial challenge to the onto-epistemic formation embedded in the current dominant form of capitalist modernity. It is this conceptual and ethical positioning that separates transition visions from more commonly established social change frameworks. This chapter provides a context for the epigraphs with which it starts. How did the leading design thinkers quoted above come to think about design as a space for such significant transformations? How did their design visions come to link into a single framework seemingly disparate elements such as place, distributed agency, paradigm change, planetary dynamics, and a new mind-set for the designer?

The chapter is divided into two parts. The first presents a range of transition visions that have been emerging with clarity and force in recent years, in both the Global North (e.g., degrowth, commoning, and the Transition Town Initiative) and the Global South (Buen Vivir, postdevelopment, transitions to postextractivism, and others). They stem from a wide spectrum of contexts and fields. Taken as a whole, these transition discourses may be said to constitute a new field, *transition studies,* which thus becomes an invaluable input for the transition design frameworks. The second part focuses on two such frameworks linking design and transitions: the transition design doctoral program being developed at Carnegie Mellon University (CMU), and Ezio Manzini's elaborate conceptualization of design for social innovation. To these, we should add Tony Fry's (2012, 2015) proposal for moving from Enlightenment to Sustainment, presented in the previous chapter. By bringing under a single roof transition narratives from the North and the South, usually kept separate, and combining these with transition design visions, this chapter hopes to present a convincing argument for the significance of transition thinking for design studies.

If the first part is intended as a contribution to the visioning element of the transition design frameworks, the second is purposely presented as a contribution to the evolving ontological design field. The emphasis on place-making and collaborative practice, as well as the unambiguous grounding of transition design in an ecological vision, is an important element of the political ontology of design.

Discourses of Transition

The formulation of transition imaginaries has been taking place for several decades, as exemplified by Ivan Illich's (1973) argument for a transition from industrial to convivial societies. However, it has intensified during the past decade. In fact, the forceful emergence of transition narratives, imaginaries, and proposals in multiple sites of academic and activist life over the past decade is one of the most anticipatory signs of our times. Transition discourses (TDs) take as their point of departure the notion that the contemporary ecological and social crises are inseparable from the model of social life that has become dominant over the past few centuries, whether categorized as industrialism, capitalism, modernity, (neo)liberalism, anthropocentrism, rationalism, patriarchy, secularism, or Judeo-Christian civilization. Shared by most TDs is the contention that we need to step outside existing institutional and epistemic boundaries if we truly want to strive for worlds and practices capable of bringing about the significant transformations seen as needed.

While talk of crises and transitions has a long genealogy in the West, TDs are emerging today with particular richness, diversity, and intensity. Notably, as even a cursory mapping of TDs would suggest, those writing on the subject are not limited to the academy; in fact, the most visionary TD thinkers are located outside of it, even if they often engage with critical academic currents. At present, TDs are emerging from a multiplicity of sites, including social movements and some nongovernmental organizations, the work of intellectuals with significant connections to environmental and cultural struggles, and that of intellectuals within alternative or dissenting scholarly traditions; TDs are prominent in the fields of culture, ecology, religion and spirituality, alternative science, food and energy, social movements research, and digital technologies.[1]

Thomas Berry explains the search for transitions in the following way: "We are in between stories. The old story, the account of how the world came to be and how we fit into it, is no longer effective. Yet we have not learned the new story" (1988, 123). The search for a new story (or rather new stories) is on; he puts it most pointedly and comprehensively: "We must describe the challenge before us by the following sentence: The historical mission of our time is to reinvent the human—at the species level, with critical reflection, with the community of life systems, in a time-developmental context, by means of story and shared dream experience" (1999, 159). This is a compelling mandate for all humans, and certainly for ontologically minded designers.

TDS in the Global North

Typically, TDs are differentiated geopolitically, between those produced in the Global North and those from the Global South, although bridges between them are being built. In the North, the most prominent include degrowth (often associated with debates on commoning and the commons; Bollier 2014; Bollier and Helfrich 2012, 2015; Nonini 2007) and a variety of transition initiatives. Debates on the anthropocene, forecasting trends (e.g., Randers 2012), interreligious dialogues, and some United Nations processes, particularly within the Stakeholders Forum, are also active spaces where TDs are being articulated. Among the transition initiatives are the Transition Town Initiative (in the United Kingdom), the Great Transition Initiative (Tellus Institute; e.g., Raskin 2012), the Great Turning (Macy and Johnstone 2012), the Great Work or transition to an Ecozoic era (Berry 1999), and the transitions from the Age of Separation (of individuals from community, and of humans from the rest of the living world) to an Age of Reunion (Eisenstein 2013), from Enlightenment to Sustainment (Fry 2012) or Enlivenment (Weber 2013), and from industrial civilization to ecological-cultural civilization (Greene 2015). In the Global South, TDs include postdevelopment and alternatives *to* development, crisis-of-civilization model, Buen Vivir and the rights of nature, communalization, and transitions to postextractivism. While the age to come is described in the North as being postgrowth, postmaterialist, posteconomic, postcapitalist, and posthuman, for the South it is expressed in terms of being postdevelopment, nonliberal, postcapitalist/noncapitalist, biocentric, and postextractivist (see Escobar 2011, 2015a, for further elaboration).

Most contemporary TDs posit a radical cultural and institutional transformation—a transition to an altogether different world. This is variously conceptualized in terms of a paradigm shift (Raskin et al. 2002; Shiva 2008); a change in civilizational model (indigenous movements); the rise of a new, holistic culture; or even the coming of an entirely new era beyond the modern dualist (Goodwin 2007; Macy and Johnstone 2012; Macy and Brown 1998; Lappé 2011), reductionist (Kauffman 2008; Laszlo 2008), economic (Schafer 2008), anthropocentric (Weber 2013; Goodwin 2007), and capitalistic (Klein 2014) age. This change is seen as already under way, although most transition proponents warn that the results are by no means guaranteed. Even the most secular visions emphasize a deep transformation of values. The most imaginative TDs link together aspects that have remained separate in previous imaginings of social transformation: cultural, politico-economic, ecological, and spiritual. These domains are newly brought together by a profound concern with human suffering and with the fate of life itself. Let us listen to a few classical statements on the transition:[2]

> The global transition has begun—a planetary society will take shape over the coming decades. But its outcome is in question. . . . Depending on how environmental and social conflicts are resolved, global development can branch into dramatically different pathways. On the dark side, it is all too easy to envision a dismal future of impoverished people, cultures and nature. Indeed, to many, this ominous possibility seems the most likely. But it is *not* inevitable. Humanity has the power to foresee, to choose and to act. While it may seem improbable, a transition to a future of enriched lives, human solidarity and a healthy planet is possible. (Raskin et al. 2002, ix)

> Life on our planet is in trouble. It is hard to go anywhere without being confronted by the wounding of our world, the tearing of the very fabric of life. . . . Our planet is sending us signals of distress that are so continual now they seem almost normal. . . . These are warning signals that we live in a world that can end, at least as a home of conscious life. This is not to say that it *will* end, but it *can* end. *That very possibility changes everything for us*. . . . This is happening now in ways that converge to bring into question the very foundation and direction of our civilization. A global revolution is occurring. . . . Many are calling it the Great Turning. (Macy 2007, 17, 140; emphasis added)

> Ecological civilization is not something to be arrived at, but something ever to be created. . . . Bringing it into being and sustaining it involves more just and cooperative relationships among humans, as well as transformed relationships of humans with the larger community of life. It is something that everyone may be involved in and in which everyone has a place. (Greene 2015, 3)

Common to many TDs, exemplified by the above quote from Raskin and colleagues, is the view that humanity is entering a planetary phase of civilization as a result of the accelerating expansion of the modern era, that a global system is taking shape with fundamental differences from previous historical phases. The character of the transition will depend on which worldview prevails. The Great Transition Initiative distinguishes among three worldviews—

evolutionary, catastrophic, and transformational—with corresponding global scenarios: conventional worlds, barbarization, and the Great Transition. In this framework, only the latter promises lasting solutions to the sustainability challenges, but it requires fundamental changes in values and novel socioeconomic and institutional arrangements. The Great Transition paradigm highlights interconnectedness and envisions the decoupling of well-being from growth and consumption, and the cultivation of new values (e.g., solidarity, ethics, community, meaning). It proposes an alternative global vision that replaces industrial capitalism with what they conceptualize as a civilizing globalization.[3]

Many TDs are keyed in to the need to move to postcarbon economies. Vandana Shiva has brought this point home with special force (see also L. Brown 2015). For Shiva (2005, 2008), the key to the transition "from oil to soil"— from a mechanical-industrial paradigm centered on globalized markets to a people- and planet-centered one—lies in strategies of relocalization based on the construction of decentralized, biodiversity-based organic food and energy systems operating on the basis of grassroots democracy, local economies, and the preservation of soils and ecological integrity. In general, TDs of this kind exhibit an acute consciousness of communities' rights to their territories and of the tremendously uneven patterns of global consumption and environmental impacts. Critiques of capitalism, cultural change, spirituality, and ecology are woven together in the various diagnoses of the problem and proposals for possible ways forward (Korten 2006; Mooney, ETC Group, and What Next Project 2006; Sachs and Santarius 2007). An "ecology of transformation" (Hathaway and Boff 2009) is seen as the route to counteract the ravages of global capitalism and construct sustainable communities; its main components include ecological justice, biological and cultural diversity, bioregionalism, rootedness in place, participatory democracy, and cooperative self-organization. Some recent TDs emphasize the idea of pansentience, that is, the notion—dear to many place-based and indigenous peoples—that consciousness and meaning are the property of all living beings (and even matter), not just of humans (Goodwin 2007; Weber 2013; Ingold 2011).[4]

The work of Thomas Berry (a self-described "geologian") has been influential for transition visions.[5] His notion of the Great Work—a transition "from the period when humans were a disruptive force on the planet Earth to the period when humans become present to the planet in a manner that is mutually enhancing" (1999, 11; see also 1988)—is one of the most prescient articulations of a transition imaginary. Berry calls the new era *Ecozoic*, tellingly meaning "house of life," a notion with which designers can surely feel great sympathy. For Berry, "the deepest cause of the present devastation is found in the mode of consciousness that has established a radical discontinuity between the humans and other modes of being and the bestowal of all rights on the humans" (1999, 4). The divide between human and nonhuman domains is at the basis of many of the critiques proposed by TDs, along with the idea of a separate self. Joanna Macy and Chris Johnstone (2012) speak of a cognitive and spiritual revolution involving the replacement of the modern self with an ecological, nondualist self that reconnects with all beings and recovers a sense of evolutionary time, which has been effaced by the linear time of capitalist modernity. Central to transition visions, thus, is the healing of dualisms. Berry's oft-quoted phrase "Earth is a communion of subjects, not a collection of objects" is one of the most eloquent statements in this regard (Berry 1987, 107, 108).

Berry's summary statement bears repeating: "The historical mission of our time is to reinvent the human—at the species level, with critical reflection, with the community of life systems, in a time-developmental context, by means of story and shared dream experience" (1999, 159). Each of the five elements of this mission has its own unique meaning and importance, spelled out throughout Berry's work, and most of Berry's vision could easily be translated into design concepts. For instance, Berry identifies four pillars keeping in place the story that needs to be replaced (governments, corporations, universities, and religions). He also described the anthropocene with great foresight.[6] He was a pioneer of bioregionalism and adopted a living-systems perspective. His critique of anthropocentrism was radical and coexisted with his insistence on "reinvent[ing] the human," much like the critiques of Tony Fry and others. And he speaks about the activation of the human imagination in ways that designers can certainly echo (e.g., 1999, 55).

There are nevertheless aspects of Berry's work that would require deeper reflection on designers' part, such as his view of the Earth as a biospiritual planet; his insistence on the need to re-create an intimacy with the Earth as essential to crafting the new story ("We cannot discover ourselves without first discovering the universe, the earth, and the imperatives of our own being"; 1988, 195); and, perhaps most difficult and controversial, the idea that central to the transition is a transrational thought guided by revelatory visions, one that is attuned to life's self-organizing potential and best accessed through myth and dreams, "indicating an intuitive, nonrational process that occurs when we awaken to the numinous powers ever present in the phenomenal world about us" (as, say, shamans have done throughout the ages; 1988, 211).

Building on Berry's work and on the tradition of process thought (largely associated with the British mathematician and philosopher Alfred North Whitehead), Herman Greene (2015) proposes a transition from an industrial-economic to an ecological-cultural age, or, shortly, to an ecological civilization (a more user-friendly term for Berry's Ecozoic). Like Berry, he emphasizes both inclusion of the Earth as an active participant in the creation of worlds and civilizational change as a new dimension for action. For Greene, given the globalization of Western civilization, it becomes imperative to revisit the intersection of human history and natural history within a cosmological scope of inquiry. Ecological civilization thus becomes a new stage of human civilization; it starts with the premise that Earth is a single sacred community bound together in interdependent relations, and that humans' role is to celebrate and care for this community in conscious self-awareness. The ecological civilization also recognizes the right to justice and fairness for all humans and all living beings; is grounded in places and bioregions, as well as in historic cultures and civilizations; protects the commons; and has the overall goal of bringing about the integral functioning and flourishing of the Earth community as a whole. Its promise is that "for centuries to come we will have a viable human future in a flourishing life community" (Greene 2015, 8). A related approach has been proposed by Phillip Clayton in association with the Institute for Postmodern Development in China, where the notion of an ecological civilization is being developed. An interesting feature of this proposal is that besides the usual areas of concern (the economy, technology, agriculture, education, etc.) it includes spirituality and worldview as essential ingredients of the transitions. These projects explicitly theorize the reorganization of social domains necessary to achieve a civilized existence on the planet.[7]

The Transition Town Initiative, Degrowth, and the Commons: Three Emerging Spaces for Transition Design

The Transition Town Initiative (TTI), started in the town of Totnes in southern England and spearheaded by Rob Hopkins, is a main source of inspiration for the transition design framework developed at CMU, to be discussed shortly. Taken together, the TTI, degrowth, and the commons may be seen as constituting a somewhat unified space for the further development of the theory and practice of transition design. In the next section, I will propose a similar set of notions from Latin America, including postdevelopment, Buen Vivir, the rights of nature, and transitions to postextractivism, as important spaces for advancing transition design.

The TTI is one of the most concrete proposals for a transition to a post–fossil fuel society (Hopkins 2008, 2011). This compelling vision uses post–peak oil scenarios to propose a path for towns to move along a transition timeline. The relocalization of food, energy, housing, transportation, and decision making is a crucial element of the TTI. The TTI contemplates the reinvigoration of communities so that they become more self-reliant, a carefully planned but steady "powering down" or "energy descent" in human activity, and tools for rebuilding ecosystems and communities eroded by centuries of delocalized, expert-driven economic and political systems. Resilience is the TTI's alternative to conventional notions of sustainability; it involves seeding communities with diversity and social and ecological self-organization, strengthening the capability to produce locally what can be produced locally, and so forth. The TTI is indeed "one of the most important social experiments happening anywhere in the world at the moment" (Hopkins 2011, 13). Like other TDs, it is based on a new story positing a radical shift in society within the time frame allowed by the ecological crisis. One of the cornerstones of the approach is that of building community resilience as "a collective design project" (45). Rethinking resilience through localization practices is, in fact, one of the main contributions of the initiative. This real-life social-innovation design experiment has become a large network with transition initiatives in more than thirty-four countries by now.[8]

The notion of degrowth is creating a visible transition imaginary and movement, particularly in parts of Europe, and has the potential to become an important ingredient in transition design frameworks. As its name implies, the degrowth movement is based on the critique of economic growth as the number-one goal and arbiter of what societies do. As ecological economists and others have demonstrated, growth cannot continue indefinitely, nor for much longer at current levels, before many more ecosystems collapse. Degrowth articulates a political vision of radical societal transformation, appealing to broad philosophical, cultural, ecological, and economic critiques of capitalism, the market, growth, and development. Its sources are diverse, from Illich's (1973) critique of industrialism and expert institutions and Polanyi's (1957) analysis of the disembedding of the economy from social life, to bioeconomics and sustained attention to economic and ecological crises. Degrowth has a strong ecological basis (from sustainable degrowth to strong sustainability), but its most farsighted variants encompass a range of cultural and nonmaterial concerns. As some degrowth advocates provocatively put it, degrowth is not about doing "less of the same" but about living with less *and* differently, about downscaling while fostering the flourishing of life in other terms (Kallis, Demaria, and D'Alisa 2015).[9]

Degrowth is described as "a way to bring forward a new imaginary, which implies a change of culture and a rediscovery of human identity which is disentangled from economic representations" (Demaria et al. 2013, 197). The new imaginary involves displacing markets from their centrality in the organization of human life and developing an entire range of different institutions for the relocalization and reinvention of democracy. To this end, degrowth considers a broad array of strategies and actors, from oppositional activism and the construction of alternative economies to various types of reformism. Rather than voluntary simplicity, which has proven controversial, degrowth theorists prefer the notion of conviviality as a descriptor of the aims and domains of degrowth (tools, commons, economies, etc.). Degrowth's goal thus becomes "a transition to convivial societies who live simply, in common and with less" (Kallis, Demaria, and D'Alisa 2015, 11). Degrowth also deals with population, although somewhat obliquely, emphasizing the need to link population issues to feminist emancipatory politics.

The movements around the defense and re-creation of the commons brings together northern and southern TDs, contributing to dissolving this very dichotomy. As David Bollier (2014) points out, the commons entail a different way of seeing and being, an alternative model of socionatural life. Struggles over the commons are found across the Global North and the Global South, from forests, seeds, and water to urban spaces and cyberspace, and the interconnections among them are increasingly visible and practicable (see, e.g., Bollier and Helfrich 2012, 2015). Debates about the commons are one of those instances in which diverse peoples and worlds have an interest in common, which is nevertheless not the same interest for all involved, as the visions and practices of the commons are place based and world specific (de la Cadena 2015). Reflection on commons and commoning tends to reveal commons-destroying dualistic conceptions, particularly the dualisms between humans and nonhumans, the individual and the communal, and mind and body; these discussions resituate the human within the ceaseless flow of life in which everything is inevitably immersed. Commons have this tremendous life-enhancing potential at present.

Degrowth and commoning are emergent movements that contribute to the deconstruction of the individual and the economy. Working toward a "commons-creating economy" (Helfrich 2013) means working toward re-embedding the economy in society and nature and calls for the reintegration of persons within the community, the human within the nonhuman, and knowledge within the inevitable coincidence of knowing, being, and doing. These are key issues for ontologically oriented design practices.

Postdevelopment, Buen Vivir, the Rights of Nature, and Civilizational Transitions

There is likely no other social and policy domain where the paradigm of growth has been most persistently deployed than that of development. Development continues to be one of the main discourses and institutional apparatuses structuring unsustainability and defuturing. It is crucial for transition designers to resist the intellectual and emotional force of this imaginary, even more so now when the "international community" (a self-serving and self-appointed elite group intent on keeping the world going without major changes) is gearing itself up for fifteen more years of bland and damaging policy prescriptions in the name of so-called sustainable development.

The golden age of development was the decades from the 1950s to the end of the 1970s, when the dream of poor third-world countries catching up with the rich West still captured the imaginations of most world leaders. Starting in the late 1980s, cultural critics in many parts of the world started to question the very idea of development, arguing that development was a discourse that operated as a powerful mechanism for the cultural, social, and economic production of the Third World by the West (Rist 1997; Escobar 2011). These analyses entailed a radical questioning of the core assumptions of development, including growth, progress, and instrumental rationality. Some started to talk about a "postdevelopment era" as an extension of these critiques, meaning three interrelated things: first, development is displaced from its centrality in the representations of conditions in Asia, Africa, and Latin America. A corollary of this first goal was to open up the discursive space to other ways of describing those conditions, less mediated by the premises of development. Second, discursive space is created to think about the end of development and to identify alternatives *to* development, rather than development alternatives, as a concrete possibility. Third, awareness is cultivated of the acute need to transform development's order of expert knowledge and power. To this end, postdevelopment advocates proposed that useful ideas about alternatives could be gleaned from the practices of grassroots movements.

Debates on postdevelopment and alternatives *to* development have gained force in Latin America over the past decade, in connection with the existing progressive regimes, although the main force behind this resurgence has been the social movements. Two key areas of debate closely related to postdevelopment are the notions of Buen Vivir ("Good Living," or collective well-being according to culturally appropriate conceptions; *sumak kawsay* in Quechua and *suma qamaña* in Aymara) and the rights of nature. Defined as a holistic, de-economized view of social life, Buen Vivir "constitutes an alternative *to* development, and as such it represents a potential response to the substantial critiques of postdevelopment" (Gudynas and Acosta 2011, 78). Very succinctly, Buen Vivir grew out of indigenous struggles as they articulated with the social-change agendas of peasants, Afrodescendants, environmentalists, students, women, and youth.[10] Crystallized in the Ecuadorian and Bolivian constitutions (of 2008 and 2009, respectively), Buen Vivir "presents itself as an opportunity for the collective construction of a new form of living" (Acosta 2010, 7; see also Gudynas 2014, 2015).

Buen Vivir subordinates economic objectives to the criteria of human dignity, social justice, and ecology. The most substantive versions of Buen Vivir in the Andes reject the linear idea of progress, displace the centrality of Western knowledge by privileging the diversity of knowledges, recognize the intrinsic value of nonhumans (biocentrism), and adopt a relational conception of all life. It should be emphasized that Buen Vivir is not purely an Andean cultural-political project, as it is influenced by critical currents within Western thought and aims to influence global debates. Debates about the form Buen Vivir might take in modern urban contexts and in other parts of the world, such as Europe, are beginning to take place. Degrowth and Buen Vivir could be "fellow travelers" in this endeavor.[11]

Comparing Degrowth and Postdevelopment as Transition Imaginaries

It is useful to contrast degrowth and postdevelopment in order to clarify their potential incorporation into transition design framings. The strategies for reaching postgrowth, postcapitalism, and postdevelopment are somewhat different in the postdevelopment and degrowth frameworks. For degrowth advocates, these goals have fostered a genuine social movement, understood in terms of the construction of an alternative interpretive frame of social life (Demaria et al. 2013, 194). Regardless of whether this is a sufficient criterion to identify a social movement, it is fair to say that postdevelopment, rather than being a social movement in itself, operates through and with social movements. At their best, degrowth and postdevelopment will be more effective when they function on the basis of *societies in movement* (Zibechi 2006), or even *worlds in movement* (Escobar 2014). One important convergence concerns the relation between ecology and social justice. Joan Martínez-Alier (2012) emphasizes the fact that the considerable environmental justice movements in the Global South (including climate and water justice, ecological debt, and so forth) can serve as strong bridges with degrowth. Patrick Bond (2012) and Naomi Klein (2014) have similarly argued that climate justice will be tackled effectively only through transnational networks of movements and struggles.

Both movements agree that markets and policy reforms, by themselves, will not accomplish the transitions needed. Shared as well is a substantial questioning of capitalism and liberalism as arenas for advancing sustainable degrowth, postdevelopment, or Buen Vivir. Degrowth's emphases, such as energy descent and the redefinition of prosperity, are rarely considered in the South, being seen as inapplicable or even ridiculed (there are exceptions, such as the growing movement of *ecoaldeas* [ecovillages] in Latin America, which involves dimensions of spirituality and frugality). These concerns could buttress the critique of overconsumption among the Latin American middle classes, and elsewhere in the Global South, which has barely started. The bias toward the small and the place-based, under the banner of relocalization, is another feature bringing together degrowth and postdevelopment. An important concern for both schools of thought is the emphasis on local autonomy, which reveals a certain predilection for anarchist political imaginaries.

Finally, degrowth and postdevelopment confront overlapping challenges. On the postdevelopment side, the clearest challenge is the appropriation of Buen Vivir and the rights of nature by the State in countries like Ecuador and Bolivia while continuing to pursue aggressive extractivist policies and, not infrequently, the repression of environmentalist and grassroots organizations. Also noticeable is the trend for local communities to acquiesce, under pressure, to conventional development projects with corporations, nongovernmental organizations, or the State (e.g., for Reduced Emissions from Deforestation and Forest Degradation [REDD] projects). On the degrowth side, a main risk is the subversion of its meaning through green-economy and postgrowth schemes that leave untouched the basic architecture of economism. Finally, a partnership between degrowth and postdevelopment could contribute to dispelling the idea (in the North) that while degrowth is fine for the North, the South needs development, and, conversely (in the South), that the concerns of degrowth are only for the North and not applicable to the South.

Transitions to Postextractivism

One of the most concrete and well-developed proposals for transitions to come out of South America is the framework of "transitions to postextractivism." Originally proposed by the Centro Latinoamericano de Ecología Social (Latin American Center for Social Ecology, CLAES) in Montevideo, Uruguay, it has become the subject of intense intellectual-activist debate in many South American countries (Alayza and Gudynas 2011; Massuh 2012; Velardi and Polatsik 2012; Gudynas 2015; Svampa 2012). The point of departure is a critique of the intensification of extractivist models based on large-scale mining, hydrocarbon exploitation, or extensive agricultural operations, particularly for agrofuels, such as soy, sugarcane, or oil palm. Whether these activities take the form of conventional—often brutal—neoliberal extractivist operations, as in countries like Colombia, Peru, and Mexico, or follow the neo-extractivism of the leftist regimes, they are often legitimized as the most efficient growth strategies. Given the avalanche of highly destructive extractivist projects in much of the world, the usefulness of the transitions-to-postextractivism framework to buttress critiques of the growth model, its relevance to transition design and movements such as degrowth and postdevelopment, must be taken seriously. In fact, according to its proponents, this framework, while offering guidelines to organizations wishing to slow down extractivism, locates itself within the epistemic and political space of alternatives *to* development and hence also points beyond modernity.

The postextractivism framework does not endorse a view of untouched nature, nor a ban on all mining or larger-scale agriculture, but rather the significant transformation of these activities so as to minimize their environmental and cultural impact. It posits a horizon with two main goals: zero poverty and zero extinctions, to which we need to add, from a political ontology perspective, zero worlds destroyed. It proposes a typology that differentiates among predatory extractivism (activities taking place without regard for environmental and social impacts), sensible extractivism (those that obey existing environmental and labor regulations), and indispensable extractivism. The latter category includes those activities that are genuinely necessary to support Buen Vivir and that fully comply with environmental and social conditions. As Eduardo Gudynas concludes in his comprehensive book on the subject, the imaginary of postextractivism "opens up the path to alternatives capable of breaking away from the shackles of anthropocentrism and utilitarianism. It is time to start treading other paths, framed by plural ethics, inclusive of the rich and diverse valuations of people and nature. Once again, it is the value of life itself that is in question" (2015, 434).

To sum up: TDs from both the Global North and the Global South advocate for a profound cultural, economic, and political transformation of dominant institutions and practices. This transformation is often imagined to take place in tandem with those communities where the regimes of the individual, ontological separation, and the market have not yet taken complete hold of socionatural life. In emphasizing the interdependence of all beings, transition visions bring to the fore one of the crucial imperatives of our time: the need to reconnect with each other and with the nonhuman world. The relocalization of food, energy, and the economy is seen as essential for the transitions, and TDs often endorse diverse economies with strong communal bases, even if not bound to the local (Gibson-Graham 2006; Gibson-Graham, Cameron, and Healy 2013). Degrowth, commoning, Buen Vivir, and the search for nonextractivist models of the economy are offered as guiding imaginaries and tangible goals for moving along transition pathways while upholding the radical questioning of growth and development. These notions map a whole domain— concrete issues, dimensions, and goals—for transition design initiatives.

Designs for Transitions

Considering the great transition that might be unfolding, Italian design theorist Ezio Manzini wrote:

> So today, we must expect to be living this turbulence for a long time, in a double world where two realities live together in conflict: the old "limitless" world that does not acknowledge the planet's limits, and another that recognizes these limits and experiments with ways of transforming them into opportunities. . . . [A] continent is emerging. . . . It is a transition (long for us, but short for world history) in which we must all learn to live, and live well, on the new islands, and in doing so, anticipate what the quality of life will be like on the emerging continent. (2015, 2–3)

Manzini deliberately refers to the long-standing cultural background within which a design practice appropriate to the transitions is beginning to take shape. It resonates with Berry's auspicious reading of the coming of the new age: "The universe," Berry writes, "is revealing itself to us in a special manner just now" (1988, 215). According to climate scientists, humans may have a narrow window of opportunity (perhaps only three decades) to change direction radically in order to avoid the catastrophic effects that will come about with an increase in the Earth's temperature above two degrees Celsius. The space evolving from such a dire predicament is already being populated by myriad tiny transition islands where unsustainability and defuturing are being held at bay. But there is still a long way to go until such islands give rise to the new continents where life might again flourish.

The literature on transitions makes it clear that transitions are not designed but emergent; they depend on a mix of interacting dynamic processes, both self-organizing and other-organized (by humans). Emergence, and this is one of its key principles, takes place on the basis of a multiplicity of local actions that, through their (largely unplanned) interaction, give rise to what appears to an observer to be a new structure or integrated whole (say, a new social order or even civilization), without the need for any central planning or intelligence guiding the process.[12] Systems views of the transition emphasize that the paths and character of the transitions cannot be predicted in advance. Transition scenarios are a tool to inquire about possible paths and futures, and of course not all of them lead to satisfactory outcomes, as the Great Transition Initiative's helpful analyses illustrate. Hence, it is important to change the way we think about change itself. Ideas about emergence, self-organization, and autopoiesis (chapter 6) can be important elements in rethinking theories of social change (Escobar 2004). One thing is certain: most transition thinkers are adamant that the transition is happening. Many social movements have a lucid awareness of this realization. We are riding the cusp of the transition.

At a recent workshop on transition design, the notion that transitions are not designed but emergent led to reflection about the most appropriate category for the design imagination being born at the intersection of transition thinking and critical design studies.[13] Whatever the category adopted—whether transition design, design for transitions, design for social innovation, or what have you—there is a shared understanding that the transitions are emergent and plural. In what follows, I present two evolving but already well-structured frameworks: the transition design graduate program at CMU's School of Design, and the conceptualization of design for social innovation and transition proposed by Manzini in his most recent book.[14]

The Transition Design Framework at CMU

The transition design project at CMU has a clear mission statement: "Transition Design acknowledges that we are living in 'transition times' and takes as its central premise the need for societal transitions to more sustainable futures and the belief that design has a role to play in these transitions" (Irwin, Tonkinwise, and Kossoff 2015, 2). This premise is spelled out in two major ways: by demarcating a subfield of transition design within the school's graduate program, but with implications for design studies as a whole, and by proposing a preliminary but well-thought-out conceptualization of transition design. The school's graduate program structure is based on overlapping "design tracks" (products, communications, and environments) and "areas of focus," including design for service ("design within existing paradigms and systems in which moderate positive change can be achieved"), design for social innovation ("design *within* and *for* emerging paradigms and alternative economic models leading to significant positive social change"), and transition design ("design *of* and *within* new paradigms that will lead to radical positive social and environmental change"). Both the tracks and the areas of focus are placed within an overarching umbrella, "Design for Interactions" (among people, the built world, and the natural environment). Tellingly, the approach explicitly identifies the natural world as the context for all design activities, not only for the transition design focus area.[15]

The transition design framework constitutes a significant intervention into design discourse and education, at a moment when many design schools are feeling the pressure to adapt to the mounting ecological and social challenges of today's world. This is of course easier said than done in a field that, since the Bauhaus, has been so wedded to the making of unsustainable modern styles of living. The CMU group's identification of an area of design research, education, and practice committed to radical social change in the face of structural unsustainability can thus be seen as the group's most courageous and proactive intervention, not only within the design field but within the academy as a whole. The intitiative to form a transition design track can be considered a particular attempt at reorienting design, perhaps parallel to but different from those cited in chapter 1 (such as those by John Thackara; Anthony Dunne and Fiona Raby; and Pelle Ehn, Elizabeth Nilsson, and Richard Topgaard). The group's transition design imagination, in fact, goes beyond the changes currently being implemented in the social sciences and humanities, or within interdisciplinary fields such as global and environmental studies, at least in the Anglo-American academy. (In my view, most major universities are bowing to the pressures to train people to be allegedly successful in what is described without much reflection as an increasingly globalized and interconnected world; this means preparing individuals to compete in market economies, and many of these individuals will carry on the mandate of unsustainability and defuturing.) Let us see, then, how this new area is being conceptualized.

The framework is based on a heuristic model structured around four different and interrelated areas (see figure 5.1), and it has some unique features. First, it is a design approach oriented to longer time horizons and explicitly informed by visions of sustainable futures. The creation of *visions* of and for transitions is the cornerstone of the approach. This component of the framework is under development; it focuses on tools and methods for facilitating discussion about alternative futures (e.g., scenario development, forecasting, and speculative design), rather than on a full-blown strategy for the critical study and articulation of visions. It embraces some of the trends discussed in chapter 1 and in the first part of the present chapter, such as the necessarily place-based character of much transition design work, and design's relation to the transformation of everyday life. The "visions" dimension also appeals explicitly to a few of the TDs already discussed, particularly the TTI and the Great Transition Initiative.

A second unique feature of the framework is its explicit incorporation of theories of social change as central to design strategies for the transition. These are intended to instill in designers an always-evolving attitude of critical learning about the world. One of the key theories espoused by the transition design track is living-systems theory, a body of knowledge that explains the dynamics of self-organization, emergence, and resilience taking place within natural and social systems (see the recent tome by Frijof Capra and Pier Luigi Luisi [2014] for an outstanding and comprehensive account of this theory). This body of thought is central to a number of TDs (e.g., those of Joanna Macy, Brian Goodwin, Erwin Laszlo, and the Great Transition Initiative), although it remains relatively marginal within the life sciences and is practically unknown within established theories of social change, with few exceptions (Taylor 2001; B. Clarke and Hansen 2009). Working within the holistic perspective of living-systems theory, Gideon Kossoff, from the transition design team at CMU, develops a relational conceptualization of the domains

A vision for the transition to a sustainable society is needed. It calls for the reconception of entire lifestyles that are human scale and place based but globally connected in their exchange of technology, information, and culture. It calls for communities to be in a symbiotic relationship with their ecosystem.

New ways of designing will help realize the vision but will also change/evolve it. As the vision evolves, new ways of designing will continue to be developed.

The vision of the transition to a sustainable society will require new knowledge about natural, social, and built/designed systems. This new knowledge will, in turn, evolve the vision.

Vision for Transition

Ideas, theories, and methodologies from many varied fields and disciplines inform a deep understanding of the dynamics of change in the natural and social worlds.

The transition to a sustainable society will require new ways of designing.

New Ways of Designing

Theories of Change

Changes in mind-set, posture, and temperament will give rise to new ways of designing. As new design approaches evolve, designers' temperaments and posture will continue to change.

A new theory of change will reshape designers' temperaments, mind-sets, and postures. And these "new ways of being" in the world will motivate the search for new, more relevant knowledge.

Posture and Mind-set

Living in and through transitional times requires a mind-set and posture of openness, mindfulness, a willingness to collaborate, and "optimistic grumpiness."

5.1 CMU's Transition Design Framework. The four areas represented co-evolve and mutually reinforce each other. Source: Irwin (2015: 5). Redrawn based on diagram by Terry Irwin, Gideon Kossoff, and Cameron Tonkinwise.

of everyday life in terms of nested structures (household, village, city, region, and planet), each with its own dynamics of self-organization around collaborative networks. "The transition to a sustainable society," Kossoff explains, "will require the reconstitution and reinvention of households, villages, neighborhoods, towns, cities, and regions everywhere on the planet as interdependent, nested, self-organised, participatory and diversified wholes. This will essentially be the transition from counterfeit to authentic holism in everyday life. The result will be a decentralized and diversified structure of everyday life which is in contrast to the centralized and increasingly homogenized structure that we have become accustomed to. It will . . . embody the communion not just of people, but of people, their artifacts, and nature, and will come into being at multiple, interrelated levels of scale" (2015, 36). This conceptualization endows transition visions with a scalar imagination that avoids the conventional vertical hierarchy of scales, which inevitably gives too much weight to the global and too little to the local or the place-based. With their emphasis on relocalization and recommunalization, all transition initiatives aim to reverse this hierarchy. Thinking in terms of nested structures and networks provides the basis for a distributed understanding of agency.

The theories-of-change dimension of the framework appeals to postnormal science (the science that takes seriously the knowledge of nonexperts) with the goal of making designers actively reflect on their taken-for-granted ideas about change. In some versions it incorporates design theories and methods that embed an understanding of change (e.g., Richard Buchanan's four orders of design and Arnold Wasserman's heuristic design framework; see Scupelli 2015). Many questions remain insufficiently addressed, however, by the theories of change incorporated into the framework thus far; these questions include design-specific issues such as how to disentangle the coexistence of futuring and defuturing in most human actions, the role of key agents such as business, and so forth (Scupelli 2015). There are other issues that remain insufficiently theorized; the reliance on systems and complexity theories, for instance, poses challenges for dealing with a range of questions that critical social theories (whether of Marxist or poststructuralist provenance) have routinely dealt with, in particular questions about history and context, power and politics, and domination and resistance.[16] This incompleteness, however, is indicative of the current impasse in modern social theory as a whole. As we discussed in chapter 2, notions of networks and assemblages have gone a long way to deconstruct taken-for-granted notions of agency but have yet to provide compelling accounts of what social theory calls domination, resistance, class/gender/race, and so forth, within a posthumanist landscape.[17]

Transition design thus proposes design-led societal transformations toward more sustainable futures. By applying an understanding of the interconnectedness of social, economic, political and natural systems, it aims to address problems that exist at all levels of scale in ways that improve quality of life, including poverty, biodiversity loss, decline of community, environmental degradation, resource, and climate change.

The remaining two dimensions of the framework are design specific. The dimension "posture and mind-set" is of utmost interest since it calls on transition designers to develop "a new way of 'being' in the world" (Irwin 2015, 8).

This involves both a particular value system and new practices of relating to others and to the world. This aspect of the proposal openly problematizes design ethics and practice, favoring the development of relational ethics. Here we find a variation of Francisco Varela's (1999) question of how best to foster nondualist rationalities in the West. What does it mean to take seriously the insights of relationality in design work? As the CMU group contends, it requires active inner work on the transition designer's part. In other words, transition design seeks to imbue design with a nondualist imagination. Again, this is easier said than done, given our entrenched dualist ways of thinking, being, and doing and the fact that they are embedded—indeed, "concreted-in," to use Cameron Tonkinwise's (2013b, 12) fitting metaphor—in the forms, norms, and structures of our capitalistic everyday life. The collective discussion of the challenges entailed by this dimension of the project might become an integral part of how it is carried forward. This debate takes the transition designer along the path of the transitions, as the questions likely to be raised in these discussions—for example, of the individual versus the communal, embedded reflexivity versus abstract knowledge, single versus multiple reals, and so forth—will be unsettling.

It is necessary to reiterate that learning how to take seriously the insights of relationality is one of the most intractable issues modern humans, particularly those qualified as experts, have to confront. What does "nondualist existence" mean in everyday life? An entry point into this question, and a sequitur of this book's ontological analysis, is the phenomenological insight that we are not just, or even primarily, detached observers but rather participants and designers who engage the world by being immersed in it. Knowing is relating. As the Mapuche poet and *machi* (shaman) Adriana Paredes Pinda puts it in a lecture at Chapel Hill (2014), *"we have to relearn to walk the world as a living being."* Engaging with people's lifeworlds and attaining again a certain intimacy with the Earth are essential to this endeavor. This inner work is led not only by analytical knowledge but also by what Chicana feminist Gloria Anzaldúa (2002) called *conocimiento*, which involves embodied knowledge, reflexivity, intuition, and emotion. In other words, the inner work demanded for a relational practice of living and designing requires other tools than (or besides) those of theoretical reflection.

Finally, the fourth dimension envisages "new ways of designing." Here the group makes a rich and challenging set of contributions. Some of these were already mentioned in the previous chapter when discussing Fry's (2012) work, such as elimination design and the debates on de/futuring and the dialectic of creation and destruction inherent in all design work. The questions arise: how can designers become newly aware of the fact that design careers often result in the use of vast amounts of materials that contribute to ecosystem destruction and pose risks to fellow humans? That "designers do a lot of material destroying on their way to being creative" (Tonkinwise 2013a, 5)? New habits—essential if different design futures are the desired outcome—need to involve ecological literacy and a renewed attention to materiality as inputs into radical sustainability design; rethinking of innovation beyond conventional business, commercial, and service design consulting and toward transformative kinds of social innovation; new pathways for design and its expansion into explicitly change-oriented domains; the relocalization of sustainable innovations; and, of course, foregrounding of the role of visioning in designing.[18] It is no surprise that at this level the transition design framework is seen as fostering "a paradigm shift and an entirely new way of understanding households and understanding societies" (Tonkinwise 2012, 8). Besides changes in mind-set, one might thus expect the creation of skill sets appropriate to the transition design task. Transition design is thus conceived as a new area of design methodology, practice, and research, and it is offered as such for further discussion. The following is an apt summary of the approach: Transition design

> (1) Uses living sytem theory as an approach to understanding/addressing wicked problems; (2) Designs solutions that protect and restore *both* social and natural ecosystems; (3) Sees everyday life/styles as the most fundamental context for design; (4) Avocates place-based, globally networked solutions; (5) Designs solutions for varying horizons of time and multiple levels of scale; (6) Links existing solutions so that they become steps in a larger transition vision; (7) amplifies emergent, grassroots solutions; (8) Bases solutions on maximizing satisfiers for the widest range of needs; (9) Sees the designer's own mindset/posture as an essential component of the design process; (10) Calls for the reintegration and recontextualization of diverse transdisciplinary knowledge. (Irwin, Kossoff, and Tonkinwise 2015, 3)

This statement implies a major transformation of design. Design itself becomes a project in transition. It joins other theoretical-political projects seeking to enrich our understanding of life and the human.

Design for Social Innovation:
Design, When Everybody Designs

Design, When Everybody Designs: An Introduction to Design for Social Innovation (Manzini 2015) is about the relation between design and social change, and the best way to enact such a relation in practice. It is based on a particular but sophisticated vision of what social life is and might come to be.[19] The work can also be seen as a sustained reflection on the increasingly contested modern cultural practice that design is, explicitly approached from the perspective of design's potential contribution to what he also sees as a "great transition" (2015, 2). The book starts with four propositions. (1) We live in a world where everybody has to design and redesign their existence; hence, the goal of design becomes the support of individual and collective life projects. (2) The world is undergoing a great transition; design may contribute to fostering a culture of cosmopolitan localism that effectively links the local and the global through resilient infrastructures that bring production and consumption closer together, building on distributed systems. (3) People's actions to change their everyday life conditions increasingly take place through collaborative organizations; design experts thus become part of creating the conditions for collaborative social change. (4) All of the above takes place within an international conversation on design, intended to transform the cultural background for both expert and nonexpert design work. Four interrelated propositions, then: everybody designs; this designing is integral to significant transitions that are under way, operating on the basis of distributed agency; collaborative organizations are central to designing; and all of this means that a new culture of design is emerging. Taken together, these four statements—concerning the agent, historicity, form, goals, and culture of design—ground a powerful vision of design for social innovation. Let us see how.

The contemporary landscape of social practice is full of examples of collaborative projects where local actions create new functions, practices, and meanings. Strategies for the relocalization of food are one of the best-known examples, but one could cite here a whole range of transition activities, including in the sectors of energy, infrastructure, construction, and many aspects of the economy. What is interesting to note is that many of these innovations take place through a new logic, that of distributed systems. In essence, this refers to the fact that, unlike the dominant centralized, top-down modern systems and infrastructures (representing a hierarchical model of organization and social life), distributed systems operate on the basis of decentralized elements that become mutually linked into wider networks. An insightful design implication of distributed agency is the fact that "the more a system is scattered and networked, the larger and more connected is its interface with society and the more the social side of innovation has to be considered" (Manzini 2015, 17). The result of increasingly networked action is more resilient systems and a redefinition of work, relations, and well-being (akin to Buen Vivir) and, eventually, "a new civilization" (3). This can be considered to be the case, says Manzini, at least as a design hypothesis (26), with design participating proactively in the social construction of the civilization's meaning.

To substantiate this hypothesis, Manzini introduces two useful distinctions: first, between two dimensions of design, namely, problem solving and sense making; and, second, between diffuse and expert design—*diffuse design* refers to the fact that everybody is endowed with the ability to design, *expert design* to professional design knowledge. In between problem solving and meaning making, and diffuse and expert design, there opens a space for rethinking "design in a connected world," as the title of chapter 2 states. In Manzini's model this space functions as a heuristic device allowing the visualization of design modes, from "cultural activism" engaged in diffuse design and meaning making to technological agency focused on expert-led problem solving (see Manzini's diagram on p. 40). These modes often overlap, nurturing new design cultures out of their convergence in particular places and situations. The aim of these new cultures is the construction of a new ecology of places and regions (perhaps along the lines of Sustainment). New practices of codesign, participatory design, and design activism (to which we will add autonomous design in the next chapter) become the stuff of a new model of design for social innovation. New design approaches are to be based on a positioning that is both critical of the current state of things and constructive, in terms of actively contributing to broad cultural change.

Discussing social innovation from design perspectives enriches the social science understanding of how change happens and at the same time radicalizes design practice. Examples could again be drawn from many parts of the world and areas of social life.[20] There are many lessons to be learned from open-ended codesign processes, including the iterative character of research and knowledge production, the ways in which local initiatives might generate general visions (e.g., for the transformation of an entire practice, such as that of cultivating food and eating with the slow food movement), and visions for the reimagining of a region (see chapter 6 of this book). From here follows the definition of design for social innovation as "*everything that expert design can do to activate, sustain, and orient processes of social change towards sustain-ability*" (62; italics in the original). Not all design, of course, needs to fit this definition; a great deal of it will continue to adhere to conventional ("big-ego" and "post-it") design models. Clearly, the principle of dialogic collaboration makes a huge difference in this respect. This dialogism might take place across worlds or ontologies, making design for social innovation genuinely pluriver-sal.[21] Its practices are conducive to the design of coalitions in which visionary capacity, dialogic process, and diffuse and expert design knowledge are all in-terwoven, with designers playing the role of facilitator, activist, strategist, or cultural promoter, depending on the circumstances and the character of the coalition at play.

Collaborative organizations are vital to design for social innovation. In a world that is both loaded with problems and highly connected, social innova-tion happens "when people, expertise, and material assets come into contact in a new way that is able to create new meaning and unprecedented oppor-tunities" (77). Oftentimes these conditions materialize at the intersection of grassroots organizations or local communities and digital networks, enabling new bottom-up, top-down, and peer-to-peer practices and their combination. The amalgamation of face-to-face and virtual interactions creates propitious conditions for the reexamination of people's collective life projects. "Collab-orative life projects" have become salient in modern life in recent times, in part as a corrective to the excessively individualistic lifestyles promoted by the modern ontology and as a response to the disabling effect of expert-based systems in health, education, transportation, and so forth.[22] Embedded within the concept of collaborative life projects is therefore a critique of these central aspects of modernity; said otherwise, the concept takes seriously the anthro-pological insight that individual actions occur within meaning systems that are ineluctably historical and collective. As such, "*collaborative organizations should be considered as bottom-up initiatives not because everything happens at grassroots level, but because the precondition for their existence is the active involve-ment of the people concerned*" (83).

Manzini's concept of collaborative life projects resonates with the concept of life projects that some indigenous peoples in the Americas have been pro-posing in contradistinction to development projects (Blaser, Feit, and McRae 2004). The indigenous concept is meant to make visible the notions of the good life emerging from their own experience *in their place*, and the ways it differs from the allegedly universal vision of the good life offered to them by development projects. In doing so, indigenous peoples are rendering visible the heterogeneity of visions of the good life among place-based groups on the planet (Blaser forthcoming).[23] They do so precisely as a way to defend their territories and relational ontologies. While these communities also create collaborative organizations at times, their real strength lies in the fact that their cultural-political mobilization for the defense of their life projects stems from their long-standing historical experience of cultural autonomy, even if under harsh conditions of domination. There are thus bridges to be built at this level between various ways of conceiving the nature and organization of the communal, with their respective "relational intensities" (Manzini 2015, 103).

Collaborative organizing for social innovation gives rise to a whole set of design tools and practices, whether new or adapted and redefined from existing repertoires, which Manzini develops throughout the book based on an array of examples from Europe and North America, from housing co-ops and community-supported agriculture to digital storytelling and urban-planning ecolabs. They include tools for mapping collaborative encounters; heuristics for discussing types and degrees of involvement on the designer's part; collaborative scenario building; mapping and visual tools to facilitate social conversations; and the generation of metavisions of alternative, although as yet unrealized, forms of living. Scenarios take on a double character: they are based on social innovation, and they are also intended to create the conditions for social innovation. What results is "an ecology of collaborative encounters" (118); in this context, society becomes "a laboratory for new ways of being and doing" (132).

Generating auspicious conditions for collective life projects demands the creation of supportive environments through appropriate "infrastructuring." Enabling infrastructures—the result of codesign—are intended to counter the defuturing infrastructures at the basis of most modern activities, subverting them from within (e.g., through retrofitting, broadly understood) or from without (via new designs). Making codesign possible requires a multiplicity of elements, from research, experimentation, and prototyping to platforms, local networking, and community-oriented tool kits. An interesting aspect of the framework is the idea that diffuse design capabilities can also be enhanced through these tools and practices, and that this might be an important step in making codesign effective. Enabling solutions will arise in accordance with the strength of codesign tools and methodologies. *"Enabling solutions are product-service systems providing cognitive, technical, and organizational instruments that increase people's capacities to achieve a result they value"* (167–168). They stem from a seemingly straightforward question: how can we achieve the life we want to live? Here again we find the strong relevance of the notion of life projects and the importance of visioning.

Strategies function at two levels: first, through projects aimed to make the general context more favorable, by creating larger visions and different meaning frameworks (say, within the same social domain or through geographical expansion); and, second, through local projects in support of the desired enabling solutions. While solutions may remain local and place based, they are also open to networking. Given that "today *the small is no longer small* and *the local is no longer local*" (178), the potential for gaining strength through connection is huge. This main lesson of the notion of distributed systems—for example, distributed infrastructures, power, and production, as well as, one may add, distributed activism (Papadopolous 2015; Escobar 2004)—constitutes a new ground for social innovation: small, local, open, and connected (SLOC) (Manzini 2015, 178).[24] By coordinating with others through networking, local projects might achieve scalar effects at the neighborhood and regional levels. The resulting configurations may rightly be considered instances of *cosmopolitan localism* (202).

Design for social innovation decidedly locates place making and the re/creation of communities at the heart of the design mission. Far from being a neutral and allegedly objective position, it is an ethical and political position that takes a stand on the side of a particular understanding of life and a particular style of world making that privileges localization, self-organization, and a collaborative social praxis. In advocating for a new civilization, it directs our attention away from the "big dinosaurs of the twentieth century" (193), namely, those hierarchical systems underlying Berry's four defuturing institutional structures (governments, corporations, universities, and religions), toward the emergence of "territorial ecologies"—assemblages of ecosystems, places, and communities—where open-ended codesign processes might function with greater ease. Manzini is perfectly aware that place-based politics can lead to exclusionary tendencies and regressive localisms. If these tendencies can be held at bay, however, "the resulting localities and communities are exactly what is needed to promote not only a new territorial ecology and a resilient ecosystem, but also a sustainable well-being" (202). Toward the end of his book, Manzini articulates this option at its most wide-ranging: "Place building can therefore carry considerable weight in the definition of a new idea of well-being. . . . I think that what social innovation is indicating, with its idea of well-being based on the quality of places and communities, is the seed of a new culture. Or better, of a metaculture which could be the platform for a multiplicity of cultures [a pluriverse?]" (202).

This statement resonates with the Latin American debates on Buen Vivir. But perhaps one of the most noteworthy aspects of the transition imaginaries that have inhabited this chapter is their willingness to bring back a politics of place into the picture as a central aspect of progressive and perhaps radical politics (e.g., Harcourt and Escobar 2005). This will become an important theme in the next chapter. Before tackling this task, let us pause for a moment to listen once again to Berry, as he articulates the stakes embedded in the call for transitions at their most fundamental; in the last chapter of *The Great Work: Our Way into the Future*, appropriately entitled "Moments of Grace," he puts it thus:

> We are now experiencing a moment of significance far beyond what any of us can imagine. What can be said is that the foundations of a new historical period, the Ecozoic era, have been established in every domain of human affairs. The mythic vision has been set into place. The distorted dream of an industrial technological paradise is being replaced by the more viable dream of a mutually enhancing human presence within an ever-renewing organic-based Earth community. The dream drives the action. In the larger cultural context the dream becomes the myth that both guides and drives the action.
>
> But even as we make our transition into this new century we must note that moments of grace are transient moments. The transformation must take place within a brief period. Otherwise it is gone forever. (1999, 201)

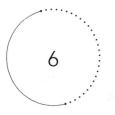

Autonomous Design and the Politics of Relationality and the Communal

6

La tierra manda, el pueblo ordena, y el gobierno obedece. Construyendo autonomía.

"The earth commands, the people order, and the government obeys. Constructing autonomy."

· **Zapatista slogan**

Cambiar el mundo no viene de arriba ni de afuera.

"Changing the world does not come from above or from outside."

· **Tramas y mingas para el Buen Vivir,** Popayán, Colombia, June 2013

In fact, the key to autonomy is that a living system finds its way into the next moment by acting appropriately out of its own resources.

· **Francisco Varela,** *Ethical Know-How: Action, Wisdom, and Cognition*

On June 9–11, 2013, the second Tramas y mingas para el Buen Vivir (Conspiracies and Collaborations for Buen Vivir) took place in the city of Popayán, about two hours south of Cali, in Colombia's southwest. Sponsored by the masters in interdisciplinary development studies (a bastion of Latin American decolonial thought, despite its name) at the Universidad del Cauca and held every other year, the event is carried out as a *cátedra abierta* (open university) where dialogues between academics, intellectuals, and activists from outside the academy can take place. Attended by several hundred participants, largely from social movements and grassroots communities from all over the southwest, the Tramas y mingas para el Buen Vivir is an amazing space of interepistemic conversation. The contributions of indigenous and Afrodescendant intellectuals and activists are particularly pointed and enriching, but the interventions by workers, women, environmentalists, peasants, and urban activists are also significant. It is a tremendously inspiring event, perhaps not too uncommon for the Global South, where this type of hybrid space is sometimes cultivated even as part of academic work. Let us listen to some of the sound bites that emerged from the event, of direct relevance to this chapter's themes:

> It is time to lose fear about designing our dreams, always with
>   our feet on the earth.
> We must not renounce the right to fall in love with the territory.
> Autonomies are not institutions but forms of relation.
> We need autonomy precisely because we are different.
> We are building a community of communities.
> Decommercialize speech.
> The secret is being like children and like water: joyful,
>   transparent, creative, and in movement.

And perhaps the two most revealing propositions: "No podemos construir lo nuestro con lo mismo" ("We cannot build our own realities with more of the same") and "Lo possible ya se hizo; ahora vamos por lo imposible" ("We already accomplished the possible; let us now go for the impossible!").

These statements are the tip of the iceberg of the irruption of what in Latin America is called *pensamiento autonómico*, or autonomous thought. This chapter inquires whether the Latin American notion of *autonomía* (autonomy), along with the parallel notion of *comunalidad*, or the recrafting of communal forms of being, and their associated practices, can be seen as laying the ground for a particular kind of design thought. Buen Vivir, transitions to postextractivism, and the *Planes de Vida* (life plans or life projects) envisioned by indigenous, Afrodescendant, and peasant communities are part of this trend as well, and so are the experiences of territorial defense in so many locations where brutal forms of extractive globalization are taking place, such as the defense of seeds, commons, mountains, forests, wetlands, lakes and rivers, and so forth.

It should be mentioned at the outset that many, if not most, of these experiences are, despite their commitment, inevitably undermined by the antagonistic contexts in which they take place; in their search for autonomy, some slide back into developmentalism, others are subverted from within by their own leaders, still others reinscribe older forms of oppression or create new ones, and not infrequently the mobilizations peter out under the incredible weight of the pressures of the day, or owing to outright repression. Be that as it may (and these aspects will be discussed no further in this chapter), the upsurge is on. In fact, one could posit as a hypothesis the idea that at this historical juncture "Abya-Yala/Afro-America/Latino-America," a land with an intense historical dialectic of commonality and diversity, might be offering to the rest of the world particularly valuable elements for the *pensamiento para la transición* (the thought for the transition).

It is worth recalling that in the context of many grassroots communities, design would take place under conditions of ontological occupation. The concept of autonomous design outlined in this chapter should thus be seen in terms of ontological struggles for the defense of people's territories and lifeworlds. The question remains, is it possible to think about design under the conditions of repression and violence that often affect such communities? It is precisely in those cases that the idea of autonomy is flourishing and the hypothesis of design for autonomy is taking on the timeliest meaning. I will examine the notions of autonomy emerging in these contexts shortly. For now, it is useful to reflect for a moment on Francisco Varela's minimalist definition of autonomy, quoted in the third epigraph above. Finding one's way into the next moment by acting appropriately out of one's own resources applies as much to organisms as to persons and communities or even worlds. For communities under ontological occupation, while this principle reveals the dire conditions under which their struggle take place, since an important aspect of those resources is precisely what the occupation seeks to destroy, it might also become a guiding notion for strategies for survival and flourishing.

This does not mean that this hypothesis is beyond questioning. As already mentioned in the introduction, is *autonomous design* not an oxymoron? To state it prospectively, the possibility I am trying to ascertain is whether ontologically oriented design could be design for, and from, autonomy. To restate the case, this would require extricating design from its dependence on unsustainable and defuturing practices and redirecting it toward other world-making projects. What would this mean in terms of the design of tools, interactions, contexts, and languages in ways that fulfill the ontological design principle of changing the ways in which we deal with ourselves and things so that futuring is enabled? This chapter broaches these questions by laying down the rudiments of autonomous design, largely based on intellectual-activist debates taking place in Latin America at present.

The first part of the chapter journeys again to a theoretical register by returning to Humberto Maturana and Francisco Varela (1980, 1987), focusing this time on their well-known notion of autopoiesis; as will be shown, what these authors call *biological autonomy* may provide useful guidelines for autonomous design. We then move, in the second part, to discuss current Latin American debates on autonomy and the communal. Out of these various threads will emerge a particular conception of autonomous design, as well as a broad idea of what is entailed by the realization of the communal. This idea is complemented, in the third and last part of the chapter, by a description of two experiences. The first, in which I was involved, took place in 1998; it consisted in the development and implementation of a workshop on ecological river basin design for communities in the Pacific rain forest region, using a systems methodology centered on autonomy. The second experience presents the seed of a transition design exercise for a particular region in Colombia's southwest, ravaged by over a century of capitalist development but potentially ripe for a transition imagination. Let me add two caveats before moving forward: first, that this chapter is offered in the spirit of a hypothesis: that design and autonomy can indeed be brought under a common roof; and, second, that it is derived from Latin American experiences and ideas.

Autopoiesis and Biological Autonomy

Beyond a theory of cognition and of the biological roots of human understanding, Maturana and Varela's work constitutes a theory of the organization of the living as a whole. It is both biology and philosophy, a system of thought in the best sense of the term.[1] Their approach to the living is all-embracing, from the cellular level to evolution and society. Perhaps it can be said that it is an attempt to explain life "from the inside" (that is, in its autonomy), without relying primarily on observer-generated concepts of what life is or does, whether in terms of "functions" (like the functions performed by a cell or an organ), "inputs," or "outputs," or the organism's relation to its environment. Their theory is a departure from these well-known biological approaches; it explains living systems as self-producing and self-contained units whose only reference is to themselves. The approach stems from the insight that cognition is a fundamental operation of all living beings and that it has to do not with representations of the world but with the effective action of a living being in the domains in which it exists (chapter 3). From this it follows that the essential character of the living is to have an autonomous organization that enables such operational effectiveness, for which Maturana and Varela coin the term *autopoiesis*: "Our proposition is that living beings are characterized in that, literally, they are continually self-producing. We indicate this process when we call the organization that defines them an *autopoietic organization*" (1987, 43). It is worth quoting the original, albeit a bit technical, definition. An autopoietic system is that unit which is organized "*as a network of processes of production (transformation and destruction) that produces the components which: (i) through their interactions and transformations continuously regenerate and realize the network of processes (relations) that produced them; and (ii) constitute it (the machine) as a concrete unity in the space in which they (the components) exist by specifying the topological domain of its realization as such a network*" (1980, 79).[2]

I find it useful to think about "organization" in this context as a system of relations among components (e.g., biophysical, cellular, biochemical, nervous, etc., just to think in biological terms for now) whose continued interaction produces the composite unit itself. All living systems have to maintain this basic organization in order to continue being the living systems they are; losing that organization leads to their disintegration. It follows that all relations among living units have to respect the criteria of conservation of autopoiesis. This takes place through what Maturana and Varela call structural coupling; all living systems interact with their environment through such coupling. The key issue here is that the environment does not dictate the relation; rather, it is the organization of the unit (its basic system of relations) that determines its interaction with the environment. Another way of saying this is that living systems have "*operational closure* in their organization: their identity is specified by a network of dynamic processes whose effects do not leave the network" (1987, 89); yet another way to refer to this feature is to say that living systems are structurally determined ("machines," in the above definition) in that their changes are determined by their organization (in order to conserve autopoiesis; e.g., 1987, 95–100; 1980). But again it is not the perturbations of the environment that determine what happens to the living being but the latter's organization; the former only triggers the changes.

This is a key feature of both biological and social or cultural autonomy; systems can undergo structural changes and adopt various structures in response to interactions with the environment, but they have to maintain a basic organization in order to remain as the units they are. Historical interaction among autopoietic units (worlds, one might say) often takes on a recurrent character, establishing a pattern of mutually congruent structural changes that allows the respective units to maintain their organization (pluriversal interactions). This eventually leads to the coordination of behavior, communication, and social phenomena through co-ontogenies, resulting in all kinds of complex units (codesign); in humans, this process takes place through language.[3]

Before I move on to link this to social movements and design, however, it is prudent to address the question of why we talk about "systems." Poststructuralists might find questionable the use of this concept, which, like those of structure, identity, and essence, has been heavily criticized and deconstructed for its connections to organicity, totality, and lawlike behavior, without even mentioning the military-industrial applications of systems analysis. This criticism is important, yet here again we find an example of poststructuralism deconstructing too much and not reconstructing enough; networks and assemblages have, of course, been important reconstructive agendas (e.g., Latour 2007; de Landa 2006), but I think it is fair to say that the question of wholes, form, and coherence remains unsolved in social theory. Complexity theory offers useful clues in this regard. As Mark Taylor put it in discussing precisely this issue, "after considering the logic of networking, it should be clear that systems and structures—be they biological, social, or cultural—are more diverse and complex than deconstructive critics realize. Emergent self-organizing systems do act as a whole, yet do not totalize. . . . Far from repressing differences [as deconstructivists fear], global [i.e., systemic] activity increases the diversity upon which creativity and productive life depends" (2001, 155).[4]

Neomaterialist and neorealist scholars might find some unsuspected allies in the lessons of complexity. For instance, complexity theory might be useful for ascertaining how certain socionatural configurations (including capitalism, patriarchy, and modernity) gain stability, despite their changing character. Is it possible to think about nontotalizing configurations that do not behave like conventional systems but that nevertheless act as wholes? Crudely stated, systems thinking is predicated on the idea that the whole emerges from the interplay of the parts. Over the past three decades, theories of emergence and self-organization have underscored the fact that these processes result in complex systems that are in no sense fixed and static but open and adaptive, often existing within conditions of instability and far from equilibrium (poised between order and chaos). When biologists pose the question, why does order occur?, and discover certain basic dynamics underlying the organization of all living systems (from the cellular and the organismic to the social levels), they are rearticulating the question of the *coherence and wholeness* of the perceived order of the world (see, e.g., Kauffman 1995; Solé and Goodwin 2000; Goodwin 1994, 2007); they find coherence and creativity in natural processes, including emergence and complexity, fractal patterns, and self-similar formations. These are questions of intensive differences and morphogenesis, of the relationship between the form of life and the life of form (Goodwin 2007). These might be useful concerns for designers as much as for neomaterialist and postdualist theorists.[5]

To highlight some elements from the theory of autopoiesis: living beings are autonomous entities in that they are autopoietic, that is, self-producing; they generate themselves through the recursive interaction among their components. This is the definition of biological autonomy. Autopoietic systems are wholes that relate to their environment through structural coupling. They are both open to their environments and operationally closed; indeed, the system is open to its environment in proportion to the complexity of its closure (its degree of autonomy), that is, the complexity of the basic system of relations that makes the system what it is. This operational closure is the basis of the organism's (or the system's or assemblage's) autonomy.

One caveat before we consider the application of these principles to the domain of the communal form of living and politics: don't claims about autopoiesis and autonomy negate claims about relationality? I do not think so. First, and perhaps the easier point, Latin American conceptions of autonomy are predicated on a radical notion of relationality. Alterity, within a rigorously pluriversal conception, is a constitutive dimension of relationality, not merely the other. Second, as for autopoiesis, it too relies on a conception of the universe as flux.[6] Autopoietic entities do not preexist their environments; they are mutually constituted but according to certain processes and rules. Autopoiesis reconceptualizes the relations of determination, requiring active engagement with other beings (what Maturana and Varela actually call love). Autopoiesis names a type of self-creation that is anything but autonomous in the modernist sense; it is not about self-sufficiency. To say it colloquially, autonomy and autopoiesis spell out the conditions that prepare systems (beings, communities) for confident relating and greater sharing. In the case of subaltern communities, this preparation takes a lot of conjunctural thinking and strategizing (at times engaging in what to outside observers might appear like strategic essentialism or the defense of culture).

Autonomy in the Social and Cultural Domain

Ever since the irruption of the Zapatistas and their cry of *Ya Basta!* (Enough Is Enough!), the struggle for autonomy has raged in Latin America, principally among indigenous peoples but also among other rural and urban groups. "Que se vayan todos, que no quede ninguno!" ("Let them all go away, let not one remain"), shouted the Argentinean unemployed to all the politicians and economic elites in whose representations, the protesters claimed, nobody could ever be trusted again after the economic collapse of 2001. Similar calls have been heard since, for instance, among the Indignados movement of southern Europe and the Occupy protesters in the United States. In Latin America the call for autonomy involves not only a critique of formal democracy but an attempt to construct an altogether different form of rule anchored in people's lives, a struggle for liberation and for a new type of society in harmony with other peoples and cultures (Esteva 2015).

The Mexican development critic Gustavo Esteva has provided the following useful distinction from the perspective of the tenacious resistance to development, modernity, and globalization by indigenous and peasant communities in southern Mexico. He distinguishes among three situations in terms of the norms that regulate the social life of a collectivity:[7]

- Ontonomy: When norms are established through traditional cultural practices; they are endogenous and place specific and are modified historically through embedded collective processes.
- Heteronomy: When norms are established by others (via expert knowledge and institutions); they are considered universal, impersonal, and standardized and are changed through rational deliberation and political negotiation.
- Autonomy: when the conditions exist for changing the norms from within, or the ability to change traditions traditionally. It might involve the defense of some practices, the transformation of others, and the veritable invention of new practices.

"Changing traditions traditionally" could be a description of autopoiesis; its correlate, "changing the way we change," designates the conditions required to preserve it, that is, to shift back from heteronomy to autonomy and ontonomy, from allopoiesis to autopoiesis (for instance, from heteronomous developmentalism to life projects). So understood, autonomía (autonomy) describes situations in which communities relate to each other and to others (say, the State) through structural coupling while preserving the community's autopoiesis. It tends to occur in communities that continue to have a place-based (not place-bound), relational foundation to their existence, such as indigenous and peasant communities, but it could apply to many other communities worldwide, including those in cities who are struggling to organize alternative life projects.[8]

The crucial elements for maintaining a mode of existence that is both relational and communal include particular types of relations among persons, relations to the Earth and to the supernatural world, forms of economy, food production, and of nurturing plants and animals, healing practices, and forms of deliberation and decision making. The concept of *territory*, as utilized by some social movements, is a shorthand for the system of relations whose continuous reenactment re-creates the community in question. In the context of the long historical resistance of indigenous and Afrodescendant peoples in countries like Colombia, autonomía is a cultural, ecological, and political process. It involves autonomous forms of existence and decision making. Its political dimension is incontrovertibly articulated by indigenous organizations in Colombia during the past two decades: "When we fail to have our own proposals we end up negotiating those of others. When this happens we are no longer ourselves: we are them; we become part of the system of global organized crime"[9] The statement also points at the continuous slippage between autonomy and heteronomy, particularly in social movements' relations to the State. There is no absolute autonomy in practice; rather, autonomía functions as a theoretical and political horizon guiding political practice.

Autonomía in these cases involves the ontological condition of being communal. The Zapatista put it well in their remarkable Sixth Declaration from the Lacandon Jungle in 2005: "[our] method of autonomous government was not simply invented by the Ejército Zapatista de Liberación Nacional (EZLN); it comes from several centuries of indigenous resistance and from the Zapatistas' own experience. It is the self-governance of the communities" (Subcomandante Marcos and the Zapatistas 2006, 77–78). In describing the autonomous movements in Oaxaca during the same period, Esteva similarly writes, "It is a social movement that comes from afar, from very Oaxacan traditions of social struggle, but it is strictly contemporary in its nature and perspectives and view of the world. It owes its radical character to its natural condition: it is at the level of the earth, close to the roots. . . . It composes its own music. It invents its own paths when there are none. . . . It brings to the world a fresh and joyful wind of radical change" (2006, 36–38). Autonomía is thus exercised within a long historical background, which has led some researchers to argue that, particularly in cases of indigenous-popular insurrection such as those that have taken place in southern Mexico, Bolivia, and Ecuador over the past two decades, it would be more proper to speak of societies in movement rather than social movements (Zibechi 2006). We can go farther and speak of *worlds in movement* (Escobar 2014). These societies/worlds in movement are moments in the exercise of cultural and political autonomy—indeed, of ontological autonomy.[10]

This characterization of autonomía is a response to the *current conjuncture of destruction of communal worlds by neoliberal globalization.* Interestingly, the aim of autonomous movements is not so much to change the world as to create new worlds (community, region, nation) *desde abajo y a la izquierda* (from the bottom and to the left), as the Zapatistas like to put it. Autonomía is not achieved by "capturing the State" but by taking back from the State key areas of social life it has colonized. Its purpose is to create spheres of action that are autonomous from the State and new institutional arrangements to this end (such as the well-known Juntas de Buen Gobierno, or Councils of Good Government, in Zapatista territories). At its best, autonomía seeks to establish new foundations for social life. Zapatista autonomy, for instance, involves the transformation of the procurement of key social functions, particularly in the following domains: eating, learning, healing, dwelling, exchanging, moving, owning (collective ownership of land), and working (Esteva 2013; Baschet 2014). While it would be impossible to analyze here how the practices in each of these domains have been transformed along the axis heteronomy-autonomy, making them more autonomous, in all likelihood this experience constitutes the best example of design for autonomy.[11]

Autonomía often has a decided territorial and place-based dimension. It stems from, and re/constructs, territories of resistance and difference, as the cases of black and indigenous movements in many parts of the Americas show; however, this applies to rural, urban, forest, and other kinds of territories in different ways. In the case of the well-known movements of the unemployed in Buenos Aires after the crisis of 2001, the exercise of autonomy included both a critique of capitalism and the creation of new forms of life (from daycare centers and urban gardens to free clinics, the restructuring of public schools, and the recovery and self-management of abandoned factories); in other words, it involved the creation of noncapitalist spaces and other forms of territoriality. New practices began to emerge, such as workplace democracy and horizontality in the self-managed factories, and communitarian values rather than market values in the communities. The goal of the movements was to produce in different ways and to create nonexploitative labor relations, not so dependent on capital and the State, over an entire range of activities involving production and social reproduction. In urban movements one can see the interplay among territorial organizing, collective identities, and the creation of new forms of life that is often at the core of autonomy (Mason-Deese 2015; Sitrin 2014).[12]

The place-based dimension of autonomía often entails the primacy of decision making by women, who are historically more likely than men to resist heteronomous pressures on their territories and resources and to defend collective ways of being (e.g., Harcourt and Escobar 2005; Conway 2013). There is often, in autonomía-oriented movements, the drive to re/generate people's spaces, their cultures and communities, and to reclaim the commons. These processes involve epistemic disobedience and foster cognitive justice (Santos 2014). Some say that autonomía is another name for people's dignity and for conviviality (Esteva 2005, 2006); at its best, *autonomía is a theory and practice of interexistence and interbeing, a design for the pluriverse.*

It is important to remark, however, that the capacity of communities to create and maintain their autonomy depends on their transversal skillful coordination of efforts at many levels, from the local and regional to the transnational. For autonomy to take root, "there has to obtain the conjunction of a local regime of autonomy, understood as the basis for the self-government of social life, and a planetary network open to the collaborative interconnection of living entities" (Baschet 2014, 72). As they free themselves from the State form, autonomous collectives tend to self-organize as a plurality of worlds through intercultural planetary networks. As the salience of the Planes de Vida and life projects of communities reveals, control over a basic level of production is indispensable for an effective translocal politics of articulation. For Baschet, this basic production infrastructure is a sine qua non for liberated spaces to grow and go beyond their determination by capital, the dominant economy, and the law of value.

Colombian anthropologist Astrid Ulloa (2010, 2011, 2012) similarly sees territorial autonomy as a multiscalar process. We already cited her work with indigenous groups in the Sierra Nevada de Santa Marta in the Colombian northwest. Based on the strategies of these groups, she suggests the notion of indigenous relational autonomy, stemming from the confrontation between indigenous groups and local and translocal actors. Anchored in the ontology of the circulation of life (chapter 2), indigenous groups develop strategies in their dealings with diverse actors, from the direct local intermediaries of extractive operations and regional megadevelopment projects to transnational legal regimes that not infrequently act as mechanisms of symbolic appropriation, given the neoliberal understanding of nature and forms of ecogovernmentality they often deploy through, say, carbon markets and Reduced Emissions from Deforestation and Forest Degradation (REDD) schemes. In so doing, as she proposes, the Arhuaco, Kogui, Kankuamo, and Wiwa peoples engage in a complex interepistemic and interontological geopolitics aimed at creating alternative territorialities that might result, to the greatest extent possible, in an effective articulation of territory, culture, and identity for the defense of their lifeworlds.[13]

The Realization of the Communal: Nonliberal Forms of Politics and Social Organization

Let us consider an important concept of the Nasa mobilization, the Minga social y comunitaria (Social and Communal Collective Work). "The word [*la palabra*] without action is empty. Action without the word is blind. The word and the action outside the spirit of the community are death."[14] Notions of community are making a comeback in diverse epistemic-political spaces, including indigenous, Afrodescendant, and peasant mobilizations, particularly in Mexico, Bolivia, Colombia, Ecuador, and Peru; this rekindled interest in things communal is also present in some urban struggles throughout the continent. The communal has also become an important concern for decolonial feminism. It is also found in some transition-related approaches, for instance, those that speak of commoning and community economies (e.g., Gibson-Graham, Cameron, and Healy 2013). Talk of community in Latin America may take a number of forms: comunalidad (communality), the communal, the popular-communal, struggles for the common, communitism (community activism), and so forth. Here I will use *the communal* or *communal logics* to encompass this range of concepts.

The historical background of this "return of the communal," if we are allowed to put it in these terms, is very complex; for the case of Latin America, it includes the emergence of indigenous movements after 1992, the political turn to the left and the rise of progressive regimes after 1998, and the particularities of the indigenous-popular insurrections in countries like Bolivia and Ecuador. A recounting of this context is beyond the scope of this book, as is a discussion of the many critiques raised against communal notions—from charges of romanticism and going back to the past to warnings about the repressive character of communities (see Escobar 2010a, 2014, for a detailed account of both the context of these critiques and the responses to them).[15]

Communal thought is perhaps most developed in Mexico, based on the experiences of social movements in Oaxaca and Chiapas. For Esteva, *la comunalidad* (the condition of being communal) "constitutes the core of the horizon of intelligibility of Meso-American cultures.... It is the condition that inspires communalitarian existence, that which makes transparent the act of living; it is a central category in personal and communitarian life, its most fundamental *vivencia*, or experience" (n.d., 1). As Oaxacan activist Arturo Guerrero puts it,

> *comunalidad* is a neologism that names a mode of being and living among the peoples of the Sierra Norte of Oaxaca, plus other regions in this state of southeastern Mexico. It expresses a stubborn resistance to all forms of development that have arrived to the area, which has had to accept diverse accommodations as well as a contemporary type of life that incorporates what arrives from afar, yet without allowing it to destroy or dissolve what is one's own (*lo propio*).... Communality is the verbal predicate of the We. It names its action and not its ontology. Incarnated verbs: eat, speak, learn ... These are collectively created in specific places. It only exists in its execution.... We open ourselves to all beings and forces, because even if the We comes about in the actions of concrete women, men and children, in that same movement, all that is visible and invisible below and on the Land also participates, following the principle of *complementarity* among all that is different. The communal is not a set of things, but an *integral* fluidity. (forthcoming, 1)[16]

The Mexican sociologist Raquel Gutiérrez Aguilar has recently proposed the concept of *entramados comunitarios* (communitarian entanglements) as opposed to "coalitions of transnational corporations," two contrasting modes of the organization of the social. By *communitarian entanglements* she means "the multiplicity of human worlds that populate and engender the world under diverse norms of respect, collaboration, dignity, love, and reciprocity, that are not completely subjected to the logic of capital accumulation even if often under attack and overwhelmed by it" (2012, 12). As she explains on the same page, "such community entanglements . . . are found under diverse formats and designs. . . . They include the diverse and immensely varied collective human configurations, some long-standing, others younger, that confer meaning and 'furnish' what in classical political philosophy is known as 'socionatural space.'" Gutiérrez Aguilar's distinction also aims to make visible "the *gigantic and global confrontation* between diverse and plural communitarian entanglements, with a greater or lesser degree of relationality and internal cohesion, on the one hand; and, on the other, the most powerful transnational corporations and coalitions among them, which saturate the global space with their police and armed bands, their allegedly 'expert' discourses and images, and their rigidly hierarchical rules and institutions" (13).

It is important to emphasize, however, to return to Guerrero, that communality can be understood only in its relation with the noncommunal exterior; "this is the *outside spiral*: it begins with an external *imposition*, which unleashes, or not, an internal *resistance*, and develops into an *adaptation*. This result is *lo propio* (what is one's own), and the We" (Guerrero forthcoming, 2). In other words, the communal does not refer to an ontological condition that preexists a social group's interactions with its surrounding worlds *but is the very product of such interactions.* Said otherwise, the "We" is never produced in isolation but is always coproduced through an interplay among heteronomy, autonomy, and ontonomy. At the same time, it is clear that communitarian entanglements involve a type of human relation centered on *lo común* (the common), always attempting to overflow their determination by capital.

The massive mobilizations and popular insurrections that took place in Bolivia during the years before the election of the country's first indigenous president, Evo Morales, in 2006 have been another fertile ground for the theorization of autonomía and the political. The literature is already vast and cannot be summarized here (Escobar 2010a); only a few contributions of particular relevance for this chapter's purposes will be presented, based on the work of indigenous and nonindigenous intellectuals. In her important work on liberalism and modernity in Bolivia from indigenous perspectives, the Bolivian scholar Silvia Rivera Cusicanqui (1990, 2014) interprets indigenous struggles, starting with the famous rebellion of Tupac Amaru and Tupac Katari in 1780–1781, in terms of the tension between liberal and communal forms of life and social organization. The tension between these forms, as she states, has shaped much of Bolivia's history, as they are interwoven "in a chain of relations of colonial domination" (Rivera Cusicanqui 1990, 20). It remains so today, as shown by the intense insurrections of 2000–2005, before Morales's election, when the collective memory of the events of 1781, including the dismemberment of Katari and the exhibition of his lifeless body parts in different public spaces in La Paz, yielded a desire "for the reunification of the fragmented body politic of indigenous society" (2014, 9). Rivera Cusicanqui gestures at a crucial dimension of politics in relation to communal groups, namely, their nonlinear conception of time and history and yet their strict contemporaneity.

It is against this background that El Alto, the largely Aymara city close to La Paz that grew to close to a million people in less than three decades, heavily populated by peasant migrants expelled by the neoliberal reforms of the 1980s (largely on the advice of Jeffrey Sachs, which was adopted by the military ruler of the time), became, for sociologist Félix Patzi Paco, a school for communal thought. For this Aymara intellectual, the transformation pursued by these movements took place "from the perspective of their own philosophy and their own economic and political practices" (2004, 187–188). Similarly, writing about the insurrections against neoliberal reforms in 2000–2005, Pablo Mamani (2005) speaks of an "indigenous-popular world" in movement, stemming from a society different from liberalism, and Gutiérrez Aguilar (2008) writes about the fracture of the liberal paradigm effected by the communal-popular forms. As she concludes, the insurrections demonstrated "the possibility of transforming social reality in a profound way in order to preserve, transforming them, collective and long-standing lifeworlds and to produce novel and fruitful forms of government, association, and self-regulation. In some fashion, the central ideas of this path can be synthesized in the triad: dignity, autonomy, cooperation" (2008, 351).

These interpretations unveiled the existence of a Bolivian society "characterized by noncapitalist and nonliberal social relations, labor forms, and forms of organization" (Zibechi 2006, 52). The main features of nonstatist and nonliberal regulation include deliberative assemblies for decision making, horizontality in organizations, and rotation of assignments. The struggles created forms of self-organization aimed at the construction of non-State forms of power. These forms appeared as *micro-gobiernos barriales* (neighborhood microgovernments) or *anti-poderes dispersos*, that is, diffuse and quasi-microbial, intermittent forms of power (Mamani 2005). The struggles (a) aimed to reorganize society on the basis of local and regional autonomies; (b) set in movement noncapitalist and nonliberal forms of organization, particularly in urban areas; (c) introduced self-managed forms of the economy, organized on communal principles, even if articulated with the market; and (d) engaged with the State, but only to dismantle its colonial rationality. The objective was not to control the State but "organizarse como los poderes de una sociedad otra" ("to become organized on the basis of the powers of an other society"; Zibechi 2006, 75).

Emerging from this interpretation is a fundamental question, that of "*being able to stabilize in time* a mode of regulation outside of, *against, and beyond* the social order imposed by capitalist production and the liberal state" (Gutiérrez Aguilar 2008, 46).[17] Patzi Paco's concept of the communal system spells out this hypothesis: "Our point of departure for the analysis of communal systems is doubtlessly the indigenous societies. In contradistinction to modern societies, indigenous societies have not reproduced the patterns of differentiation nor the separation among domains (political, economic, cultural, etc.); they thus function as a single system that relates to both internal and external environments [*entorno*]. . . . The communal system thus presents itself as opposed to the liberal system. The communal system can appropriate the liberal environment without this implying the transformation of the system [and vice versa]" (2004, 171–172). One can relate this conceptualization to the theory of autopoiesis and autonomy.[18] In the communal economy, as practiced by urban and rural indigenous groups, natural resources, land, and the means of labor are collectively owned, although privately distributed and utilized. The entire system is controlled by the collectivity. The political dimension is just as important as the economic dimension; power is not anchored in the individual but in the collectivity. In the communal form of politics, "social sovereignty is not delegated; it is exercised directly" through various forms of authority, service, assembly, and so on; in short, the representative "manda porque obedece," or rules through obedience (Patzi Paco 2004, 176), which is also a main Zapatista principle.

The proposal of the communal system implies three basic points: (1) the steady decentering of the capitalist economy and the expansion of communal enterprises and noncapitalist forms of economy; (2) the decentering of representative democracy in favor of communal forms of democracy, or *comunalocracia* (Guerrero in press); and (3) the establishment of mechanisms for genuine interculturality (Patzi Paco 2004, 190). Patzi Paco is emphatic in stating that the communal system is not predicated on excluding any group. It utilizes the knowledge and technological advances of liberal society but subordinates them to the communal logic; in the process, the communal system itself becomes more competitive and fairer. The proposal is not a call for a new hegemony but for an end to the hegemony of any system, for taking leave of the universals of modernity and moving into the pluriverse of interculturality. To achieve this goal may perhaps require a refounding of the societies of the continent based on other principles of sociability. Patzi Paco's conceptualization of the communal system offers persuasive principles for autonomy-oriented redesign.

To sum up: in lieu of state-driven development based on imputed needs and market-based solutions, autonomía builds on ways of learning, healing, dwelling, producing, and so forth that are freer from heteronomous commands and regulation. This is crucial for design projects intended to strengthen autonomy. Thus, autonomía means living, to the greatest extent possible, beyond the logic of the State and capital by relying on, and creating, nonliberal, non-State, and noncapitalist forms of being, doing, and knowing. Yet it also requires organization, which tends to be horizontal in that power is not delegated, nor does it operate on the basis of representation; rather, it fosters alternative forms of power through types of autonomous organization such as communal assemblies and the rotation of obligations. Autonomía is anticapitalist but not necessarily socialist. If anything, it can be described in terms of radical democracy, cultural self-determination, and self-rule. In linking design and democracy, design theorist Gui Bonsiepe (2005) actually defines democracy as the reduction of heteronomy, that is, of domination by external forces, and the process by which dominated citizens transform themselves into subjects, opening spaces for self-determination and autonomous projects.

This does not mean autarky or isolation; on the contrary, autonomía requires dialogue with other peoples, albeit under conditions of greater epistemic and social equality. Moreover, it requires alliances with other sectors or groups in struggle—strategies of localization and interweaving not intended to insert "the local" into "the global," following conventional views, but a type of place-based globalism (Osterweil 2005) that connects autonomous movements with each other. These alliances are seen in terms of "walking the word" (*caminar la palabra*), a concept developed by the Colombian Minga social y comunitaria to point at the need to come into visibility, make demands on society, and collectively weave knowledges, resistances, and strategies with other movements.

One final caveat about the notions of community and the communal: as the Buenos Aires militant research collective Colectivo Situaciones put it, rather than being a preconstituted entity or an "unproblematic fullness," the community "is the name given to a particular organizational and political code, a singular social technology"; in resisting being rendered an anachronism by the modern, the community summons "actualized collective energies"; as such, and "against all common sense, the community produces dispersion," and this dispersion could become central to the invention of amplified non-statist modes of cooperation (Colectivo Situaciones 2006, 212, 215). The appeal to community itself is thus not anachronistic, as moderns often dismissively reply; on the contrary, "the community summons actualized collective energies. . . . Communal doings and their openness to internal contradictions and ambivalence are a reflection of the radical contemporaneity of communities with respect to other modes of organization and cooperation"—including, one might say, standard modern forms that are by now more anachronistic (213, 215).

To speak of "communities in resistance" does not imply an essentialist or homogenizing vision of the community, as some critics adduce. It means understanding how, despite communities' fracture and fragmentation, communal actions might reveal "transition paths, beyond the dualism between modernity and postmodernity, universalism and communitarianism. . . . [They reveal] collective biographies of microrevolutions for self-determination" (P. Botero 2015, 17–19). That said, it is important to investigate exactly how, in the midst of the conflicts and heterogeneity that inevitably shape these communities because of their subaltern condition, there appear in them new forms of life, solidarity, and militancy. While the internal diversity of the communities might generate strife and disorganization under the pressure of intense repression and displacement, it often also yields types of intercultural diversity capable of broadening the processes by which they endow their worlds with meaning. These dynamics usually escape the attention of researchers too intent on finding antagonist oppositions in the midst of communities in struggle (which of course are also there). To go beyond this habitual research behavior requires a different epistemic positioning, one in which the researcher genuinely sees herself or himself as part of the collective action she or he is studying, as well as the willingness to interact with it. Far from disappearing, in many communities in struggle the collective dimension is woven out of plurality and disagreement (P. Botero and Perdomo 2013).

There is perhaps no clearer example of the openness of the communal at present than the decolonial and communitarian feminisms that are emerging in some popular and ethnic communities. For the Aymara intellectual-activist Julieta Paredes, communitarian feminism is a strategy for pursuing the twin goals of depatriarchalization (in relation to both autochthonous and modern patriarchies) and decolonization (in relation to liberal, modernizing, and capitalistic hegemonies, including individualizing Western feminisms). In this framework, the community is seen as "the inclusive principle for the caring of life" (Paredes 2012, 27). The community "is another manner of understanding and organizing society and of living otherwise. . . . It is an alternative proposal to that of individualistic societies" (31). This is why it implies an entire *tejido* (weave) of complementarities, reciprocities, and forms of autonomy and interculturality that include, for rural communities, relations to urban communities and transnational groups and, of course, the entire range of nonhumans. The community links together body, space, memory, and movement within a dynamic cyclic vision; this is the complex process that anchors the *Vivir Bien*, or collective well-being.

In all of these experiences, the community is thus understood in deeply historical, open, and nonessentialist terms. If anything, there is an emphasis on the creation of new spaces for the communal. It follows that the realization of the communal is always an open-ended historical process. In Maturana and Varela's (1980) language, as social systems, communities are third-order autopoietic entities whose "operational closure" (often coded in terms of "the defense of our culture" by locals) is maintained throughout the communities' relation to their "environment" (the sociopolitical and ecological context, broadly speaking); through this always-ongoing form of relating (structural coupling), communities may undergo structural changes of various types (e.g., by adopting the use of information and communication technologies or novel market practices); however, the basic system of relations has to be maintained for the community to preserve its autopoiesis, that is, its capacity for self-creation. *Autonomy* is the name given to this process.

Needless to say, communities' exercise of autonomy takes place today under astonishingly inimical conditions. The ongoing war on things communal also means that communal-based transition initiatives and territorial struggles indeed prefigure potential worlds to come (like the musics they sometimes create), yet they have to realize themselves within incredibly hostile environments that relentlessly undermine their efforts. This is the political ontology—held in place by capitalism, corporate coalitions, expert institutions, repressive and police states, and dualist rationalities—within which autonomous initiatives have to struggle. They surely cannot flourish in isolation, but perhaps the strategies of interweaving being tried out across myriad tiny islands of attempted autonomy might result in the renovated continents, however small for the time being, imagined by transition activists and designers. Can autonomous design contribute to this pluriversal realization of the communal?

This long historical, political, and theoretical background on autonomía and the communal has been necessary to convey the importance of placing autonomy within the scope of design, on the one hand, and of constructing the communal as a design space for ontologically oriented design, on the other. It was also a way to convey what the Latin American struggles' specific contributions to the *pensamiento* (thought) of transition might be.

An Outline of Autonomous Design

The remainder of this chapter will lay down additional elements for thinking about the relations among autonomy, design, and the realization of the communal. This will be done in three parts. The first identifies some principles for autonomous design, drawing on a particular experience in Colombia in the late 1990s; the second extends these lessons based on the chapter's discussion of autonomy and the communal. The third, finally, sketches a transition imagination exercise for a particular region in the Colombian southwest.

Autonomous design—as a design praxis with communities that has the goal of contributing to their realization as the kinds of entities they are— stems from the following presuppositions (slightly modified from PCN and Escobar 1998):[19]

1   *Every community practices the design of itself*: its organizations, its social relations, its practices, its relation to the environment. If for most of history communities practiced a sort of "natural design" independent of expert knowledge (ontonomy, spontaneous coping), contemporary situations involve design based on both detached and embodied forms of reflection.

2   Every design activity must start with the strong presupposition that *people are practitioners of their own knowledge* and from there must examine how people themselves understand their reality. This epistemological, ethical, and political principle is at the basis of both autonomy and autonomous design. (Conventional development planning is intended to get people to practice somebody else's knowledge, namely, the experts'!)

3   What the community designs, in the first instance, is *an inquiring or learning system about itself*. As designers, we may become co-researchers

with the community, but it is the latter that investigates its own reality in the codesign process.

4 Every design process involves a *statement of problems and possibilities* that enables the designer and the group to generate agreements about objectives and to decide among alternative courses of action (concerning the contamination of the river, the impact of large-scale mining, a particular food-production project, landlessness, the struggle to defend place and culture, discrimination against women, availability of water, etc.). The result should be a series of scenarios and possible paths for the transformation of practices or the creation of new ones.[20]

5 This exercise may take the form of building a model of *the system that generates the problem of communal concern*. Given this model, the question that every autonomous design project must face is: what can we do about it? The answer will depend on how complex the model of reality is. The concrete result is the design of a series of tasks, organizational practices, and criteria by which to assess the performance of the inquiry and design task.[21]

In building the model for the particular concern, it is important to recognize that *problem statements always imply solution statements*; problems never stand as neutral statements about reality; the entire process is political since any construction entails choices that affect people in particular ways. Problem statements are by the same token necessarily partial. The group's perception of the problem is continuously evolving as the conceptualization of it becomes more complex in light of new thinking, new information, more involved experimentation, and the like. The more complex the conceptualization of the system that produces the problem, the sharper the sense of purpose and of what needs to be done. Problem statements need to address the question, "Why do we/I see this as a problem?," and to follow each "because . . ." with another "why" until participants' values are made explicit. The design process also needs to broach the questions, What/who needs to change? Why is this change not happening now? What consequences would follow if such changes were to happen? And these inquiries must be repeated at various scales, including the household, community, and regional (e.g., river basin) levels and beyond.[22]

A problem statement is thus the *expression of a concern* that the group has about people's condition (ideally shared by the designer). In the last instance, what the autonomous design process wants to accomplish is to make not only the community but also the larger society more sensitive and responsive to the newly articulated concerns of the collectivity. This can be seen in terms of generating, out of the breakdowns that the systems' exercise unveils, a range of possibilities for disclosing new spaces for the exercise of community autonomy as the group deals with the problems at hand. It should be apparent by now that, according to this perspective, the ideal situation for autonomous design obtains when the client, the designer, the decision maker, and the guarantor of the system are the same entity (Churchman 1971), namely, the community and its organizations.

The workshop's systems methodology might seem a bit dated now, yet it is useful as a starting point for understanding autonomous design practices. In this particular instantiation in the Colombian Pacific, the workshop contributed to the creation of concepts and scenarios that, eventually, resulted in a framework developed by Afrodescendant movements (to some extent in conversation with indigenous activists) and provided the basis for a sophisticated political ecology by the movement, which I have analyzed at length elsewhere (Escobar 2008). Some of the key notions included that of the Colombian-Ecuadorian Pacific as a "region-territory of ethnic groups," the conceptualization of the territory as the space for the "life projects of the communities," a framework for the conservation of biodiversity based on the defense of territory and culture (very different from the established frameworks designed by conservation biologists and economists), and a set of guiding principles for the region's own vision of development and perspective on the future (Escobar 2008). Autonomía became central to the entire process. Figure 6.1 is a representation of the process (see PCN 2000, 2004).

We can recognize in this model the pillars of a design imagination centered on autonomy and the realization of the communal. Autonomía involves the articulation of the life project of the communities, centered on the *Vivir Bien* (the well-being of all, humans and nature), with the political project of the social movement, centered on the defense of the region-territory. (Notably, the notion of Vivir Bien in this framing is very similar to that of Buen Vivir that become well known in the 2000s, discussed in the last chapter.) While the life project is grounded in the long-standing relational ontology of the river communities (referred to as *cosmovision* during those years), the political project is based on the work of ethnoterritorial organizations, requiring the effective appropriation of the territories and guided by the communities' own vision of the future. Would it be too far-fetched to suggest that this particular social movement was pursuing a strategy of autonomous, ontologically ori-

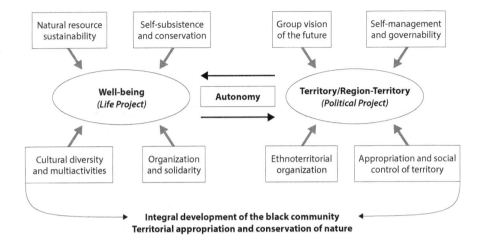

6.1 Basis for a culturally and ecologically sustainable development and perspective of the future. Redrawn based on diagram from PCN (2000: 5; 2004: 38).

ented design? In this and similar cases, one could argue that a codesign process is at play in which communities, activists, and some outside participants (including expert designers) engage in a collaborative exercise, with planner, designer, decision maker, and guarantor coinciding to a great extent with the communities and the movement.

It is noteworthy that this experience was based on the organizational principles agreed on by the Proceso de Comunidades Negras (Black Communities Process, PCN) since 1993 (and which remain in force to this day, even if in an enriched form that nevertheless maintains their basic structure). These principles include the affirmation of identity (the right to be black); the right to the territory (as the space for the exercise of being); autonomy (as the right to the conditions for the exercise of identity); the right to their own vision of the future, including the communities' right to choose their own model of development and of the economy according to their cosmovision; and the right to historical reparations (see Escobar 2008, 221–227). These principles anchor not only the internal decision making of the organization but its relation to the State and to other actors. In cases such as this, *it is of crucial importance for designers to develop a profound understanding of the political project of the movement* (not necessarily to share it in its entirety but to apprehend it fully) and to be willing to submit all codesign activities to the same principles. This is a sine qua non for working with political (say, ethnoterritorial) organizations under the rubric of autonomous design.

A Few Additional Features of Autonomous Design

From the theoretico-political discussion that occupied most of this chapter we can propose the following additional elements for thinking about autonomous design (again particularly for the Latin American context). Autonomy-oriented design

- Has as its main goal the realization of the communal, understood as the creation of the conditions for the community's ongoing self-creation and successful structural coupling with their globalized environments.
- Embraces ancestrality, as it emanates from the history of the relational worlds in question, and futurality, as a statement about futures for communal realizations.
- Privileges interventions and actions that foster nonliberal, non-State-centered, and noncapitalist forms of organization.
- Creates auspicious spaces for the life projects of communities and the creation of convivial societies.
- Considers the community's engagement with heteronomous social actors and technologies (including markets, digital technologies, extractive operations, and so forth) from the perspective of the preservation and enhancement of the community's autopoiesis.
- Takes seriously the transition design imperatives of place building, re-localization, renewed attention to materiality and nonhumans, and the creation of interepistemic collaborative organizations.
- Gives particular attention to the role of commoning in the realization of the communal; conversely, it devises effective means to encourage diverse economies (social and solidarity economies, alternative capitalist and noncapitalist economies).
- Articulates with the trends toward Buen Vivir and the rights of nature and with related trends elsewhere (e.g., degrowth, commons).
- Fosters pluriversal openings; it is, to this extent, a form of design for the pluriverse, for the flourishing of life on the planet.
- Thinks deeply about, and creates spaces for, strengthening the connection between the realization of the communal and the Earth (its relational weave at every place and everywhere), in ways that enable humans to

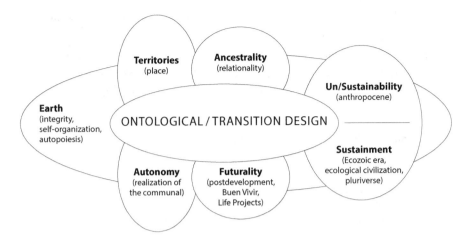

6.2 Autonomy, Transition, Sustainment. A framework for autonomous design and design for transitions.

relearn to dwell on the planet with nonhumans in mutually enhancing manners.

· Gives hope to the ongoing rebellion of humans and nonhumans in defense of relational life principles.

Conceived in this fashion, autonomous design can be considered a response to the urge for innovation and for the creation of new forms of life arising out of the struggles, forms of counterpower, and life projects of politically activated relational ontologies. This is, indeed, too much to place at the doorstep of any given theoretico-political imaginary. To restate, what is at stake here is not so much, or not only, how things are but how things can be. As Esteva puts it, "hope is not the conviction that something will happen, but the conviction that something makes sense, whatever happens" (2009, 22).

Figure 6.2 is a particular rendition of the framework presented thus far. By this point, the explanation of the diagram should be straightforward: the starting point of all design process for transition toward Sustainment, or toward an Ecozoic era, should be the Earth itself, the preservation of its integrity and self-organization. For the case of design with communities and social movements struggling for the defense of territory and place, the goal of the design process should be the strengthening of the community's autonomy and its continued realization. This design process takes place by building on the ancestrality of the community (its long-standing relational practices, however contradictorily they happen to take place) and orients itself toward futurality, embodied in the community's Life Project. The design process also takes place in resonance with the broad struggles of the day, such as those for postdevelopment and Buen Vivir. In the last instance, the aim is to transform the conditions that create unsustainability and defuturing and, hence, to provide a pluriversal alternative to the human-created anthropocene.

A Transition Imagination Exercise for the Cauca Valley Region in Colombia

Many regions in the world could be said to be ready to embark on significant cultural and ecological transitions, although few might be prepared for it. Afrodescendant movements in the Colombian Pacific have been engaging in this type of process since 2000, in a limited way given the onslaught of developmentalist and defuturing projects (Escobar 2008, 2014). In this region, the recalcitrant regional elites and State institutions continue to push economic strategies that will only increase eco-social devastation, violence, and unrest—against all scientific evidence and ecological, social, and cultural common sense. This region is in fact a prime laboratory for local and regional transition projects, and as such it can provide rich lessons for alternative pluriversal articulations.

On the other side of the western Andean cordillera, traveling eastward from the main Pacific port city of Buenaventura, lies the fertile Cauca River valley; this region could well be considered a poster child of development gone awry. Capitalist development based on sugarcane plantations in the plains and extensive cattle ranching on the Andean hillsides started to take hold in the late nineteenth century. It gained force in the early 1950s with the setting up of the Corporación Autónoma Regional del Cauca (Cauca Regional Autonomous Development Corporation), patterned after the famous Tennessee Valley Authority, with the support of the World Bank. By now it has become clear not only that this model of development based on sugarcane and cattle is exhausted but that it has caused massive ecological devastation of hills, aquifers, rivers, forests, and soils, besides profoundly unjust and painful social and territorial dislocation of the region's peasants and Afrodescendant communities. The region can easily be reimagined as a veritable agroecological stronghold of organic fruit, vegetable, grain, and exotic plant production and as a multicultural region of small and medium-size farm producers, a decentralized network of functioning towns and medium-size cities, and so forth. Other attractive futures can surely be imagined for this region.

Nevertheless, these futures are at present *unthinkable*, such is the strength of the hold the developmentalist imaginary has on most of the region's people and, of course, the power of elite control. While the region is ripe for a radical transition, this proposition is unthinkable to elites and most locals, and certainly to its middle classes, whose intensely consumerist lifestyle is inextricably tied to the model. Under these conditions, is a transition design exercise even possible? Moreover, could it have some real bearing on policy, mind-sets, actions, and practices? To raise this question means to put this chapter, and this book, on trial, so to speak. I am interested in showing, even if tentatively and again as a hypothesis, that even under such antagonistic conditions a transition design imagination can be set in motion. Let us see how.

The Cauca River Valley: Regional Development Gone Awry

The Cauca River, Colombia's second most important waterway, runs for 1,360 kilometers, flowing northward from its origin in the Colombian Massif, a group of high Andean mountains in Colombia's southwest. Seventy percent of Colombia's freshwater is said to originate in the massif. It is there also that the Andean mountain chain splits into three, giving origin to inter-Andean valleys, such as the Cauca Valley. The valley opens up progressively in between the western and central cordilleras (the latter has several snowy peaks above five thousand meters). The first part of the larger Cauca River basin (the focus of this exercise, known as the Alto Cauca, or upper Cauca) widens progressively, following the river for more than five hundred kilometers, covering an area of 367,000 hectares; its width ranges between fifteen and thirty-two kilometers. It is an incredibly beautiful valley, flanked by the two cordilleras and traversed by many smaller rivers and streams. The flat plains have an altitude of a thousand meters and an average temperature of twenty-five degrees centigrade. A traveler looking at the valley with a relational gaze in the 1950s would no doubt conclude that it could easily support a very pleasant and culturally and ecologically rich existence. Locals actually refer to the valley with the name of the most famous colonial hacienda still standing: El Paraíso (Paradise). This future, however, was being foreclosed by the 1950s as the defuturing forces gained speed and strength.

In terms of administrative divisions, most of the valley falls within the Valle del Cauca department, but an important area lies in the Cauca department to the south. The Alto Cauca starts at the Salvajina Dam, constructed in the mid-1980s by the Cauca Regional Autonomous Development Corporation to regulate the water flow of the river and to generate electricity for the growing agroindustrial complex centered in the city of Cali (population: 2.5 million) and for the city's growing middle classes. The geographic Cauca Valley is a bio-region also shaped by up to forty smaller river basins, several lagoons, and extensive wetlands, many of which were destroyed or severely impacted by cane cultivation. Its soils are very fertile, well drained, and of relatively low salinity. Superficial and deep aquifers have been a rich source of high-quality water for both agricultural use and human consumption. Historically, this ecological complex of mountains, forests, valley, rivers, and wetlands has been home to hundreds of plant and animal species. All of these features have been systematically undermined by the agroindustrial operations.

Even if the majority of the population of the region is mestizo, the Afrodescendant presence is very significant. There are several predominantly black municipalities in the Norte del Cauca (including the municipality of Buenos Aires, within the sphere of influence of the Salvajina Dam; the community of La Toma, whose resistance to gold mining was described in chapter 2, is also located in this municipality). Up to 50 percent of Cali's population is black, according to some estimates, which is largely the result of migration and forced displacement from the Pacific region over the past thirty years, making Cali's black population the second largest in urban Latin America after that of Salvador da Bahia (Brazil). This is an amazingly important social fact for any design project. Most of the black population is poor; at the other end of the spectrum there lies a small white elite, extremely wealthy, who pride themselves on their European ancestry. This elite has traditionally controlled most of the land and owned the largest sugar mill operations. In 2013, 225,000 hectares were planted in cane and 53,000 in pastures for cattle. Although only about sixty holdings are over five hundred hectares, this figure is deceiving since the large landholders also lease land or buy the cane produced on a large number of smaller farms exclusively dedicated to cane. The use of water in sugarcane cultivation is intensive, about 10,300 cubic meters per hectare in the region. This sector uses up 64 percent of all surface water and 88 percent of subterranean water. Over 670,000 hectares of hillsides (more than half of the total area) have been affected by extensive cattle ranching.[23]

Traveling up and down the valley on the main highway one sees what most locals consider a beautiful green landscape: hectare after hectare of sugarcane in the plains, almost without interruption, and cattle leisurely roaming the foothills. But this landscape is the result of more than a hundred years of ontological occupation of the valley by a heterogeneous assemblage made up of the white elite, cattle, cane, water (the dam, allegedly intended to control floods and regularize irrigation, plus the ubiquitous irrigation canals in the cane fields), chemicals (the tons of pesticides and fertilizers used in sugarcane cultivation), the State (the political elite, completely wedded to the model), experts (the Cauca Regional Autonomous Development Corporation in particular), global markets (demand for white sugar), and, of course, the black cutters, without whom the entire operation (despite increasing mechanization) would have been impossible. The black cutters actually refer to sugarcane as the green monster and associate it with the devil; for them it is far from a beautiful landscape (Taussig 1980). The entire assemblage is "concreted in" by a large network of roads, trucks (the *trenes cañeros*, or long trailer trucks loaded with cane, impossible to avoid if you are traveling by car, as sugarcane is cultivated year-round), and, of course, the entire industrial, financial, and service infrastructure in Cali and nearby towns.[24]

After more than a century of allegedly smooth functioning, of well-oiled operations by this heterogeneous assemblage—touted as a *milagro del desarrollo* (development miracle) by local elites and celebrated in folk culture in multiple ways, from soap operas to salsa music—its profoundly defuturing effects are finally becoming visible. They are visible in the exhaustion of soils, sedimentation of rivers, and contamination of aquifers; in the desiccation of wetlands, the erosion of biodiversity, the deforestation and severe erosion of hills and mountainsides, the respiratory health problems of black workers and nearby populations because of the ash they inhale during the periodic burning of the cane after cultivation, the repression against black workers' attempts to organize for better conditions, and the persistence of racism and profound inequality, all integral to the cane model.

Linked to inequality and the poverty of 60 percent of the population, as its inevitable result, is the high degree of "insecurity" and "delinquency" decried by the middle classes, who attempt to find security by living in heavily surveilled apartment complexes and gated communities, and by restricting a great deal of their social lives to the ubiquitous, well-policed, globalized shopping centers.[25] One wonders how the model goes on, year after year, despite its blatant and obvious failings, failings that some activists and a handful of academics and intellectuals are already beginning to identify, despite the apparent unawareness of most of the population and the absence of any critical voice in the dominant media, which continues to celebrate the model day in and day out, in so many forms. This is the challenging backdrop (not uncommon for regions in the Global South) against which any transition design strategy will have to be crafted. Let us discuss a few of the major aspects of this endeavor.

Generating a Transition Design Imagination
for the Cauca Valley

Even a purely theoretical transition design exercise for a region such as this is a daunting task, and even more so if one hopes for some degree of implementation. Yet considering the huge number of actual cases of impactful regional re/development and revitalization worldwide (including the famed Tennessee Valley Authority in the United States, and of course the Cauca Valley after the construction of the Salvajina Dam, all considered tremendously successful from a capitalistic perspective), the question arises, why not? Conventional regional re/development, it goes without saying, has the advantage of relying on the naturalized histories of capitalist development, whereas the type of regional transition envisioned here would go against the grain of such histories. Many of the design ideas discussed in previous chapters may, of course, be invoked in support of the exercise in question. However, as Colombian design theorist Andrea Botero, from the media lab at Aalto University in Helsinki, argues, "despite these advancements, our understanding of how to go about setting up, carrying on, and more broadly, sustaining collaborative and open-ended design processes in explicit ways is still limited" (2013, 13). As she goes on to say, there is a great need for methods that enable collaborative design over longer periods than usual, that elaborate on the evolving roles of designers under this extended temporality (beyond, say, being initiators or facilitators), and that take to heart the distributed nature of design agency, including, one needs to add, nonhumans. The articulation of design-in-use practices in the context of temporally extended collective design activities is particularly important at this point in time.

It is relatively easy for ecologists and transition activists and designers to propose scenarios to trigger the design imagination. I have proposed one such scenario above. Recall, first, the overwhelming landscape of omnipresent sugarcane and cattle, and their in/visible effects. Then try to reimagine it "as a veritable agroecological stronghold of organic fruit, vegetable, grain, and exotic plant production and as a multicultural region of small and medium-size farm producers, a decentralized network of functioning towns and medium-size cities, and so forth." Easy to imagine, perhaps, but still locally unthinkable. What follows are some elements that might go into a transition design exercise for the Cauca Valley to take place over a number of years (let's call it the *Cauca River Valley Transition Project*).[26]

There are two crucial tasks to be accomplished at the start of the project: gathering a codesign team and creating a design space with which the collaborative design team would coevolve. Creating an attractive identity for the design space might be useful, but that is just the start. The importance of the design space cannot be underestimated, as rightly underlined by Andrea Botero, Kari-Hans Kommonen, and Sanna Marttila (2013). These design theorists understand the design space "as the space of possibilities for realizing a design, which extends beyond the concept design space into the design-in-use activities of people" (186). The design space involves tools for mapping design activities aimed at locating participants' possibilities in a continuum from consumption to active creation. The design space is always coconstructed and explored by multiple actors through their social interactions involving technologies, tools, materials, and social processes. Through ongoing design activity, it becomes "the space of potentials that the available circumstances afford for the emergence of new designs" (188). The concept thus goes well beyond the focus on objects, workplaces, and design briefs to embrace design-in-use in all of its complexity, including of course the multiple users' inputs and designs. This expanded notion of design spaces might be particularly effective in what Botero calls "communal endeavors," those that "stand midway between being the project of a recognized community of practice or teams [say, La Toma's territorial organization] and being simply the coordinated actions of unidentifiable collectives or ad-hoc groups" (2013, 22).

In this dialogic space, design coalitions would create a new, radical vision for the valley and a vision for large-scale change, well beyond the business-as-usual adjustments. In the first year or two of the project, the coalitions and collaborative organizations involved would be tasked with the construction of an initial vision and framework for the transition(s). One could think of the design space as a kind of lab or set of labs where vision making and codesign meet, resulting in organized conversations for action (for instance, a Valle del Cauca Lab but also a Cali Lab, given the city's commanding presence in the valley; or labs focused on specific domains of social and ecological actions, whether soils, wetlands, workers, or what have you).

Given this overall objective (and the politically highly charged and controversial character that the process will take on as it evolves), at least in the initial phases of the Cauca River Valley Transition Project process, the actors involved in the codesign team will be limited. It will be essential that the main actors share the fundamental goals of the exercise in the broadest sense. That said, the actors should include at least the following sectors: social movement organizations (urban and rural, Afrodescendant, indigenous, peasant, and various urban groups); organizations of women and youth, particularly from marginalized rural and urban areas; the academy and intellectual life; arts and alternative communications and media. It will also be essential that this team be seeded with epistemic, social (in terms of race/ethnicity, gender, generation, class, and territorial basis), and cultural (ontological) diversity from the get-go, since this will be the only reasonable guarantee of a genuinely pluriversal design outcome. Activists, intellectuals, people from nongovernmental organizations, and academics, including those in the natural and physical sciences, are all in principle good candidates for the team (it should be said that it is not uncommon in Latin America for individuals to perform several of these roles, simultaneously or sequentially; in the Cauca Valley, there is a significant natural reservoir of persons already quite adept at carrying out interepistemic conversations). It will also be crucial for this team to develop the ability to think communally and relationally, in onto-epistemic terms (although of course not necessarily in these theoretical terms).[27]

The actual transition exercise would start to evolve from this initial process, and it would have to include both the continued *generation of contexts* capable of nourishing the idea of a transition and concrete projects intended to develop particular aspects of the design for social innovation (Manzini 2015).[28] Some of the goals and activities of this phase might include the following:

- Making visible the "civilizational breakdowns" and defuturing practices of the current model. What are the main ecological and social manifestations of unsustainability and defuturing (e.g., effects on water and soils, the systematic impoverishment of black workers, rampant consumerism, and destructive forms of extractivism, including gold mining, just to mention a few)? It will be necessary to map the political geology and ecology of sugarcane and cattle in newly creative ways, from the perspective of their materialist ontologies.
- Creating a sense of the region different from the "folk" regional narrative that prevails, particularly in Cali, dominated by sugarcane, salsa music, sports, and commerce. This would require articulating a *pluriversal bioregional notion* for the entire Alto Cauca, beyond the purely geographical or folk concept.

- Getting a sense of the diverse life projects of the communities and collectivities involved, including those in marginalized urban areas and even those seemingly without place and community.
- Promoting a diversity of actions, such as digital platforms to enable broader participation in the codesign process; thematic clusters and design labs; traveling interactive exhibits and labs to encourage and facilitate the generation of new imaginaries about and for the region in smaller towns and the countryside; compendia of realistic cases (particularly useful to demonstrate that "other economies are possible"); competing metastories; the collective creation of scenarios, whether grounded in existing cases extrapolated to fulfill the vision of a particular community or speculatively imagined to elicit open-ended design reflections.[29]
- Envisioning actions that privilege bottom-up, horizontal, and peer-to-peer methodologies and design tools, yet involve top-down elements as needed, although always subordinated to the goals arising from the communal dialogues. There will surely be many methodological hurdles to work through. For instance, how can one design spaces where collaborative organizations might create the conditions to dignify the manifold memories of the past, acknowledge the multiple overlapping worlds and reals, and consequently provide resonance for the numerous futures that populate the discursive and emotional space of the broad range of Cauca River valley inhabitants?
- Creating a series of "Cali Labs" intended to ascertain the range of answers to the question, "What do you want Cali to be?," to be followed by scenario building where the various visions can be put on display, along with potential transition and speculative design imaginaries developed by the codesign team—so that more and more people come to entertain an image of Cali as a truly hospitable space for dwelling, rather than an unsustainability machine that is rapidly destroying even its own rivers.
- Designing methods and tools to activate the multiple communal design histories (vernacular, diffuse, autonomous), found among so many rural and urban groups and in so many places throughout the valley, and their intersections with expert design.
- Assessing the impact of climate change on the various local worlds (peoples and ecosystems) by learning from the many transition initiatives in the world that are dealing with this question, such as the Transition Town Initiative, and strategically invoking broad transition imaginaries such as Buen Vivir and degrowth. This design aspect potentially touches

on everything: agriculture (as Via Campesina [2009] is fond of saying, "small farmers cool down the earth"), energy and transportation (diminishing the exponential growth of private cars and moving toward alternative light, decentralized transportation systems), city planning, commons (parks and recreation), and so forth. The concept of resilience, resituated in the ontological context of autonomous worlds, might be important in this area.

- Creating art and communications media and digital platforms for the transitions. Performance art (including about nonhumans, for example, about how to "liberate" the exhausted soils and bring them back to life), transition music and dance (building on the region's strong musical traditions, including salsa and the black musics from the Pacific and Norte del Cauca regions), social media, and new mainstream media contents that destabilize the folk discourse about the region and position the new one in the collective imaginary will all be integral to the design task. This aspect will build on strong popular education and communication sectors that have been present in the region since the 1980s. There is a great potential in the transition imagination to generate an unprecedented wave of cultural activism.

There is a whole range of other issues that could be considered from the viewpoint of transition design frameworks, such as the relation between diffuse and expert design; the creation of knowledges that might travel from one location to another; the learning process as the project moves on; the role of design research; the use of prototypes and maps; the creation of scenarios under rubric of small, local, open, and connected strategies (Manzini 2015); digital and live storytelling; the design of tool kits from and for communal spaces; smart media campaigns; and questions of scale, among others.

This presentation is of course extremely tentative and general. It is offered more as an indication of the kind of design inquiries that might be at play in transition efforts than as an actual road map to be followed. I am perfectly aware of the overly ambitious nature of the proposal. Let us say that it was intended largely as a theoretical exercise and, as such, as a contribution to critical design studies. It was also intended to buttress the idea that "another design is possible," a design for the pluriverse. At the same time, it might be considered an example of the dissenting design imagination that, as this book has tried to show, is emerging in various design domains. Perhaps, in the last instance, this effort was my imperfect attempt at making a political-ontological statement by relying on those ultradesigned spaces we call the academy and the book.

Let us listen once again to the words of Nasa activists of the Northern Cauca region as a way to conclude; they bring to the fore both the stakes and the kind of alliances that might be forged:

> As we said in 2005 and say again now, the releasing (*la desalambrada*, or getting rid of the barbed wire) of Uma Kiwe (Mother Earth) will depend on uncoiling the heart (*desalambrar el corazón*). And uncoiling the heart is going to depend on uncoiling Mother Earth. Who would have believed it: heart and earth are one single being. That is what we know and feel in this moment. Being this way, should we get on the train of progress? . . . Looking at it clearly, we are left with but one path: we have been saying it for years, but now it gains strength: au-ton-o-my. It is not difficult to see it if the heart is awake. And, speaking of autonomy, it is something very simple: to live as we like and not as is imposed on us. To take life where we want it to go and not where a boss—whoever he might be—says we have to be. But we cannot live autonomy without a territory. And there cannot be territory without Mother Earth. And there is no Mother Earth as long as she is enslaved. . . . That is why we have returned to our farms since December 2014. This is why these are our farms and not others. . . . In that way we return to the path of autonomy, and we open the trail to the freedom of Uma Kiwe. We know . . . that we are capable of a little, and that we can only learn and triumph as an entanglement, a heap (*en montonera*). Not only of male and female Indians: *una motonera* (a swarm) with peasants, with Afrodescendants, with people from the city. It is true that the doubt is sown and is strong. We invite you to turn off the television and look at one another face-to-face: our history, our struggle, our words, which are clumsy but sincere. . . . Turn on your flashlight and illuminate well. Then you will see clearly that this struggle is out of Northern Cauca and not from or for Northern Cauca. Out of the Nasa people but not of the Nasa people. Every freed farm, here or in any corner of the world, is a territory that adds up to reestablish the equilibrium of Uma Kiwe. It is our common house, our only one. There it is, yes: come in, the door is open.[30]

In this incredibly lucid statement lies the basis for autonomous and transition design praxes, to be developed a bit further in the conclusion. *The door is open.*

Coda: The Communal in the Case of the Peoples without Community

Tell me how the universe came about, and I will tell you who you are.

We can choose who we wish to become when we have decided on an in principle undecidable question.

· **von Foerster,** "Ethics and Second-Order Cybernetics"

It is often said that the notions of relationality and the communal apply only to rural or indigenous peoples, or to those cases where people maintain an attachment to a territory; in other words, they do not apply to urban moderns always on the move. This is a partial truth at best, for we all exist within the pluriverse. For those of us who live in the delocalized and intensely liberal worlds of middle-class urban modernity, the historical imperative is clearly that of recommunalizing and reterritorializing. New territories of existence and novel forms of being communal need to be imagined, many of them unprecedented, appropriate to the age of unsettlement. For those of us without an ancestral mandate to help our worlds persevere, the question becomes, how do we recreate and recommunalize our worlds? How do we develop forms of knowing that do not take words and beings and things out of the flow of life—that is, forms of knowing and being that do not recompose nature as external to us, as dead or unsentient matter? What kinds of rituals might we develop to this end? How do we render our inevitable existential condition of being *entre mundos*, between worlds, into a hopeful praxis of living, a space for contributing to stitch worlds together within a pluriversal ethics?

The fact is that we are not just individuals; while each of us is indeed a singular person, we inevitably exist as knots or relays in networks—nay, weaves—of relations. The communal is the name we give to these entanglements and weaves. There is no contradiction between the singular person and the communal as the space within which she or he always exists in relation. As Ivan Illich liked to put it (Gustavo Esteva, pers. comm., July 28, 2015), for those of us who were not born in the midst of a community and who have been constructed as individuals by our histories, there is always friendship and love as the seeds to forge new commons.

Gloria Anzaldúa refers to the condition currently faced by many people as "living in nepantla, the overlapping space between different perceptions and belief systems" (2002, 541), or living between worlds. This condition renders conventional categories of identity obsolete, calling for new paradigms and narratives that enable creative engagement with each other and the Earth. For Anzaldúa, being a *nepantlera* means inhabiting a zone of possibility, not a cause for fear or closing borders. It is an occasion for imagining and creating a "new tribalism" (560), one that avoids the old story or either assimilation or separation. She calls on us to move from the militarized zone of divisions to a roundtable that always ackowledges the kinship among all things and people. "When you relate to others, not as parts, problems, or useful commodities, but from a connectionist view, compassion triggers transformation" (569). Herein lies an ethical principle for relational recommunalization.

Conclusion

Tanto vivir entre piedras,
Yo creí que conversaban.
Voces no he sentido nunca,
Pero el alma no me engaña.

Algún algo han de tener
Aunque parezcan calladas.
No en vano ha llenado Dios
De secretos la montaña.

Algo se dicen las piedras.
A mí no me engaña el alma.
Temblor, sombra o qué sé yo,
Igual que si conversaran.

Ah, si pudiera algún día
Vivir así, sin palabras.

I lived among stones so long,
I thought I heard them talking.
It wasn't exactly with voices,
But something more gently rocking.

They've got something going on
As they sit there so discreetly.
Not in vain did God, after all,
Load the mountain with secrets.

Something they say to each other
I feel it within my soul
A tremor, a shadow, who knows what,
The same as if they were talking

Ah! If only I could live just like that,
someday, speechless.

· Argentinean poet and folk singer
Atahualpa Yupanki

Atahualpa Yupanki's poem transports us to a universe where even stones have a life of sorts. Yupanki's songs incarnate a philosophy of place, territory, and landscape. These cosmovisions animate the thought for the transitions of many communities. Transition ideas are being elaborated explicitly by many groups. As Guillermo Palma, a Rarámuri indigenous activist, puts it, "tenemos que autopensarnos a nosotros mismos para defendernos" ("we have to auto-think ourselves in order to defend ourselves").[1] While each social group, or socionatural assemblage, needs to broach this process out of its own resources and historical circumstances, no single social formation has the complete onto-epistemic architecture necessary to deal with the hydra of global capitalism, as the Zapatista call it. In some instances, designers can build on, and help catalyze, the emergent transitions in their own locations through situated transition design practices.

Rather than summing up or even revisiting the book's main arguments, I would like to rearticulate some of the questions that will undoubtedly remain a matter of debate as a way to conclude. These questions bring forth the highest stakes for design. In a way, they make the book unravel as it ends, hopefully to be rewoven by others in their own ways, or at least return its arguments to their status as hypotheses. Before tackling these questions, however, I start this conclusion in an epistemic-political register to propose a principle for transition thinking and design, that of the Liberation of Mother Earth. This is followed by brief remarks on "designs from the South," and finally a discussion of open questions, including modernity, technology, futures, and the university.

The Liberation of Mother Earth as Transition Design Principle

A new statement travels the world: *La Liberación de la Madre Tierra* (the Liberation of Mother Earth). Recently expressed by the Nasa people, it echoes in many corners of the planet and announces other worlds to come. "But we say—as long as we continue to be indigenous, in other words, children of the earth—that our mother is not currently free for life, but she will be when she returns to being the soil and collective home of the peoples who take care of her, respect her, and live with her. As long as it is not this way, neither will we be free, her children. All peoples are slaves along with the animals and all beings of life, as long as we do not achieve that our mother recovers her freedom."[2]

It is somewhat paradoxical that statements of this sort are uttered in contexts of war and aggression against communities. But it is precisely because what is at stake in these contexts is the defense of life that the emphasis on the complementarity between humans and nonhumans emerges with particular clarity and force ("who would have believed it: heart and earth are one single being").[3] These narratives of communities in resistance evince a kind of knowledge that, "while a reflection of ancestral wisdom, is not an issue of essential identities, but rather signals the possibility of widening the meaning and practices of togetherness within a process of collective weaving" (P. Botero 2013, 50). Ancestrality, in the view of many of these collectives, implies actively looking at the future.

What I am proposing is that all transition thinking needs to develop this attunement to the Earth. In the end, it seems to me that a plural sense of civilizational transitions that contemplates—each vision in its own way—the *Liberation of Mother Earth* as *a fundamental transition design principle* is the most viable historical project that humanity can undertake at present. Elsewhere, in an article about the state of Latin American critical thought, I argued that critical thought today is an interweaving of three threads: leftist thinking, autonomous thought, and the thought of the Earth. While these threads overlap, they are distinct. The Left's concerns with exploitation, domination, inequality, and social justice are as important as ever, yet much leftist thinking continues to be anthropocentric, patriarchal, ethnocentric, and universalizing, and its view of transitioning to socialism or postcapitalism is limiting. Many of the autonomy thinkers, for their part, maintain ontological commitments to unexamined forms of anthropocentrism, hence the need to imbue autonomous thought with a strong notion of relationality. Finally, the thought of the Earth—or rather, *sentipensar con la Tierra*, thinking-feeling with the Earth (Escobar 2014)—does not refer so much to ecological thinking as to the profound conviction of our indissoluble connection with the Earth and with everything that exists in the universe, the unity of all beings.

The thought of the Earth has its own implications, eloquently expressed by the nasa activists in the same text: "Nos liberamos con la tierra para convivir. Este es nuestro llamado y compromiso. Esto significa no solo liberar la tierra y empoderarse de la lucha, sino también liberar el pensamiento, el corazón, las voluntades, la identidad, la alegría, la conciencia y la esperanza." (We free ourselves as we free the Earth so that we can live together well. This is our call and our commitment. This does not mean only to liberate the land and empower ourselves through the struggle, but to free up the thought, the heart, the will, identity, happiness, consciousness, and hope.) Like in Bob Marley's stunningly political "Redemption Song," each person and each group will need to reflect on this call in her or his own way.[4]

Building Bridges between Design for Transitions in the Global North and in the Global South

In *The Darker Side of Western Modernity*, the decolonial theorist Walter Mignolo (2011) identifies five global trajectories that, in his view, shape possible futures: de-Westernization, re-Westernization, reorientations of the Left, spiritual options, and decolonial options. The latter two can be seen as "roads to re-existence delinking from the belief that development and modernity are the only way to the future" (64). Which future prevails will depend on the struggles and negotiations among these trajectories, likely without a winner. "If there is a winner," Mignolo adds, "it would be the agreement that global futures shall be polycentric and noncapitalist. Which means that a struggle for world domination . . . would yield to pluriversality as a universal project" (33–34). Citing Humberto Maturana's maxim that "when one puts objectivity in parentheses, all views, all verses in the multiverse are equally valid. Understanding this, you lose the passion for changing the other" (27), Mignolo goes on to expound the decolonial option as the clearer path toward the pluriverse. This is a hopeful vision. It seems to me that one could explicitly posit emergent visions of transitions as another historical force within the spectrum of trajectories. Transition thinking may be found in the leftist, spiritual, and decolonial pathways imagined by Mignolo; however, in the senses discussed here—as an array of explicit discourses and imaginations—it cannot be encompassed within any of them.

This book is about redesigning design from within and from without, a project on which a number of design thinkers, as we have seen, are already embarked. Little is known about how this process is taking place in the Global South, and in this book I have dealt with this issue only obliquely, through my discussion of transition narratives and autonomous design. The process of building bridges between transition design visions in the Global North and the Global South has already commenced. This goal is present, for instance, in Colombian design theorist Alfredo Gutiérrez Borrero's (2015a) conceptual framework that explicitly speaks about "el sur del diseño y el diseño del sur" (the south of design and the design of the south), where *south* stands as an onto-epistemic border where pluriversal theoretico-practical design projects might emerge. In contradistinction with much northern design practice, with its instrumental and commercial orientation, such projects would explore viable designs stemming from communal worlds, where each community would practice the design of itself on the basis of local, decolonial knowledges (Gutiérrez Borrero 2014, 2015a, 2015b). Knowledges and ontologies from the South would act as alternative operating systems enabling autonomous forms of design. This sort of "anti-industrial design"—or, rather, way of provincializing industrial design as one possibility among many—explicitly aims at designs for conviviality.

Diseños del sur also stands for the rich variety of *diseños otros* (other designs and design otherwise) associated with notions that name the onto-political thrust of groups embarked on their own alternatives to hegemonic modernity, such as Buen Vivir, *ubuntu*, swaraj, or degrowth (Kothari, Demaria, and Acosta 2015). Finding inspiration in the Lakota principle of *mitakuye oyasin* that posits that not only humans are persons but also rocks, soil, rivers, plants, and even things, Gutiérrez Borrero goes on to posit southern forms of design based on a relational ontology of multiple personhood. From here he draws a vital question:

> What happens, then, when we design on the basis of design thinking based on other notions and by other names, of sciences which are not such, in order to create alternatives to development with technologies and industries that are something else? We are confronted by older idioms that we are just beginning to hear anew, and by epistemologies in search of aliases. Designs from the south were always there, albeit with other names, we are just starting to perceive them. It takes time to recognize them. Now we need to begin the task of designing with them and of letting ourselves be designed by them. (2015a, 126)

This listening to design's idioms from the Global South animates a recent set of essays assembled under the concept of "design in the borderlands" (Kalantidou and Fry 2015). Explicitly conceived from the perspective of the geopolitics of design knowledge, and in full acknowledgment of design's Eurocentrism and its status as a global force, the volume attempts to "unconceal the way that design operates within a global world order" and, conversely, to ascertain the role that design can play in creating decolonial futures (Pereira and Gillett 2015, 109). While paying attention to both "the globalization of Eurocentric power by design" and "the design of globalization by the Eurocentric mind"

(Fry and Kalantidou 2015, 5), the volume argues for the existence of "contra-Western understandings of design" (6) and illustrates instances of place-based design practices that enact such counterdiscourses. One learns in the volume about resourceful vernacular design practices by other names (for instance, in Africa), the emergence of the design profession in various parts of the world, the possibilities for ontological redesigning in the Global South, and the helpful notion of "designing for creative ontological friction" in a way that "explicitly and reflexively recognizes ontological difference across different social formations" (James 2015, 93). The result is both a pluralization of the history of design and the beginning of a genealogy of decolonial design practices.

The borderlands are strategically important spaces for the reconstitution of an ethics and praxis of care in relation to what ought to be designed, and how. For Tony Fry (2017), this would be an ontology of repair of the broken beings and broken worlds that have resulted from centuries of defuturing designing and their alleged accumulated outcome, the anthropocene. Herein lies the possibility of, and ground for, the reconstitution of design in, for, and from the South, not as a total rejection of design but as "critical selection and local innovation" (46) involving the creation of structures of care toward the Sustainment:

> The central issue and project for design of/by and for the South is another kind of ontological designing—one based on the creation of structures of care able to constitute the Sustainment. . . . How can a designer be designed to be a provider of care via the designing of things that ontologically care? The answer to this question requires acknowledging that a new kind of designer depends upon the arrival of a transformed habitus. . . . [It requires an] understanding of design's implication in the state of the world and the worlds within it. To gain this understanding means fully grasping the scale and impact of design as an ontological force of and in the world in its making and unmaking. . . . Acquiring such knowledge leads the proto-designer to learn how to read what is brought into being by design causally. Thereafter, what design serves is the creation of a future with a future. (28, 29)

The constitution of a field of "design for/by/from the Global South" is thus a very welcome and timely call, for two main reasons: first, because much of what goes on under the banner of design in the Global North is not appropriate for design in the South (and increasingly inappropriate to a North in crisis as well); and, second, because there is great potential in design's reorientation to serve a range of theoretical and political projects in the South.

The convergence between transition design narratives in the North and in the South can also be explored by positing the existence of two converging dynamics responding to the defuturing and delocalization effected by the global order: the first dynamic is Ezio Manzini's *cosmopolitan localism*, "capable of generating a new sense of place," as a historical condition of communities (2015, 25). This dynamic occurs more readily within the Global North, given the extent of the decommunalization of societies and the specific imperative of relocalization that ensues. Cosmopolitan localism entails a dynamic reinvention of the communal through a multiplicity of activities concerning food, the economy, crafts, and care. Many of these activities can also be seen in the Global South. Yet, and this is the second dynamic, there are other, somewhat specific dynamics in the Global South where old (vernacular) and new forms of design combine, yielding an entire range of situations, from improvisational design for survival to the design of urban neighborhoods out of displacement, and from alternative capitalist and noncapitalist economies to autonomous struggles for Buen Vivir. Would it be too far-fetched to see in these twofold, albeit glaringly uneven, dynamics a convergence of the sort intuited by Manzini? "All of these ideas, the activities they refer to, and the relationships they generate seem to me beautiful islands of applied cultural and socioeconomic wisdom. They are islands in the sea of unsustainable ways of being and doing that is, unfortunately, still the mainstream throughout the world. The good news is that the number of these islands is growing and generating a wide archipelago. An archipelago that could be seen as the emerging dry land of a rising continent: the already visible expression of a new civilization" (26).

These convergences are of course not guaranteed. Transition design needs to deepen its critique of capitalism and liberalism and its awareness of the ways in which it still shelters modernist commitments such as belief in the individual, anthropocentrism, and reliance on political processes that depend, by their very nature, on the ontology of subjects and objects.[5] Northern transition design visions need to think decolonially and postdevelopmentally, as discussed in chapter 5. Conversely, autonomous design, diseños otros, and designs from the South need to broach the questions of innovation and technoscience in earnest. In this it has a lot to learn from ecological design in northern visions. To return to Manzini: "I think that what social innovation is indicating, with its idea of a well-being based on the quality of places and communities, is the seed of a new culture. Or better, a metaculture which could be the platform for a multiplicity of cultures [a pluriverse] . . . the culture of a society in which places and communities are not isolated entities but become nodes in a variety of networks . . . helping to create a resilient planet where it would be possible for us and for future generations to live, and hopefully to live well" (207). The convergence of transition design, design for autonomy, and diseños otros might prove to be a powerful force for counteracting the centuries-old but ongoing ontological occupation of people's lives (communities, territories, places) by the nonconvivial technologies of patriarchal capitalist modern designs. By connecting to each other, they might extend like rhizomes, possibly emerging into local and regional topologies of partially connected worlds, eventually leading to the rising continents of relational living envisioned by Manzini and others.

Some Open Questions

Finally, I would like to tackle a set of interrelated questions concerning modernity, technology, futures, the communal, the pluriversal, and the university as a way to conclude. What follows is offered in the spirit of a counterpoint to what has already been said, that is, by getting at the issues from somewhat different vantage points as a way to giving them a different form.

The Question of Modernity

First, the question of modernity. To paraphrase: it is easier to imagine the end of the world than the end of modernity. This is a question that does not go away completely. As Humberto Maturana and Gerda Verden-Zöller say, "our human existence is one in which we can live whatever world we bring about in our conversations, even if it is a world that finally destroys us as the kind of being that we are" (2008, 143). Might the civilizational conversation called modernity be at risk of reaching this point? If modernity is ineluctably all we have to go on, then this book's propositions could legitimately be qualified as romantic or utopian (as they inevitably will be by many).

Let me attempt, however, two final displacements of modernity's centrism. We already encountered Ashis Nandy's telling reversal that the pathologies of science-driven modernity have already proven to be more lethal than the pathologies of traditions. Beyond a handful of philosophical treatises, we in the Global North rarely entertain seriously the end of modernity; actually, most scholars react strongly and disdainfully against such a proposition, disqualifying it as utopian or even reactionary. It is, however, implicit (though rarely stated out loud) in most transition discourses. None other than the revered Buddhist teacher Thich Nhat Hanh has spoken openly about it in his critique of consumerism: "This civilization of ours will have to end one day. But we have a huge role to play in determining when it ends and how quickly. . . . Global warming may be an early symptom of that death" (2008, 43–44). He goes further, inviting us to actively accept the end of our civilization by meditating on this thought: "*Breathing in, I know that this civilization is going to die. Breathing out, this civilization cannot escape dying*" (55). This is the call that the transition "bells of mindfulness" makes to us: to move beyond a civilization that has become so antithetical to the ontology of interbeing.[6]

There is a second tactic we can take in relation to modernity, akin to J. K. Gibson-Graham's analysis of capitalism and political economy (Gibson-Graham 2006; Gibson-Graham, Cameron, and Healy 2013); this would include three steps: first, to deconstruct the modern centrism of most social theory, that is, the way in which social theory's lenses inevitably endow modernity with the ability to fully and naturally occupy the field of the social, so as to make invisible or secondary other ways of constructing societies; second, to reconstruct our understanding of the social by positing the existence of modern, alternative modern, and nonmodern (or amodern) forms of being, knowing, and doing; and, third, to inquire into how we can foster the alternative modern and nonmodern forms collectively. This would include the question of how we might cultivate ourselves as subjects who desire noncapitalist, nonliberal, and nonmodern forms of life. For under the visible part of the iceberg of the social (what is perceivable as conventionally modern) there lies an entire set of practices that can hardly be described as modern and that perhaps can be theorized as nonmodern or amodern (besides those that are clearly anti-modern). This is a theoretico-political project that still remains to be done.[7]

A common strategy by critical scholars is to pluralize modernity. There is a risk, however, in doing so. While it makes a lot of sense to speak about alternative or multiple modernities worldwide—different European modernities, Latin American modernities, Chinese or Arab modernities, or what have you—the risk is to reintroduce, through the back door of the premise of a single shared world or real, the universality of dominant modern ways of seeing. A second danger is to absolve modernity from any wrongdoing, since after all many of those who are "differently modern" (say, among peripheral or nondominant European regions or cultures) will argue that they never were part of the dominant modern order (from which they have nonetheless benefited immensely). To avoid these risks, the pluralization of modernity will have to be done decolonially—that is, keeping in sight three processes: dominant modernity's negation of other worlds' difference, the resistance and excess constituted by subaltern subjects at the fractured locus of the colonial difference (Lugones 2010b; de la Cadena 2015), and the challenges to the dominant modern core stemming from nondominant modern sources. In other words, *all worlds need to broach the project of remaking themselves from the critical perspective of their historical location within the modern/colonial world system.*[8]

For moderns, actively facing the ontological challenges posed by the idea of the end of modernity—of a world significantly or radically different from the current one—is not easy; it induces a type of fright that is deeply unsettling. Ontologically oriented design needs to articulate this civilizational anxiety in effective ways. After all, most other worlds have had to exist (and still do) with the fright and, not infrequently, the reality of their vanishing. An important element in the strategy of nondominant or alternative moderns would be to *effectively activate* their specific critique of the dominant modern (which would place them in the position of fellow travelers, not enemies, of those who uphold more explicitly positions that are "beyond modernity").

Rationality, Technoscience, and the Real

Closely related is the thorny assessment of science and its rationality. Is technoscience even partially adaptable or reversible, as all transition narratives implicitly assume? Is this not also a rather baseless and naive desire? Any redesigned design philosophy must articulate a critique of the rationalistic tradition and reconstruct its own mode of rationality, open to the plurality of modes of consciousness that inhabits the pluriverse. But is this really possible? This does not mean an antiscience position; in fact, none of the authors invoked in these pages sustains such a position. Nandy's approach is illustrative: "Modernity knows how to deal with those who are anti-science or anti-technology; it does not know how to deal with those using plural concepts of science and technology" (1987, 137), which is the case for most of our authors, from Ivan Illich and Francisco Varela to Enrique Leff and Val Plumwood.[9] The social movements invoked here openly allow for creative, critical uses of modernity within traditions, but they insist on doing so from the perspective of local autonomy, subordinating science and technology to buen vivir and to strengthening the convivial fabric of life. The same holds for engagement with markets and the economy: these should be subordinated to buen vivir according to place-based criteria, rather than the other way around. To argue that the critics and activists believe otherwise is to perform a travesty of their actual concepts and practices.

Always at play in these debates is the question of the real. By its very nature, this question will remain unsettled. The position I have taken in this book is consistent with a philosophy of strong relationality: an epistemology and ontology *without* subjects, objects, and processes that are inherently or intrinsically existent by themselves—what biologist Kriti Sharma (2015) calls radical contingentism. It is our epistemologies and ontologies that sustain "both the sense of *separateness* of objects from subjects and the sense of *interaction* of objects with subjects" (100). Subjects, objects, processes, structures, essential properties and identities, and so forth depend on these assumptions. This folk essentialism is stronger for those of us who go on living in the Cartesian theater. Some spiritual traditions like Buddhism and animism and many traditional cosmologies have ways to diffuse these essentialisms or hold them at bay (through particular practices and rituals but often through mundane daily practices of interbeing). Shifting our existence—our bodies, minds, and souls—into a relational ontology challenges any objectifying notion of a real. To listen to Sharma once more:

> Sometimes when we come across a spider's web, it can be difficult to find where it's anchored; yet the assumption is that it is anchored somewhere; it is easy to assume that the dense net of experiences is anchored somewhere—in a world of objects, or a body, brain, or soul. We often believe that the regularities we experience must be grounded in some kind of substance *beyond* them—material, spiritual, or mental. However, it is entirely possible that the net is aloft, that it is not tethered to anything outside of it. In fact, as far as anyone can tell, the net is *all there is*, so there can be nothing outside of it that could serve as a tether. (100–101)

So-called traditional peoples have no problem living with this realization. For the Kogui of the Sierra Nevada de Santa Marta, each act of living is an act of weaving—one weaves life in thought as much as on the land, and certainly in resistance; indeed, it is in the loom that all the elements of the world come together. The Kogui, moreover, live with the conviction that their weaving is essential for the balance of the universe as a whole. In the Fanti-Ashanti tradition from the Gulf of Benin, the bisexual spider god/goddess Anansi incessantly weaves life from her own material and cognitive resources (Lozano 2015; Arocha 1999). Since the conquest and slavery, her threads unite Africa and America, and in the Colombia Pacific, Anansi is said to have created the fractal jungle and the meandering estuaries with threads she pulled out of her belly. She or he continues to link each newborn to the territory through the practice of the *ombligada*, which in the Pacific is carried out by midwives.[10] For Betty Ruth Lozano (2015), Anansi is a metaphor of survival and self-sufficiency, and midwives must be seen as practitioners of reexistence and as spiritual leaders who embody an insurgent imagination. It is thus that these relational worlds struggle to persevere as the kind of worlds they are, even if under ferocious attack.

Those of us who inhabit the liberal worlds of "real realities" and "autonomous individuals" can certainly come to understand the profound insights of relationality theoretically; yet conceptual analysis can carry us only partway in the journey toward more relational living. To the theoretical work we need to add some form of practice that takes us into other habits and modes of living and interexisting, of being in a world that is made up of things that are real yet not inherently independent.[11] Shifting to the terrain of practice places us in a situation, from the realists' perspective, where the question of the real can never be ultimately settled, so it shall remain so.

Do "Traditional Communities" Design? Toward a Practice of *Disoñar* (Designing-Dreaming)

This brings me to one of the most intractable questions about nondualist approaches to design, which I have bracketed thus far. The question has two corresponding, though seemingly unconnected, sides. First, is it really possible to come up with a notion of nondualist design that avoids the modern ontology of Enframing, within which everything that exists does so as "standing reserve" for instrumental human purposes (Heidegger 1977)? In other words, is *nondualist design* not an oxymoron, for is design not always about human projects and goal-oriented change, about an analytics and ethics of improvement and an inescapable ideology of the *novum*, that is, of development, progress, and the new? Moreover, why use the word *design* at all, especially for nonmodern contexts? This is the other side of the concern: is it advisable to use the concept of design in connection with struggles for autonomy by communities and collectives struggling precisely to keep dualist ontologies and instrumentalizing technologies at bay? Would it not make more sense to declare these communities "design-free territories"? After all, is not the utopia of some of them that of preserving their ability to live outside of, or beyond, the damaging designing effected by patriarchal capitalist modern life?[12]

The question of designless communities is posed indirectly by Maturana and Verden-Zöller:

Our ancestors in non-patriarchal cultures lived in a systemic dynamic interconnectedness within a cosmos that they were aware of and able to integrate. And as they lived their cosmic interconnectedness, they lived it in a systemic thinking of multidimensional coherences that they knew how to evoke but could not describe in detail. In that way of living they were not concerned with controlling the different aspects of their existence. *They just lived them*; and they did so through the conservation of practices that both conserved and realized their harmonious participation in the cosmic dynamics of their daily living in the human community to which they belonged. (2008, 126; emphasis added)

We find related arguments in ethnographic engagements with nonmodern peoples. Amazonia ethnology, for instance, shows how elders throughout the region used to hold—some still do, though more precariously—a complex shamanic knowledge of the entire Amazon basin, without ever having traveled far from their own places, and despite their different locations and languages, from Colombia and Peru to Brazil. This knowledge was grounded in a tight relation between the level of thought (*pensamiento*) and that of practice. The practices—concerning community spaces, water and plant worlds, cultivation and food, fishing and hunting, healing, and so forth—simply enacted what was already known in thought (this is the "they just lived them" part of the above quote, but according to a systemic knowledge of the world). There used to be agreement among the various groups on how to live and manage the territory. All of this points to the existence of a lived knowledge out of which entire worlds were (and to some extent still are) constructed. As some designers argue, there is a design process in these knowledge practices, even if without any explicit design concept. Much of this came under attack with colonialism, evangelization, and development, and even more so today with extractivism in indigenous territories.[13]

My argument is that the conditions for spontaneous relational living only partially exist at present; hence, designlessness as such is a forgone historical possibility, even if it can still be posited as a desirable horizon. Said otherwise, while many territorial communities could be said to live life according to implicit relational knowledge (akin to Varela's ethical know-how), it is also the case that all communities are variously thrown into the process of having to practice both embodied and detached reflexivity about their historical circumstances, sometimes even as a matter of sheer survival. How to design without instrumentalizing relations (especially without pushing these relations further into an objectifying and individualizing mode of hierarchy and control) becomes a crucial question. Caroline Gatt and Tim Ingold's (2013) nonteleological and open notion of design offers one such approach, one capable of giving direction to collective processes without fixed end points, pathways without targets, weavings rather than blueprints, *planes de vida* (life projects) rather than conventional plans, and so forth. It seems to me that the frameworks of transition design, design for social innovation, autonomous design, and diseños otros aim in this direction, even if often falling short of the task, whether because of the demands of strategy, lack of clarity about what is at stake, organizational pressures, or what have you.

That said, I believe the issue of whether indigenous communities design should remain an open question. But from this provisional discussion we can rearticulate the question in a way that applies to communities and social groups in many parts of the world: how do we make *effective weavings* and foster mutually enhancing entanglements of worlds *in the face of the catastrophe* visited on the planet by the current global capitalist One-World order? Earth's territories, including cities, are where we, humans and not, go on weaving life together. *Design can thus become an open invitation for us all to become mindful and effective weavers of the mesh of life.* To do so, design needs to contribute to creating conditions that dampen our impulse to think and act like modern individuals—to interrupting our "self-alchemization" based on notions of self-improvement in favor of an ethics of autonomous interexistence, albeit without negating our capacity to operate in modern worlds at the same time. This calls for designs that foster convivial reconstruction and that promote "healthy and enabling instrumentalizations" for behaving responsibly toward "the assemblages in which one finds oneself participating" (Bennett 2010, 12, 36).

Gatt and Ingold's perspective would have designers follow "the ways of the world as they unfold" (145). It argues for a type of flexibility that "lies not only in finding the ways of the world's becoming—the way it wants to go—but also in bending it to an evolving purpose. It is not, then, only a matter of going with the flow, for one can give it direction as well. Designing for life is about giving direction rather than specifying end points. It is in this regard that it also involves foresight [futuring]" (2013, 145). To realist ears, this sounds like phenomenological utopia, perhaps nonsense, even more so if one attends to this notion's sequitur: "*Design, in this sense, does not transform the world, it is rather part of the world transforming itself*" (146; emphasis added).

It might be that all communities are poised today, to varying degrees, between living according to their embodied and place-based norms, on the one hand, and giving explicit and effective direction to their collective life, on the other. The issue is how to do it from within a culture of relationality and a biology of love by working at the level of the collective emotioning that is the basis of the social life of a collectivity, while avoiding falling back into established categories and merely utilitarian "preferred solutions"—in other words, by continually renewing the will to be communal. Perhaps this is what is meant by *disoñar* (to embed design with dreams, to dream in order to create), a concept used by some groups in Colombia to signal a practice that is different from, and goes well beyond, the well-intentioned but ultimately self-defeating projects of "saving the planet" and "helping others."[14] To these slogans, one might counter with this one: *A disoñar, a re-diseñar, a recomunalizar!* Dream-design, redesign, recommunalize!

Back to the Pluriverse and Political Ontology

Does the concept of the pluriverse, and the field of political ontology that attends to it, have a future with futures? Or will these concepts, and ontological design itself, become yet one more academic endeavor, interesting but defuturing in relation to enabling worlds, knowledges, and lives otherwise? The answer will depend on the extent to which the notions of the pluriverse and political ontology can sustain their effort to disentangle themselves, perhaps not completely but significantly, from the modern episteme. We raised this issue in passing in the discussion of the politics of the ontological turn in chapter 2. I would like to offer a few additional comments from the perspective of how worlds relate to each other and of the limits of modern knowledge's ability to understand what makes the modern and the nonmodern different yet not entirely separate, partially connected yet also divergent in relation to each other.

The concept of partial connection is useful to enable the analysis of how worlds appear to be shaped, and even encompassed, by each other while remaining distinct (de la Cadena 2015, 33). It provides a conceptual means to understand the ontological complexity of "really existing" partially connected worlds, of how worlds can be part of each other and radically different at the same time. It is necessary to start by emphasizing that radical difference is not something "indigenous people have" (275) but designates relational existence under conditions of partial connection, where every world is more than one (not complete or total unto itself) but less than many (that is, we are not dealing with a collection of interacting separate worlds); all worlds are, in short, within the pluriverse.[15] The question remains, however, of how to make explicit the onto-epistemic politics of translation going on between worlds under conditions of partial connection that are also asymmetrical relations.[16]

One way to think about this difference, as Marisol de la Cadena (2015) meticulously exemplifies in her recent ethnography of multiply interacting "Andean worlds," is in terms of the ontological excess that subaltern worlds continue to exhibit in relation to dominant worlds. There is, for instance, much in Andean indigenous worlds that does not abide by the divide between humans and nonhumans, even if the divide is also present in many of their practices. The question thus arises of how to understand worlds that clearly live partly outside of the separation between nature and humanity but who also live with it, ignore it, are affected by it, utilize it strategically, and reject it—all at the same time. A pluriversal attitude in relating to indigenous groups who defend mountains or lakes on the basis that they are "sentient beings" or "sacred entities" (our modern translation) would allow mountains or lakes to be what they are, not mere objects or independently existing things; above all, it would suspend the act of translating these arguments into "beliefs," which is the main way in which moderns can accommodate them from the perspective of an ontology of intrinsically existent objects or nonhumans. Clarity about these issues of partial connection and translation is essential in design activities in pluriversal contexts.

A timely question for all those worlds that never wanted, or no longer want, to abide by allegedly universal rules is that of how to relate with dominant worlds that do not want to relate. To develop tools that enable going beyond the modern notion of politics based on the partition of reality into discrete and unconnected subjects and objects is crucial; this implies recognizing that while worlds are connected to one another, they diverge at the same time— indeed, such divergence, and not only homogenization, is a sign of our times. In fact, subaltern worlds need to diverge in order to live in partial connection with dominant ones. A decolonial politics would allow for this divergence to take place, "with no other guarantee than the absence of ontological same- ness" (de la Cadena 2015, 281). Is this enough to go on, at least for those of us who inhabit dominant worlds and yet are committed to an ethics of con- tributing to bringing about more favorable conditions for the perseverance of the relational worlds under attack? Are these ideas enough in order to de- sign/struggle in tandem with the worlds of the peoples-territory discussed in chapter 6? With communities in the Global North also determined to embark on their own transition path toward the pluriverse? How do we let ourselves be affected by these worlds? How can we "disrupt the composition through which the world as we know it constantly makes itself homogenous" (de la Cadena 2015, 282), by building on what in each world challenges the One-World World's ability to fulfill itself?

Let's quote Mario Blaser at length to close this question for now:

> Political ontology is intended neither as a pedagogic project to illuminate a reality that deficient theorizing cannot grasp, nor as a proselytizing project to show the virtues of other, nonmodern blueprints for a good life. Such readings would confuse an attempt to carve out a space to listen carefully to what other worldings propose with an attempt to rescue and promote those worldings as if we knew what they are about. Political ontology is closer to hard-nose pragmatism than to the liberal desire to understand everyone; the *pax moderna* no longer holds (if it ever truly did), and dominance without hegemony is a costly proposition when ontological differences become politically active. (2013, 559)

Political ontology is thus not a new approach for another realist claim on the real; in fact, one may say that the worlds briefly described in this book are not "really existing" ontologies "out there" but a manner of foregrounding the array of ways of conceiving what exists so as to make palpable the claim of multiple ontologies or worlds. Political ontology is, in a way, a "foundationless foundational" field (Blaser 2013, 551) with a particular political sensibility, an open-ended ethical and theoretico-political proposition, rather than a hard-nosed claim on the real. Political ontology is a way of telling stories differently, in the hope that other spaces for the enactment of the multiple ontologies making up the pluriverse might open up.

As the scale and pace of destruction continue to expand through the massive extractive operations needed to keep the capitalist industrial system going, these issues take on added meaning. Environmental conflicts are often ontological conflicts; patriarchal capitalist modernity entails the ontological occupation of the existential territories of humans and nonhumans; and people's struggles are thus ontological struggles. Hence the importance of placing design within this ontological politics, including the negotiation of what counts as political and real.

Design with/out Futures? Take II: From Crisis to Reexistence

Design, it is often stressed, is about (preferred) futures. But is not the notion of future, and even futures and the futural, inevitably modern? There is no need to rehearse here the arguments about the existence of multiple temporalities among social groups for whom the notion of linear, cumulative time does not make much cultural sense, where even life and death are so intermingled as not to mark beginnings and ends. Moreover, is not the notion of the future inevitably compromised in representations of the Global South, where poor countries always end up at the losing end of the "uneven distribution of apocalyptic futures" so central, for instance, to climate change discourses?[17] Why, then, use *future(s)* at all? Let us see if we can gain further clarity on the issue of future(s) that has remained unproblematized in this book so far.

We hinted in the introduction at the idea of the bifurcation taking place regarding the question of "posthuman" futures. This is the open question par excellence, regardless of the certainty with which the proponents of the most visible answer to the posthuman uphold their views. This bifurcation involves two paths, which we may call "return to Earth" and "the human beyond biology."[18] By the first I mean—in the company of the many sages, activists, and intellectuals from territorialized communities; wise elders from "an alternative West"; and ecological and feminist thinkers—something more than merely ecological or environmentally correct living. Returning to Earth implies developing a genuine capacity to live with the profound implications entailed by the seemingly simple principle of radical interdependence. To return to the notion of the biology of love (recall that for its proponents this is not a moral precept but a way to name the structural dynamics of interdependence they discover at the foundation of all life; call it "care" if you prefer): "The biology of love, the manner of living with the other [human and nonhuman] in the doings or behaviors through which the other arises as a legitimate other in coexistence with oneself, and in which we human beings take total responsibility for our emotions and for our rational doings, is not a coexistence in appropriation, control or command" (Maturana and Verden-Zöller 2008, 118).

Living with the Earth within the biology of love supposes a mode of existence in which relations of mutual care and respect are *spontaneously realized*—a mode of living that involves our whole life and that can take place only within what we have called the communal. It means cultivating this principle not only theoretically but by living it autonomously. It means being actively cognizant of how "patriarchality through mistrust and control, through manipulation and appropriation, through domination and submission, interferes with the biology of love, pushing humans away from the domain of collaboration and mutual respect towards the domain of political alliances, mutual manipulation, and mutual abuse" (119). Sounds familiar, right? "*And as the biology of love is interfered with, our social life comes to an end*" (119; emphasis added). This is because the biology of love is the principle of all successful sociality. From many territorial groups at present we learn the chief political implications of this lesson: that the care of communal territories/worlds is the fundamental political task of our times.[19]

Let us now look at the second scenario, by most counts the most likely to gain the upper hand. This is the overcoming and total transcendence of the organic basis of life dreamed up by the technopatriarchs of the moment. This scenario necessitates an ongoing legitimation of the ontology of separation. It would not have such a hold on the popular imagination were it not for the fact that its pivotal constructs—the individual, markets, expert knowledge, science, material wealth—are paraded every night for hours on end on CNN and the like and in the annual rituals of the Davos men and World Bank and International Monetary Fund economists, as if they *truly represented the fundaments of human life.* Be that as it may, the technological imagination is powerful, even more so perhaps when depicting the final alchemic fantasy of a world that no longer depends on nature. The entire panoply of biological, material, and digital technologies is placed at the service of this imaginary. Sure, the bodies of animals and plants might tolerate a high level of manipulation if certain fundamental cellular features are respected, so to this extent these developments may justifiably be seen as feasible. The corollary of this possibility, however, is, literally, earth-shattering. A question becomes imperative: "in doing all this, will human-ness be conserved or lost?" (Maturana and Verden-Zöller 2008, 116). These authors continue:

> Acceptance of the legitimacy of the manipulation of the biosphere in gen-eral, and of human life in particular, becomes the norm in the service of technology through the blindness of non-systemic [nonrelational] think-ing. Does it matter? If technology becomes the most fundamental and central feature of human endeavors, then indeed it does not matter that in the technological expansion and complication of human activities human beingness as *Homo sapiens-amans* should be lost to be replaced by the conservation of some new being like *Homo sapiens agressans,* or *Homo sapiens arrogans,* for example. The conservation of some new *Homo sapiens* identity will change the course of history, and human beingness as *Homo sapiens-amans* shall disappear, or it will remain hidden in some distant pockets of primitive life. . . . But if loving humanness remains important and valuable for us as human beings, then technology will not determine

human life, and the biology of intimacy [interconnectedness] will not be lost or destroyed but will be conserved. (119)

We are confronted here with the rise of a posthuman quite different from that envisioned by posthumanist social theory. The human would not disappear as such, as many environmentalists dread (rightly so), but would mutate into another type of being. The stakes are clear. How shall ontologically oriented design face the quandaries of life beyond biology? Will designers be able to resist the seduction of this powerful imaginary? For the technoworlds created by these imaginations are unfailingly loaded with the promise of unlimited growth, novelty, power, adventure, and wealth (as if these were the ultimate criteria of a good life), albeit at the cost of alienating us ever more from our participation in the life of Earth. Will designers be able to contribute to dissuading unreflective publics from succumbing to the virtual realities offered by the patriarchal and capitalistic technological imaginations of the day?[20]

Is the fundamental question of design today then about diverging imaginations of the future? One thing is certain, that despite the fact that design has often maintained an utopian tendency, today's professional practice of design has a strong propensity "to abdicate from futuring," in the face of which it makes sense for transition designers to counter "with a revived insistence on design taking responsibility for the futures it materializes" (Tonkinwise 2015, 88). As Fry argues, Sustainment "can only be realized by being constituted as a project with a specific agenda that is based on a rupture with the *telos* of past world-making" (2015, 63; see also Stewart 2015). This notion of the futural goes against the constitutive teleology of patriarchal capitalist modernity. Perhaps it is only thus that one can hope to counter the pervasive defuturing of worlds effected throughout the centuries by the instrumentations of the Enlightenment project. Moving from the historical (a renewed understanding of our current ontologies and social systems) to the futural might provide some openings to address the question of genuinely open futures.

Many people, doubtlessly many environmentalists, feel an immense sadness when confronted with the devastation of life. How can one accept a life without the anaconda, the jaguar, or the elephant, or so many birds and millenarian trees, rivers, landscapes, and snowy peaks, or even the smallest living beings that go unnoticed altogether? How can one think about the reconstruction of the House of Life (the Ecozoic) so as to avoid such futures? Can one bring back beauty and harmony into the world, so undermined in the name of urban comfort and efficiency? There is no doubt that beauty—which for some theorists has actually been an important piece of evolution, perhaps even its telos (Goodwin 2007; Lubarski 2014)—has been a major victim of the anthropocene; in fact, one may posit that the systematic exile of beauty from modern life is one of its most salient dimensions. These, too, are relevant questions for contemporary design.

Optimistic readings of the anthropocene are of course welcome if they push against the boundaries of the techno-capitalistic liberal mind-set. Writer and eco-philosopher Diane Ackerman (2014), for instance, constructs one such hopeful view based on her analysis of human agency in the face of eco-logical disasters, focusing on those human responses that for her represent a rising consciousness of our partaking of the natural world (green-belt cor-ridors; successful ecosystem restoration programs; recovery of species in extinction through genetic science; constructive wilderness management schemes; advances in neuroscience, robotics, nanotechnology, biomateri-als, and regenerative medicine; and so forth). Such analyses, it seems to me, need to take into account *simultaneously* the other side, as it were, of the kind of global modernity in which we currently live—the dialectic of the incredible complexity of the current system of global capital under cor-porate control, on the one hand, and the brutal simplicity of its results, on the other, the simplicity that condemns millions of people and species to constant destruction, displacement, incarceration, and expulsion, as Saskia Sassen (2014) so eloquently has shown. At stake are veritable "predatory formations" (much more than just rapacious elites) characterized by un-heard-of systemic capacities that generate sustained expulsions through novel structures of rule bringing together technological, financial, market, and legal innovations, a global operational space to which most governments acquiesce as the said formations go on performing ever more extensive re-source grabs (of land, water, the biosphere), leaving human and ecological devastation in their wake. It is these geographies of destruction that we need to pair with our more optimistic readings of human agency, lest our analyses end up contributing to more of the same or, worse, widening the space of the expelled.

We should be clear about something: the anthropocene does not start with capitalism and modernity (hence, it is not enough to speak about a "capitalo-cene"); it stems from much farther back. While it might not be appropriate to speak about a "patriarchocene," it is important to acknowledge that it was in the long history of patriarchy that life's constitutive relationality began to be systematically broken down, and hence it is there that we find the long-standing source of the crisis.

How about the University?

One final question: does the university have any positive role to play in relation to transition and autonomous design? Is the university not irremediably ensconced within the Enlightenment project just alluded to, with its liberal, anthropocentric, and capitalistic trademarks? Stated in terms of political ontology, is the university not one of the most effective *occupying forces* of people's lives and territories, along with the State, the police, and the army?[21] Can the university really move beyond its inexorable ties to the cultures of expertise so decried by Illich throughout his entire oeuvre so that it can serve convivial visions? Can designers and those engaged in the recommunalization of life "escape (disabling) education" so that they can design and learn "within grassroots cultures" (Prakash and Esteva 2008), those cultures for whom conventional education has meant only the devaluation of their forms of knowledge and lives? Answers to these questions go in all directions, from those who advocate for giving up on the university as the site of life-affirming practices to those who would fight for its epistemic decolonization and pluralization, especially in the face of the unrelenting corporatization of the academy going on in so many countries.

Anne-Marie Willis's constructive provocation to the doctoral transition design program at Carnegie Mellon University helps us here. For this design thinker, transition design "is reformist, not revolutionary. . . . It doesn't capture the extent of divestments needed for a significant cultural shift towards Sustainment. . . . There is a problem in branding and marketing a radical postgraduate program, a program intending, if it is serious, to dismantle the system" (2015, 70). This is so because of the pervasive commodification, instrumentalization, and corporatization of higher education. Founded on the principles of separation and disconnection from the natural world, academic knowledge in general seems unprepared to provide us with the earth-wise knowledge needed for the integral functioning of humans and the Earth. Neither does it seem capable of accommodating the rooted, incarnated vernacular knowledges of the "refusenik cultures" with their wisdom about dwelling, presence, and place that is essential for the reclaiming of the commons and the rerooting of worlds (Prakash and Esteva 2008).

Can academic knowledge be made less hierarchical and elitist? In the Latin American decolonial theory grammar, this is known as *epistemic decolonization*.

Epistemic decolonization involves critically assessing "which concepts are we moved by and how we move those concepts and theories that are presupposed in the decisions that affect us day in and day out" (P. Botero 2013, 44). Within this perspective—aptly called "collective research and action"—"the communities are an integral part of knowledge as researchers, and the researchers are part of the collective doing" (44).[22]

This reflection gives me pause to return to the location of the present work. Is not this book also part of the same academy? No doubt it is, in both its language and its mode of construction. Could it also be part of the decolonizing effort? Perhaps, although this will depend on the decolonizing practices and discourses in which it might successfully participate. I want to emphasize, more than anything, that this book is not another attempt, no matter how well intentioned, to teach others how to be or what to do, especially not those communities struggling for their autonomy. They know what to do better than anybody else. In this sense, the book is not proselytizing nor developmentalist. I have presented these ideas as a working hypothesis, more pertinent perhaps for those of us who spend most of our lives in the spaces most directly shaped by the individualizing and objectifying modern categories, from which we are ever attempting to disentangle ourselves, with limited success at best. Let us say, in the spirit of cultural studies, that the ideas contained here are shaped by my reading of the current conjuncture; it is, however, a historical reading that pertains to many people and groups, albeit not to all.

Revisiting the Stakes

At the other extreme from the views of the techno-fathers and the marketers, we find complexity theory biologist Brian Goodwin's vision of "the great transformation":

> I am optimistic that we can go through the transition as an expression of the continually creative emergence of organic form that is the essence of the living process in which we participate. Like the caterpillar that wraps itself up in its silken swaddling bands prior to metamorphosis into a butterfly, we have wrapped ourselves in a tangled skein from which we can emerge only by going through a similar dramatic transformation. In the world of insects, this transformation occurs as a result of a self-digestion, a meltdown of the caterpillar in which only a few living foci of living tissue, the imaginal discs, remain intact. It is from this that the legs, wings, antennae, body segments and other structures of the adult form emerge as an integrated, transformed

being, the butterfly. What the cultural correspondences of this metaphor might mean we can only speculate. (2007, 177)

For some indigenous and other subaltern peoples in Latin America, this great transformation is none other than the *pachakuti*: a profound overhaul of the existing social order, not as a result of a sudden act or a new great synthesis of knowledge or novel agreements, but of an expansive and steady, albeit discontinuous, effort to permanently unsettle and alter the established order. The pachakuti, or the great cycles of the Mayan calendar, are long-standing concepts of peoples who are strictly contemporaneous, that is, peoples for whom "there is no 'post' nor 'pre' because their vision of history is neither linear nor teleological; it sketches a path without ceasing to return to the same point" (Rivera Cusicanqui 2014, 6). The pachakuti "evokes an inversion of historical time, the insurgency of a past and a future that might culminate in catastrophe or renewal. . . . What is experienced is a change of consciousness and a transformation in identities, modes of knowing, and modes of conceiving of politics" (6).

It seems daring to apply these concepts to the transitions into which we are being thrown at present, but I find in them a more constructive way of thinking about human futures than in the prescriptions in vogue given to us by established institutions, such as the impoverished post-2015 sustainable development agenda or, even less so, the technological alchemies of the day, which would most certainly cause even greater destruction of the Earth with their offering of illusive futures.

Perhaps we can hear the rumblings of the pachakuti in the transition initiatives and grassroots struggles for autonomy in so many parts of the world, as in Arundhati Roy's poetic evocation of it, "*Another world is not only possible, she is on her way. On a quiet day, I can hear her breathing*" (quoted in Macy 2007, 17). For this process to take off on a surer footing, albeit in unpredictable directions, the dream of fitting all worlds into one has finally to be put on hold.

Epilogue

Rethinking design from the vantage point of relationality, and vice versa, was a major aspect of this book, as was the proposition that autonomy (again, in the contemporary Latin American sense, not as found in Kantian moral philosophy or in classical liberalism) can be an expression of the radical relationality of life. Together, these two lines of argumentation—on design and autonomy—allowed me to propose a praxis space generated by the interplay of an ethics of world making and a politics of social existence, and to bring a processual and relational ethics into design itself and into all we do.

The propositions presented in this book have oscillated between a politics of the real and a politics of the possible—between pragmatism and utopianism, if you wish. The politics of the real, as should be clear, redefines the politics of the possible, and vice versa; this is one of the strong arguments of neorealism. By adopting a perspective of radical relationality one not only multiplies the reals but redraws the maps of what is possible. Yet this does not do away with the dire questions of political strategy posed by the current conjuncture. What are the best ways of going about the redesign of those institutions that keep unsustainability, growing inequality, and odious, unacceptable levels of injustice in place? Of Thomas Berry's (1999) four institutional formations responsible for unsustainability (governments, universities, organized religions, and corporations), it is clearly the fourth that continues to gain the upper hand—in fact, one of its major triumphs has been to deploy its central logics in the midst of the other three, as attested by the steady corporatization of higher education and the State that has taken place over the past three decades.

There is an imperative need to fight over governments, universities, and spiritualties by reimagining them through the lens of relationality, lest we continue to be subject to the logic underlined by Walter Benjamin long ago, that "*even the dead* will not be safe from the enemy if he wins. And this enemy has not ceased to be victorious" (1968, 264). In the same oft-quoted thesis, Benjamin redefines the politics of the real: "To articulate the past historically does not mean to seize it 'as it really was'. . . . It means to seize hold of a memory as it flashes up in a moment of danger. . . . In every era the attempt must be made anew to wrest tradition anew from a conformism that is about to overpower it" (265). Tell this to the coalition of Native Americans at the Standing Rock Sioux reservation so courageously and brilliantly opposing the construction of the Dakota Access Pipeline; they have long known what it means to be the victims of naturalized traditions of dominance, for they have faced a politics of genocide and erasure that seems never to come to an end, an enemy that continues to be victorious. Through their struggle, they summon the past in order to shake up our established politics of the possible and the real.

The return of the Right occurring in so many countries on every continent is not so much an indication that the immediately preceding regimes were much better—they stemmed from the same traditions Benjamin spoke about, those of dominant modernities—but of the pains to which such traditions go to achieve self-reproduction. The resulting structures of rule being set in place at present might end up being even more exclusionary and damaging than those they are seeking to replace; if this proves to be the case, nineteenth- and twentieth-century modernity would indeed look in retrospect like benign, well-intentioned, and enlightened social orders, as their founders and defenders claim. Nevertheless, as the social basis for dispossession widens (proliferating extractivism, truly massive displacement and expulsion, xenophobia, growing incarceration . . .), so do the fields of potential antagonisms multiply, and thus so might the seeds of potentially important transformations.

This is the source from which the *digna rabia* (rightful anger) springs, the forceful outrage that so many people, from all walks of life, feel in Donald Trump's United States, Mauricio Macri's Argentina, or Michel Temer's Brazil, to speak only of the most flagrant cases in the Americas. Thinking about the effective redesign of institutions in this context becomes one of the most pressing cultural-political projects in which the academy can engage; at its best, it will do it by joining forces with on-the-ground struggles fighting for justice and the active acknowledgment of the value of all forms of life in the world.

Notes

1 Unlike engineering, conventional economics completely forgot that the economy is about flows of matter and energy; this is the so-called metabolism of the economy that ecological economists have placed at the center of their economic analysis; see, e.g., Martínez-Alier (2002); Healy et al. (2013); Bonaiuti (2011). Such a materials perspective is essential to ecologically oriented design and to those concerned with degrowth and energy-descent strategies.

2 The popular communications movement in Cali was spearheaded by two professors from the Universidad del Valle, Alvaro Pedrosa (nonformal education) and Jesús Martín Barbero (communications). In the mid-1980s, Pedrosa set up a nongovernmental organization, Fundación HablaScribe, devoted to research and activism in the nascent field and staffed by a young cadre of self-defined *comunicadores populares* (popular communicators). The foundation thrived for at least a decade and became a hotbed for the diseño de culturas with grassroots groups all over the Colombian southwest. The theoretical foundations of the movement were rather eclectic (ranging from Karl Marx, Ivan Illich, Marshall McLuhan, and Serge Moscovici to Michel Foucault, Néstor García Canclini, and even biologists like James Lovelock, Lynn Margulis, Konrad Lorentz, and Howard Odum). Equally broad were the range of issues considered pertinent, including orality and literacy, the role of paper and recording and computer technologies (Atari and Commodores at that point!), the history of cultures, and the relation between *diseño popular* (popular design), publicity, and elite art. I am indebted to Pedrosa for this recollection.

3 This group included Brooke Thomas, Alan Goodman, Alan Sweedlund, Tom Leatherman, Lynnette Leidy, and Lynn Morgan at the nearby Mount Holyoke College, and Merrill Singer in Hartford, plus a strong group of PhD students.

4 For the Spanish edition, see Winograd and Flores (1989). Flores lived in Berkeley in the 1980s, where I met him; besides talking with him a number of times, I also attended one of his two- to three-day seminars on ontological coaching. This book is still partly an outcome of this relation, for which I am grateful.

5 In one example of a moment of inspiration, the provisional but entire outline of another book on which I have been working for some years, tentatively titled *Everything Has to Change: Earth Futures and Civilizational Transitions*, "downloaded" on my mind at a concert in Chapel Hill with Cuban singer Omara Portuondo sometime in 2011. I usually take a small notebook with me to concerts (whether of classical, popular, or experimental music) since being at a concert hall seems to trigger such moments of creativity, which I describe with the digital metaphor of the download. (Some fiction writers describe their inspiration in somewhat similar terms.)

6 Courtney Shepard has (2015) written a fine honors thesis at the University of North Carolina on the "refashioning movement" by women *refashionistas* who, in blogs and face-to-face events, are creating a vibrant movement; refashioning is related to the larger makers' movement.

7 Note that *How the Leopard Changed Its Spots* is the title of one of Goodwin's well-known books on complexity (2007).

Introduction

1 This kind of two-way introduction to concepts and literatures might frustrate some readers wishing for more in-depth treatment of one or another aspect of the concepts and trends reviewed. I will point to additional readings in notes when appropriate for those wishing to follow up on the debates in question.

2 The title of the Spanish edition of this book is actually *Autonomía y diseño: La realización de lo communal* (Autonomy and design: The realization of the communal). Readers acquainted with Maturana and Varela's work will realize that this subtitle mimics that of their book *Autopoiesis and Cognition: The Realization of the Living* (1980). In the preface to the second edition of the Spanish original (entitled *De máquinas y seres vivos*), Maturana explains, however, that the book's full title should have been *Autopoiesis: La organización de lo vivo* (Autopoiesis: The Organization of the Living) (Maturana 1994, 9).

3 "Real Situation" is the second track from the LP *Uprising* (Bob Marley & The Wailers. Kingston, Jamaica: Tuff Gong Studio/Island Records, 1980).

4 This and other translations are my own. Quotes from Illich are from a recently reedited version of the Spanish-language edition first published in 1978 (Illich 2015), although slightly modified by me in some instances after comparison with the English text. For the English-language version, see Illich (1973). The book was based on essays originally written in Spanish and some notes in English, which were eventually published in both languages, with some differences between the editions (Gustavo Esteva, personal communication, November 20, 2015).

5 Contrary to what could be gathered from Illich's reputation, Illich was not antitechnology per se. In his view, many tools (say, the telephone, formal education, and, we may

add, the Internet) are convivial in principle. The point for him was not to get rid of modern science and technology, or bureaucracy, but to eliminate them as obstacles to other modes of living. He called for a balance between mass production, to satisfy demand, and convivial production. He believed that science and technology could be enlisted in the service of more efficacious convivial tools and designs, so that technology serves humans rather than humans being at the service of the machine and its societal instrumentations. There should be an integration of modern science with "tools that are utilizable with a minimum of learning and common sense" (2015, 87). Here lies a challenge for product, service, and interface design. Illich's work can be placed side by side with those of historians and critics of technology and of advanced industrial society such as Jacques Ellul, Lewis Mumford, Erich Fromm, Herbert Marcuse, Paul Goodman, and Paul Virilio.

6 Von Werlhof's development of what she terms a critical theory of patriarchy has spanned several decades, starting in the 1970s in collaboration with Maria Mies and Veronica Bennholdt-Thomsen. I am drawing here primarily on a Spanish selection of her essays published recently in Oaxaca (hence all translations from this source are mine). Some of these essays can also be found in her English-language book from 2011. See also von Werlhof (2001, 2013) for important articles. She founded the Research Institute for the Critique of Patriarchy and for Alternative Civilizations in Innsbruck, Austria, where she lives. It should be noted that this research program and perspective are quite independent and distinct from the established critical feminist theories in much of the Anglo-American and French academies. It increasingly dovetails with Latin American decolonial and autonomous feminisms (chapter 2). For related perspectives, see Merchant (1980) and Federici (2004). One final caveat: there was a heated debate in the 1970s in Anglo-American feminist anthropology and elsewhere (going back to Friedrich Engels's *Origin of the Family, Private Property and the State*) about whether genuine matriarchies ever existed. My sense is that the approaches reviewed here differ in their ontological (not merely politico-economic and cultural) orientation.

7 We will return to the discussion of black, indigenous, and modern patriarchies and feminisms in chapter 2. Some of the main authors in this debate include María Lugones, Rita Segato, Silvia Rivera Cusicanqui, Betty Ruth Lozano, Sylvia Marcos, Aura Cumes, Irma Alicia Velásquez Nimatuj, Julieta Paredes, Aída Hernández, Yuderkis Espinosa, Diana Gómez, Karina Ochoa, Brenny Mendoza, Karina Bidaseca, Ochy Curiel, Natalia Quiroga, and Xochitl Leyva.

8 Paul Virilio concurs here: "To progress would be to accelerate. After the break with the geocentrism of Ptolemy and the Copernican delocalization of the 'eternal truths,' we would see the exponential development of techno-industrial arsenals giving priority to artillery and explosives, but also to horology, optics, mechanics . . . all things necessary for the elimination of the present world" (2012, 15). Also attentive to tools and machines, Virilio describes "the parody of Progress of knowledge" that starts in the Italian quattrocento and results in a (patriarchal) ideology of "humanity's escape from its incompleteness, from its dissatisfaction with being oneself" (38), preventing us from living in place and trapping us via "simulators of proximity" such as the web. Virilio does not spare angry words in diagnosing the situation; for him, we are confronted with a

"global suicidal state" based on Darwinist progress, technocracies, and endless war. See also Virilio (1997).

9 Maturana defines cultures as closed networks of conversations through which the consensual coordination of coordination of behaviors takes place. He has maintained an original and active research and practice on matristic cultures and the biology of love with collaborators in Santiago de Chile for many decades. See his Matríztica School blog and organization, cofounded with Ximena Dávila Yáñez: http://matriztica.cl/Matriztica/. Verden-Zöller's work centers on the determining role of mother-child relations in early life from the perspective of play, defined as a corporeal relation in which the mother or parent is absolutely present to the child, which is fundamental to all successful future coexistence by the child. The Brazilian psychologist Evânia Reichert has written a fine book on child pedagogy (2011) based on the work of Wilhelm Reich, Lev Vygotsky, Jean Piaget, Claudio Naranjo, and Maturana's biology of love. The implications for the *practice* of child rearing are enormous (needless to say, they go against the grain of most approaches to it at present!).

10 Far from being a moral value, *love* is defined by these authors as "the domain of those relational behaviors through which the other arises as a legitimate other in coexistence with oneself" (Maturana and Verden-Zöller 2008, 223). As such, it is a basic fact of biological and cultural existence. They add, "Love is visionary, not blind, because it liberates intelligence and expands coexistence in cooperation as it expands the domain in which our nervous system operates" (138). They counterpose this biology of love to patriarchal coexistence in appropriation and control.

11 *Abya Yala* means "Continent of Life" in the language of the Gaundule (Kuna) peoples of Panama and Colombia (or "land in full maturity" in other versions). It is the name for the continent preferred by indigenous peoples from Latin America, akin to Turtle Island, the name given by Native Americans to the North American continent.

12 The idea of a technological singularity has been popularized by futurist Ray Kurzweil (2005); see his home page, http://www.singularity.com/. Singularity debates have taken place at Stanford University. Kurzweil situates the onset of the Singularity in 2045.

13 With regard to technology's capacity for destruction, witness, for instance, the expansion of large-scale mining worldwide with ever more devastating effects, even to secure a few grams of gold, diamonds, or the minerals that go into the making of digital devices, for which entire communities and ecosystems are sacrificed without much reservation.

14 Readers familiar with Manzini's latest book will realize that this point parallels closely that author's fourth summary point of his argument (2015, 5).

Chapter 1: Out of the Studio and into the Flow of Socionatural Life

Epigraphs: Mau and the Institute without Boundaries, *Massive Change* (2004), 23; T. Brown, *Change by Design* (2009), 3; Manzini, *Design, When Everybody Designs* (2015), 1, 31.

1 The following wonderful quote from a text from 1973 by Georges Perec (which recalls Norbert Elias) may suffice to illustrate this point about the intimacy of design and every-

day life: "What we need to question is bricks, concrete, glass, our table manners, our utensils, our tools, the way we spend our time, our rhythms. To question that which seems to have ceased forever to astonish us. We live, true, we breathe, true; we walk, we open doors, we go down staircases, we sit at a table in order to eat, we lie down on a bed in order to sleep. How? Where? Why?" (quoted in Blauvelt 2003, 21). One can easily connect this statement to interface design (e.g., Laurel 1989) and to the problematization of objects at the intersection of art and design (including anything from silverware to shoes but well beyond these examples; see, e.g., Lukic and Katz 2011).

2 See, for example, the well-known works by Bruce Mau, *Life Style* (2000) and *Massive Change* (2004); see also the Museum of Modern Art's *Design and the Elastic Mind* (2008).

3 I must confess, however, that I have always felt a certain delight at García Márquez's description of the reaction of Macondo's people to the inventions; his vindication of live music versus its mechanical reproduction; his apparent defense of real-life, face-to-face interactions as compared to the surrogate experience of the cinema; his admiration for the older, earthier imagination of the magical time of the gypsies. There are lessons here, too, for thinking critically about the multiple impacts of today's ubiquitous digital devices.

4 Argentinian cultural critic Beatriz Sarlo has similarly written a wonderful book (1992) showing how the products of modern technology (the radio, the telephone, the telegraph, and the movies, among other phenomena) not only helped to shape notions of modernity in Argentinian society but effected a significant intellectual and cultural reorganization, albeit with internal and class contradictions. There is an English version of this book (2008).

5 See chapter 6 for an explanation of the distinctions among ontonomy, heteronomy, and autonomy.

6 As in all epochs of design, the development of new materials (metals, woods, plastics) was crucial at this stage. In the transition from traditional craft schools to modern industrial design, the aim was to create functional and affordable products for all. While theorists like Walter Gropius emphasized a new unity between art and technology, function and form, design itself became increasingly rational and Cartesian, especially after World War II. The German company Braun best exemplified the new approach to "good design" (according to Bürdek, 2005: 57, the idea that "Less design is more design" was adapted by German designer Dieter Rams from architect Mies van der Rohe's well-known adage "Less is more," eventually influencing a number of companies, though not without controversy). Not until the 1960s, with the Frankfurt school's critique of alienation in postindustrial society, did functionalism see a rollback, and a new move to the art of design (also in architecture) ensued in various ways. For background on the history and theory of product design (largely in western Europe and the United States but with some attention to other regions of the world), see the excellent treatise by Bernhard Bürdek (2005). A sweeping history of design from 1400 to the present, covering all major world regions and highlighting the evolution of style, form, materials, and techniques, is the lavishly illustrated volume edited by Pat Kirkham and Susan Weber (2013).

7 Many designers in the early twentieth century actually had a socialist sensibility, espousing a mix of rationalism and utopianism (particularly after the devastation caused by the

Great War). Le Corbusier's design of functional buildings for the working class is a case in point. The socialists' modernist aesthetics and commitments, however, have not always yielded happy results, as is well known.

8 Personal communication by email, July 7, 2015.

9 As John Thackara (2004) reports, 80 percent of the environmental impact of products and services is determined at the design stage. The United States produces a million pounds of waste per person per year. This "million-pound backpack" is industrial society's ecological rucksack, as ecological economists put it.

10 See Antonelli's keynote speech at the Solid Conference in 2014, "The New Frontieres of Design," published May 22, 2014, by O'Reilly Media, 14.10 min: https://www.youtube .com/watch?v=u6mDAEOfGWQ. See also her TED Talk, "Treating Design as Art," published January 22, 2008 by TedTalks, 18.11 min: https://www.youtube.com/watch?v= -bdfiNnDZ8M.

11 Thackara's Doors of Perception Conference is a good source for design debates with a critical edge from several world regions from within the profession; see http://wp.doors ofperception.com/.

12 See the special issue of *Design Studies*, "Interpreting Design Thinking" (vol. 32 [2011]), organized by the Design Thinking Research Group at the University of Technology, Sydney, based on the group's eighth symposium.

13 Tim Brown's (2009) book is worth reading as an introduction to design thinking, with illustrative examples from the government, service, nongovernmental organization, and corporate sectors. Some of the topics and concepts dealt with include spaces of innovation; smart teams, including a new breed of ethnographers; the role of intuition, insight, and empathy in design; convergent and integrative thinking (another trope in much design literature); user-generated content and open-source innovation; storytelling; and prototyping. Many of these notions are found in one way or another in a number of design books at present.

14 It should be mentioned, however, that architects have always been attuned to the value of theory as a means to reflect on their practice, at least from the days when Marxism, existentialism, structuralism, and phenomenology vied for influence in the theoretical landscape. See, for instance, the Barcelona architect Josep Maria Montaner's (2013) retrospective analysis of the relation between architecture and critical theory. As he suggests, however, with the advent of poststructuralism and deconstruction, this relation shifted to a new level. See also Mitrovic (2011).

15 On Koolhaas's earlier projects with the Office for Metropolitan Architecture in New York, including the famous mega-volume *S, M, L, XL* (OMA, Koolhas, and Mau 1995), see Foster (2002b); Kwinter (2010); Montaner (2013).

16 Aravena (winner of the Pritzker Architecture Prize in 2016) became well known for his participatory design of "half of a good house" in poor settlements, to be completed by the owners when resources become available. For the tiny house movement, see the website for "The Tiny Life," http://thetinylife.com/what-is-the-tiny-house-movement/. See also the current proposals by "eco-restorative designer" Tim Watson of Hillsborough, North Carolina, for tiny houses in the website of his EarthWalk Alliance (http://earthwalkalliance

.org/). One finds in Victor Papanek a brief discussion of a "postindustrial vernacular" (1984, 13, 17). Perhaps Paolo Soleri's famous Arcosanti might be considered an example of that (https://arcosanti.org/).

17 Takasaki Masaharu (2012), based in Tokyo, puts this concern most acutely by poetically describing his architecture practice as attempting "to instill spirit and soul into objects from the perspective of creating things and nurturing people.... I hope to make the flowers inside people's hearts blossom through objects which I have put all my mind and soul into to create. I also pursue lively, vibrant architecture by forming relationships with animals, plants, and nature as well as with spiritual things"; in his view, architecture participates in the making of "chains of existence." His "architecture of cosmology" and "animated design" have yielded a set of unusually creative structures and shapes (e.g., egg-shaped forms). Two other examples at the exhibition joined vernacular forms and collaborative design, including computers. The first included a fog-harvesting device designed to emulate the traditional uses of the *warka* (fig) tree in Ethiopia, designed by computer but with a traditional basketlike shape and constructed locally from bamboo; besides providing water for the locals, subsequent prototypes are expected to include solar panels for illumination and community Internet. The second example involved an integrated project in Kigutu, Burundi, designed to foster community self-reliance and off-the-grid sustainability through the integration of cultural forms (including those of the built environment), the landscape, aesthetics (local patterns, including drumming), energy production, community gardens, and so forth, all within the spirit of communal collaboration. See the entries "Architecture and Vision" (40–42) and "Louise Braverman" (56–58) in the exhibition catalog (Biennale Architettura 2012). The exhibition, held on August 29–November 25, 2012, included fifty-seven works from most regions of the world. I happened to be in Venice for a degrowth conference and spent time at some of the exhibits.

18 How about the following lesson for ontological design: "The primeval architectural images are, in order of their ontological appearance, ground, roof, walls, doors, windows, fireplace, stairs, bed, table, bathroom. Each of them can be analyzed from an ontological point of view, from the perspective of its phenomenological encounter" (Pallasmaa 2016, 102). Many of us have had the experience of being in an old house designed with these principles in mind (a "Bachelardian house," one might say, one that ontologically dreams). Yet today "architectural form has lost its ontological fundaments, and architecture has become a practice of formal invention" (105).

19 The English version of this book dates from 1933. "Our cuisine harmonizes with the shadows; there exist indestructible bonds between them.... Our ancestors, forced to live, whether they wanted or not, in dark houses, discovered the beauty that lies in the heart of the shadows, and it didn't take them long to utilize them to achieve aesthetic effects" (Tanizaki 1994, 42). While this surely sounds like a wholesale endorsement of an ahistorical Japanese ontology, it does point at features many people have come to admire about certain Japanese cultural practices.

20 Here one might mention the phenomenon of celebrity architects like Spain's Santiago Calatrava, Mexico's Luis Barragán, and Italy's Enzo Piano, besides Gehry and Koolhaas.

21 The Arki Research Group at the Media Lab, Aalto University, in Helsinki, led by Kommonen, has been developing a framework for digital design, as well as a notion of "design ecosystems" (systems of connected and interacting designs) applied to a broad vision of "The Design of Everyday Life" and "Design for a Society in Transformation." See the Arki Group's blog and website, "Arki," http://arki.mlog.taik.fi/; Kommonen (2013a, 2013b).

22 Halpin and Monnin have worked with philosopher of technology Bernard Stiegler in Paris. See Halpin, Clark, and Wheeler (2010); Halpin (2011); Halpin and Monnin (2014). Fry (2012) draws on Stiegler in his exploration of the role of technology in evolution and design.

23 The best treatise on the subject, in my view, remains van der Ryn and Cowan ([1996] 2007). See also Hester (2006); Orr (2002). For more technical treatises, see Yeang (2006) and the large and well-documented tome by Paul Hawken, Amory Lovins, and L. Hunter Lovins (1999). There are, of course, many books on concrete aspects of green or ecological design by now. A prominent and influential example is permaculture, for which there is a vast specialized literature. The concepts of biomimicry (Benyus 1997) and cradle-to-cradle (Braungart and McDonough 2002) are garnering attention in product design. In Latin America, agroecology has become a gathering space for peasant agriculture and ecological design, often in tandem with social movements such as La Vía Campesina.

24 This is not the place to even adumbrate a critique of mainstream approaches to global climate change and sustainability, such as carbon markets, geoengineering, or the green economy. However, these are crucial ecological design issues. The best recent critiques, in my view, are by climate justice activists Naomi Klein (2014), Patrick Bond (2012), and Larry Lohman (e.g., 2011). For a critique of geoengineering, see the work of the ETC Group, in their website: http://www.etcgroup.org/. See also Shiva (2008); Bassey (2012).

25 One of the most eloquent and visionary examples of radical cultural and social change based on the principles of natural design that I know of is by the late complexity theorist Brian Goodwin (2007). Goodwin's remains a marginal view within biology, however.

26 There are many well-known examples of this type of design by now; a common one is the design of sewage treatment plants that use constructed marshes to simultaneously purify water, reclaim nutrients, and provide habitats and landscape. There are lots of cases of restoration, successful urban renewal, the parallel restructuring of energy and transportation (in Germany and Denmark, for instance), and the design of landscapes, ecotones, and so forth. Transition-town initiatives are rich with examples of this kind.

27 I am referring to the work of anthropologist Cassandra Hartblay (2015), whose engaged ethnography explores in detail the social, political, cultural, and material configurations that account for the meaning and practice of disability in the post-Soviet Russian context from a design perspective. Toward the end of her dissertation, she develops design implications for the approach called crip theory (from the reclaimed category of subordination), raising anew the power relations at play in the question of who designs, and showing how subjects creatively redesign their living quarters into nondisabling spaces. She entertains the notion of the coemergence of social forms and

material infrastructures, which holds promise as a foundation for nonableist forms of design.

28 A caveat is in order: while I emphasize design's relation to capitalism, design's implication with other social and political orders must be mentioned, certainly twentieth- and twenty-first-century socialisms, and even centrally planned empires in antiquity, such as Rome, Egypt, or imperial China. In this book I focus on the intersection of modernity, capitalism, colonialism, and patriarchy (known by the somewhat cumbersome Latin American decolonial theory rubric of "the capitalist patriarchal modern/colonial world system").

Chapter 2: Elements for a Cultural Studies of Design

Epigraphs: Anne-Marie Willis, "Transition Design: The Need to Refuse Discipline and Transcend Instrumentalism" (2015), 72–73; Caroline Gatt and Tim Ingold, "From Description to Correspondence: Anthropology in Real Time" (2013), 147; Michel Foucault, *The Order of Things* (1970), 373, 378, 386.

1 Following Grossberg, too, I differentiate this project from CDS, as discussed in the previous chapter. As Grossberg (2010) underscores, the project of cultural studies goes beyond critique to embrace the specificity of the concrete. It examines design's intricate location within formations of culture and power but also ways it might contribute to other world-making projects. A cultural studies of design also differs from CDS because of the centrality of culture and, as we shall add in this book, ontology in the former.

2 There are parallel trends in geography, which I cannot review here; one of the more noted is GeoDesign, as a practice that brings geographic analysis (ecological, spatial, GIS, modeling) into design.

3 The preconference publication prototype in 2010 was coordinated by Christopher Kelty, Alberto Corsín Jiménez, and George Marcus. On the history, concept, and uses of prototypes from design (rather than anthropological) perspectives, see the contributions by Michael Guggenheim, Alex Wilkie, and Nerea Calvillo in this collection of short essays (ARC Studio 2010).

4 See the project's website, "Rethinking Ethnography as a Design Process," Center for Ethnography, UCI School of Social Science, http://www.ethnography.uci.edu/programs/design.php, and Murphy (2016) for a more satisfactory review of this trend.

5 Introductory remarks for the session, "Design for the Real World: But Which World? What Design? What Real?," American Anthropological Association Annual Meeting, San Francisco, November 14, 2012.

6 There are several interesting groups working at the anthropology/design intersection (for instance, a three-day workshop at Aberdeen in 2009 on design anthropology, convened by James Leach and Caroline Gatt, and an interdisciplinary group bringing together scholars from the Parsons School of Design and Cornell University on the subject of Ecology, Critical Thought, and Design). The next few years will surely see a number of new volumes at the intersection of anthropology, ecology, and design.

7   Design Studio for Social Intervention, http://www.ds4si.org/.

8   See the website for the Boston-based Design Studio for Social Intervention, http://ds4si.org/storage/ds4si_whatwedo.pdf (accessed September 1, 2012). Another interesting group in this vein is the School for Designing a Society (http://www.designingasociety.net/). See also Chin's "Laboratory of Speculative Ethnography" (http://elizabethjchin.com/projects-2/).

9   A number of interesting NGOs are working hands-on on design for development and sustainability, again with various degrees of self-awareness of "poking at the edges," largely in Europe or with an international scope (see, e.g., the Center for Sustainable Design, http://cfsd.org.uk; the International Development Design Summit, http://iddsummit.org/; the Social Design Site, http://www.socialdesignsite.com/content/view/30/58/; Design That Matters, http://www.designthatmatters.org/; and Design for the World, http://www.designfortheworld.org).

10 Schwittay's article examines codesign experiences promoting financial inclusion and savings among poor communities that have been spearheaded by the Institute for Money, Technology and Financial Inclusion at the University of California, Irvine. As she reports, staff at the institute were very much aware of the tensions in the programs. While microfinance is still touted by many as an effective solution to poverty, the critiques are mounting. For a critique of microfinance and of the approach created by Muhammad Yunus, founder of the Grameen Bank, see the well-documented book by Bangladeshi anthropologist Lamia Karim (2011). One of Karim's main findings is that the loans contribute to undermining communal mechanisms of self-reliance, which are precisely what needs to be strengthened from an autonomous design perspective.

11 Linked to the Millennium Development Goals was the high-profile but patently dubious Millennium Village Project concocted by Jeffrey Sachs—the darling of neoliberal privatizers in Latin America and eastern Europe in a previous era, now turned "savior" of "Africa's poor"—the outrageous claims of which have been heavily criticized, even by the World Bank! (e.g., Munk 2013).

12 This is not a comprehensive review by any means. There are many schools of PE (sometimes not earmarked as such), going back to the 1970s, in many parts of the world, including Latin America and South Asia, Catalonia, France, Germany, Scandinavia, North America, and the United Kingdom. Most reviews in English to date focus on the Anglo-American traditions. See Escobar (2010b) for additional references; and Bryant (2015) for an excellent comprehensive international collection on contemporary PE. See also Dove, Sajise, and Dolittle (2011); Harcourt and Nelson (2015); Biersack and Greenberg (2006); and Robbins (2004).

13 For instance, see the early and influential critiques of the concept of sustainable development by Michael Redclift (1987) and Enrique Leff (1986).

14 I will not review here the debates on the ontological turn, particularly in Anglo-American anthropology, but rather give my own sense of what it is from the perspective of my joint work on political ontology with Mario Blaser and Marisol de la Cadena. As de la Cadena says, more than being an already-accomplished "turn," political ontology is interested in the theoretical and political openings that appealing to ontology might perform. Those

wishing to peruse the debates might refer to recent fora in journals such as *Cultural Anthropology*, HAU: *Journal of Ethnographic Theory*, and *American Ethnologist* involving writers such as Eduardo Viveiros de Castro, David Graeber, Martin Holbraad, Morten Pedersen, Lucas Bessire, and David Bond.

15 Think, for instance, of the works of Dianne Rocheleau, Paige West, Laura Ogden, Wendy Harcourt, Sarah Whatmore, Anna Tsing, J. K. Gibson-Graham, Susan Paulson, and Jane Bennett, among others. In retrospect, one may also argue that materialist ecofeminists like Vandana Shiva, Maria Mies, Ariel Salleh, and Mary Mellor were attuned to some of the ontological dimensions of ecology among capital, gender, and nature through their attention to embodiment and women's knowledges. Salleh's emphasis on embodied materialities, from which she derived her original concept of embodied debt (the debt owed to women worldwide for their unpaid reproductive and care work), is a case in point (Salleh 2009a). A similar argument could be made about the cultural ecofeminists of the 1970s and 1980s with their attention to culture and spirituality (think of Susan Griffin and Carolyn Merchant).

16 Remarks made as discussant in the panel on Contemporary Theory in Environmental Anthropology, at the American Anthropological Association Annual Meeting, Washington, DC, December 2014.

17 I am grateful to María Lugones and Yuderkis Espinosa for bringing this point to my attention with particular insight (conversation in Buenos Aires, November 2012).

18 In what follows I use a number of ES formulations from various sources; I have amended them slightly in some cases, which is why I do not present them as exact quotations. This section is *not* intended as a comprehensive or systematic presentation of ES; rather, I highlight a few of its principles that will allow me to underscore the ontological and design implications of the framework.

19 In her most recent book, Saskia Sassen (2014) identifies the expulsion of peoples, places, enterprises, and the biosphere from their locations as the fundamental worldwide logic of contemporary global capitalism. Expulsions, in her compelling analysis, unveil a set of novel subterranean trends driving the systemic forces of brutality and complexity at play in global capital. She adamantly argues that these processes can no longer be understood with conventional social science categories, a point also underscored in the present book. Expulsion and occupation are, I believe, articulated logics. What is expelled, as much as what is occupied, is often an entire way of worlding. The paradigmatic case of the logic of occupation is of course the Israeli occupation of Palestinian territories, yet the modalities and types of occupation are quite diverse. On occupation as a main logic of globalization, see Visweswaran (2013).

20 I have in mind here, of course, Gilles Deleuze and Félix Guattari's (1987) discussion of rhizomes and Laura Ogden's (2011) remarkable extension of this concept to the human/nonhuman assemblages in the Florida Everglades.

21 Statement by Francia Márquez of the Community Council of La Toma, taken from the three-minute trailer for the documentary *La Toma*, by Paula Mendoza (2010), accessed May 20, 2013, http://www.youtube.com/watch?v=BrgVcdnwUoM. Most of this brief section on La Toma comes from meetings I participated in with La Toma leaders in 2009,

2012, 2014, and 2015, as well as campaigns to stop illegal mining in this ancestral territory and accounts of the march to Bogotá in November 2014. All translations are mine.

22 From the trailer of Mendoza's documentary *La Toma*.

23 Francia Márquez, "Situación que carcome mis entrañas. A propósito de la orden de bombardear el Cauca," open letter, April 18, 2015. An English version of this letter is found on the website of the First Afro-Diasporic Gathering of Black Women Defenders of Rights and their Territories, http://www.blackwomensmarch.org/news/letter-from-francia-marquez.

24 Francia Márquez, "A las mujeres que cuidan de sus territorios como a sus hijas e hijos. A las cuidadoras y los cuidadores de la Vida Digna, Sencilla y Solidaria," open letter, April 14, 2015. Content related to this letter is found on the website of the Latin America Working Group; see "We Are Defenders of Life—Francia Elena Marquez Mina," http://www.lawg.org/action-center/lawg-blog/69-general/1607-qwe-are-defenders-of-lifeq—francia-elena-marquez-mina.

I should note that the reference to the umbilical cord refers to the long-standing practice among rural and forest Afrodescendant communities of burying the placenta and umbilical cord to create an indissoluble link with the territory, so that humans become an integral part of it, and a bit more than human, too.

25 The Nasa are the second-largest indigenous group in the country (about 140,000 people). Their territory involves seventy-two *resguardos* (collective lands), most of which date back to the colonial period (seventeenth and eighteenth centuries). They have maintained a radical militancy in relation to the State. The Misak inhabit the Ancestral Resguardo of Guambía, most of which is located in the Silvia municipality), although their collective territory is discontinuous. They total about twenty-three thousand members, with a strong and distinct language and cultural identity. This means that the Norte del Cauca is an intensely intercultural region made up of indigenous, Afrodescendant, and mestizo communities. Their territories have always been coveted because of their resources, and this is even more so today. Over the past three decades, the region has been one of the most intense scenes of the armed conflict between the State, left-wing guerrillas, and right-wing paramilitaries. It is in this adversarial context that indigenous and black communities are struggling for their territories, Life Plans, and autonomy.

Chapter 3: In the Background of Our Culture

Epigraphs: Maturana and Varela, *The Tree of Knowledge: The Biological Roots of Human Understanding* (1987), 241; Plumwood, *Environmental Culture: The Ecological Crisis of Reason* (2002), 4–5; Albán Achinte, *Más allá de la razón hay un mundo de colores* (2013).

1 A word about the authors in question: the three main ones are Humberto Maturana, Francisco Varela, and Fernando Flores. Maturana and Varela are known as the originators, beginning in the late 1960s, of the Chilean school of cognitivism. Their main intervention has been to propose a theory of cognition that contrasts sharply with established positions. Beyond cognition, they have proposed an entire conceptual framework for understanding living beings, based on the notion of autopoiesis (self-creation). As they state in their landmark study (1980; originally published in Spanish in 1973), their

work can be considered an original and complete system of thought, a theoretical biology. While Varela in the 1980s sought to refine his approach through a dialogue with Buddhism (see Varela, Thompson, and Rosch 1991; Varela 1999), Maturana continued working on what he calls a biology of love—love as a biological and social phenomenon. The root of their work is their early neurobiological research, but they are deeply influenced by phenomenology. While their work is increasingly being recognized worldwide, it remains relatively marginal outside some strands of cognitivism, systems theory and cybernetics (yet see B. Clarke and Hansen 2009 for a collection devoted to Varela's work). Based on Maturana and Varela, along with Heidegger and Hans-Georg Gadamer, Flores and Terry Winograd proposed their ontological approach to design. Flores has also collaborated with philosophers in his effort to develop non-Cartesian frameworks for social action (Spinosa, Flores, and Dreyfus 1997).

2 Readers acquainted with the work of Heidegger will obviously recognize these notions (being-in-the-world, readiness-to-hand, thrownness, and background of understanding), and likewise some of Gadamer's and Maurice Merleau-Ponty's notions. Again, let me underscore that while these are important sources for Maturana and Varela, so is their biological understanding, along with, in Varela's case, Buddhist philosophy of mind.

3 The Buddhist literature on the mind is so vast that it is almost ludicrous to mention any particular sources. However, for useful introductions to the question of mind by an esteemed Buddhist teacher who also engages with Varela's work, see Mingyur Rinpoche (2007); for the notions of mindfulness and interbeing, see Nhat Hanh (1975, 2008). A key foundational Buddhist text from the twelfth century is found, with contemporary commentary, in Thrangu Rinpoche (2003, see especially ch. 17, "The Perfection of Wisdom-awareness"). A classical guide in Tibetan Buddhism for dealing with the nonexistence of the self and achieving freedom from ego clinging (a guide to the practice of cultivating compassion, known as *lojong*) is found in Kongtrul (2005). Central to Buddhist meditation practice are the notions of interrelation and interdependency, impermanency, and compassion. Joanna Macy draws on these notions to develop her vision of transition, to be discussed in chapter 5 (Macy 2007; Macy and Johnstone 2012).

4 Varela, Evan Thompson, and Eleanor Rosch refer to the various realist and foundationalist forms of cognitivism as being trapped within "the Cartesian anxiety" (see ch. 7 of *The Embodied Mind* [1991]).

5 Maturana and Verden-Zöller (1993) emphasize the importance of consciously accepting or rejecting the notions of objective reality and universal truth. Deciding to reject these notions means opting for the pluriverse, that is, for the idea of multiple legitimate domains of reality and multiple explanations of them by observers.

6 The best traditions of folk music articulate powerfully the popular wisdom of attachment to place and landscape within the flow of life. Think, for instance, of the poet, composer and singer from Northern Argentina Atahualpa Yupanki, for the Latin American context.

7 Von Foerster goes on to draw a set of revealing implications from this analysis, including that objectivity is "a popular device for avoiding responsibility" (1991, 5). For him, objectivity can ground a set of moral codes but not a compelling ethics. This was an exciting development that brought together pioneers of information, communications, and cultural theory

such as Margaret Mead, Gregory Bateson, Stafford Beer, Warren McCulloch, W. Ross Ashby, and Humberto Maturana and that influenced the notions of self-organization, autonomy, autopoiesis, and self-referentiality. These debates anticipated much of what was discussed in the 1980s under the headings of constructivism and postmodernism. I have taken the above quotes from von Foerster (1991), https://pdfs.semanticscholar.org/7ff9 /4a923a0111eb9bcc3f08b3f01109e790a732.pdf. A published version of the conference talk is included in a collection of essays by von Foerster (2010).

8 I am drawing here largely on Ashis Nandy (1987, 1988, 2012). The group includes, among others, Shiv Visvanathan; Claude Alvares; some of the critics of development, such as Rajni Kothari, D. L. Shet, and Smitu Kothari; and the iconoclastic chemical engineer C. V. Sheshadry ("a classicist scientist, a crank who . . . saw the autobiography, the laboratory, and the constitution as thought experiments, a visionary who felt India could transform the idiocies of globalisation into something life giving," according to Visvanathan [2002, 2163]). Visvanathan wrote one of the first ethnographies of laboratory science (1985). Some of the subaltern studies scholars have been associated with the group, as have at times the works of Vandana Shiva and Veena Das (e.g., Shiva 2005, 2008; Das 2007, 2015).

9 The landmarks of the invention of the economy and its relation to the rise of markets have been eloquently traced by Karl Polanyi, Louis Dumont, Fernand Braudel, and Michel Foucault as well as historians of capitalism such as Maurice Dobb and E. P. Thompson. This is, of course, a central aspect of what Polanyi (1957) so aptly called "the great transformation." In a different vein, I would say that economics is a cogent academic tradition that many of its practitioners find exciting (like, say, physics or mathematics or indeed any branch of academic knowledge). The problem, however, is that when exercised via policy as a hegemonic form of truth, it becomes a pillar of structured unsustainability and social inequality.

10 This thus means that ontology is historical; an amusing thought is that it might even be species specific: "Even the most hard-nosed biologist . . . would have to admit that there are many ways the world is—indeed even different worlds of experience—depending on the structure of the being involved and *the kinds of distinctions it is able to make*" (Varela, Thompson, and Rosch 1991, 9; emphasis added).

11 Foucault (1970: xi) describes the episteme as "a positive unconscious of knowledge"; he differentiates among three epistemes in post-Renaissance Europe, the last being the modern episteme that crystallized in the late eighteenth century with the figure of Man as its center: Man as the foundation, subject, and object of all knowledge. In this modern episteme, the analysis of life, labor, and language took on the forms of modern biology, economics, and linguistics, respectively. This is different from epistemology; the natural, social, and human sciences have seen three contending epistemologies: positivist (dominant in the physical and natural sciences), dialectical (Marxist approaches), and constructivist.

12 For a presentation of the decolonial perspective and a set of references, see Escobar (2008, ch. 4); Mignolo and Escobar (2010). The main names associated with it are Enrique Dussel, Aníbal Quijano, and Walter Mignolo, but it includes a network of scholars,

intellectuals, and activists particularly in the Andean countries and the United States. It should be emphasized that this perspective is not the same as postcolonial theory.

13 Here *we* refers to ongoing work on relational ontologies I am doing with Mario Blaser and Marisol de la Cadena; see, e.g., Blaser (2014); de la Cadena (2010, 2015); Blaser, de la Cadena, and Escobar (2014); Escobar (2014).

14 This is a partial list of perspectives, largely from cultural theory (see Escobar 2010b for a review of this literature). Along with these trends has come a renewed attention to certain authors (a new list of influences), including Spinoza, Bergson, Nietzsche, Whitehead, the pragmatists (William James) and romantic writers (Emerson, Whitman, Thoreau), Deleuze and Guattari, and Merleau-Ponty; a few of these authors also appeal to complexity, evolutionary, and biological theories by Vladimir Vernadsky, Pierre Teilhard de Chardin, Lynn Margulis, and Susan Oyama, and to cognitivism, including Varela. A state-of-the-art collection on these trends is de la Cadena and Blaser (2017), largely drawn from the perspectives of science and technology studies.

15 I think the following practices are the most central in the modern episteme within which mainstream and critical social theories alike function: the parceling out of the uninterrupted complexity of the flow of socionatural life into allegedly separate and autonomous domains, such as the economy, society, nature, culture, the polity, the individual, and so forth; the attachment of a discipline to one or another of these domains, the truth of which they are supposed to reveal (economics, sociology, psychology, political science, anthropology, etc.); and the existence of three main approaches and epistemologies: liberal, Marxist, and poststructuralist. This space is, of course, always being challenged from without by artistic and social movements (e.g., romanticism, anticolonialism, surrealism) and from within by critical currents. However, my argument is that *taken as a whole* the academy, including critical cultural and social theory, systematically reproduces this epistemic space.

16 A strictly Foucauldian perspective would ask whether the figure of "Man" that is at the center of the modern episteme has been removed from its centrality. I can only say for now that most tendencies still show lingering forms of anthropocentrism, androcentrism, and Eurocentrism and continue to function within the oww.

17 In *Decolonizing Methodologies: Research and Indigenous Peoples*, the Maori scholar Linda Tuhiwai Smith thoughtfully ponders the risks incurred when indigenous peoples use academic writing to discuss their history and situation of oppression; in doing so, she asks, do they not run the risk of writing about indigenous peoples "as if we really were 'out there,' the 'Other,' with all the baggage that this entails"? (1999, 36; see also Walsh 2012). As she adds, "academic writing is a form of selecting, arranging and presenting knowledge. . . . [It reinforces and maintains] a style of discourse that is never innocent" (36). I believe this concern with logocentric writing is close to Varela's. The condition of possibility of academic writing is still a certain Western *ratio*, a feature that characterizes the entire system of the human and social sciences within the modern episteme (Foucault 1970, 377, 378).

18 The conversations established by these authors between Western and Buddhist scholars on the mind, including the Dalai Lama, have been very fruitful and are chronicled in various projects and books.

19 Karl Marx's concepts of commodity fetishism and alienation were already an argument about disconnection—in his case, the invisibility of the social labor embedded in the commodity and the way this is central to profit making.

20 Well known is the example of the flower given by the Buddhist teacher Thich Nhat Hanh; the flower does not exist in isolation but interexists with the plant, the soil, the water, the pollinating insects, and even the sun, which are all essential to its existence (e.g., Nhat Hanh 1975, 2008). As Sharma adds, "the sense of a flower's continuity over time is a kind of experience, not an autonomous feature of an external world" (2015, 12). In Buddhism, meditation on interdependence goes along with equally important reflections on imper-manence and compassion; only then can the insight of interbeing be fully realized. The ultimate aim is to be able to *practice interdependence*, not to get caught up in philosophical reflection on it.

21 This is an intellectual approximation to relationality, of course; grasping its nature more fully, according to some, demands transrational forms of engagement with the real, such as contemplative, hallucinatory, or shamanic experiences.

Chapter 4: An Outline of Ontological Design

Epigraphs: Virilio, *The Administration of Fear* (2012), 46, 72; Willis, "Ontological Designing—Laying the Ground" (2006), 80; Winograd and Flores, *Understanding Computers and Cognition* (1986), xi.

1 "Can We Auto-Correct Humanity?" by Prince Ea, posted online on September 29, 2014 by Prince Ea, 3.27 min: https://www.youtube.com/watch?v=dR18EIhrQjQ (accessed on January 10, 2017, when it had over eighteen million views).

2 As the mantra goes, "Because we live in an increasingly globalized, rapidly changing, and interdependent world" (the slogan of Public Radio International). One should always add "increasingly devastated" to this facile mantra. In this seemingly slight addition we find an expression of the challenges and politics of design.

3 I am drawing here on the insightful short book on the political geology of media tech-nologies by Finnish theorist of digital culture Jussi Parikka, *The Anthrobscene* (2016). See also Gibson-Graham, Cameron, and Healy (2013, 95–104) for a discussion of the ethical and economic implications of the market in so-called conflict minerals.

4 Virilio is likely the most enlightening critic of new technologies. He is most well known as a philosopher of speed, or, more precisely, of the relations among speed, power, and tech-nology. In his view, information and communication technologies, operating in real time, alter dramatically our long-standing experience of place, body, time, and space, inaugurating a dromosphere, a space of living ruled by speed (see, e.g., Virilio 1997, 1999, 2012). The gener-alized delocalization caused by these technologies, and taken to its ultimate applications by military technology, reveals for Virilio that what is at stake is contrasting conceptions of the world (diverging ontologies). Of his work he says that it "is that of a 'resister' because there are too many 'collaborators' who are once again pulling the trick of redemptory progress, emancipation, [humans] liberated from all repression, etc." (1999, 80). Virilio

attended Maurice Merleau-Ponty's lectures in Paris for a time, which intensified his interest in phenomenology. I will return to the question of technology in the conclusion.

5   The most insightful of the cyberpunk novels was, to my mind, William Gibson's *Neuromancer* (1984), where the term *cyberspace* was actually coined. In this and several of his subsequent novels, Gibson explores the changed body politics enacted by technology, in particular the largely male fantasies of total disembodiment (see Escobar 1994 for further discussion).

6   This aspect of the book draws heavily on Martin Heidegger and Hans-Georg Gadamer. A tradition is a pervasive background or preunderstanding within which we act in, and interpret, the world; it is concealed by its obviousness; it is historically produced and impossible to describe in its entirety (the hermeneutic circle). As Humberto Maturana and Francisco Varela put it, referring to how they came up with the novel concept of autopoiesis, "we could not escape being immersed in a tradition, but with an adequate language we could orient ourselves differently and, perhaps, from the new perspective generate a new tradition" (1980, xvii). The novelty of their work lies precisely in the invention of a new lexicon for talking about biological existence, particularly cognition, as we shall see in the last chapter.

7   Throughout the book Spinosa, Flores, and Dreyfus discuss exemplary figures of this type of skill, such as Martin Luther King Jr. and the group Mothers against Drunk Driving. I have applied these concepts to the case of the activists in the movement of the black communities of the Colombian Pacific, whose activism can genuinely be seen as a practice of skillful disclosing and history making in the midst of a sustained attack on their territories and culture by developmentalist actors (Escobar 2008, 229–236).

8   An important part of Winograd and Flores's framework is the development of a linguistic approach to the work of organizations based on "directives" (orders, requests, consultations, and offers) and "commissives" (promises, acceptances, and rejections). In the 1980s Flores developed a software program for organizations, called the Coordinator, based on the idea that organizations are networks of commitments operating in language. See Winograd and Flores (1986, chs. 5 and 11) and Flores and Flores Letelier (2013). Its objective was "to make the interactions transparent—to provide a ready-to-hand tool that operates in the domain of conversations for action" (1986, 159). Anthropologist Lucy Suchman (1994) has proposed a cogent critique of Winograd and Flores's reliance on speech act theory for their theory of organizations. In her opinion, their framework veers perilously close to the imposition of a Foucauldian disciplinary order by a group of allegedly enlightened designers. This leaves untouched organizations' links to power, while people's actions get normalized in the name of a higher form of rationality. In other words, she casts doubts on Winograd and Flores's claim that their approach constitutes an emancipatory alternative. I agree with most of this critique, although I am trying to recover the political potential of their view of ontological design through my interpretation, going beyond language.

9   What else is the anthropocene if not the result of design choices, a design itself perhaps?

10 This is a very partial account of Fry's sustained attempt at providing a new foundation for design, developed through a number of major books and multiple articles. Fry's view

articulates particular readings of evolutionary theory, sociotechnics, Nietzschean genealogy, and Heideggerian phenomenology. There is a practical side to Fry's work, particularly in urban design (besides design education, of course). This account is largely based on Fry's three main books of the last few years. (I will not discuss here aspects of Fry's work that are less convincing to me, such as his Nietzschean notion of the humax.)

11 See also Fry's current project, The Studio at the Edge of the World, http://www.thestudioattheedgeoftheworld.com/.

12 Besides Heidegger and Maturana, Ehrenfeld draws on the critique of industrial society by early Frankfurt school writers (particularly Erich Fromm), the Chilean critic of development Manfred Max-Neef, and Anthony Giddens's theory of structuration. Tellingly, he acknowledges Flores for introducing him to Heidegger and Maturana "through an intensive program in ontological design" in the Bay Area in the late 1980s (2009, xxii). Those versed in contemporary critical social theory might find peculiar or problematic the combination of theoretical sources (say, going back to Fromm, who was indeed an enlightened critic of modernity), or the focus on addictive behavior, which might be seen as harking back to much-criticized psychological approaches, but here again I will encourage the more theoretically minded readers to consider Ehrenfeld's effort as a salient instance of ontological thought on design.

13 Ehrenfeld cites the local food movement and new toilets that instruct users about flushing decisions, which he sees as eventually inducing a more profound change of consciousness. The approach remains largely theoretical, however, and does not deal explicitly with politics. That said, the notions of flourishing, presencing (of Heideggerian and Buddhist derivation, a concept we will encounter again when discussing the work of Otto Scharmer and Katrin Kaufer below), and care are all elements of an emergent design lexicon.

14 Fry envisions seven possible types of human beings emerging, the character of which can be gleaned from the labels: homotecs (radically pro-technology), neo-nomads, war-takers, hoarder survivalists, scavengers, gatherers, and palingensiaists (keepers and re-creators of knowledge). See Fry (2012, 205–211) for his discussion of these "people of the future."

15 This is an inadequate presentation of these authors' ideas. See their work at the Presencing Institute (https://www.presencing.com/). Their ideas are influenced by Heidegger and Varela as well as by organizational scholars Peter Senge and Brian Arthur. A problem with this framework that is often discussed (e.g., by PhD students in my graduate seminar on design) is the risk of co-optation owing to a lingering individualist orientation and the absence of a more explicit sense of politics. There is also a certain teleology in how the authors present the models of "economic evolution": the State-driven "Society 1.0," market-driven "Society 2.0," stakeholder-driven "Society 3.0," and ecosystem-driven "Society 4.0," or the "con-creative economy." As in much of this otherwise-creative work in the United States, there is very little explicit critique of capitalism, and an insufficiently examined willingness to work with corporations. On the positive side, I would say that this theory is unusual in that it tackles the inner work designers need to do in order to take seriously the challenges of presencing and nondualism.

16 For a related argument about moving beyond the autonomous individual that instead draws on historical and contemporary Western sources, see Dreyfus and Kelly (2011).

17 On care, see Boff's (2002) work; his argument about care as a fundamental ontological structure is based on Heidegger, religious thought, and the everyday actions of common people. There is a voluminous feminist literature on care, from economists who focus on the care economy to scholars in science and technology studies who introduce ethical care concerns into the domain of relations between human and nonhuman (e.g., Haraway 2008). María Puig de la Bellacasa (2015) brings an original angle into the care debates, that of the existing tension between the productivist time of capitalism, innovation, and technoscience (and, one might add, design as usual), on the one hand, and the temporalities required for an effective ethics of caring for the webs of relationality that maintain life, across the entire spectrum of material, human, and nonhuman forms, on the other.

18 *Sociedades abigarradas* is a difficult term to translate; it can mean "motley, variegated, jumbled, or heterogeneous societies."

19 While these fusions bring together musics from practically all world regions, there are some places that constitute particularly rich musical sources at present, such as West Africa (Mali and Senegal); Cuba, Colombia, and Brazil in Latin America; and Europe and North America (in some of their folk traditions). (The London-based magazine *Songlines* is dedicated to these fusions.) I am afraid I know little about world musics from other world regions.

20 *Fusion* is actually a misnomer for what musicians mean. As the well-known Flamenco singer Diego el Cigala says, the concept of fusion implies the disappearance of worlds, yet in musical collaborations the worlds do not disappear but are reenacted in dialogue. In support of this idea, el Cigala mentions a conversation with salsa musician Bebo Valdés: "Tu canta como ese gitano que eres que yo tocaré como el cubano que soy" ("you go ahead and sing like the Gypsy you are, and I will play like the Cuban I am"). See the program with El Cigala, "Diego el Cigala. Encuentro en el estudio," published by Canal Encuentro, Buenos Aires, August 21, 2014, 55.26 min: https://www.youtube.com/watch?v=10yhpNCqn9Y. Collaborations are found across all kinds of musics, including within classical, popular, and folk musics; witness, for instance, the fascinating collaboration *Uniko* (2004/2011) between the San Francisco–based Kronos Quartet and the Finnish musicians Kimmo Pohjonen (accordion and voice) and Samuli Hosminen (voice sampling, live loops, and digital interfaces). Interestingly, musicians often describe collaborations as doing "what is best for the music" when they collaborate (as in jam sessions, but more pointedly in intergenre productions). Two explicit conversations in this regard that I happen to know of are that among the Venetian electronic music composer Luigi Nono, the director Claudio Abbado, and the pianist Murizio Pollini (see the documentary *A Trail on the Water*, directed by Bettina Ehrhardt [2001]), and, in a very different vein, that among Argentinean folk musicians Peteco Carabajal, the duo Coplanacu, and Raly Barrionuevo (see the DVD of their collaboration, *La Juntada* (Carabajal, Coplanacu and Barrionuevo 2004).

21 Attali bases his argument about composition on avant-garde composers such as Luciano Berio, John Cage, Luigi Nono, and Pierre Boulez but also on American free jazz, a mixture of African American popular music and European experimental music.

Chapter 5: Design for Transitions

Epigraphs: Irwin, "Transition Design: A Proposal for a New Era of Design Practice, Study and Research" (2015), 1, 4; Tonkinwise, "Design's (Dis)Orders and Transition Design" (2014), 12; Manzini, *Design, When Everybody Designs: An Introduction to Design for Social Innovation* (2015), 2.

1 I use the term *transition* rather than *transformation* since that is the actual term used by most of the frameworks discussed here. Some of the TDs can be criticized on many grounds (e.g., their lack of attention to questions of power and domination in terms of class, gender, and race, or their continued reliance on modernist premises). However, most imply a radical notion of transformation at many levels. In some cases, the meaning of *transition* is similar to Karl Polanyi's (1957) notion of "the great transformation"; in others, a transition is seen as entailing many types of transformation. Most exhibit a profound open-endedness and awareness of being one of many possible stories. In contrast to well-known areas of transition research in the social sciences (e.g., transitions to postsocialism, postcapitalism, or postconflict), the TDs presented here bracket straightforward teleologies, even if they, too, tell a story with a "from" and a "toward." Some explicitly appeal to nonlinear dynamics, emergence, and self-organization.

2 The TDs cited here represent a segment of the literature. They range from the more cultural and spiritual to the explicitly political; they appeal to a broad array of concepts and tropes, from the dystopian (collapse, decline and descent, survival, apocalypse, etc.) to the reconstructive (e.g., conscious evolution, collective intelligence, sacredness, saving the planet and humans, and so forth). There is lots to be learned from these visions and proposals, which academics and designers rarely consider. The entire field of spiritual ecology can be seen as a space for TDs.

3 The Great Transition Initiative is a network devoted to the systematic study and promotion of transition ideas and strategies, housed at the Tellus Institute in Boston. Its origins date back to 1995, with the creation of the Global Scenario Group by Paul Raskin and the Argentinean modeling expert Gilberto Gallopín. See the initiative's website, http://www.greattransition.org/.

4 This is an exciting and growing area, even in some critical strands of the academy. Within the West, it has predecessors in the works of Vladimir Vernadsky and Pierre Teilhard de Chardin, among others, but also in the traditions of immanence, vitalism, and process thought. It should be emphasized that a sentient universe is a core idea—indeed, a reality— in many indigenous cosmologies.

5 See the work of the Center for Ecozoic Societies in Chapel Hill (http://www.ecozoic societies.org/), directed by Herman Greene, which is largely devoted to Berry's work.

6 Berry actually posited a definition of the anthropocene *avant la lettre*; in an essay from 1988, beautifully entitled *The Dream of the Earth*, he wrote, "We are acting on a geologi-

cal and biological order of magnitude. We are changing the chemistry of the planet. . . . The anthropogenic shock that is overwhelming the earth is of an order of magnitude beyond anything previously known in human historical or cultural development." (206, 211).

7 For the project led by Greene, see Center for Ecozoic Societies, http://www.ecozoic societies.org/; for Clayton's, see Ecological Civilization International, http://colleges .org/networks/ecological-civilization-international/. For related projects, see Seizing and Alternative. Toward an Ecological Civilization, http://www.ctr4process.org /whitehead2015/; Pando Populus, http://www.pandopopulus.com/.

8 There are close to five hundred communities worldwide (largely in the North) engaged in transition plans inspired by the TTI. The primer for transition initiatives is detailed and feasible. See the Transition Network's website, https://transitionnetwork.org/.

9 The references to degrowth in this section are largely based on the theoretical contributions of a group of ecological economists and degrowth scholars within ICTA (Institut de Ciència i Tecnologia Ambientals, Universitat Autònoma de Barcelona); this group's scholarly production is an impressive effort at building a comprehensive framework for degrowth. See especially Schneider, Lallis, and Martínez-Alier (2010); Martínez-Alier (2009); Kallis (2011); Kallis, Kerschner, and Martínez-Alier (2012); Cattaneo et al. (2012); Sekulova et al. (2013); Demaria et al. (2013); Asara, Profumi, and Kallis (2013); and D'Alisa, Demaria, and Kallis (2015).

10 For analyses of the notions of Buen Vivir and the rights of nature, see the useful short volumes by Alberto Acosta (2010) and Acosta and Esperanza Martínez (2009a, 2009b); and the valuable overviews in Eduardo Gudynas's (2014, 2015) works. There is a considerable literature on these topics; see Escobar (2015a) for a list of pertinent references. The monthly journal *América Latina en Movimiento* is an excellent source of intellectual-activist writings on these subjects, with special issues on Buen Vivir (452, 462), transitions (473), postdevelopment (445), and so forth (http://www.alainet.org). I should make it clear that for reasons of space I will not discuss the application of the notions of Buen Vivir and the rights of nature by progressive regimes like those in Ecuador and Bolivia; as is well known in the region, this application has been selective and contradictory.

11 There are related notions in the South, such as the southern African notion of *ubuntu*, which cannot be discussed here. For a comparison of degrowth, swaraj, and Buen Vivir, see Kothari, Demaria, and Acosta (2015).

12 The literature on emergence and self-organization is huge, and I will not even try to summarize it here. See, e.g., Capra and Luisi (2014) for a very useful and up to date summary account; Varela (1999); Escobar (2004; 2008, ch. 6) for a short summary. At the Transition Design Workshop to be discussed shortly, Manzini discussed this concept by analyzing the emergence of capitalism and the collapse of the Soviet Union as two contrasting instances of emergence.

13 The meeting, called the Doctoral Reviews and Transition Design Symposium, was held at CMU in Pittsburgh on March 6–7, 2015; it gathered about fifty participants, including the main faculty affiliated with the program (Terry Irwin, Cameron Tonkinwise, Gideon Kossoff, and Peter Scupelli), five current PhD students, former PhD students from the

school, and outside guest speakers. Anne-Marie Willis and Ezio Manzini gave the symposium's main talks. I also attended the meeting.

14 The presentation is largely based on the following texts and on my participation at the symposium: Irwin 2015; Irwin, Kossoff, and Tonkinwise 2015; Kossoff 2011, 2015; Scupelli 2015; Tonkinwise 2012, 2013a, 2013b, 2014, 2015; Irwin et al. 2015; and Manzini 2015. I will not refer to specific texts in this presentation, except for explicit quotations. While most of the presentation in this section and the next will be straightforward (that is, based on the ideas found in the sources), some of it will take the form of the "point counter point" described by one of the main characters (a writer) in Aldous Huxley's self-described "novel of ideas" from 1928 with the same title: "The modulations, not merely from one key to another, but from mood to mood. A theme is stated, then developed, pushed out of shape, imperceptibly deformed, until, though still recognizably the same, it has become quite different" ([1928] 1996, 293–294). This dynamic of "contrapuntal plots" often operates in academic writing.

15 See the interesting and unique Carnegie Mellon School of Design framework, from the School's website, http://design.cmu.edu/content/program-framework.

16 This point was made emphatically by Damian White, from the Rhode Island School of Design, during the symposium, and it is discussed in his paper (2015).

17 Besides living-systems theory, the current Theories of Change component includes social-practice theory, some critiques of modernity (e.g., that of Illich), and poststructuralist analysis of dominant discourses such as development. In my view, one strategy to enrich the Theories of Change dimension of the framework is to selectively identify proposals that in one way or another are likely to illuminate particular roadblocks or difficult steps in moving transition design forward. A key issue is how to rethink the economy, and the most developed proposal in this area, to my mind, is J. K. Gibson-Graham's diverse economies framework, which I would say has a design-friendly imagination (Gibson-Graham 2006; Gibson-Graham, Cameron, and Healy 2013), and the Latin American social and solidarity economy (e.g., Coraggio and Laville 2014; Coraggio, Laville, and Cattani 2013). Epistemological issues could be constructively discussed with the help of the *Epistemologies of the South* framework, decolonial thinking, and political ontology, discussed in chapter 2. This could buttress the non-Eurocentric spirit of the project. It seems to me also that there is a great need for the framework to incorporate some of the work in science and technology studies and feminist political ecology dealing with key questions of importance to design, such as bodies, materiality, and the reconstruction of technoscience.

18 As Tonkinwise puts it, "most designers focus on merely improving existing life styles or ways of working. This is design as business-as-usual enhancement" (2014, 7). The transition designer would opt for a different ethics.

19 Phenomenologically speaking, the book can be said to be the product of a practitioner who has become a master at his practice, that is, one who practices design at its best.

20 Manzini's examples include collaborative services and housing programs in the United Kingdom and Italy, as well as the slow food and democratic psychiatry movements in Italy. He draws throughout the book on the rich experience of the Design for Social Innovation and Sustainability Network, based in Milan but with participant nodes (affili-

ated university and design school labs) in a number of countries (see http://www.desis
-network.org/).

21 This is a feature that Manzini clearly adumbrates, even if he does not elaborate on it; for
him, the emergent new civilization takes place within a complex pluriverse; see, e.g., p. 23
of his book.

22 Whether implicitly or explicitly, there is a clear cultural critique of both individualism
and disabling expert-driven institutions in Manzini's vision, echoing Illich's radical critiques of the same systems.

23 The Life Projects Network is coordinated by Mario Blaser in Newfoundland, Canada. As
its portal describes, it is intended "to access a variety of ongoing experiments across the
Americas that seek to foster the various practices of a good life that emerge from particular places, historical trajectories and conceptions of reality. The term 'Life Projects' is
fundamentally a place holder that stands for practices of a good life that in one way or
another differ from 'Development Projects' (in both, Right and Left wing versions), that
is, visions and practices of a good life premised on the primacy of the 'Human.'" See their
website, The Life Projects Network, https://www.lifeprovida.net/index.php?lang=en.

24 Manzini underscores an important element in this dynamic: "This means that the capacity of people and communities cannot be increased from the bottom up only, by distrib-
uting dedicated toolkits. It is necessary to combine different kinds of intervention, based
on different strategies. It follows that the toolkits we are talking about must be part of a
wider set of services and communicative artifacts that compete not only to foster their
own good use, but also to reinforce motivations to use them" (2015, 184). Elsewhere (Escobar 2001), I have spoken about subaltern social movements engaging in a twofold set of
strategies: strategies of localization (place based), for the defense of their territories and
cultures, and strategies of interweaving with other struggles, against shared structuring
conditions of domination; the latter might be explained today in terms of distributed
power and agency.

Chapter 6: Autonomous Design and the Politics of Relationality and the Communal

Epigraphs: Zapatista slogan included at the end of the "Ten Principles of Good Government" at the entrance of one of the Zapatista autonomous communities (see "Junta
del Buen Gobierno Corazón del Arco Iris," August 9, 2012, from the website of the
Confederación General del Trabajo [CGT-España], Chiapas, http://www.cgtchiapas.org
/denuncias-juntas-buen-gobierno-denuncias/jbg-morelia-denuncia-ataque-orcao-con
-arma-fuego-bases); Olver Quijano, "Cambiar el mundo no viene ni de arriba ni de afuera.
Resumen del Congreso Tramas y Mingas por el Buen Vivir, Popayán, Junio 9-11, 2013"
(Quijano 2013); Varela, *Ethical Know-How: Action, Wisdom, and Cognition* (1999), 11.

1 This point is made by the legendary systems theorist Stafford Beer, who worked with
Flores on Project Cybersyn during the Allende presidency in Chile, in his preface to Maturana and Varela's *Autopoiesis and Cognition* (1980). Project Cybersyn was a pioneering

attempt at applying cybernetics and computing to the Chilean economy during the Allende socialist period (1970–1973); there is a full-fledged account of the project by historian of science Eden Medina (2011). The point of departure of Maturana and Varela's work was Maturana's neurophysiological studies of vision from the late 1950s, which led to several important publications in the 1960s; these formed the basis of *Autopoiesis and Cognition* (1980), originally published in Spanish in 1973. There followed a radical reinterpretation of key biological concepts, including ontogeny, phylogeny, reproduction and heredity, evolution, and, of course, cognition and the nervous system.

2 Readers have pointed out the circularity of this definition. In fact, the cover of the first Chilean edition of the book, titled *De máquinas y seres vivos* (1973), included the ancient symbol of the *uroboros*, apparently of Egyptian origin, which depicts a serpent eating its tail. The uroboros represents the self-referentiality of the living that is at the core of the notion of autopoiesis—matter and energy always folding in on themselves (as in Teilhard de Chardin's notion of consciousness folding in on itself as the central dynamic of evolution). I thank Gustavo Jiménez Lagos for telling me about the cover (personal communication, July 12, 2014).

3 It should be clear that this perspective depends on making a distinction between two units or structures, the living being and its environment. Maturana and Varela's epistemological discussion of this distinction is complex, and I have bracketed it here (see Escobar 2008, 294–295, for a discussion). In the preface to the fifth edition of the Spanish version, Varela speaks of *co-definición* (codetermination) between system and environment. Maturana and Varela's work was influenced by the vibrant debates on systems, cybernetics, information, and self-organization of the 1950s and 1960s (see Escobar 2008, ch. 6, for this background).

4 Taylor's is one of the few works linking critical theory and theories of emergence and self-organization; his argument is that complexity theories can help in rearticulating some of poststructuralism's unsolved questions. He charges that deconstructivists reproduce the totalizing gesture they impute to systems theorists (that systems totalize and thus repress differences), since they leave differences irremediably fragmented and without any hope of recomposition. To my knowledge, the only sustained application of the concept of autopoiesis to social systems is by Niklas Luhmann, discussed in B. Clarke and Hansen (2009).

5 This section should have a more adequate account of complexity, emergence, and self-organization and their relevance to social theory; I hope the remarks offered above might entice others to undertake such a task. For those worried about the importation of natural science idioms into social theory, I would suggest that one may think of social and biological life in terms of assemblages, coherence, and wholes from a continuum of experience and matter that is both self-organized and other-organized (a pluriverse); in this way, there would not be separate biological and social worlds, nature and culture. One could then read the insights of complexity as lessons from one kind of theory to another and not from some pregiven biological realm whose truths biologists are finally getting right.

6 Out of this flux there emerge observer-generated systems. Varela, in the Introduction to Heinz von Foerster's *Observing Systems* (1983, xv), writes, "There is still virtually no chal-

lenge to the view of objectivity understood as the condition of independence of descriptions, rather than a circle of mutual elucidation. Further, there is little acceptance yet that to make these points of view scientific programmes is the operational closure of cognitive systems, living or otherwise." In other words, *operational closure does not entail independent existence.* As he sums up, aphoristically, "the logic of the world is the logic of the description of the world. . . . Objectivity: the properties of the observer shall not enter in the description of the observation. Post-objectivity: the description of observations shall reveal the properties of the observer" (Varela 1983, xvi.).

7 I heard Esteva make this distinction in a lecture in the mid-2000s. A version of it is found in Esteva (2015). This entire issue of the *Latin American and Caribbean Ethnic Studies* journal is devoted to indigenous autonomy in Latin America.

8 These features of autonomía emerge from discussions by and about social movements particularly in southern Mexico (Chiapas, Oaxaca), southwestern Colombia (black and indigenous movements), and parts of South America, especially Bolivia and Ecuador. There are resonances with themes in contemporary theory (e.g., Gilles Deleuze and Félix Guattari, 1987) and with anarchist thought.

9 From a document signed by the main indigenous organizations of Colombia (Organizaciones Indígenas de Colombia 2004). Downloaded June 6, 2017, from the website Minga Informativa de los Movimientos Sociales, http://www.movimientos.org/es /show_text.php3%3Fkey%3D3282.

10 In fact, social movements can be considered autopoietic units; established theories see movements as allopoietic, that is, produced by and referring to another logic, whether capital, the State, nationalism, or what have you (Escobar 1992).

11 According to Jerôme Baschet (2014), rebellious autonomy is the general principle of both Zapatista organizing and their actions aimed at the reconstruction of life beyond capitalism.

12 The case of the *piqueteros* in Argentina is one of the most well-known cases of autonomous politics in urban Latin America. See the excellent dissertation by Elizabeth Mason-Deese (2015).

13 I should make it clear that I am discussing here the Latin American perspectives on autonomía. There are many other sources for the concept, including in anarchism and Italian autonomous Marxism. The alter-globalization movements of the late 1990s and early 2000s did much to bring the question of autonomy into discussion. See, for instance, Conway (2013); Osterweil (2013); Grubacic and O'Hearn (2016).

14 This principle is repeated frequently in Nasa writings, particularly those by the Asociación de Cabildos Indígenas del Norte del Cauca (ACIN). See, for example, the call for the "Tercer Congreso ACIN, junio 15–21, 2017," https://nasaacin.org/30-congreso-acin-cxhab-wala-kiwe/.

15 The theoretico-political expressions of autonomy and the communal stem first of all from a variety of grassroots collectives and movements. These notions are being actively conceptualized by a number of intellectuals and activists, including Gustavo Esteva, Raquel Gutiérrez Aguilar, Xochitl Leyva, Silvia Rivera Cusicanqui, Raúl Zibechi, Manuel Rozental, Vilma Almendra, Patricia Botero, Astrid Ulloa, John Holloway, Carlos Walter Porto Gonçalves, el Colectivo Situaciones, Luis Tapia, Catherine Walsh, Janet Conway,

and Jerôme Baschet; the Aymara intellectuals Pablo Mamani, Julieta Paredes, Felix Patzi, and Simón Yampara; and a diverse group of researchers, intellectuals, and activists centered in the city of Popayán, with the active participation of indigenous and Afrodescendant communities. Many of these actors converged at the recent meeting in Puebla, Mexico, the First International Congress on Comunalidad, convened by Gutiérrez Aguilar and collaborators (October 26–29, 2015). The doctoral program in Latin American cultural studies at the Universidad Andina Simón Bolívar in Quito, headed by Catherine Walsh, is also important in this regard.

16 The term *comunalidad* was coined at the end of the 1970s by two Oaxacan thinkers, Floriberto Díaz Gómez and Jaime Martínez Luna. Esteva also introduces *comunalitario*, or communalitarian, different from the well-established *comunitario* (communitarian). This neologism is helpful in establishing some distance from the association of the communal with what is often described as "communitarian violence" in South Asia.

17 There has been a clear fallback into statist and developmentalist positions in Bolivia in recent years, certainly at the level of the State.

18 Patzi Paco's conceptual framework includes a distinction between system and environment reminiscent of Maturana and Varela's.

19 This part is based on a weeklong workshop on ecological river basin design that I designed and implemented in 1998 in the port city of Buenaventura, in the Colombian Pacific, together with the activists of the Proceso de Comunidades Negras (Process of Black Communities), under the explicit rubric of autonomous design. The participants were leaders of grassroots river organizations and activists in the social movement of the black communities. The background to the exercise was the need for river communities to develop their own *plan de ordenamiento territorial* (territorial action plan), mandated by the government. The workshop workbooks are available, although they were never published (see PCN and Escobar 1998). The workshop followed my own version of a systems approach, significantly influenced by C. West Churchman and Leonard Joy (mentioned in the book's preface).

20 For Victor Papanek, "the most important ability that a designer can bring to his work is the ability to recognize, isolate, define, and solve problems" (1984, 151). Today everybody agrees that design goes beyond problem solving, and that inquiring into problems needs to be participatory. To be fair, Papanek advocated for "integrated, comprehensive, anticipatory design" (322), arguing against narrow problem definitions and planning.

21 The further one departs from established Cartesian methodologies, the more engaging the discussions leading to what I have called a model (surely not the best term) become. By *engaging* I mean an intense, open-ended conversation that brings forth, and at its best challenges, the cultural background of the collectivity. This type of engaging conversation is well known in community assemblies or social movements' political meetings, which often go on for hours, seemingly without a concrete agenda. Planners miss this dynamic altogether with their fixed routines, or they consider it a waste of time.

22 These questions stem from Joy's systems approach to food and nutrition planning (from class notes, University of California, Berkeley, summers of 1978 and 1979; Joy 1978).

23 I am grateful to David López Mata and Douglas Laing for some of the information in this section.

24 In his remarks during a tribute to him which took place in Cali on October 28, 2015, don Luis Enrique Dina Zape, an elder from the black town of Puerto Tejada in the heart of the sugarcane-growing region, referred to the early period of cane expansion as "the time when the bandits arrived." The cane systematically destroyed the independent farms based on cocoa and a diversity of crops that black farmers had maintained, in some cases, until the mid-twentieth century, thus bringing to an end a period of independent, autonomous black farming communities (see also Mina 1975).

25 According to the excellent study by anthropologist Arlene Dávila (2016), Latin America is the world region where the construction of globalized shopping malls is proceeding fastest; this trend significantly affects cultural practices (increasingly centered on consumption), socioeconomic structures, and identity processes. The design of shopping centers is an effective machine for defuturing and unsustainability.

26 In a recent proposal (Escobar 2015b), I envisioned the process as taking place over a ten-year period. See the proposal for additional theoretical justification of the project. It should be made clear that the Cauca River valley refers in this section to the entire geographic region (sometimes also called Alto Cauca), not to the administrative department.

27 Ezio Manzini (2015, 89) speaks about the importance of the initial "creative community" in collaborative design experiences.

28 Manzini's discussion of design for social innovation (chapter 3) is very useful for thinking about many of these aspects; see especially his discussion of the Slow Food Movement.

29 "Other Economies Are Possible" was actually the title of a four-day workshop designed and organized by Proceso de Comunidades Negras (PCN) and held in Buga, north of Cali, in July 2013, with the participation of seventy activists from Norte del Cauca and the southern Pacific, plus a handful of academics, including me. The goal was to discuss the very idea that other economies are possible and to showcase examples of autonomous economic projects by communities. The workshop was sponsored in part by a grant from the Paul K. Feyerabend Foundation (see http://pkfeyerabend.org/en/).

30 From the document, "Libertad para la Madre Tierra," May 28, 2010, from the Asociación de Cabildos Indígenas del Norte del Cauca (ACIN) website, http://www.nasaacin.org /libertar-para-la-madre-tierra/50-libertad-para-la-madre-tierra. For background on this indigenous movement and the recent actions, see "El desafío que nos convoca," May 28, 2010, http://www.nasaacin.org/el-desafio-no-da-espera (same webpage). See also, from the website Pueblos en Camino, "Lo que vamos aprendiendo con la liberación de Uma Kiwe," January 19, 2016, http://pueblosencamino.org/?p=2176; Vilma Almendra, "La paz de la Mama Kiwe en libertad, de la mujer sin amarras ni silencios," August 2, 2012, http:// pueblosencamino.org/?p=150. From the blog Libertad para la Madre Tierra, see "Liberar y alegría con Uma Kiwe: Palabra del proceso de liberación de la Madre Tierra," http:// liberemoslatierra.blogspot.es/1481948996/libertad-y-alegria-con-uma-kiwe-palabra-del -proceso-de-liberacion-de-la-madre-tierra/.

Conclusion

The opening poem was translated by John Chasteen, Department of History, University of North Carolina at Chapel Hill.

1 Remark made at one of the events on the Mexican crisis convened under the rubric "Defending Our Common House," organized by Gustavo Esteva and held in Mexico City on November 16–21, 2015. The Rarámuri were formerly known as Tarahumara.

2 "Lo que vamos aprendiendo con la Liberación de Uma Kiwe," from the website of the Tejido de Comunicación Asociación de Cabildos del Norte del Cauca, http://anterior. nasaacin.org/index.php/nuestra-palabra/7987-lo-que-vamos-aprendiendo-con-la -liberaci%C3%B3n-de-uma-kiwe, accessed June 8, 2017.

3 "Lo que vamos aprendiendo."

4 "Emancipate yourselves from mental slavery, none but ourselves can free our minds. . . . Won't you help to sing these songs of freedom, it's all I ever had, redemption songs." From the album *Uprising* (1980).

5 Yet one finds statements critical of capitalism in the transition design literature, for instance, from Cameron Tonkinwise: "Within design thinking there is an idealistic drive toward anti-capitalism, or at least anti-business-as-usual" (2012, 14). At the same time, the same author warns that design "tends to be ameliorative rather than politically pursuing structural change" (2015, 87).

6 This idea has found a recent lucid expression in the domain of insurrectionary politics: "The biggest problem we face is a philosophical one: understanding that this civilization is *already dead*. . . . [Its end] has been clinically established for a century" (Invisible Committee 2015, 29). Talk of crisis is a surrogate for the realization that it is the West that is the catastrophe—nobody is out to destroy the West; it is destroying itself.

7 I owe the idea of extending Gibson-Graham's analysis of capitalism to modernity to Nicolás Sánchez, who suggested it in one of the sessions of my Anthropology of Design graduate seminar in the spring of 2016.

8 My concern with the risks of pluralizing modernity has benefited greatly from discussions with friends in several parts of the world. These friends rightly point, conversely, at two risks in the pluriversal position: the alterization of difference (locating difference, and hope for change, in the more clearly identifiable subaltern groups, such as ethnic minorities) and the tendency to treat modernity as hegemonic and homogeneous. All worlds have to be historicized deeply—all worlds (whether traditional or modern) contain a judicious mix of the good, the bad, and the ugly.

9 Nandy's remark was made in reference to Gandhi. For Nandy, one of the paradoxical implications of Gandhi's thought was that "it is more civil not to be civilized in the modern sense" (Nandy 1987, 146).

10 The ritual of *la ombligada* (*ombligo* means "navel") refers to the act of burying the umbilical cord and the placenta after a child is born near the house or under a tree by the edge of the forest (for girls and boys, respectively). The navel of the newborn is subsequently filled with a pulverized natural substance—animal, plant, or mineral—in such a way as to

transmit the substance's properties to the individual. In so doing, the newborn is deeply connected to the territory and made to partake in some fashion of the rest of the natural world. See Escobar (2008, 113–115) for a description and analysis of this ritual, including the main ethnographic studies of it in the Colombian Pacific.

11   "Contingentists preserve the world's reality"—concludes Sharma—"*just by* their refusal to posit an order that is radically external to subjects, a truth that perceivers will never attain, or a reality from which subjects are forever separated" (2015, 98). This is consistent with Maturana and Varela's solution, already quoted in chapter 3, of finding "a *via media*: to understand the regularity of the world we are experiencing at every moment, but without any point of reference independent of ourselves that would give certainty to our descriptions and cognitive assertions" (1987, 241).

12   We discussed this question intensely with a group of ten doctoral students at my week-long seminar on the anthropology of design at the Universidad del Cauca in Popayán in October 2015. I thank all the seminar participants for their insights. Thanks also to Enrique Leff and Gustavo Esteva for conversations on the same issue, held in Mexico City in November 2015, and to Walter Mignolo (conversation in Durham, North Carolina, May 26, 2016). The position taken here is, of course, mine.

13   The points about Amazonian knowledge became clear to me after presentations and discussions with don Abel Rodríguez, an indigenous botanist and healer from the Nonuya nation (Colombian Amazon), and with don Abel's partners, the anthropologists Carlos Rodríguez and María Clara van der Hammen, from Tropenbos International in Bogotá (http://www.tropenbos.org/country_programmes/colombia). These conversations also included designer and visual artist Fernando Arias, from More Art, More Action (http://www.masartemasaccion.org/), and anthropologist Astrid Ulloa. The conversations took place at Duke University and at the University of North Carolina at Chapel Hill on March 31–April 1, 2016. See also van der Hammen (1992).

14   *Disoñar* is made up of two words, *diseñar* (to design) and *soñar* (to dream); the intention is to bridge those two activities, formulate new utopias, and come up with creative solutions to livelihood problems. The concept started to be used in Cali by the poet and environmentalist León Octavio in the late 1980s (conversation with Cristina Ríos, Chapel Hill, April 2016, and with León Octavio, Cali, October 2016). According to Adolfo Albán Achinte, from the Universidad del Cauca, the concept has been in use among groups in Cauca since the late 1980s (conversation in Popayán, October 2015). It is now used by a few groups in several countries in Latin America; there is a periodic "International Encounter of *Disoñadores*" and meetings of *disoñadores para el Buen Vivir* (*Disoñadores* for Buen Vivir). Every year, peasant activists and intellectuals gather in Manizales, Colombia, for an annual gathering called Ecovida (EcoLife), whose purpose is to disoñar the territory and the defense of life. See the *Proceedings of the Gathering of Disoñadores del Futuro*, held in Nariño, Colombia, in 1996 (Asociación Para el Desarrollo Campesino 1996).

15   The pluriverse, one can say, is fractal, or endowed with self-similarity: anywhere you look at it, and at any scale, you find similar (yet not the same) configurations, meshes, assemblages . . . that is, the pluriverse.

16 The concept here is that of "controlled equivocations" (originally proposed by Eduardo Viveiros de Castro), a condition obtained when one becomes aware of what might be lost in translation because the worlds in question only partially share their categories, or not at all (see de la Cadena 2015, 116).

17 The perceptive notion of the "uneven distribution of apocalyptic futures" was proposed by Saydia Kamal, a recent PhD graduate at UNC–Chapel Hill from Bangladesh, in expressing her concern with the many lopsided representations that paint her country as the poster child of food crises and climate change effects, thus calling for an entire politics of intervention and governance by international nongovernmental organizations in the name of adaptation (conversation in Chapel Hill, March 2016). My thanks to Saydia and other students present for this enlightening discussion on the risks of speaking about future(s).

18 I am doing a play on words with the subtitle of Kurzweil's book *The Singularity Is Near: When Humans Transcend Biology* (2006). Tonkinwise exemplifies this bifurcation in terms of "smart green future cities" and "cyborgian singularity" (2015, 88).

19 It is also, a bit unexpectedly perhaps, the lesson drawn by insurrectionary anarchists: "The first duty of revolutionaries is to take care of the worlds they constitute" (Invisible Committee 2015, 194).

20 Will we even know the difference between the two (or perhaps more) posthuman scenarios? "*The inferno of the living is not something that will be; if there is one, it is what is already here, the inferno where we live every day, that we form by being together. There are two ways to escape suffering it. The first is easy for many: accept the inferno and become such a part of it that you can no longer see it. The second is risky and demands constant vigilance and apprehension: seek and learn to recognize who and what, in the midst of the inferno, are not inferno, then make them endure, give them space*" (Italo Calvino, 1972, 165). Or, for one final music tribute, another expression of the same thought: "So, do you think you can tell Heaven from hell, blue skies from pain? Can you tell a green field from a cold steel rail? A smile from a veil? Do you think you can tell?" (Pink Floyd, "Wish You Were Here," 1975).

21 I am aware that this is a very strong statement. While there are certainly hundreds of worthy endeavors and life-affirming examples of academic knowledge, *taken as a whole* the academy, I say, is an instrument of ontological occupation. This is particularly true for elite universities. The more elite the university (e.g., the Ivy League in the United States and like-minded institutions), the closer to power circles, the more distant from poor people's lives and emotions, and the more invested they are in maintaining business-as-usual options.

22 The collective research and action is based on the notion of "social theory in movement," a kind of theory that "takes the quotidian resistance of the communities as its point of departure in order to crystallize actions conceived from the communal locus of enunciation, as the communities weave plural collective meanings from within their own diversity; in doing so, such theory constructs a place of counter-power to homogeneous theorizing with its modeling of the world in terms of progress, order, and development" (P. Botero 2013, 30). Here we find an alternative understanding of theory and its role in research for social transformation.

References

Ackerman, Diane. 2014. *The Human Age: The World Shaped by Us*. New York: W. W. Norton.

Acosta, Alberto. 2010. *El Buen Vivir en el camino del post-desarrollo: Una lectura desde la Constitución de Montecristi*. Quito: Fundación Friedrich Eber.

Acosta, Alberto, and Esperanza Martínez, eds. 2009a. *El Buen Vivir: Una vía para el desarrollo*. Quito: Abya-Yala.

Acosta, Alberto, and Esperanza Martínez, eds. 2009b. *Derechos de la naturaleza: El futuro es ahora*. Quito: Abya-Yala.

Adas, Michael. 1989. *Machines as the Measure of Men*. Ithaca, NY: Cornell University Press.

Alayza, Alejandra, and Eduardo Gudynas, eds. 2011. *Caminos para las transiciones post extractivistas*. Lima: RedGE.

Albán Achinte, Adolfo. 2013. *Más allá de la razón hay un mundo de colores*. Santiago de Cuba: Editorial Oriente.

Anzaldúa, Gloria. 2002. "Now Let Us Shift . . . the Path of Conocimiento. . . . Inner Work, Public Acts." In *This Bridge We Call Home: Radical Visions for Social Transformation*, edited by Gloria Anzaldúa and Analouise Keatin, 540–578. New York: Routledge.

Arocha, Jaime. 1999. *Ombligados de ananse: Hilos ancestrales y modernos en el Pacífico colombiano*. Bogotá: Editorial Universidad Nacional.

Asara, Viviana, Emanuele Profumi, and Giorgos Kallis. 2013. "Degrowth, Democracy and Autonomy." *Environmental Values* 22:217–239.

Asociación de Cabildos del Norte del Cauca (ACIN). 2009. "Historia de la Asociación de Cabildos Indígenas del Norte del Cauca, *Cxhab Wala Kiwe* (Territorio del gran pueblo)." Unpublished manuscript, Corinto, Cauca, Colombia.

Asociación para el Desarrollo Campesino. 1996. *Memorias Encuentro Disoñadores del Futuro*. Pasto, Colombia: Asociació para el Desarrolo Campesino.

Attali, Jacques. 1985. *Noise: The Political Economy of Music.* Minneapolis: University of Minnesota Press.

Austerlic, Silvia. 1997. "New Tendencies in Design in Latin America." *Organization* 4 (4): 620–627.

Bachelard, Gaston. 1969. *The Poetics of Space.* Boston: Beacon.

Baksh, Rawwida, and Wendy Harcourt, eds. 2015. *The Oxford Handbook of Transnational Feminist Movements.* Oxford: Oxford University Press.

Balsamo, Anne. 2011. *Designing Culture: The Technological Imagination at Work.* Durham, NC: Duke University Press.

Baschet, Jerôme. 2014. *Adiós al capitalismo: Autonomía, sociedad del buen vivir y multiplicidad de mundos.* Buenos Aires: Futuro Anterior Ediciones.

Bassey, Nnimmo. 2012. *To Cook a Continent: Destructive Extraction and the Climate Crisis in Africa.* Cape Town: University of Kwa Zulu Natal Press.

Battaglia, Debbora, ed. 1995. *Rhetorics of Self-Making.* Berkeley: University of California Press.

Beer, Sir Stafford. 1980. "Preface." In Humberto Maturana and Francisco Varela, *Autopoiesis and Cognition: The Realization of the Living*, 63–72. Boston: D. Reidel.

Benjamin, Walter. 1968. *Illuminations.* New York: Schocken Books.

Bennett, Jane. 2010. *Vibrant Matter: A Political Ecology of Things.* Durham, NC: Duke University Press.

Benyus, Janine. 1997. *Biomimicry: Innovation Inspired by Nature.* New York: Harper Perennial.

Berglund, Eeva. 2012. "Design for a Better World; or, Conceptualizing Environmentalism and Environmental Management in Helsinki." Paper presented at the 2012 conference of the European Association of Social Anthropology, Nanterre, France, July 10–13.

Berglund, Eeva. 2011. "Hiding in the Forest; or, the Cultural Economy of Finnish Architecture and Finnish Design Now." Paper presented at the Economy Conference, Welsh School of Architecture, Cardiff University, July.

Berry, Thomas. 1999. *The Great Work: Our Way into the Future.* New York: Bell Tower.

Berry, Thomas. 1988. *The Dream of the Earth.* San Francisco: Sierra Club Books.

Berry, Thomas. 1987. "The Determining Features of the Ecozoic Era." In Anne Lonergan and Caroline Richards, eds. *Thomas Berry and the New Cosmology*, 107–108. New London, CT: Twenty-Third Publications.

Bichard, Jo-Anne, and Rama Gheerawo. 2011. "The Designer as Ethnographer: Practical Projects from Industry." In *Design Anthropology: Object Culture in the 21st Century*, edited by Alison Clarke, 45–55. New York: Springer Vienna.

Biennale Architettura. 2012. *Traces of Centuries and Future Steps.* Palazzo Bembo, Venice. Exhibit Catalogue. Leiden: GlobalArtAffairs Foundation.

Biersack, Alleta, and James Greenberg, eds. 2004. *Reimagining Political Ecology.* Durham, NC: Duke University Press.

Blaser, Mario. Forthcoming. "Life Projects." In *The Postdevelopment Dictionary*, edited by Ashish Kothari, Federico Damaria, Alberto Acosta, Arturo Escobar, and Ariel Salleh. London: Zed Books.

Blaser, Mario. 2013. "Ontological Conflicts and the Stories of Peoples in Spite of Europe: Towards a Conversation on Political Ontology." *Current Anthropology* 54 (5): 547–568.

Blaser, Mario. 2010. *Storytelling Globalization from the Chaco and Beyond.* Durham, NC: Duke University Press.

Blaser, Mario. 2009. "The Political Ontology of a Sustainable Hunting Program." *American Anthropologist* 111 (1): 10–20.

Blaser, Mario, Marisol de la Cadena, and Arturo Escobar. 2014. "Introduction: The Anthropocene and the One-World." Unpublished manuscript.

Blaser, Mario, Harvey Feit, and Glenn McRae, eds. 2004. *In the Way of Development: Indigenous Peoples, Life Projects, and Globalization.* London: Zed Books.

Blauvelt, Andrew, ed. 2003. *Strangely Familiar: Design and Everyday Life.* Minneapolis, MN: Walker Art Center.

Boellstorff, Tom. 2008. *Coming of Age in Second Life.* Princeton, NJ: Princeton University Press.

Boff, Leonardo. 2002. *El cuidado esencial.* Madrid: Editorial Trotta.

Boff, Leonardo. 1997. *Cry of the Earth, Cry of the Poor.* New York: Orbis Books.

Bollier, David. 2014. *Think Like a Commoner: A Short Introduction to the Life of the Commons.* Gabriola Island, BC: New Society.

Bollier, David, and Silke Helfrich, eds. 2015. *Patterns of Commoning.* Amherst, MA: Off the Commons Books.

Bollier, David, and Silke Helfrich, eds. 2012. *The Wealth of the Commons: A World beyond Market and State.* Amherst, MA: Leveller Press.

Bonaiuti, Mario, ed. 2011. *From Bioeconomics to Degrowth: Georgescu-Roegen's "New Economics" in Eight Essays.* London: Routledge.

Bond, Patrick. 2012. *Politics of Climate Justice: Paralysis Above, Movement Below.* Cape Town: University of Kwa Zulu Natal Press.

Bonsiepe, Gui C. 2005. "Design and Democracy." Paper presented at the Metropolitan University of Technology, Santiago de Chile, June.

Bonsiepe, Gui C. 2000. "Design as Tool for Cognitive Metabolism." Paper presented at the International Symposium on the Dimensions of Industrial Design Research, Ricerca+Design, Politecnico di Milano, Milan, May 18–20.

Botero, Andrea. 2013. *Expanding Design Space(s).* Helsinki: Aalto Art Books.

Botero, Andrea, Kari-Hans Kommonen, and Sanna Marttila. 2013. "Expanding Design Space: Design-in-Use Activities and Strategies." In *Expanding Design Space(s),* by Andrea Botero, 186–199. Helsinki: Aalto Art Books.

Botero, Patricia, ed. 2015. *Resistencias: Relatos del sentipensamiento que caminan la palabra.* Manizales, Colombia: Universidad de Manizales.

Botero, Patricia. 2015. "Presentación: Antología de los pueblos en resistencia." In *Resistencias: Relatos del sentipensamiento que caminan la palabra,* edited by Patricia Botero, 13–25. Manizales, Colombia: Universidad de Manizales.

Botero, Patricia. 2013. "Teoría social en movimiento: Aportes desde los procesos de investigación y acción colectiva—IAC—y algunas experiencias de investigación militante." In *La utopía no está adelante: Generaciones, resistencias e institucionalidades emergentes,* edited by Patricia Botero and Alicia Itatí Perdomo, 31–61. Manizales, Colombia: Consejo Latinoamericano de Ciencias Sociales/Centro de Estudios Avanzados en Niñez y Juventud.

Botero, Patricia, and Alicia Itatí Perdomo, eds. 2013. *La utopía no está adelante: Generaciones, resistencias e institucionalidades emergentes*. Manizales, Colombia: Consejo Latinoamericano de Ciencias Sociales/Centro de Estudios Avanzados en Niñez y Juventud.

Bourdier, Jean-Paul, and Trinh T. Minh-ha. 2011. *Vernacular Architecture of West Africa: A World in Dwelling*. London: Routledge.

Bratton, Benjamin. 2014. "The Black Stack." *e-flux*, no. 53. http://www.e-flux.com/journal/the-black-stack/.

Braungart, Michael, and William McDonough. 2002. *Cradle to Cradle: Remaking the Way We Make Things*. New York: North Point.

Brown, Lester. 2015. *The Great Transition: Shifting from Fossil Fuels to Solar and Wind Energy*. New York: W. W. Norton.

Brown, Tim. 2009. *Change by Design*. New York: Harper.

Bryant, Raymond, ed. 2015. *The International Handbook of Political Ecology*. London: Elgar.

Bürdek, Bernhard. 2005. *Design: History, Theory and Practice of Product Design*. Basel: Birkäuser Publishers for Architecture.

Cabildo, Taitas, and Comisión de Trabajo del Pueblo Guambiano. 1994. *Plan de vida del Pueblo Guambiano*. Territorio Guambiano-Silvia, Cauca: Cabildo del Pueblo Guambiano.

Cabildo Indígena de Guambía. 2007. "Misak Ley: Por la defensa del derecho mayor, patrimonio del pueblo misak." Unpublished manuscript, typescript.

Calvino, Italo. 1972. *Invisible Cities*. San Diego: Harcourt Brace Jovanovich.

Capra, Fritjof, and Pier Luigi Luisi. 2014. *The Systems View of Life. A Unifying Vision*. Cambridge: Cambridge Universty Press.

Carabajal, Peteco, Dúo Coplanaco, and Raly Barrionuevo. 2004. *La Juntada*. Buenos Aires: Distribuidora Belgrano Norte. DVD.

Cattaneo, Claudio, Giacomo D'Alisa, Giorgos Kallis, and Christos Zografos. 2012. "Introduction: Degrowth Futures and Democracy." *Futures* 44 (6): 515–523.

Chapman, Jonathan. 2005. *Emotionally Durable Design: Objects, Experiences and Empathy*. London: Earthscan.

Chin, Elizabeth. 2017. "Using Fiction to Explore Social Facts: The Laboratory of Speculative Ethnology." In *Routledge Companion for Digital Ethnography*, edited by Larissa Hjorth, Heather Horst, Anne Galloway, and Genevieve Bell, 478–489. New York: Routledge.

Chin, Elizabeth, Morgan Marzec, Cayla McCrae, and Tina Zeng. 2016. "Caminemos Juntos: Design, Digital Media and Participatory Storytelling with Homeless Youth." In *Participatory Visual and Digital Research in Action*, edited by Aline Gubrium, Krista Harper, and Marty Otañez, 243–258. New York: Routledge.

Churchman, C. West. 1971. *The Design of Inquiring Systems*. New York: Basic Books.

Clarke, Alison, ed. 2011a. *Design Anthropology: Object Culture in the 21st Century*. New York: Springer Vienna.

Clarke, Alison. 2011b. "Introduction." In *Design Anthropology: Object Culture in the 21st Century*, edited by Alison Clarke, 1–15. New York: Springer Vienna.

Clarke, Bruce, and Mark Hansen, eds. 2009. *Emergence and Embodiment: New Essays on Second-Order Systems Theory*. Durham, NC: Duke University Press.

Colectivo Situaciones. 2006. "Epílogo: Notas sobre la noción de 'comunidad' a propósito de *Dispersar el poder.*" In *Dispersar el poder,* edited by Raúl Zibechi, 211–220. Buenos Aires: Tinta Limón.

Connolly, William. 2011. *A World of Becoming.* Durham, NC: Duke University Press.

Conway, Janet. 2013. *Edges of Global Justice: The World Social Forum and Its "Others."* London: Routledge.

Coole, Diana, and Samantha Frost, eds. 2010. *New Materialisms: Ontology, Agency, and Politics.* Durham, NC: Duke University Press.

Coraggio, José Luis, and Jean-Louis Laville, eds. 2014. *Reinventar la izquierda en el siglo XXI: Hacia un diálogo norte-sur.* Buenos Aires: Universidad Nacional de General Sarmiento/Consejo Latinoamericano de Ciencias Sociales.

Coraggio, José Luis, Jean Louis Laville, and David Cattani, eds. 2013. *Diccionario de la otra economía.* Buenos Aires: Universidad Nacional de General Sarmiento.

Corsín Jiménez, Alberto. 2013. "The Prototype: More than Many and Less than One." *Journal of Cultural Economy* 7 (4): 381–398.

Cross, Nigel. 2011. *Design Thinking.* London: Bloomsbury.

D'Alisa, Giacomo, Federico Demaria, and Giorgos Kallis, eds. 2015. *Degrowth: A Vocabulary for a New Era.* London: Routledge.

Das, Veena. 2015. *Affliction: Health, Disease and Poverty.* New York: Fordham University Press.

Das, Veena. 2007. *Life and Words: Violence and the Descent into the Ordinary.* Berkeley: University of California Press.

Dávila, Arlene. 2016. *El Mall: The Spatial and Class Politics of Shopping Malls in Latin America.* Berkeley: University of California Press.

de la Cadena, Marisol. 2015. *Earth Beings: Ecologies of Practice across Andean Worlds.* Durham, NC: Duke University Press.

de la Cadena, Marisol. 2010. "Indigenous Cosmopolitics in the Andes: Conceptual Reflections beyond Politics." *Cultural Anthropology* 25 (2): 334–370.

de la Cadena, Marisol, and Mario Blaser, eds. 2017. *Indigenous Cosmopolitics: Dialogues about the Reconstitution of Worlds.* Durham, NC: Duke University Press.

de Landa, Manuel. 2006. *A New Philosophy of Society: Assemblage Theory and Social Complexity.* New York: Continuum.

Deleuze, Gilles, and Félix Guattari. 1987. *A Thousand Plateaus.* Minneapolis: University of Minnesota Press.

Demaria, Federico, François Schneider, Filka Sekulova, and Joan Martínez-Alier. 2013. "What Is Degrowth? From an Activist Slogan to a Social Movement." *Environmental Values* 22:191–215.

Dilnot, Clive. 2015. "The Artificial and What It Opens Towards." In *Design and the Question of History,* by Tony Fry, Clive Dilnot, and Susan Stewart, 165–203. London: Bloomsbury.

Dimpfl, Mike. 2011. "Dualism(s) Flush Toilets: The Potential of an Eco-Ethics of Toileting in the Domestic US." Research paper for Political Ecology graduate seminar, Department of Anthropology, University of North Carolina, Chapel Hill.

DiSalvo, Carl. 2012. *Adversarial Design.* Cambridge, MA: MIT Press.

Domínguez Rubio, Fernando, and Uriel Fogué. 2015. "Unfolding the Political Capacities of Design." In *What Is Cosmopolitcal Design? Design, Nature and the Built Environment*, edited by Albena Yaneva and Alejandro Zaera Polo, 143–160. London: Routledge.

Dove, Michael, Percy Sajise, and Amity Dolittle, eds. 2011. *Beyond the Sacred Forest: Complicating Conservation in South East Asia*. Durham, NC: Duke University Press.

Dreyfus, Hubert. 2014. *Skillful Coping: Essays on the Phenomenology of Everyday Perception and Action*. Oxford: Oxford University Press.

Dreyfus, Hubert. 1979. *What Computers Can't Do: The Limits of Artificial Intelligence*. New York: Harper Colophon Books.

Dreyfus, Hubert, and Sean Kelly. 2011. *All Things Shining: Reading the Western Classics to Find Meaning in a Secular Age*. New York: Free Press.

Dunne, Anthony, and Fiona Raby. 2013. *Speculative Design: Design, Fiction, and Social Dreaming*. Cambridge, MA: MIT Press.

Ehn, Pelle, Elizabeth Nilsson, and Richard Topgaard, eds. 2014a. *Making Futures: Marginal Notes on Innovation, Design, and Democracy*. Cambridge, MA: MIT Press.

Ehn, Pelle, Elizabeth Nilsson, and Richard Topgaard. 2014b. "Introduction." In *Making Futures: Marginal Notes on Innovation, Design, and Democracy*, edited by Pelle Ehn, Elizabeth Nilsson, and Richard Topgaard, 1–16. Cambridge, MA: MIT Press.

Ehrenfeld, John. 2009. *Sustainability by Design*. New Haven, CT: Yale University Press.

Ehrhardt, Bettina, dir. 2001. *A Trail on the Water: Abbado, Nono, Pollini*. Ratingen, Germany: TDK. DVD.

Eisenstein, Charles. 2013. *Sacred Economics: Money, Gift and Society in the Age of Transition*. Berkeley, CA: Evolver Editions.

Escobar, Arturo. 2015a. "Degrowth, Postdevelopment, and Transitions: A Preliminary Conversation." *Sustainability Science* 10:451–462.

Escobar, Arturo. 2015b. "*Transiciones*: A Space for Research and Design for Transitions to the Pluriverse." *Design Philosophy Papers* 13 (1): 13–23.

Escobar, Arturo. 2014. *Sentipensar con la tierra: Nuevas lecturas sobre sobre desarrollo, territorio y diferencia*. Medellín: UNAULA.

Escobar, Arturo. 2011. *Encountering Development: The Making and Unmaking of the Third World*. 2nd ed. Princeton, NJ: Princeton University Press.

Escobar, Arturo. 2010a. "Latin America at a Crossroads: Alternative Modernizations, Postliberalism, or Post-development?" *Cultural Studies* 24 (1): 1–65.

Escobar, Arturo. 2010b. "Postconstructivist Political Ecologies." In *International Handbook of Environmental Sociology*, edited by Michael Redclift and Graham Woodgate, 91–105. 2nd ed. Cheltenham, UK: Elgar.

Escobar, Arturo. 2008. *Territories of Difference: Place~Movements~Life~Redes*. Durham, NC: Duke University Press.

Escobar, Arturo. 2004. "Other Worlds Are (Already) Possible: Self-Organisation, Complexity, and Post-capitalist Cultures." In *The World Social Forum: Challenging Empires*, edited by Jai Sen, Anita Anad, Arturo Escobar, and Peter Waterman, 349–358. Delhi: Viveka.

Escobar, Arturo. 2001. "Culture Sits in Places: Reflections on Globalism and Subaltern Strategies of Globalization." *Political Geography* 20:139–174.

Escobar, Arturo. 1994. "Welcome to Cyberia: Notes on the Anthropology of Cyberculture." *Current Anthropology* 35 (3): 211–231.

Escobar, Arturo. 1992. "Imagining a Postdevelopment Era? Critical Thought, Development, and Social Movements." *Social Text* 31/32:20–56.

Espinosa, Yuderkis, Diana Gómez, and Karina Ochoa, eds. 2014. *Tejiendo de otro modo: Feminismos, epistemología y apuestas decoloniales en Abya Yala.* Popayán, Colombia: Universidad del Cauca.

Esteva, Gustavo. n.d. "La noción de comunalidad." Unpublished manuscript, Oaxaca.

Esteva, Gustavo. 2015. "The Hour of Autonomy." *Latin American and Caribbean Ethnic Studies* 10 (1): 134–145.

Esteva, Gustavo. 2013. "Nuevas formas de la revolución." Unpublished manuscript, Oaxaca.

Esteva, Gustavo. 2009. "What Is Development?" Unpublished manuscript, Universidad de la Tierra, Oaxaca.

Esteva, Gustavo. 2006. "The 'Other Campaign' and the Left: Reclaiming an Alternative." Unpublished manuscript, Oaxaca, Mexico.

Esteva, Gustavo. 2005. "Celebration of Zapatismo." *Humboldt Journal of Social Relations* 29 (1): 127–167.

Esteva, Gustavo, and Madhu Suri Prakash. 1998. *Grassroots Post-modernism: Remaking the Soil of Cultures.* London: Zed Books.

Federici, Silvia. 2004. *Caliban and the Witches. Women, the Body, and Primitive Accumulation.* Brooklyn, NY: Autonomedia.

Fletcher, Kate, and Lynda Grose. 2011. *Fashion and Sustainability: Design for Change.* London: Laurence King.

Flores, Fernando, and María Flores Letelier. 2013. *Conversations for Action and Collected Essays.* North Charleston, SC: CreateSpace.

Foster, Hall. 2002a. "The ABCs of Contemporary Design." *October,* no. 100:191–199.

Foster, Hall. 2002b. *Design and Crime (and Other Diatribes).* London: Verso.

Foucault, Michel. 1970. *The Order of Things.* New York: Vintage Books.

Fry, Tony. 2017. "Design for/by the Global South." *Design Philosophy Papers* 15(1): 3–37.

Fry, Tony. 2015. *City Futures in the Age of a Changing Climate.* London: Routledge.

Fry, Tony. 2012. *Becoming Human by Design.* London: Berg.

Fry, Tony. 2011. *Design as Politics.* London: Berg.

Fry, Tony, Clive Dilnot, and Susan Stewart. 2015. *Design and the Question of History.* London: Bloomsbury.

Fry, Tony, and Eleni Kalantidou. 2015. "Design in the Borderlands: An Introduction." In *Design in the Borderlands,* edited by Eleni Kalantidou and Tony Fry, 1–11. London: Routledge.

Gatt, Caroline, and Tim Ingold. 2013. "From Description to Correspondence: Anthropology in Real Time." In *Design Anthropology: Theory and Practice,* edited by Wendy Gunn, Ton Otto, and Rachel Smith, 139–158. London: Bloomsbury.

Gibson, William. 1984. *Neuromancer.* New York: Ace Books.

Gibson-Graham, J. K. 2006. *A Postcapitalist Politics.* Minneapolis: University of Minnesota Press.

Gibson-Graham, J. K., Jenny Cameron, and Stephen Healy. 2013. *Take Back the Economy: An Ethical Guide for Transforming Our Communities.* Minneapolis: University of Minnesota Press.

Goodwin, Brian. 2007. *Nature's Due: Healing Our Fragmented Culture.* Edinburgh: Floris Books.

Goodwin, Brian. 1994. *How the Leopard Changed Its Spots: The Evolution of Complexity.* Princeton, NJ: Princeton University Press.

Greene, Herman. 2015. *The Promise of Ecological Civilization.* Anoka, MN: Process Century Press.

Grossberg, Lawrence. 2010. *Cultural Studies in the Future Tense.* Durham, NC: Duke University Press.

Grosz, Elizabeth. 2010. "Feminism, Materialism, and Freedom." In *New Materialisms: Ontology, Agency, and Politics,* edited by Diana Coole and Samantha Frost, 139–157. Durham, NC: Duke University Press.

Grubacic, Andre, and Dennis O'Hearn. 2016. *Living at the Edges of Capitalism: Adventures in Exile and Mutual Aid.* Berkeley: University of California Press.

Gudynas, Eduardo. 2015. *Extractivismos: Economía, ecología y política de un modo de entender el desarrollo y la naturaleza.* Cochabamba, Bolivia: Centro de Documentación e Información Bolivia/Consejo Latinoamericano de Ciencias Sociales.

Gudynas, Eduardo. 2014. *Derechos de la naturaleza, ética biocéntrica y políticas ambientales.* Lima: Programa Democracia y Transformación Global/Red Peruana por una Globalización con Equidad/Consejo Latinoamericano de Ciencias Sociales.

Gudynas, Eduardo, and Alberto Acosta. 2011. "La renovación de la crítica al desarrollo y el buen vivir como alternativa." *Utopía y Praxis Latinoamericana* 16 (53): 71–83. http://www.gudynas.com/publicaciones/GudynasAcostaCriticaDesarrolloBVivirUtopia11.pdf.

Guerrero, Arturo. Forthcoming. "Comunalidad." In *The Postdevelopment Dictionary,* edited by Ashish Kothari, Federico Damaria, Alberto Acosta, Arturo Escobar, and Ariel Salleh. London: Zed Books.

Gunn, Wendy, Ton Otto, and Rachel Smith, eds. 2013. *Design Anthropology: Theory and Practice.* London: Bloomsbury.

Gutiérrez Aguilar, Raquel. 2012. "Pistas reflexivas para orientarnos en una turbulenta época de peligro." In *Palabras para tejernos, resistir y transformar en la época que estamos viviendo,* by Raquel Gutiérrez Aguilar, Raúl Zibechi, Natalia Sierra, Pablo Dávalos, Pablo Mamani, Oscar Olivera, Héctor Mondragón, Vilma Almendra, Emmanuel Rozental., 9–34. Oaxaca, Mexico: Pez en el Árbol.

Gutiérrez Aguilar, Raquel. 2008. *Los ritmos del Pachakuti: Movilización y levantamiento indígena-popular en Bolivia.* Buenos Aires: Tinta Limón.

Gutiérrez Borrero, Alfredo. 2015a. "Resurgimientos: Sures como diseños y diseños otros." *Revista Nómadas* 43:113–129.

Gutiérrez Borrero, Alfredo. 2015b. "El sur del diseño y el diseño del sur." In *Actas del Coloquio Internacional Epistemologías del Sur,* edited by Boaventura de Sousa Santos and Teresa Cunha, 745–759. Coimbra, Portugal: Proyecto Alice.

Gutiérrez Borrero, Alfredo. 2014. "Compluridades y multisures: Diseños con otros nombres e intenciones." Paper presented at the Tercer Encuentro Nacional de Diseño, Cuenca, Ecuador, November 20.

Habermas, Jurgen. 1987. *The Philosophical Discourse of Modernity*. Cambridge, MA: MIT Press.

Halpin, Harry. 2011. "Sense and Reference on the Web." *Minds and Machines* 21:153–178.

Halpin, Harry, Andy Clark, and Michael Wheeler. 2010. "Toward a Philosophy of the Web: Representation, Enaction, Collective Intelligence." Paper presented at the ACM Conference on Web Science, Raleigh, NC, April 26–27.

Halpin, Harry, and Alexandre Monnin, eds. 2014. *Philosophical Engineering: Towards a Philosophy of the Web*. Oxford: Wiley Blackwell.

Haraway, Donna. 2008. *When Species Meet*. Minneapolis: University of Minnesota Press.

Haraway, Donna. 1997. *Modest_Witness@Second_Millennium: FemaleMan_Meets_Onco-Mouse*. New York: Routledge.

Harcourt, Wendy. 2009. *Body Politics in Development*. London: Zed Books.

Harcourt, Wendy, ed. 2016. *The Palgrave Handbook of Gender and Development: Critical Engagements in Feminist Theory and Practice*. London: Palgrave Macmillan.

Harcourt, Wendy, and Arturo Escobar, eds. 2005. *Women and the Politics of Place*. Bloomfield, CT: Kumarian.

Harcourt, Wendy, and Ingrid Nelson, eds. 2015. *Practicing Feminist Political Ecology: Moving beyond the Green Economy*. London: Zed Books.

Hartblay, Cassandra. 2017. "Good Ramps, Bad Ramps: Centralized Design Standards and Disability Access in Urban Infrastructure." *American Ethnologist* 44 (1): 9–22.

Hathaway, Mark, and Leonardo Boff. 2009. *The Tao of Liberation: Exploring the Ecology of Transformation*. Maryknoll, NY: Orbis Books.

Hawken, Paul, Amory Lovins, and L. Hunter Lovins. 1999. *Natural Capitalism: Creating the Next Industrial Revolution*. New York: Little, Brown.

Healy, Hali, Joan Martínez-Alier, Leah Temper, Mariana Walter, and Julian-François Gerber, eds. 2013. *Ecological Economics from the Ground Up*. New York: Routledge.

Heidegger, Martin. 1977. *The Question concerning Technology*. New York: Harper and Row.

Heidegger, Martin. 1962. *Being and Time*. New York: Harper and Row.

Helfrich, Silke. 2013. "Economics and Commons? Towards a Commons-Creating Peer Economy." Paper presented at the Economics and the Commons Conference, Berlin, May 22. http://www.boell.de/sites/default/files/ecc_report_final.pdf.

Hester, Randolph. 2006. *Design for Ecological Democracy*. Cambridge, MA: MIT Press.

Hopkins, Rob. 2011. *The Transition Companion: Making Your Community More Resilient in Uncertain Times*. White River Junction, VT: Chelsea Green.

Hopkins, Rob. 2008. *The Transition Handbook: From Oil Dependency to Local Resilience*. White River Junction, VT: Chelsea Green.

Horst, Heather, and Daniel Miller, eds. 2012. *Digital Anthropology*. London: Bloomsbury.

Huxley, Aldous. (1928) 1996. *Point Counter Point*. Normal, IL: Dalkey Archive Press.

Illich, Ivan. 2015. *La convivencialidad*. Oaxaca, Mexico: El Rebozo.

Illich, Ivan. 1973. *Tools for Conviviality*. London: Marion Boyars.

Ingold, Tim. 2011. *Being Alive: Essays on Movement, Knowledge, and Description.* New York: Routledge.

Ingold, Tim. 2000. *The Perception of the Environment.* London: Routledge.

Invisible Committee. 2015. *To Our Friends.* Cambridge, MA: MIT Press.

Irani, Lilly, Janet Vertesi, Paul Dourish, Kavita Philip, and Rebecca Grinter. 2010. "Postcolonial Computing: A Lens on Design and Development." *CHI* (April 10–15): 1311–1320.

Irwin, Terry. 2015. "Transition Design: A Proposal for a New Era of Design Practice, Study and Research." Unpublished manuscript, School of Design, Carnegie Mellon University.

Irwin, Terry, Gideon Kossoff, and Cameron Tonkinwise. 2015. "Transition Design Provocation." *Design Philosophy Papers* 13 (1): 3–11.

Irwin, Terry, Cameron Tonkinwise, and Gideon Kossoff. 2015. "Transition Design Symposium Provocation." Carnegie Mellon School of Design. https://www.academia.edu/11439480/Transition_Design_Symposium_Provocation_abbreviated_version.

Irwin, Terry, Gideon Kossoff, Cameron Tonkinwise, and Peter Scupelli. 2015. "Transition Design Bibliography." Unpublished manuscript. https://www.academia.edu/13108611/Transition_Design_Bibliography_2015.

Jackson, Mark. 2014. "Composing Postcolonial Geographies: Postconstructivism, Ecology, and the Overcoming Ontologies of Critique." *Singapore Journal of Tropical Geography* 35:72–87.

James, Paul. 2015. "Urban Design for the Global South: Ontological Design in Practice." In *Design in the Borderlands*, edited by Eleni Kalantidou and Tony Fry, 91–108. London: Routledge.

Johnson, Norris. 2012. *Tenryu-ji: Life and Spirit of a Kyoto Garden.* Berkeley, CA: Stone Bridge.

Joy, Leonard, ed. 1978. *Food and Nutrition Planning: The State of the Art.* Guilford, England: IPC Science and Technology Press.

Julier, Guy. 2014. *The Culture of Design.* 3rd ed. London: Sage.

Kalantidou, Eleni, and Tony Fry, eds. 2015. *Design in the Borderlands.* London: Routledge.

Kallis, Giorgos. 2011. "In Defence of Degrowth." *Ecological Economics* 70:873–880.

Kallis, Giorgos, Federico Demaria, and Giacomo D'Alisa. 2015. "Introduction: Degrowth." In *Degrowth: A Vocabulary for a New Era*, edited by Giacomo D'Alisa, Federico Demaria, and Giorgos Kallis, 1–18. London: Routledge.

Kallis, Giorgos, Christian Kerschner, and Joan Martínez-Alier. 2012. "The Economics of Degrowth." *Ecological Economics* 84:172–180.

Karim, Lamia. 2011. *Microfinance and Its Discontents: Women in Debt in Bangladesh.* Minneapolis: University of Minnesota Press.

Kauffman, Stuart. 2008. *Reinventing the Sacred.* New York: Basic Books.

Kauffman, Stuart. 1995. *At Home in the Universe.* Oxford: Oxford University Press.

Kelty, Christopher, Alberto Corsín Jiménez, and George E. Marcus, eds. 2010. *Prototyping Prototyping.* Anthropological Research on the Contemporary (ARC) Studio. https://limn.it/wp-content/uploads/ARCEpisode3-Prototyping.pdf.

Kirkham, Pat, and Susan Weber, eds. 2013. *History of Design: Decorative Arts and Material Culture, 1400–2000.* Bard, NY: Bard Graduate Center.

Klein, Naomi. 2014. *This Changes Everything: Capitalism vs. the Climate*. New York: Simon and Schuster.

Kommonen, Kari-Hans. n.d. "In Search of Digital Design." Unpublished manuscript, Media Lab, Aalto University, Helsinki.

Kommonen, Kari-Hans. 2013a. "Design Ecosystems and the Design of Everyday Life." Unpublished paper, Arki Group, Media Lab, Aalto University, Helsinki. http://www.scoop.it/t/design-of-everyday-life.

Kommonen, Kari-Hans. 2013b. "Design Ecosystems and the Landscapes for Co-creation." Unpublished paper, Arki Group, Media Lab, Aalto University, Helsinki. http://arki.mlog.taik.fi/files/2014/05/Design-ecosystems-as-the-landscapes-for-co-creation-final.pdf.

Kongtrul, Jagmon. 2005. *The Great Path of Awakening*. Boston: Shambhala.

Koolhaas, Rem. 2004. *Content*. Cologne: Taschen.

Korten, David. 2006. *The Great Turning: From Empire to Earth Community*. Bloomfield, CT: Kumarian.

Kossoff, Gideon. 2015. "Holism and the Reconstitution of Everyday Life: A Framework for Transition to a Sustainable Society." *Design Philosophy Papers* 13 (1): 25–38.

Kossoff, Gideon. 2011. "Holism and the Reconstitution of Everyday Life: A Framework for Transition to a Sustainable Society." In *Grow Small, Think Beautiful: Ideas for a Sustainable World from Schumacher College*, edited by Stephan Hardin, 122–142. Edinburgh: Floris Books.

Kothari, Ashish, Federico Demaria, and Alberto Acosta. 2015. "Buen Vivir, Degrowth, and Ecological Swaraj: Alternatives to Sustainable Development and the Green Economy." *Development* 57 (3/4): 362–375.

Kurzweil, Ray. 2005. *The Singularity Is Near*. New York: Viking Books.

Kwinter, Sanford. 2010. *Requiem for the City at the End of the Millennium*. Barcelona: Actar.

Kwinter, Sanford. 2007. *Far from Equilibrium: Essays on Technology and Design Culture*. Barcelona: Actar.

Lappé, Francis Moore. 2011. *Eco-Mind: Changing the Way We Think, to Create the World We Want*. New York: Nation Books.

Laszlo, Ervin. 2008. *Quantum Shift in the Global Brain: How the New Scientific Reality Can Change Us and Our World*. Rochester, VT: Inner Traditions.

Latour, Bruno. 2007. *Reassembling the Social*. Oxford: Oxford University Press.

Latour, Bruno. 1993. *We Have Never Been Modern*. Cambridge, MA: Harvard University Press.

Laurel, Brenda, ed. 2003. *Design Research: Methods and Perspectives*. Cambridge, MA: MIT Press.

Laurel, Brenda. 2003. "Introduction: Muscular Design." In *Design Research: Methods and Perspectives*, edited by Brenda Laurel, 16-19. Cambridge, MA: MIT Press.

Laurel, Brenda. 2001. *Utopian Entrepreneur*. Cambridge, MA: MIT Press.

Laurel, Brenda, ed. 1989. *The Art of Human-Computer Interface Design*. Reading, MA: Addison-Wesley.

Law, John. 2011. "What's Wrong with a One-World World." *heterogeneities*, September 25, http://www.heterogeneities.net/publications/Law2011WhatsWrongWithAOneWorldWorld.pdf.

Law, John. 2004. *After Method: Mess in Social Science Research*. London: Routledge.

Leff, Enrique. 2015. *La apuesta por la vida*. Mexico, D.F.: Siglo XXI.

Leff, Enrique. 2012. "Political Ecology: A Latin American Perspective." Unpublished manuscript, Mexico City.

Leff, Enrique. 2002. *Saber Ambiental*. Mexico City: Siglo XXI.

Leff, Enrique. 1986. *Ecología y capital*. Mexico, D.F.: Universidad Nacional Autónoma de México (UNAM).

Lisifrey, Ararat, Luis A. Vargas, Eduar Mina, Axel Rojas, Ana María Solarte, Gildardo Vanegas y Anibal Vega. 2013. *La Toma. Historias de territorio, resistencia y autonomía en la cuenca del Alto Cauca*. Bogotá: Universidad Javeriana y Consejo Comunitario de La Toma.

Lohmann, Larry. 2011. "The Endless Algebra of Climate Markets." *Capitalism, Nature Socialism* 22 (4): 93–116.

Lozano, Betty Ruth. 2015. "Pedagogías para la vida, la alegría y la reexistencia: Pedagogías de mujeres negras que curan y vinculan." Unpublished manuscript, Cali.

Lubarski, Sandra. 2014. "Living Beauty." In *Keeping the Wild*, edited by George Wuerthner, Eileen Crist, and Tom Butler, 188–196. Washington, DC: Island Press.

Lugones, María. 2010a. "The Coloniality of Gender." In *Globalization and the Decolonial Option*, edited by Walter Mignolo and Arturo Escobar, 369–390. London: Routledge.

Lugones, María. 2010b. "Toward a Decolonial Feminism." *Hypatia* 25 (4): 742–760.

Luisetti, Federico. 2011. *Una vita: Pensiero selvaggio e filosofia dell'intensità*. Milan: Mimesis.

Lukic, Branko, and Barry M. Katz. 2010. *Nonobject*. Cambridge, MA: MIT Press.

Lunenfeld, Peter. 2003. "The Design Cluster." In *Design Research: Methods and Perspectives*, edited by Brenda Laurel, 10–15. Cambridge, MA: MIT Press.

Macy, Joanna. 2007. *World as Lover, World as Self: Courage for Global Justice and Ecological Renewal*. Berkeley, CA: Parallax.

Macy, Joanna, and Molly Brown. 1998. *Coming Back to Life: Practices to Reconnect Our Lives, Our World*. Gabriola Island, BC: New Society.

Macy, Joanna, and Chris Johnstone. 2012. *Active Hope: How to Face the Mess We're in without Going Crazy*. Novato, CA: New World Library.

Mamani, Pablo. 2005. *Geopolíticas indígenas*. El Alto, Bolivia: CADES.

Manzini, Ezio. 2015. *Design, When Everybody Designs: An Introduction to Design for Social Innovation*. Cambridge, MA: MIT Press.

Marley, Bob & The Wailers. 1980. *Uprising*. Kingston, Jamaica: Tuff Gong Studio/Island Records. LP.

Martínez-Alier, Joan. 2012. "Environmental Justice and Economic Degrowth: An Alliance between Two Movements." *Capitalism, Nature, Socialism* 23 (1): 51–73.

Martínez-Alier, Joan. 2009. "Socially Sustainable Economic De-growth." *Development and Change* 40 (6): 1099–1119.

Martínez-Alier, Joan. 2002. *The Environmentalism of the Poor: A Study of Ecological Conflicts and Valuation*. London: Elgar.

Marvin, Carolyn. 1999. "When Old Technologies Were New: Implementing the Future." In *The Media Reader: Continuity and Transformation*, edited by Hugh Mackay and Tim O'Sullivan, 58–72. New York: Sage.

Marvin, Carolyn. 1988. *When Old Technologies Were New*. Oxford: Oxford University Press.

Masaharu, Takasaki. 2012. "Architecture of Living Things." In *Traces of Centuries and Future Steps*. Exhibit Catalogue, Biennale Architettura, Palazzo Bembo, Venice. Leiden: GlobalArtAffairs Foundation.

Mason-Deese, Elizabeth. 2015. "The Unemployed in Movement: Struggles for a Common Territory in Argentina's Urban Peripheries." PhD diss., University of North Carolina at Chapel Hill.

Massey, Doreen. 2004. "Geographies of Responsibility." *Geografiska Annaler* 86B (1): 5–18.

Massuh, Gabriela, ed. 2012. *Renunciar al bien común: Extractivismo y (pos)desarrollo en América Latina*. Buenos Aires: Mardulce.

Maturana, Humberto. 1997. *Metadesign*. Santiago, Chile: Instituto de Terapia Cognitiva. http://www.inteco.cl/articulos/006/texto_ing.htm.

Maturana, Humberto. 1994. "Prefacio a la quinta edición." In H. Maturana and F. Varela, *De máquinas y seres vivos: Autopoiesis; La organización de lo vivo*. 5th ed., 9–33. Santiago, Chile: Editorial Universitaria/Editorial Lumen.

Maturana, Humberto, and Francisco Varela. 1987. *The Tree of Knowledge: The Biological Roots of Human Understanding*. Berkeley, CA: Shambhala.

Maturana, Humberto, and Francisco Varela. 1980. *Autopoiesis and Cognition: The Realization of the Living*. Boston: Reidel.

Maturana, Humberto, and Francisco Varela. 1973. *De máquinas y seres vivos. Autopoiesis: La organización de lo vivo*. Santiago, Chile: Editorial Universitaria.

Maturana, Humberto, and Gerda Verden-Zöller. 2008. *The Origin of Humanness in the Biology of Love*. Charlottesville, VA: Imprint Academic.

Maturana, Humberto, and Gerda Verden-Zöller. 1993. *Amor y juego: Fundamentos olvidados de los humano*. Santiago de Chile: J. C. Sáez.

Mau, Bruce. 2000. *Life Style*. New York: Phaidon.

Mau, Bruce, and the Institute without Boundaries. 2004. *Massive Change*. London: Phaidon.

McCullough, Malcolm. 2004. *Digital Ground*. Cambridge, MA: MIT Press.

McHarg, Ian. 1969. *Design with Nature*. New York: Natural History Press.

McMichael, Philip. 2013. "Rethinking Land Grab Ontology." *Rural Sociology* 79 (1): 34–55.

Medina, Eden. 2011. *Cybernetic Revolutionaries: Technology and Politics in Allende's Chile*. Cambridge, MA: MIT Press.

Merchant, Carolyn. 1980. *The Death of Nature: Women, Ecology, and the Scientific Revolution*. New York: Harper and Row.

Mignolo, Walter. 2011. *The Darker Side of Western Modernity*. Durham, NC: Duke University Press.

Mignolo, Walter. 2000. *Local Histories/Global Designs*. Princeton, NJ: Princeton University Press.

Mignolo, Walter, and Arturo Escobar, eds. 2010. *Globalization and the Decolonial Option*. London: Routledge.

Milczarek-Desai, Shefali. 2002. "Living Fearlessly with and within Difference: My Search for Identity beyond Categories and Contradictions." In *This Bridge We Call Home: Radical*

Visions for Social Transformation, edited by Gloria Anzaldúa and Analouise Keatin, 126–135. New York: Routledge.

Mina, Mateo. 1975. *Esclavitud y libertad en el valle del rio Cauca*. Bogotá: La Rosca de Investigación.

Mingyur Rinpoche, Yongey. 2007. *The Joy of Living*. New York: Harmony Books.

Mitchell, William, Alan Inouye, and Marjory Blumenthal, eds. 2003. *Beyond Productivity: Information Technology, Innovation, and Creativity*. Washington, DC: National Academies Press.

Mitrovic, Branko. 2011. *Philosophy for Architects*. New York: Princeton Architectural Press.

Mol, Annmarie. 1999. "Ontological Politics: A Word and Some Questions." In *Actor-Network Theory and After*, edited by John Law and John Hassard, 74–89. Oxford: Blackwell.

Montaner, Josep Maria. 2013. *Arquitectura y crítica*. Barcelona: Gustavo Gil.

Montoya, Michael. 2013. "Potential Futures for a Healthy City: Community, Knowledge, and Hope for the Sciences of Life." *Current Anthropology* 54 (S7): S45–S55.

Mooney, Pat, ETC Group, and What Next Project. 2006. *The What Next Report 2005–2035: Trendlines and Alternatives*. Stockholm: Dag Hammarskjöld Foundation.

Munk, Nina. 2013. *The Idealist: Jeffrey Sachs and the Quest to End Poverty*. New York: Doubleday.

Murphy, Keith. 2016. "Design and Anthropology." *Annual Review of Anthropology* 45:433–449.

Murphy, Keith. 2015. *Swedish Design: An Ethnography*. Ithaca, NY: Cornell University Press.

Museum of Modern Art. 2008. *Design and the Elastic Mind*. New York: Museum of Modern Art.

Nandy, Ashis. 2012. "Theories of Oppression and Another Dialogue of Cultures." *Economic and Political Weekly* 47 (30): 39–44.

Nandy, Ashis, ed. 1988. *Science, Hegemony and Violence: A Requiem for Modernity*. New Delhi: Oxford University Press.

Nandy, Ashis. 1987. *Traditions, Tyrannies and Utopias: Essays in the Politics of Awareness*. New Delhi: Oxford University Press.

Nhat Hanh, Thich. 2008. *The World We Have: A Buddhist Approach to Peace and Ecology*. Berkeley, CA: Parallax.

Nhat Hanh, Thich. 1975. *The Miracle of Mindfulness*. Boston: Beacon.

Nonini, Donald, ed. 2007. *The Global Idea of "the Commons."* New York: Berghahn Books.

Norgaard, Richard. 1995. *Development Betrayed*. New York: Routledge.

Ochoa Gautier, Ana María. 2014. *Aurality: Listening and Knowledge in Nineteenth-Century Colombia*. Durham, NC: Duke University Press.

Ochoa Gautier, Ana María. 2006. "Sonic Transculturation, Epistemologies of Purification and the Aural Sphere in Latin America." *Social Identities* 12 (6): 803–825.

Office of Metropolitan Architecture (OMA), Rem Koohas, and Bruce Mau. 1995. *S, M, L, XL*. New York: Monacelli Press.

Ogden, Laura. 2011. *Swamplife: People, Gators, and Mangroves Entangled in the Everglades*. Minneapolis: University of Minnesota Press.

Organizaciones Indígenas de Colombia. 2004. "Propuesta política y de acción de los pueblos indígenas." August 26. http://www.movimientos.org/es/show_text .php3%3Fkey%3D3282.

Orr, David. 2002. *The Nature of Design: Ecology, Culture, and Human Intention*. Oxford: Oxford University Press.

Osterweil, Michal. 2013. "The Italian Anomaly: Place and History in the Global Justice Movement." In *The European Social Movement Experience: Rethinking "New Social Movements," Historicizing the Alterglobalization Movement and Understanding the New Wave of Protest*, edited by Cristina Fominaya and Laurence Cox, 33–46. London: Routledge.

Osterweil, Michal. 2005. "Place-Based Globalism: Locating Women in the Alternative Globalization Movement." In *Women and the Politics of Place*, edited by Wendy Harcourt and Arturo Escobar, 174–189. Bloomfield, CT: Kumarian.

Otto, Ton, and Rachel Smith. 2013. "Design Anthropology: A Distinct Style of Knowing." In *Design Anthropology: Theory and Practice*, edited byWendy Gunn, Ton Otto, and Rachel Smith, 1–31. London: Bloomsbury.

Pallasmaa, Juhani. 2016. *Habitar*. Barcelona: Gustavo Gil.

Pandey, Gyanendra, ed. 2014. *Unarchived Histories: The "Mad" and the "Trifling" in the Colonial and Postcolonial World*. London: Routledge.

Papadopolous, Dimitris. 2015. "Staking Ontologies: More than Social Movements in Technoscience." Paper presented at the Sawyer Seminar Workshop "The Uncommons," University of California, Davis, July 28–31.

Papanek, Victor. 1984. *Design for the Real World*. Chicago: Academy Chicago.

Paredes, Julieta. 2012. *Hilando fino desde el feminismo comunitario*. La Paz: DED (Deutscher Entwicklungsdienst).

Paredes Pinda, Adriana. 2014. "Historia y cultura Mapuche." Conferencia y lectura de poemas, Institute for the Study of the Americas, University of North Carolina, Chapel Hill, October 31.

Parikka, Jussi. 2016. *The Anthrobscene*. Minneapolis: University of Minnesota Press.

Patzi Paco, Félix. 2004. *Sistema comunal: Una propuesta alternativa al sistema liberal*. La Paz: Comunidad de Estudios Alternativos.

PCN (Proceso de Comunidades Negras). 2004. *Construyendo Buen Vivir en las comunidades negras del río Yurumanguí y en Pílamo, Cauca*. Cali, Colombia: PCN/Solsticio.

PCN (Proceso de Comunidades Negras). 2000. *Fortalecimiento de las dinámicas organizativas del Proceso de Comunidades Negras del Pacífico Sur Colombiano, en torno al ejercicio de los Derechos étnicos, culturales y territoriales*. Proyecto PCN-Solsticio. Segundo informe técnico trimestral, Septiembre—Noviembre 2000. Cali, Colombia: PCN.

PCN (Proceso de Comunidades Negras) and Arturo Escobar. 1998. *Taller de capacitación sobre diseño de sistemas de ríos*. Buenaventura, Colombia: PCN.

Pereira, Helder, and Coral Gillett. 2015. "Africa: Designing as Existence." In *Design in the Borderlands*, edited by Eleni Kalantidou and Tony Fry, 109–131. London: Routledge.

Pink Floyd. 1975. *Wish You Were Here*. New York: Columbia Records. LP.

Pink, Sarah, Elisenda Ardèvol, and Dèbora Lanzeni, eds. 2016. *Digital Materialities: Design and Anthropology.* London: Bloomsbury.

Plowman, Tim. 2003. "Ethnography and Critical Design Practice." In *Design Research: Methods and Perspectives,* edited by Brenda Laurel, 30–38. Cambridge, MA: MIT Press.

Plumwood, Val. 2002. *Environmental Culture: The Ecological Crisis of Reason.* New York: Routledge.

Polanyi, Karl. 1957. *The Great Transformation.* Boston: Beacon.

Povinelli, Elizabeth. 2001. "Radical Worlds: The Anthropology of Incommensurability and Inconceivability." *Annual Review of Anthropology* 30:319–334.

Prakash, Madhu Suri, and Gustavo Esteva. 2008. *Grassroots Postmodernism.* New York: Peter Lang.

Puig de la Bellacasa, María. 2015. "Matters of Care: Speculative Ethics in More than Human Worlds" (chapter 5 of book in progress). Paper presented at the Sawyer Seminar Workshop "The Uncommons," University of California, Davis, July 28–31.

Quijano, Olver. 2013. "Cambiar el mundo no viene ni de arriba ni de afuera. Resumen del Congreso Tramas y Mingas por el Buen Vivir, Popayán, Junio 9-11."

Quijano, Olver. 2012. *Ecosimías: Visiones y prácticas de diferencia económico/cultural en contextos de multiplicidad.* Popayán, Colombia: Editorial Universidad del Cauca.

Rabinow, Paul, and George Marcus, with James Faubion and Tobias Reese. 2008. *Designs for an Anthropology of the Contemporary.* Durham, NC: Duke University Press.

Randers, Jorgen. 2012. *2052: A Global Forecast for the Next Forty Years.* White River Junction, VT: Chelsea Green.

Raskin, Paul, Tariq Banuri, Gilberto Gallopín, Pablo Gutman, Al Hammond, Robert Kates, and Rob Swart. 2002. *Great Transition: The Promise and Lure of the Times Ahead.* Stockholm: Stockholm Environment Institute. http://www.gtinitiative.org/documents/Great_Transitions.pdf.

Redclift, Michael. 1987. *Sustainable Development: Exploring the Contradictions.* London: Routledge.

Redfield, Peter. 2013. *Life in Crisis: The Ethical Journey of Doctors without Borders.* Berkeley: University of California Press.

Redfield, Peter. 2012. "Bioexpectations: Life Technologies as Humanitarian Goods." *Public Culture* 24 (1): 157–184.

Redfield, Peter, and Erica Bornstein, eds. 2010. *Forces of Compassion: Humanitarianism between Ethics and Politics.* Santa Fe: SAR Press.

Reichert, Evânia. 2011. *Infancia, la edad sagrada.* Barcelona: Ediciones La Llave.

Restrepo, Eduardo. 1996. "Los tuqueros negros del Pacífico sur colombiano." In *Renacientes del guandal,* edited by Eduardo Restrepo and Jorge I. del Valle, 243–350. Bogotá: Universidad Nacional/Biopacífico.

Rist, Gilbert. 1997. *Histories of Development.* London: Zed Books.

Rivera Cusicanqui, Silvia. 2014. *Hambre de huelga: Ch'ixinakax Utxiwa y otros textos.* Querétaro, Mexico: La Mirada Salvaje.

Rivera Cusicanqui, Silvia. 1990. "Democracia liberal y democracia de ayllu: El caso del Norte Potosí, Bolivia." In *El difícil camino hacia la democracia*, edited by Carlos Toranzo Roca, 9–51. La Paz: ILDIS.

Robbins, Paul. 2004. *Political Ecology: A Critical Introduction*. Oxford: Blackwell.

Rocha, Miguel. 2015. "Textualidades oralitegráficas y visions de cabeza en las oraliteraturas y literaturas indígenas contemporáneas en Colombia." PhD diss., University of North Carolina at Chapel Hill.

Rose, Deborah Bird. 2008. "On History, Trees, and Ethical Proximity." *Postcolonial Studies* 11 (2): 157–167.

Sachs, Wolfgang, and Tilman Santarius, eds. 2007. *Fair Futures. Resource Conflicts, Security, and Global Justice*. London: Zed Books.

Sagan, Dorion. 2011. "The Human Is More than Human: Interspecies Communities and the New 'Facts of Life.'" Paper presented at the American Anthropological Association Annual Meeting, Montreal, November 16–20.

Sagan, Dorion, Lynn Margulis, and Ricardo Guerrero. 1997. "Descartes, Dualism, and Beyond." In *Slanted Truths: Essays on Gaia, Symbiosis and Evolution*, edited by Lynn Margulis and Dorion Sagan, 172–183. New York: Springer.

Salleh, Ariel. 2009a. "Ecological Debt: Embodied Debt." In *Eco-Sufficiency and Global Justice*, edited by Ariel Salleh, 1–43. London: Pluto.

Salleh, Ariel, ed. 2009b. *Eco-Sufficiency and Global Justice*. London: Pluto.

Santos, Bōaventura de Sousa. 2014. *Epistemologies of the South: Justice against Epistemicide*. Boulder, CO: Paradigm.

Santos, Bōaventura de Sousa. 2007. *The Rise of the Global Left: The World Social Forum and Beyond*. London: Zed Books.

Sarlo, Beatriz. 2008. *The Technical Imagination*. Stanford, CA: Stanford University Press.

Sarlo, Beatriz. 1992. *La imaginación técnica: Sueños modernos de la cultura argentina*. Buenos Aires: Nueva Vision.

Sassen, Saskia. 2014. *Expulsions: Brutality and Complexity in the Global Economy*. Cambridge, MA: Harvard University Press.

Schafer, Paul. 2008. *Revolution or Renaissance: Making the Transition from an Economic Age to a Cultural Age*. Ottawa: University of Ottawa Press.

Scharmer, Otto. 2009. *Theory U: Leading from the Future as It Emerges*. San Francisco: Berrett-Koehler.

Scharmer, Otto, and Katrin Kaufer. 2012. *Leading from the Emerging Future: From Ego-System to Eco-System Economies*. San Francisco: Berrett-Koehler.

Schneider, François, Giorgos Kallis, and Joan Martínez-Alier. 2010. "Crisis or Opportunity? Economic Degrowth for Social Equity and Ecological Sustainability." *Journal of Cleaner Production* 18:511–518.

Schön, Donald. 1987. *Educating the Reflexive Practitioner. Towards a New Design for Teaching and Learning in the Professions*. San Francisco: Jossey-Bass.

Schön, Donald, and Martin Rein. 1994. *Frame Reflection: Toward the Resolution of Intractable Policy Controversies*. New York: Basic Books.

Schwittay, Anke. 2014. "Designing Development: Humanitarian Design in the Financial Inclusion Assemblage." *PoLAR: Political and Legal Anthropology Review* 37 (1): 29–47.

Scupelli, Peter. 2015. "Designed Transitions and What Kind of Design Is Transition Design?" *Design Philosophy Papers* 13 (1): 75–84.

Segato, Rita. 2015. *La crítica de la colonialidad en ocho ensayos.* Buenos Aires: Prometeo Libros.

Sekulova Filka, Giorgos Kallis, Beatriz Rodríguez-Labajos, and François Schneider. 2013. "Degrowth: From Theory to Practice." *Journal of Cleaner Production* 38:1–6.

Sharma, Kriti. 2015. *Interdependence: Biology and Beyond.* New York: Fordham University Press.

Shaw, Carolyn. 2014. "Productive Borders: African-American and African Feminist Interventions, a Personal Journey." Paper presented at the American Anthropological Association Annual Meeting, Washington, DC, December 6.

Shepard, Courtney. 2015. "Exploring the Places, Practices, and Communities of the Subculture of Refashioning Secondhand Clothing through Themes of Bricolage and Sustainability." Undergraduate honors thesis, University of North Carolina at Chapel Hill.

Shiva, Vandana. 2008. *Soil, Not Oil: Environmental Justice in an Age of Climate Crisis.* Cambridge, MA: South End.

Shiva, Vandana. 2005. *Earth Democracy.* Cambridge, MA: South End.

Simmons, Christopher. 2011. *Just Design: Socially Conscious Design for Critical Issues.* Cincinnati, OH: HOW Books.

Sitrin, Marina, and Dario Azzelini. 2014. *They Can't Represent Us! Reinventing Democracy from Greece to Occupy.* London: Verso.

Smith, Linda Tuhiwai. 1999. *Decolonizing Methodologies: Research and Indigenous Peoples.* London: Zed Books.

Solé, Ricard, and Brian Goodwin. 2000. *Signs of Life: How Complexity Pervades Biology.* New York: Basic Books.

Sparke, Penny. 2004. *Design and Culture: 1900 to the Present.* 2nd ed. London: Routledge.

Spinosa, Charles, Fernando Flores, and Hubert Dreyfus. 1997. *Disclosing New Worlds.* Cambridge, MA: MIT Press.

Stewart, Susan. 2015. "And So to Another Setting . . ." In *Design and the Question of History,* by Tony Fry, Clive Dilnot, and Susan Stewart, 275–301. London: Bloomsbury.

Stewart, Susan. 2011. "Editorial: Interpreting Design Thinking." *Design Studies* 32:515–520.

Stocking, George. 1987. *Victorian Anthropology.* New York: Free Press.

Strathern, Marilyn. 1991. *Partial Connections.* New York: Rowman and Littlefield.

Strathern, Marilyn. 1988. *The Gender of the Gift.* Berkeley: University of California Press.

Subcomandante Marcos and the Zapatistas. 2006. *The Other Campaign/La Otra Campaña.* San Francisco: City Lights.

Suchman, Lucy. 2011. "Anthropological Relocations and the Limits of Design." *Annual Review of Anthropology* 40:1–18.

Suchman, Lucy. 2007. *Human-Machine Reconfigurations: Plans and Situated Actions,* 2nd ed. Cambridge: Cambridge University Press.

Suchman, Lucy. 1994. "Do Categories Have Politics?" *Computer Supported Cooperative Work (CSCW)* 2:177–190.

Svampa, Maristella. 2012. "Pensar el desarrollo desde América Latina." In *Renunciar al bien común: Extractivismo y (pos)desarrollo en América Latina,* edited by Gabriela Massuh, 17–58. Buenos Aires: Mardulce.

Sykes, Krista, ed. 2010. *Constructing a New Agenda: Architectural Theory, 1993–2009.* New York: Princeton Architectural Press.

TallBear, Kimberly. 2011. "TallBear Discussant Remarks: Dorion Sagan, *The Human Is More than Human.*" Paper presented at the American Anthropological Association Annual Meeting, Montreal, November 16–20.

Tanizaki, Junichirō. 1994. *El elogio de la sombra.* Madrid: Siruela.

Taussig, Michael. 1980. *The Devil and Commodity Fetishism in South America.* Chapel Hill: University of North Carolina Press.

Taylor, Mark. 2001. *The Moment of Complexity: Emerging Network Culture.* Chicago: University of Chicago Press.

Thackara, John. 2004. *In the Bubble: Designing in a Complex World.* Cambridge, MA: MIT Press.

Thrangu Rinpoche, Khenchen. 2003. *Je Gampopa's The Jewel Ornament of Liberation.* Crestone, CO: Namo Buddha.

Titmarsh, Mark, and Cameron Tonkinwise. 2013. "Art vs. Design: Saving Power vs. Enframing, or a Thing of the Past vs. World-Making." *Studio Research* 1:6–17.

Tonkinwise, Cameron. 2015. "Design for Transitions—from and to What?" *Design Philosophy Papers* 13 (1): 85–92.

Tonkinwise, Cameron. [2014?]. "Against Becoming Unsustainable by Human-Centered Design: A Review of Tony Fry's *Becoming Human by Design.*" https://www.academia.edu/2985203/_Against_Becoming_Unsustainable_by_Human-Centered_Design.

Tonkinwise, Cameron. 2014. "Design's (Dis)Orders and Transition Design." https://www.academia.edu/11791137/Design_Dis_Orders_Transition_Design_as_Postindustrial_Design.

Tonkinwise, Cameron. 2013a. "Design Away: Unmaking Things." https://www.academia.edu/3794815/Design_Away_Unmaking_Things.

Tonkinwise, Cameron. 2013b. "*It's Just Going to Be a Lotta Hard Work*—Four Problematic and Five Potential Ways of Accomplishing Radical Sustainability Innovation." https://www.academia.edu/3844727/Its_Just_Going_to_be_a_Lotta_Hard_Work_Radical_Sustainability_Innovation.

Tonkinwise, Cameron. 2012. "Design Transition Expert Interview." From "The Measures Taken" (blog). https://dasaufnahme.wordpress.com/2013/11/09/design-transitions-expert-interview.

Trinh T. Minh-ha. 1989. *Woman, Native, Other: Writing Postcoloniality and Feminism.* Bloomington: Indiana University Press.

Tsing, Anna. 2015. *The Mushroom at the End of the World.* Princeton, NJ: Princeton University Press.

Tunstall, Dori. 2011. "Design Anthropology: What Can It Add to Your Design Practice?" Unpublished manuscript.

Tunstall, Elizabeth (Dori). 2013. "Decolonizing Design Innovation: Design Anthropology, Critical Anthropology, and Indigenous Knowledge." In *Design Anthropology: Theory and Practice,* edited by Wendy Gunn, Ton Otto, and Rachel Smith, 232–250. London: Bloomsbury.

Turpin, Etienne, ed. 2013. *Architecture and the Anthropocene: Encounters among Design, Deep Time, Science and Philosophy.* Ann Arbor, MI: Open Humanities Press.

Ulloa, Astrid. 2012. "Los territorios indígenas en Colombia: De escenarios de apropiación transnacional a territorialidades alternativas." *Scripta Nova: Revista Electrónica de Geografía y Ciencias Sociales* 16 (65), n.p.

Ulloa, Astrid. 2011. "The Politics of Autonomy of Indigenous Peoples of the Sierra Nevada de Santa Marta, Colombia: A Process of Relational Indigenous Autonomy." *Latin American and Caribbean Ethnic Studies* 6 (1): 79–107.

Ulloa, Astrid. 2010. "Reconfiguraciones conceptuales, políticas y territoriales en las demandas de autonomía de los pueblos indígenas en Colombia." *Tabula Rasa* 13:73–92.

Ulloa, Astrid. 2006. *The Ecological Native: Indigenous Peoples' Movements and Eco-Governmentality in Colombia.* New York: Routledge.

Ulloa, Astrid, Heidi Rubio, and Claudia Campos. 1996. *Trua Wandra.* Bogotá: OREWA/ Fundación Natura.

United Nations, Department of Social and Economic Affairs. 1951. *Measures for the Economic Development of Underdeveloped Countries.* New York: United Nations.

van der Hammen, María Clara. 1992. *El manejo del mundo: Naturaleza y sociedad entre los Yukuna de la Amazonia colombiana.* Bogotá: Tropenbos Colombia.

van der Ryn, Sim, and Stuart Cowan. (1996) 2007. *Ecological Design.* Washington, DC: Island.

Varela, Francisco. 1999. *Ethical Know-How: Action, Wisdom, and Cognition.* Stanford, CA: Stanford University Press.

Varela, Francisco. 1994. "Prefacio a la quinta edición." In H. Maturana and F. Varela, *De máquinas y seres vivos: Autopoiesis; La organización de lo vivo.* 5th ed., 35–62. Santiago, Chile: Editorial Universitaria/Editorial Lumen.

Varela, Francisco. 1981. "Introduction." In *Observing Systems,* by Heinz von Foerster, xi–xvi. Seaside, CA: Intersystems.

Varela, Francisco, Evan Thompson, and Eleanor Rosch. 1991. *The Embodied Mind: Cognitive Science and Human Experience.* Cambridge, MA: MIT Press.

Vasudevan, Pavithra. 2011. "How to Rethink Design, out of the Studio, and into the World?" Research paper for Political Ecology graduate seminar, Department of Anthropology, University of North Carolina at Chapel Hill.

Vattimo, Gianni. 1991. *The End of Modernity.* Baltimore: Johns Hopkins University Press.

Velardi, Nicoletta, and Marco Polatsik, eds. 2012. *Desarrollo territorial y extractivsimo: Luchas y alternativas en la región andina.* Cuzco: Centro Bartolomé de las Casas.

Via Campesina. 2009. "Small Scale Sustainable Farmers Are Cooling Down the Earth." http://viacampesina.net/downloads/PAPER5/EN/paper5-EN.pdf.

Virilio, Paul. 2012. *The Administration of Fear.* Los Angeles: Semiotext(e).

Virilio, Paul. 1999. *Politics of the Very Worst.* New York: Semiotext(e).

Virilio, Paul. 1997. *The Open Sky.* New York: Verso.

Visvanathan, Shiv. 2002. "The Laboratory and the World: Conversations with C V Sheshadry." *Economic and Political Weekly* 37 (22): 2163–2170.

Visvanathan, Shiv. 1985. *Organizing for Science: The Making of an Industrial Research Laboratory.* Delhi: Oxford University Press.

Visweswaran, Kamela, ed. 2013. *Everyday Occupations: Experiencing Militarism in South Asia and the Middle East.* Philadelphia: University of Pennsylvania Press.

Viveiros de Castro, Eduardo. 2010. *Metafísicas caníbales: Líneas de antropología posestructural.* Buenos Aires: Katz Editores.

von Foerster, Heinz. 2010. *Understanding Understanding: Essays on Cybernetics and Cognition.* New York: Springer.

von Foerster, Heinz. 1995. "Ethics and Second-Order Cybernetics." In "Constructions of the Mind: Artificial Intelligence and the Humanities," edited by Stefano Franchi and Güven Güzeldere, special issue, *Stanford Humanities Review* 4 (2). https://web.stanford .edu/group/SHR/4-2/text/foerster.html.

von Foerster, Heinz. 1981. *Observing Systems.* Seaside, CA: Intersystems.

von Werlhof, Claudia. 2015. *Madre Tierra o Muerte! Reflexiones para una teoría crítica el patriarcado.* Oaxaca, Mexico: El Rebozo.

von Werlhof, Claudia. 2013. "Destruction through 'Creation': The 'Critical Theory of Patriarchy' and the Collapse of Modern Civilization." *Capitalism, Nature, Socialism* 24 (4): 68–85.

von Werlhof, Claudia. 2011. *The Failure of Modern Civilization and the Struggle for a "Deep" Alternative.* Frankfurt am Main: Peter Lang.

von Werlhof, Claudia. 2001. "Losing Faith in Progress: Capitalist Patriarchy as an 'Alchemic System.'" In *There Is an Alternative: Subsistence and Worldwide Resistance to Capitalist Globalization,* edited by Veronica Bennoldt-Thomsen, Maria Mies, and Claudia von Werlhof, 15–40. London: Zed Books.

Walsh, Catherine, ed. 2012. *Pedagogías decoloniales: Prácticas insurgentes de resistir, (re)existir y (re)vivir.* Quito: Abya Yala.

Walsh, Catherine. 2009. *Interculturalidad, estado, sociedad: Luchas (de)colonials de nuestra época.* Quito: Abya Yala.

Weber, Andres. 2013. *Enlivenment: Towards a Fundamental Shift in the Concepts of Nature, Culture, and Politics.* Berlin: Heinrich-Böll-Stiftung.

White, Damian. 2015. "Metaphors, Hybridity, Failure and Work: A Sympathetic Appraisal of Transitional Design." *Design Philosophy Papers* 13 (1): 39–50.

White, Damian, Alan Rudy, and Brian Gareau. 2015. *Environments, Natures, and Social Theory: Towards a Critical Hybridity.* London: Palgrave Macmillan.

Whitemyer, David. 2006. "Anthropology in Design." International Interior Design Association. http://www.iida.org/content.cfm/anthropology-in-design.

Willis, Anne-Marie. 2015. "Transition Design: The Need to Refuse Discipline and Transcend Instrumentalism." *Design Philosophy Papers* 13 (1): 69–74.

Willis, Anne-Marie. 2006. "Ontological Designing—Laying the Ground." https://www .academia.edu/888457/Ontological_designing.

Winograd, Terry, and Fernando Flores. 1986. *Understanding Computers and Cognition.* Norwood, NJ: Ablex.

Winograd, Terry, and Fernando Flores. 1989. *Hacia la comprensión de la informática y la cognición.* Barcelona: Editorial Hispano-Europea.

World Bank. 2013. *World Development Report 2014. Risk and Opportunity—Managing Risk for Development.* Washington, DC: The World Bank.

World Commission on Environment and Development. 1987. *Our Common Future.* New York: Oxford University Press.

Yeang, Ken. 2006. *Ecodesign: A Manual for Ecological Design.* London: John Wiley.

Zibechi, R. 2006. *Dispersar el poder: Los movimientos como poderes anti-estatales.* Buenos Aires: Tinta Limón.

Index

Note: Page numbers in italics indicate figures.

240n25, 255n30, 257n13; transition design for, 194–99

commoning, 16, 144–47, 151, 176, 198–200; autonomy and, 175, 178, 188; reclaiming of, 69–70, 223; Transition Town Initiative and, 138, 140–41

communal, 116, 162, 176–84, 200–201, 208–9; autonomous design and, 74, 134, 168, 171, 184–90, *187, 189*; commitment to, 21; definition of, 219; individual versus, 146, 157, 168; rethinking of, 5

communality, 175–78, 200–201; autonomy and, 166; definition of, 177; globalization's destruction of, 174; realization of, 176–84

complexity theory, 83, 94, 115; critical social theory and, 156, 170–71, 243n15, 252n5; Goodwin on, 224–25, 236n25; Leff on, 124; Taylor on, 170, 252n4

computationalist model, 43, 80

computers, 35, 41–43, 55, 229n2; cybernetics and, 87–88, 251n1; design of, 115, 235n17; manufacture of, 107–8; social media and, 106, 111

Coplanacu (music duo), 247n20

Corsín Jiménez, Alberto, 55, 237n3

cosmopolitan localism, 137, 159, 163, 208

critical design studies, 2–3, 130, 198–99; architecture and, 36–37; critical social theory and, 27, 50–51, 54; definition of, 17; digitalization and, 41; ontological design and, 132; speculative design and, 45–46, 54–55; sustainability and, 33, 90; technology and, 18, 26; transition thinking and, 152–53

critical social theory, 27, 50–51, 54, 246n12; complexity theory and, 156, 170–71, 243n15, 252n5

Crystal Palace Exhibition (1851), 31

cultural studies, 76, 80, 224; of design, 3, 19, 46–51, 128, 237n1

cybernetics, 87–88, 96, 108–9, 241n1, 251n1

cyberspace, 35, 41–42, 108, 146, 245n5

cyborgs, 17, 258n18

Dakota Access Pipeline, 66

Dalai Lama, 243n18

Dávila, Arlene, 255n25

Dávila Yáñez, Ximena, 232n9

decolonial theory, 11, 46, 80, 133–34, 217; design and, 117, 206–8; economic development and, 62; epistemology and, 94, 97–99, 206, 223–24, 250n17; feminist, 65–66, 176, 182–83, 231n6; individualism and, 85; interdisciplinary, 166; Mignolo on, 205; political ontology and, 52; postcolonialism and, 42, 46, 80, 243n12; Varela on, 81

degrowth, 90, 144–51; autonomous design and, 188; commons and, 140, 188; Illich on, 9; transition frameworks for, 96, 138, 197–98, 206. *See also* developmentalism

de la Cadena, Marisol, xiii, 66–67, 95, 216–18; on commons, 146; on political ontology, 238n14

Deleuze, Gilles, 21, 71, 103–4, 239n20

Deloria, Vine, 97

Demaria, Federico, 148

Descartes, René. *See* Cartesianism

Descola, Philippe, 64, 102

"design designs," 4, 110–11, 131

"designer man," 52–53

Design for Social Innovation and Sustainability Network, 250n20

Design Studio for Social Intervention, 58, 238n7, 238n8

design thinking, 34, 36, 46, 48, 60–62; Berglund on, 57; Brown on, 2, 25, 234n13; Gutiérrez Borrero on, 206; Marcus on, 55–56; Scharmer on, 125–26; Stewart on, 15; Tonkinwise on, 123, 132, 256n5

developmentalism, 6–7, 95, 177, 224, 245n7; agriculture and, 66; alternatives to, 90, 96, 147–48, 154, 161–62, 205–9; autonomy and, 167, 172–73, 184; in Bolivia, 254n17; in Cauca Valley, 190–201; coloniality and, 31, 94; critics of, 242n8, 246n12, 250n17; defuturing projects and, 190–91; design

tion design, 157–58; on Koolhaas, 37; on ontological design, 117; on Sustainment, 16–17, 138, 140, 221; on types of human beings, 246n14; on urban design, 40–41

Fuerzas Armadas Revolucionarias de Colombia (FARC), 72

Fundación HablaScribe, 229n2

futurality, 9, 71, 188–90, *189*

Gadamer, Hans-Georg, 241n2, 245n6

Gallopín, Gilberto, 248n3

Gandhi, Mohandas K., 256n9

García Canclini, Néstor, 229n2

García Márquez, Gabriel, 27–31

Gatt, Caroline, 49, 52, 56–57, 237n6

Gehry, Frank, 37

GeoDesign, 237n2

geoengineering, 236n24

Gibson, William, 245n5

Gibson-Graham, J. K., 210, 239n15, 244n3, 250n17, 256n7

Giddens, Anthony, 80, 246n12

globalization, 83, 139, 239n19; destruction of communality by, 174; domination of, 69; Eurocentrism and, 206–7; Zapatistas on, 86, 174

Goethe, Johann Wolfgang von, 102

Goodman, Alan, 229n3

Goodman, Paul, 231n5

Goodwin, Brian, xii, 102, 236n25

Grameen Bank (Bangladesh), 61, 238n10

"Great Singularity," 17

Great Transition Initiative, 140–42, 154, 248n3

Greene, Herman, 141, 144, 248n5

green economy, 43–45, 95, 103, 118, 149–50, 236n24. *See also* ecological economics

Gropius, Walter, 233n6

Grose, Lynda, 44

Grossberg, Lawrence, 51, 237n1

Grupo de Académicos e Intelectuales en Defensa del Pacífico Colombiano, xvii–xviii

Guattari, Félix, 21, 71, 103–4, 239n20

Gudynas, Eduardo, 151, 249n10

Guerrero, Arturo, 177, 178, 180

Gutiérrez Aguilar, Raquel, 177–80

Gutiérrez Borrero, Alfredo, 206

Habermas, Jürgen, 32, 80

Halpin, Harry, 42, 96, 236n22

Haraway, Donna, 52, 64, 80

Harcourt, Wendy, 65

Hartblay, Cassandra, 236n27

Hathaway Mark, 142

Hawken, Paul, 44, 236n23

Hegel, G. W. F., 20

Heidegger, Martin, xiii, 20–21, 42, 80; on "Age of the World Picture," 131; sustainment and, 117; on technology, 18; terminology of, 241n2; on tradition, 245n6

Helfrich, Silke, 140, 146, 147

heteronomy, 32, 172–75, 178, 181, 188

homeless shelters, 58

Hopkins, Rob, 144–45

Hosminen, Samuli, 247n20

humanitarian aid, 59–62

Huxley, Aldous, 250n14

IDEO (design firm), 36

Illich, Ivan, 7–10, 200, 211; popular communications and, 229n2; on social transitions, 139; on technology, 230n5

Indignados movement, 69, 172

individualism, 83–85, 90–91, 183, 246n15, 251n22

industrial design, 1, 32–34, 206, 233n6

Ingold, Tim, 29, 49, 52, 56–57, 102; on One-World World, 87; on political ecology, 64

innovation, 2, 7, 18, 58, 129, 196; design, 31, 38, 47, 60, 130, 132; Manzini on, 152–53; open-source, 234n13; social, 5, 27, 67, 138, 145, 159–64; sustainable, 123, 158, 207, 215; technological, 25, 30, 110, 208, 247n17

Institut de Ciència i Tecnologia Ambientals (ICTA), 249n9

Masaharu, Takasaki, 235n17
Massey, Doreen, 82
"matristic cultures," 12–14, 17, 19, 232n9. *See also* feminisms
Matríztica School (Santiago de Chile), 232n9
Maturana, Humberto, xii, 3, 33, 79, 205, 232n9; on autopoiesis, xiv, 5, 168–72, 183; on biology of love, 13, 83, 171, 241n1; on cognition, 42, 81, 240n1, 252n1; on interconnected communities, 213–14; on "matristic cultures," 12–14; on rationalism, 82; on structural coupling, 169
Mau, Bruce, 25, 233n2, 234n15
Max-Neef, Manfred, 246n12
McHarg, Ian, 43
McLuhan, Marshall, 229n2
Médecins sans Frontières, 60
Mellor, Mary, 239n15
Merleau-Ponty, Maurice, 241n2, 245n4
microentrepreneur programs, 61, 238n10
Mies, Maria, 231n6, 239n15
Mies van der Rohe, Ludwig, 233n6
Mignolo, Walter, 205, 257n12
Millennium Development Goals, 61, 238n11
Misak people (Colombia), 73–74, 240n25
modernity, 83–91; critical analysis of, 80; design and, 32; Eurocentric, 67–68, 81, 93; Nandy on, 128; ontological dualism and, 3, 19–20; pluriverse and, 129, 200, 256n8; Santos on, 68; Varela on, 97–100; von Werlhof on, 14
Monnin, Alexandre, 42, 96, 236n22
Montaner, Josep Maria, 234n14
Montoya, Michael, 59
Morales, Evo, 178, 179
Morgan, Lynn, 229n3
Moscovici, Serge, 229n2
Mumford, Lewis, 231n5
Murphy, Keith, 47, 53–54
music, design and, 129–31

Nandy, Ashis, 89, 99–100, 128–29, 242n8, 256n9

Nasa people (Colombia), 73, 176, 199, 240n25
"natural design," 119, 184, 236n25
"negofeminism," 64–65
neoliberalism. *See* globalization
nepantleras, 65, 200–201
Nhat Hanh, Thich, 244n20
Nicholas of Cusa, 102
Nietzsche, Friedrich, 80, 246n10
Nilsson, Elizabeth, 35, 47
Nono, Luigi, 247n20, 248n21
Nonuya people (Colombia), 257n13
Northern Cauca. *See* Cauca Valley (Colombia)

Oaxaca, 173–74, 177, 253n8
Occupy movement, 69, 172
Ochoa Gautier, Ana María, 130
O'Connor, James, xiii
Octavio, León, 257n14
Odum, Howard, 229n2
ombligada ritual, 72, 213, 240n24, 256n10
One-World World (oww), 66–68, 71; Ingold on, 87; Law on, 66, 86, 131
ontological design, 48, 110–16, 131–34, *189*; agency and, 124–26; Ehrenfeld on, 45; Flores on, xiv, 42, 116, 241n1; Fry on, 117
ontological dualism, 43, 53, 81, 92–96, 104, 213; Deleuze on, 103–4; ecology and, 70, 85–86; modernity and, 3, 11, 19–20. *See also* Cartesianism
ontological turn in social theory, 20, 41, 52, 63–64, 124–25, 216
ontonomy, 32, 172–73, 178, 184
Operational closure, 169, 171, 183, 253n6

Pallasmaa, Juhani, 39
Pandey, Gyanendra, 53
Papanek, Victor, 1, 235n16, 254n20
Paredes, Julieta, 11, 182–83
Paredes Pinda, Adriana, 157
Parikka, Jussi, 244n3
Pascal, Blaise, 102

patriarchy, 63, 170, 183, 218–23; autonomous thought and, 16–18, 204, 209; of capitalist modernity, 3–4, 10–15, 20, 52, 107–8, 139; nondualist ontology and, 85–86, 91–94, 213–14

Patzi Paco, Félix, 179–81

Pedrosa, Alvaro, 229n2

Peirce, Charles, 123

Perec, Georges, 232n1

permaculture, 236n23

Pink Floyd (music group), 258n20

placenta, burial of, 72, 213, 240n24, 256n10

Planes de Vida. See Life Plans (*Planes de Vida*)

Plumwood, Val, 79, 94–95, 133–34, 211

pluriverse, 4–7, 117, 170–71, 190; autonomy of, 175, 184; bioregionalism and, 5, 45, 142, 143, 196; definitions of, xvi, 257n15; design for, 198; dialogic, 52, 161; Gutiérrez Borrero on, 205–6; of interculturality, 181; invisibility of, 68; Manzini on, 130, 164, 208; Maturana on, 205; modernity and, 129, 200, 256n8; political ontology and, 66–70, 86, 94–95, 216–18; rationality and, 211; risks in, 256n8; sustainability and, 59, *189*; transitions toward, 15–17, 188; Zhang on, 131

Pohjonen, Kimmo, 247n20

Polanyi, Karl, 145, 242n9, 248n1

political ecology (PE), 3, 62–67, 76, 186; feminist, 51–52, 65–66, 146, 250n17; Leff on, 124; postdualist, 64; schools of, 238n12

political ontology (PO), 65–69; Blaser on, 66; de la Cadena on, 238n14; definition of, 65–66; epistemologies and, 67–69, 216; of ethnoterritorial struggles, 69–76, 186–88, *187*; pluriverse and, 66–70, 86, 94–95, 216–18

Pollini, Murizio, 247n20

Portuondo, Omara, 230n5

postcolonialism, 42, 46, 80, 243n12. *See also* decolonial theory

postdevelopment, 138–40, 143–51, *189*, 190, 208, 249n10

postextractivism, 138, 140, 145, 150–51, 166–67

poststructuralism, 46, 63, 88, 234n14; complexity theories and, 252n4; epistemologies and, 92, 96, 97, 115, 243n15; Marxism and, 156; systems thinking and, 170, 250n17, 252n4

"presencing," 123, 125–26, 246n13, 246n15

Proceso de Comunidades Negras (PCN), xiv, xvii, 187, 254n19, 255n29

Project Cybersyn, 251n1

Puig de la Bellacasa, María, 247n17

Raby, Fiona, 17

Rams, Dieter, 233n6

Rarámuri people, 256n1

Raskin, Paul, 141, 248n3

Reagan, Ronald, 7

realism, 85–88, 90–92, 213, 218; economic, 197; materialism and, 170; postdualist, 96; pragmatism and, 226. *See also* Cartesianism

Redclift, Michael, 238n13

Redfield, Peter, 60

Reduced Emissions from Deforestation and Forest Degradation (REDD) projects, 149, 176

"refashionistas," 230n6

Reichert, Evânia, 232n9

Rein, Martin, 56

relationality: autonomy and, 171, 178, 204; biology of love and, 83, 216; ecology and, 12; feminism and, 65; music and, 130; nature/culture divide and, 100–104; nondualism and, 20–21, 157; political activation of, 95–97; presencing and, 125

relational ontologies, 129–31

Research Institute for the Critique of Patriarchy and for Alternative Civilizations, 231n6

Restrepo, Eduardo, 102

Rivera Cusicanqui, Silvia, 129, 178–79, 225, 231n7, 253n15

Rodríguez, Abel, 257n13

Rodríguez, Carlos, 257n13
Rosch, Eleanor, 98
Rose, Deborah Bird, 99, 103–4

Sachs, Jeffrey, 179, 238n11
Sagan, Dorion, 81, 97
Salleh, Ariel, 239n15
Santos, Boaventura de Sousa, 67, 102
Sarlo, Beatriz, 233n4
Sassen, Sakia, 222, 239n19
Scharmer, Otto, 125–26
Schön, Donald, 56
School for Designing a Society, 238n8
Schwittay, Anke, 61, 238n10
Segato, Rita, 11
Senge, Peter, 246n15
Sharma, Kriti, 91, 101, 244n20; on contingentism, 212, 257n11
Shaw, Carolyn, 64–65
Shepard, Courtney, 230n6
Sheshadry, C. V., 242n8
Shiva, Vandana, 142, 239n15
Simon, Herbert, 33
Singer, Merrill, 229n3
Sioux, 66
Smith, Linda Tuhiwai, 243n17
social-practice theory, 250n17
sociology of absences, 68
socionatural space, 178
Soleri, Paolo, 235n16
speculative design, 17, 45–46, 54–55
Spinosa, Charles, 112, 123
Spinoza, Baruch, 102
Stack ("accidental megastructure"), 42–43, 108
Stewart, Susan, 15
Stiegler, Bernard, 236n22
Strathern, Marilyn, 64, 102
structural coupling, 169, 171, 173, 183, 188
Suchman, Lucy, 57, 245n8
sumak kawsay/suma qamaña. See Buen Vivir
sustainability, 59, 225; Albán on, 33–34; by design, 43–46; fashion industry

and, 44; NGOs for, 238n9. *See also* developmentalism
Sustainment, 117–18; autonomous design of, 184–88, *187*, *189*; Fry on, 16–17, 138, 140, 221
Sweedlund, Alan, 229n3
systems thinking, 35, 62, 114, 127, 170–71; cognitivism and, 241n1; pioneers of, xii; poststructuralism and, 170, 250n17, 252n4; transition design and, 152–63, *155*. *See also* living-systems theory

TallBear, Kimberly, 97
Tanizaki, Junichiro, 39–40, 235n19
Tarahumara people, 256n1
Taylor, Charles, 80
Taylor, Mark, 170, 252n4
Teilhard de Chardin, Pierre, 248n4
Tellus Institute, 140
Tennessee Valley Authority, 190, 194
Thackara, John, 234n9, 234n11
Thatcher, Margaret, 7
Theories of Change, *155*, 156, 250n17
Thomas, Brooke, 229n3
Thompson, Evan, 98
tiny house movement, 38, 234n16
Titmarsh, Mark, 124
toilet designs, 46, 246n13
Tonkinwise, Cameron, 119, 124; on "cyborgian singularity," 258n18; on design thinking, 123, 132; on ethical design, 250n18; on transition design, 137, 157, 221, 250n18, 256n5
Topgaard, Richard, 35, 47
transition design, 4–9, 27, 47–49, 57, 124; anthropology and, 51, 208–9; at Carnegie Mellon University, 152–58, *155*; in Cauca Valley, 191–201; cosmopolitan localism and, 159, 208; definitions of, 137; emerging spaces for, 144–47; framings of, 148–58, *155*; liberation of Mother Earth as, 203–5; Manzini on, 151–52, 249n12; names for, 138; ontological, 188, *189*;

transition design (*continued*)
  social innovation and, 67, 215; Theories
  of Change and, 250n17; Tonkinwise on,
  137, 157, 221, 250n18, 256n5; Willis on, 49,
  50, 223
transition discourses (TDs), 138–43, 164,
  209
Transition Town Initiative (TTI), 138, 140,
  144–45, 154, 197–98, 236n26
Trinh Minh-ha, 37–38

Ulloa, Astrid, 74–75, 102, 176, 257n13
Ulm school of design, 32–33
Uma Kiwe (Mother Earth), 199
umbilical cord, burial of, 72, 213, 240n24,
  256n10
United Nations, 6–7
universal design, 45
urban design, 40–41, 121, 246n10
uroboros, 252n2

Valdés, Bebo, 247n20
van der Hammen, María Clara, 257n13
Varela, Francisco, xii, 3, 79–80, 167, 211;
  on autonomy, 165; on autopoiesis, xiv,
  5, 168–72, 183; Buddhism and, 241n1;
  on Cartesianism, 81; on cognition, 42,
  81, 240n1; on "ethical know-how," 110,
  126–27; on modernism, 97–100; on objectivity, 252n6; on structural coupling,
  169; on transition design, 157
Vasudevan, Pavithra, 58
Vattimo, Gianni, 80
Venice Architecture Biennale, 38
Verden-Zöller, Gerda, 83, 232n9; on
  interconnected communities, 213–14; on
  "matristic cultures," 12–14
Vernadsky, Vladimir, 248n4
Vía Campesina movement, 198, 236n23

Virilio, Paul, xiv, 105, 108–9; on progress,
  231n8; on technologies, 231n5, 244n4
virtual reality, 35, 41
Visvanathan, Shiv, 242n8
Viveiros de Castro, Eduardo, 102; on "controlled equivocations," 258n16
Vivir Bien, 183, 186, 187. *See also* Buen Vivir
von Foerster, Heinz, 88, 200, 241n7
von Werlhof, Claudia, 10–11; Berry and, 12;
  career of, 231n6; on modernity, 14; on
  "self-alchemization," 91; on Zapatistas, 14

Wasserman, Arnold, 156
Watson, Tim, 234n16
West, Paige, 64
White, Damian, 47, 62, 250n16
Whitehead, Alfred North, 102, 144
WikiLeaks, 108–9
Willis, Anne-Marie, 110–11; on ontological
  design, 105; on transition design, 49, 50,
  223
Winograd, Terry, 105, 110; on ontological de-
  sign, xiv, 42, 116, 241n1; on organizational
  theory, 245n8
Wiwa people (Colombia), 74–75, 176
World Bank development programs, 59,
  61, 190
World Social Forum, 15–16, 67
World Trade Organization (WTO), 69

yin-yang dualism, 94
Yunus, Muhammad, 238n10

Zapatistas, xvi, 7, 14, 177, 180; on autonomy,
  165, 172, 253n8; declarations of, 173–74;
  on globalization, 86, 174; Juntas de Buen
  Gobierno of, 174; World Social Forum
  and, 15–16
Zhang, Amy, 125, 130, 131